SESQUI!

1926
1776
SESQUI CENTENNIAL
EXPOSITION
PHILADELPHIA JUNE 1ST DEC 1ST
1926

SESQUI!

★ ★ ★ ★ ★

Greed, Graft, and the Forgotten World's Fair of 1926

★ ★ ★ ★ ★

THOMAS H. KEELS

TEMPLE UNIVERSITY PRESS
Philadelphia ★ *Rome* ★ *Tokyo*

FRONTISPIECE: An early promotional poster for the Sesqui, featuring Hollywood starlet Laura LaPlante. The wonders of the fair she held aloft with her shapely arms were completely illusory at the time she was photographed.

TEMPLE UNIVERSITY PRESS
Philadelphia, Pennsylvania 19122
www.temple.edu/tempress

Published 2017

Library of Congress Cataloging-in-Publication Data

Names: Keels, Thomas H.
Title: Sesqui: greed, graft, and the forgotten world's fair of 1926 / Thomas H. Keels.
Description: Philadelphia: Temple University Press, 2017. | Includes bibliographical references and index.
Identifiers: LCCN 2016022168 (print) | LCCN 2016023296 (ebook) | ISBN 9781439903292 (cloth: alk. paper) | ISBN 9781439903315 (E-book)
Subjects: LCSH: Sesqui-Centennial International Exposition (1926: Philadelphia, Pa.)
Classification: LCC T826.3.B1 K44 2017 (print) | LCC T826.3.B1 (ebook) | DDC 607/.3474811—dc23
LC record available at https://lccn.loc.gov/2016022168

♾ The paper used in this publication meets the requirements of the American National Standard for Information Sciences—Permanence of Paper for Printed Library Materials, ANSI Z39.48-1992

Printed in the United States of America

9 8 7 6 5 4 3 2 1

Contents

⋆ ⋆ ⋆

Acknowledgments

★ ★ ★

LIKE PLANNING an international exposition, writing this book was a long-term project that required the involvement of many individuals and institutions. I am deeply grateful for their generous assistance in uncovering the buried history of Philadelphia's lost world's fair.

As with past books, the knowledgeable professionals at Philadelphia's galaxy of historical and cultural institutions, along with those further afield, offered me their scholarly expertise and access to their archives. I am especially grateful to Elisa Ho of the American Jewish Archives; Carrie Hogan of the American-Swedish Historical Museum; Bruce Laverty, Jill LeMin Lee, and Sandra Tatman of the Athenaeum of Philadelphia; Ross Mitchell of the Barnes Foundation/Violette de Mazia Foundation; Alex Bartlett and Elizabeth Jarvis of the Chestnut Hill Historical Society; Mary Knapp of Freeman's Auction; Emily Afflitto and Beth Kowalchick of the Committee of 1926 at Historic Strawberry Mansion; Aurora Deshauteurs of the Free Library of Philadelphia; Willhem Echevarria of the Historical Society of Pennsylvania; Dr. Kenvi Phillips of Howard University; Aaron Dilliplane of the Japan America Society of Greater Philadelphia; Anthony S. Aiello and Robert Gutowski of the Morris Arboretum of the University of Pennsylvania; Laura Keim of the National Society of the Colonial Dames of America in the Commonwealth of Pennsylvania; David Rowland of the Old York Road Historical Society; Jane Kenealy of the San Diego History Center; William Patterson of the Sketch Club of Philadelphia; Jeff Kern of the Sports Complex Special Services District; Brenda Galloway Wright of the Temple University Urban Archives; Theresa Altieri and James P. Mundy of the Union League of Philadelphia; Maureen S. Rush of the University of Pennsylvania; William Whitaker of the University of Pennsylvania Architectural Archives; John Pollack of the University of Pennsylvania Rare Book and Manuscript Library; and Jon Grabelle Herrmann and Andrew Hohns of USA250.

I'm also grateful to the following individuals who opened their personal collections to me or who advised me on specific aspects of the manuscript: Fred Bull, Steven Camp-Landis, Cindy Charleston-Rosenberg, Emily T. Cooperman, W. Stewart Graham, Greg Heller, Pamela and James H. Hill, Pete Hoskins, Harry Kyriakodis, Charlene Mires, Daniel Rottenberg, Francis Ryan, Maureen Rush, Robert M. Skaler, Lucy Strackhouse, Ann von Schwerdtner, Cintra and Wayne Willcox, William Zulker, Charles Zwicker, and Edward Zwicker.

One of the joys of writing a book with Temple University Press is having access to the school's student body for research assistants. I was extremely lucky to have three wonderful assistants during the course of creating *Sesqui*: Matthew M. Anglin, Samantha A. Heaps, and Maureen Smith. All three did an incredible job of tracking down and summarizing research materials. I am deeply grateful to all of them for their hard work. I also wish to thank Paula Robison, associate professor at Temple, who made all three of these outstanding scholars available to me.

My deepest thanks must go to my editor at Temple University Press, Micah Kleit, who worked with me during the several permutations of this book, and who patiently guided the work to its finished form.

As always, my deepest thanks must go to my friend, colleague, partner, and husband, Lawrence M. Arrigale, who helped me overcome my own doubts and fears and bring this project to fruition.

Introduction

★ ★ ★

ASK ANY PHILADELPHIAN about the 1876 Centennial, and he or she will probably be able to tell you something about it. Most will mention Memorial Hall in West Fairmount Park, the major survivor of the fair, repurposed as today's Please Touch Museum. They may recall a visit to the Centennial exhibit in the museum basement, with its diorama of the 1876 fairgrounds. More knowledgeable Philadelphians might discourse on how the successful Centennial attracted ten million visitors and ushered the United States into the first rank of global powers. They may know that Centennial visitors were the first to witness the telephone, drink Hires root beer, and climb into the arm and torch of the Statue of Liberty, on display to raise funds to erect the rest of the colossus.

Then ask them about the 1926 *Sesqui*-Centennial and watch them stare at you blankly. Some might remember stories told them by parents or grandparents about the big ballyhoo in the summer of 1926. A few might have heard of a giant illuminated Liberty Bell that spanned Broad Street at Oregon Avenue in South Philadelphia. One or two might have Sesqui souvenirs at home, like a tattered Liberty Belle doll dressed in stars and stripes. But most Philadelphians, even those familiar with their city's history, will confess ignorance. They might ask where the fair was and what remains of it. They might ask why nobody knows about it. The Sesqui-Centennial International Exposition, held in South Philadelphia between May 31 and December 31, 1926, is the Rodney Dangerfield of World's Fairs. It don't get no respect.

The Sesqui possessed impeccable credentials. It was the first world's fair to be staged in the United States in a decade. It was the first exposition to be held in the United States since the World War of 1914–1918. It was one of only eight international expositions to take place anywhere on the globe during the 1920s, as nations struggled to rebuild after the devastation of the Great War. Once the Sesqui had survived its initial stumbles, it was described by the *New York Times* as "one of the great American international expositions . . . a fine thing to display to the nation."

Yet most books about international expositions either mention the Sesqui-Centennial briefly or skip it altogether. Books on Philadelphia history, which might be expected to pay attention to the city's second world's fair, also gloss over the Sesqui. Several doctoral dissertations by local scholars cover the fair within a larger context or focus on a specific aspect of it. Foremost among these are Martin W. Wilson's *From the Sesquicentennial to the Bicentennial: Changing Attitudes toward Tourism in Philadelphia, 1926–1976* and Ellen Freedman's *The Women's Committee and Their High Street Exhibit at the Philadelphia Sesquicentennial Exposition of 1926*.

Besides the avalanche of promotional materials issued during the fair itself, only two books are devoted to the Sesqui. *The Sesqui-Centennial International Exposition* is the fair's "official" history. Published three years after the Sesqui ended, the book is an exhaustive effort to salvage the Sesqui's tarnished reputation. In 2009 James D. Ristine authored *Philadelphia's 1926 Sesqui-Centennial International Exposition*. The slender, 128-page volume features mostly postcard views of the fair, accompanied by brief captions.

On the rare occasions when the Sesqui is cited by historians, it usually rates two comments: (1) it rained a lot, and (2) it was a financial disaster. It did rain a lot at the Sesqui: there was some precipitation on 107 days out of the fair's 184 days of operation. When it wasn't raining, it was brutally hot: that summer, the eastern half of the country was racked by a deadly heat wave. And the Sesqui-Centennial was a financial disaster. The City of Philadelphia acknowledged that it lost nearly $10 million on the fair. That's the equivalent of $106 million today, adjusted for inflation; a more realistic figure, reflecting labor costs, would be $410 million. Within weeks of the fair's closing, a $1,000 Sesqui-Centennial bond sold for $40. Not long afterward, the exposition's organizing body declared bankruptcy. Besieged by lawsuits, the city spent the rest of the decade trying to clean up the financial wreckage of the fair.

The official price tag for the Sesqui was roughly $23 million, plus another $10 million to build the Sesqui Stadium and to install an infrastructure in undeveloped South Philadelphia. Adjusted for inflation, that amount would equal $434 million today, or a whopping $1.44 billion if labor costs are included. That's about one-third of the 2016 adopted budget for the City of Philadelphia ($3.998 billion). In reality, the amount spent by Philadelphia on the Sesqui was much higher than $23 million, given the miscellaneous appropriations and special loans pushed through by City Council surreptitiously, and the money distributed clandestinely in countless insider deals. The true cost of the fair will never be known, given the concerted efforts by certain political factions to bury the Sesqui, both literally and figuratively.[1]

To be fair, most international expositions have gushed red ink. The managers of the Exhibition of the Industry of All Nations, held in New York's Crystal Palace in 1853, lost their shirts. The 1876 Centennial appeared to have made a profit of nearly $2 million, until someone read the fine print and noticed that the $1.5 million appropriation from the federal government was a loan and not a grant. Most twentieth-century fairs also ended up in the red, from the 1901 Pan-American Exposition in Buffalo (which hosted the assassination of President William McKinley to boot), up to the 1984 Louisiana World Exposition in New Orleans, which lost $120 million and declared bankruptcy *before* it closed. At least the Sesqui had the decency to go belly-up several months after closing day.[2]

Yet turning a profit was never the primary purpose of an international exposition. There were the secondary benefits of millions of visitors spending money on local hotels, restaurants, and businesses. More important, a world's fair was supposed to provide its host city with immeasurable benefits in the form of an enhanced international profile, increased opportunities for business investment, exposure to new technology and industry, and improvements to its permanent infrastructure. Without world's fairs, would Chicago and San Francisco have their art museums, or Paris its Eiffel Tower and Metro?

Staged at the southern tip of Philadelphia, the 1926 Sesqui-Centennial forced the city to spend millions to fill and grade the region's swampy land, and then to install paved roads, trolley tracks, sewers, and street lighting. Unfortunately, the city made these improvements in its most sparsely populated region, while neglecting rapidly growing areas like the Northeast. There would be few South Philadelphians to enjoy the benefits of this infrastructure until years after World War II. Meanwhile, the city canceled or postponed urgently needed improvements as it poured money into the bottomless pit of the Sesqui. A subway loop to the new Museum of Art was scratched; so were rapid transit lines to the city's northwestern and far northeastern districts. Other badly needed improvements—a municipal court, a convention center, and upgrades to the city's water supply—were delayed for years because of the Big Ballyhoo in South Philadelphia. And what did the city have to show for its expenditures? A shoddily built stadium that was a white elephant for most of its sixty-six-year existence.

Even if they lost money, most world's fairs attracted tens of millions of visitors. Extrapolating from previous fair attendance and the number of Americans living within 150 miles of Philadelphia, Sesqui planners expected between forty and fifty million guests. Fewer than five million paying visitors actually attended the fair during its six-month run. That was roughly one-half of the attendance for the 1876 Centennial held fifty years earlier, before the invention of automobiles, airplanes, electric trolleys, radio, and movies. Only the abysmal 1907 Jamestown Tercentenary Exposition (2.85 million visitors) saves the Sesqui from the ignominy of being the most sparsely attended American world's fair of the twentieth century.

Perhaps it was lucky that more people didn't come, because the Sesqui was both a financial and an imaginative failure. It was a self-satisfied celebration, designed to delight the Sinclair Lewis protagonist George F. Babbitt, reflecting his petit bourgeois love of patriotic bunting, military bands, and multicolored bathroom fixtures. Yet even Babbitts were bored by the Sesqui. It was trapped between the old and the new, following the protocol for a nineteenth-century trade fair in the increasingly consumer-oriented culture of the twentieth century. As in 1876, most Sesqui exhibits were piles of stuff, displays of manufactured goods of every variety, artfully arranged within endless rows of decorative booths in cavernous warehouses. Even the cutting-edge technology at the fair, like talking pictures and electric sound amplification, was standard stuff by 1926. Some observers carped that a visit to one of Philadelphia's department stores would have been as edifying, and would not have cost fifty cents.

With so little to recommend it, why write about this fair-to-middling fair?

The true story of Philadelphia's second world's fair is much more than financial finagling and bad weather. It's an allegory for the ongoing struggle between the yin and yang of Philadelphia, caught between the gleaming vision of William Penn's "virgin settlement" and the sordid reality of its "pay-to-play" politics, between the enlightened civic duty of some citizens and the unlimited greed of others. It's the story of planners and architects who hoped to liberate Philadelphia from its grimy industrial shell and transform it into the City Beautiful. It's also the story of the men who owned the slaughterhouses that poured filth into the Schuylkill River, and how they boycotted the Sesqui because the resulting cleanup would threaten their livelihood.

The Sesqui saga is a study of Philadelphia boss politics in the early twentieth century. The 1920s marked the high noon of the Republican Organization under William S. Vare, who rose from peddling vegetables in South Philadelphia to being elected U.S. senator from Pennsylvania. In the 1920s,

Vare emerged as the most omnipotent political boss Philadelphia had ever known, ruling the city with an iron hand that reminded observers of Benito Mussolini. Through the Organization, Vare wielded control over nearly every politician and public servant in City Hall. Among his puppets was W. Freeland Kendrick, the former pawnshop owner whom Vare raised to the mayoralty in 1923. Kendrick paid back the favor by moving the Sesqui from the Fairmount Parkway, the city's new showplace, to the swamps of South Philadelphia, Vare's political stronghold. This move alone guaranteed the fair's failure, since it added millions of dollars in development costs and delayed construction. But it brought thousands of jobs and millions of dollars to "Varesville." The price of Kendrick's loyalty to Vare was his political career. The price of Philadelphia's allegiance to Vare was its financial stability.

Looking beyond Philadelphia, the Sesqui-Centennial served as a microcosm of America during the 1920s, and the culture wars that seethed beneath its surface. Philadelphia women tested their newfound political muscle at the Sesqui, defying the Organization to create the one truly successful attraction at the fair. Cardinal Dennis Joseph Dougherty demonstrated the power of Roman Catholics by celebrating a Solemn Pontifical Mass that attracted more attendees than any other Sesqui event. Meanwhile, African Americans struggled to keep their voices from being stifled by a callously racist white establishment. Jewish leaders generously contributed their money and talent to save the Sesqui from oblivion, only to be vilified by anti-Semites. The resurgent Ku Klux Klan planned to hold its 1926 Klonvokation at the Sesqui in September, with the blessing of City Hall. A coalition of blacks, Jews, Catholics, and other thoughtful Americans finally convinced Mayor Kendrick that burning crosses were not the best way to celebrate the 150th anniversary of the Declaration of Independence.

The Sesqui attracted fewer than six million visitors. But those guests who did show up to the party included nearly everyone who made the 1920s roar, with the possible exception of Al Capone, Charles Lindbergh, and Clara Bow. There was President Calvin Coolidge. Gloria Swanson. Jack Dempsey. Herbert Hoover. Alice Roosevelt Longworth. Gene Tunney. John Philip Sousa. Marian Anderson. Gangster Arnold Rothstein. Polar explorer Richard E. Byrd. General John Pershing. Johnny Weissmuller. President Borno of Haiti. Tom Mix. Queen Marie of Romania. Damon Runyon. Leopold Stokowski. Sessue Hayakawa. "Gentleman" Jimmy Walker. Plus more governors, ambassadors, generals, admirals, and assorted dignitaries than anyone could count.

For one surreal summer, the somber streets of Philadelphia were crowded with Cossacks, cowboys, Chinese princesses, colonial Quaker maids, Tunisian Berbers, fez-wearing Persians, fez-wearing Shriners, and Great War veterans clad in every color of the rainbow. Hundreds of American and foreign flags fluttered in the air, and the streets were decked with bunting and decorations. At night, the chop-suey joints and dance halls along Chestnut Street were packed with customers, drawn by the flickering colors of that new-fangled French import, neon lighting. Atop City Hall, William Penn was swathed in electric lights that bathed him in bright red. The skies were filled with more airplanes than anyone had ever seen, along with giant dirigibles like the TC-5. Pedestrians learned to avoid South Broad Street, lest they get run over by Mayor Kendrick's limousine with its screaming siren, as he raced down to the Sesqui for yet another official reception.

At the Sesqui, Philadelphians gazed at canvases by Kandinsky and Matisse and wondered what art was coming to. They knelt on tatamis and tried to understand the differences between the Japanese and Formosan tea ceremonies. They ate blinis at the Russian Tea House, while faux-Russian musicians in silk tunics strummed balalaikas. They ate *weisswurst* at the Alpine Haus while genuine Bavarians in dirndls and lederhosen danced the *Schuhplattler*. After dark, they danced the Charleston under the stars in the Forum of the Founders, hoping to win a silver cup. And they stared in wonder at the eighty-foot-tall Liberty Bell that straddled Broad Street, studded with twenty-six thousand amber, gold, and pink lightbulbs that made it glow like molten metal. The Sesqui may have been a giant boondoggle, but it turned staid, sooty Philadelphia into a dazzling Rainbow City for six magical months.

A NOTE ON SPELLING: *Sesqui* is a Latinate term meaning "one and a half." Therefore, *sesquicentennial* means "one hundred and a half," or a 150th anniversary. The accepted spelling of this word, according to *Webster's Collegiate Dictionary*, is *sesquicentennial*. This was the spelling used by the *New York Times* in its contemporary coverage of the fair. But when John Wanamaker, the fair's foremost proponent, selected this term to refer to the 150th anniversary of American independence, he used the more archaic, hyphenated spelling of "Sesqui-Centennial." So did major Philadelphia newspapers; so did the fair's governing body, the Sesqui-Centennial Exhibition Association. So will this book, although it will also use the abbreviation "Sesqui," which quickly became Philadelphians' preferred name for their second world's fair. It's worth noting, however, that when the powers that be cannot agree on how to spell the name of a fair before the first spade of dirt is turned, there's sure to be trouble ahead.

NOTES

1. All currency projections and calculations are based on the Purchasing Power Calculator at MeasuringWorth.com. 2016 city budget from the City of Philadelphia "Open Budget" website, available at http:///www.phila.gov/openbudget/.

2. Financial data taken from Findling and Pelle, *Encyclopedia of World's Fairs and Expositions*.

Prologue

★ ★ ★

The Great Fair

IT HAD BEEN the greatest international exposition that the world had ever witnessed, and it had taken place in Philadelphia. From May 10 to November 10, 1876, nearly ten million visitors from around the globe flocked to a wonderland that had risen in mere months, on a plateau above the west bank of the Schuylkill River in Fairmount Park. There, they had been amazed by the modern miracles of the "International Exhibition of Arts, Manufactures, and Products of the Soil and Mine," known informally as the Centennial Exposition. The Centennial had easily outshone the 1853 Exhibition of the Industry of All Nations in New York's Crystal Palace, young America's first attempt at a world's fair. It had also compared favorably with the massive international gatherings staged by European powers since the initial Great Exhibition at London's Crystal Palace in 1851: the Parisian Expositions Universelles of 1855 and 1867, the Great London Exhibition of 1862, and the Vienna Weltausstellung of 1873.

The Philadelphia Centennial Exhibition was a true world's fair, with thirty-six foreign countries represented (fifty-five if you counted Canada and the other eighteen colonies of the British Empire separately). Participants ranged from the first tier of world powers – the United Kingdom, France, the German Empire, and the elite club's newest member, the United States of America – to faraway, primitive lands like Japan and China. Twenty-four American states and territories took part, including the former rebel states of Arkansas and Mississippi. The Centennial offered Americans the opportunity to tour the world, arrayed in its myriad splendor in 249 structures spread across 284 acres. It also allowed them to see their own

The twenty-acre Main Building, 1,880 feet long and 464 feet wide, was said to be the largest structure in the world in 1876.

country, unified and strong, a decade after the trauma of the Civil War had threatened to tear it apart forever.

The heart of the Centennial rested in two huge structures: the Main Building and Machinery Hall. Fair planners loved to boast that the Main Building, 1,880 feet long by 464 feet wide, was the largest structure in the world. At the same time, they were unable to explain why the edifice, meant to be exactly 1,876 feet long, had overshot its goal by four feet. Costing $1,763,600, the Main Building had been erected in only eighteen months, using the latest American techniques in prefabricated materials and modern construction.

Here, foreign countries held court in lavish enclosures, exemplified by the Moorish extravaganza designed by Philadelphia architect Frank Furness for the Brazilian Empire, the fast-growing South American counterpart to the United States. The facade of the nearby Egyptian pavilion announced that "the oldest peoples in the world send their morning greetings to the youngest nation." Americans flocked to the Japanese pavilion to admire its ornate bronzes and delicate porcelains, "the variety and beauty of which were one of the great surprises of the Exhibition." Besides the foreign enclosures, the Main Building was crowded with displays of manufactured goods, presented in the most elaborate and ingenious manners: mountains of Doulton stoneware, a castle composed of children's building blocks, and a ghostly army of buxom torsos encased in the latest corsets.

At one booth, a twenty-nine-year-old inventor from New Jersey demonstrated his latest creation: the Quadruplex Telegraph, capable of

The fourteen-acre Machinery Hall showed visitors how the Industrial Revolution had completely changed the world in a few short decades.

transmitting four messages simultaneously over a single telegraph wire. Thomas A. Edison's most noteworthy inventions, the phonograph and the incandescent lightbulb, would not meet the public eye for another year or two. Another inventor, Alexander Graham Bell, unveiled his creation only a week before closing day. It was generally dismissed as a fanciful and impractical trifle. "The telephone is a curious device that might fairly find place in the magic of *Arabian Tales*," observed a dubious New York *Tribune*. "Of what use is such an invention?"[1]

West of the Main Building, the fourteen-acre Machinery Hall demonstrated how the Industrial Revolution had thrust a once-primitive America into the pantheon of global powers. At its heart towered the Corliss Centennial Steam Engine. Channeling steam from outdoor boilers, the two massive cylinders of the forty-foot-high engine propelled a thirty-foot flywheel, generating fourteen hundred horsepower of energy. The flywheel turned a giant pinion wheel beneath the floor, which operated a vast network of shafts, pulleys, and belts throughout Machinery Hall. Crowds gathered every morning to watch attendants turn the two levers that threw the flywheel into motion, powering hundreds of secondary machines. These included the "Lightning" rotary press, capable of printing twenty thousand newspapers an hour; the Linde-Wolfe ammonia compressor, an early mechanical refrigerator; and the Otis Brothers and Co. steam elevator and freight platform. Near the Corliss Engine stood more than a dozen steam

James H. Windrim's ten-acre Agricultural Hall reminded visitors that despite America's industrial prowess, the majority of its inhabitants still lived in rural settings.

locomotives, many of them built by Philadelphia's own Baldwin Locomotive Works at Broad and Spring Garden Streets.[2]

Looking like a giant Gothic barn, Agricultural Hall sprawled at the northern tip of the fairgrounds. The nine-acre wooden structure reminded visitors that for all of America's industrial might, most of its citizens still lived on farms or in small rural towns. Besides the latest farming equipment and technology, the hall contained a bewildering array of agricultural products, foodstuffs, animals, and plants. An aquarium along the western wall contained every species of food fish from American rivers and lakes, as well as the Atlantic and Pacific Oceans. Visitors to the California Restaurant could sample the best varieties of wines produced by that state's vineyards. The rambling structure also served as a catchall for oddities like the eagle "Old Abe," elderly mascot of the Eighth Wisconsin Regiment of Infantry during the Civil War. The irascible Old Abe, who tried to sink his talons into anyone who ventured too close to his perch, delighted bystanders by devouring a live chicken once a day.[3]

The two remaining structures of the fair's five principal buildings were meant to be permanent additions to Fairmount Park. Although Horticultural Hall was the smallest of the five, it was the largest conservatory ever built, constructed at a cost of $367,073. Set at the end of a boulevard called Fountain Avenue and surrounded by thirty-five acres of ornamental gardens, it was designed as the jewel in the crown of Fairmount Park. The tall, rectangular

Schwartzmann's Horticultural Hall, a conservatory built in the Moorish style, was praised by one German critic as "that embodiment of the tales of Scheherazade!"

iron-and-glass structure, 383 feet long by 193 feet wide, was designed in the Moorish style, brightly colored inside and out and bristling with spires, onion domes, and cast-iron tracery. The soaring central hall was filled with exotic tropical plants, their foliage constantly changing colors from sunlight filtered through hundreds of tinted windowpanes.[4]

Memorial Hall was a richly decorated, rectangular building with corner towers and a central dome topped by a statue of Columbia. The 76,650-square-foot pavilion cost $1.5 million, nearly as much as the twenty-acre Main Building. Constructed of glass, iron, and granite, the "modern Renaissance" structure was meant to be completely fireproof to safeguard the collection it would house during the Centennial as the Art Gallery, and after the fair as the Pennsylvania Museum of Industrial Art. With 75,000 square feet of wall space and 20,000 square feet of floor space at his disposal, Bureau of Art Director John Sartain struggled to find room for the 3,256 paintings and drawings, 627 sculptures, 431 works of applied art, and 2,833 photographs accepted for display. Some galleries were packed with paintings from floor to ceiling. Finally, the Centennial Commission had to build an Art Annex north of Memorial Hall to provide another 60,000 square feet of wall space for paintings. The photographs were dispatched to a separate Photographic Annex, the first building ever created for this purpose.[5]

Besides the five principal structures, more than 240 other buildings dotted the fairgrounds. There were twenty-four state pavilions, ranging

Designed by H. J. Schwarzmann, Memorial Hall served as the Art Gallery for the Centennial, housing thousands of paintings and sculptures from throughout the civilized world.

from Mississippi's log cabin to the "elegant and substantial" Ohio House, constructed of stone from twenty-one quarries. Among the fifteen foreign pavilions, the Japanese complex proved to be another revelation for Westerners encountering this "primitive" culture for the first time. The Japanese had attracted ridicule during construction, when the "flat-nosed Orientals" had used "uncouth" hand tools to erect a framework that looked "like a corncrib," in the words of the *American Architect and Building News*. After its completion, the elegant and airy buildings were commended by the Centennial judges for the "beautiful treatment of wood and admirable joinery . . . graceful lines of roofs and porches, the perfect tile work . . . and the rich ornamental carving."[6]

Throughout the fairgrounds, monumental statuary commemorated historical events or represented the contributions of specific groups. Two gigantic winged horses, held in check by Amazonian maidens, framed the entrance to Memorial Hall. Rejected by the Vienna Opera House, they had been picked up for a song by Robert H. Gratz of Philadelphia while on his world tour. A magnificent Fountain of Light and Water by French sculptor Frédéric Auguste Bartholdi stood in the plaza between the Main Building and Machinery Hall. Elsewhere on the grounds was another statue by Bartholdi, or rather a fragment of a statue. A gigantic woman's hand, clutching an equally gigantic torch, stood by a lake north of Machinery Hall. The colossal arm was part of a projected statue of the Goddess of Liberty that Bartholdi hoped to erect in New York harbor. To raise funds for the rest of the statue, visitors were charged twenty-five cents to climb through the hollow arm into the base of the torch.[7]

Seeking to avoid the predatory or officious attitudes they had observed at the 1873 Vienna fair, Centennial managers evinced a genuine concern with the welfare of their guests. William Dean Howells spoke approvingly of the "perfect freedom" of the Centennial: "There are innumerable officials to direct you, to help you, to care for you, but none of them bothers you." Several police stations kept crime to a minimum, while a medical bureau cared for injured or exhausted fairgoers. Public restrooms and changing rooms were scattered liberally throughout the fairgrounds. The Department of Public Comfort provided numerous chairs and sofas, where fatigued fair-goers could relax. It also offered lavatories, dressing rooms, mail and telegraph service, a visitors' registry, a ticket bureau, coat and baggage rooms, bootblacks, and an inexpensive café.

The spirit of the Centennial extended far beyond its buildings, statues, and exhibits. Even on the steamiest summer day, there was constant spectacle and activity in the form of concerts, parades, bicycle races, shooting matches, regattas, and fireworks. Despite rainy weather, nearly 187,000 people crowded the fairgrounds on May 10, to see the fair opened by President Ulysses S. Grant and Emperor Dom Pedro II of Brazil, the first reigning monarch to visit the United States. Although an emperor seemed like an odd choice to help the world's greatest democracy celebrate its centenary, Dom Pedro was renowned as a ruler of "elevated character" with "enlightened views of government." His exuberant and easygoing manner made him more popular than the sullen Grant, whose administration was increasingly mired in the Whiskey Ring and other scandals.

Dom Pedro returned on July 4 for at a grand celebration and parade at Independence Hall (Grant did not attend, to universal criticism). The emperor was joined on the reviewing stand by General William Tecumseh Sherman, the great hero of the Civil War, and by Lieutenant General Saigo of the Imperial Japanese Army. On Pennsylvania Day, 274,919 people paid their fifty-cent notes to enter the Centennial, more than had ever attended any other international exposition on a single day. Both candidates in the upcoming presidential election, Republican Governor Rutherford B. Hayes of Ohio and Democratic Governor Samuel J. Tilden of New York, addressed crowds at the exhibition.

On November 9, the eve of the fair's closing, a dazzling fireworks display filled the night sky with magnesium stars, golden fountains, and a classical temple topped by the Goddess of Liberty, pointing to an American eagle soaring aloft with the Stars and Stripes in its beak. When the Centennial closed the next day, more than fifteen thousand spectators braved a chilling rain, hoping to catch a glimpse of President Grant and other dignitaries. Crowds packed Judges' Hall to watch President Grant give the signal to power down the great Corliss Engine and to declare the Centennial officially over.

The success of the fair was due primarily to the determination, vigor, and expertise of the U.S. Centennial Commission, led by President Joseph R. Hawley and Director-General Alfred T. Goshorn. Hawley and Goshorn were backed by a capable and talented executive committee, many of whom came from Philadelphia. Foremost among them was John Welsh, a Philadelphia merchant who had served on the city's Select Council and as a longtime commissioner of the Fairmount Park Commission. In 1864, Welsh had chaired the executive committee of the Sanitary Fair in Logan Square, a miniature exposition that raised more than $4 million for the U.S. Sanitary Commission in three weeks. As chairman of the Centennial Board of Finance, Welsh saved the 1876 fair from oblivion when initial support was in jeopardy. His prestige was such that he persuaded one hundred wealthy Philadelphians to act as guarantors for a $500,000 bond required as collateral for a $1.5 million appropriation by Congress. Easily recognizable by his flowing muttonchops, the seventy-one-year-old Welsh received one of the loudest ovations from the crowd at the opening ceremonies on May 10.[8]

Goshorn and Welsh had also been supported by a cadre of younger men, who had carved out impressive careers either as Civil War officers or as successful businessmen. Among them was a thirty-nine-year-old dry goods merchant from Philadelphia named John Wanamaker. In April 1861, only ninety-six hours before the outbreak of the Civil War, Wanamaker and his brother-in-law Nathan Brown had opened Oak Hall, a men and boys' clothing store, at Sixth and Market Streets. Despite the wartime economy, the business prospered. After Brown's death in 1868, Wanamaker established a second store on upscale Chestnut Street. Within ten years, Wanamaker had expanded Oak Hall and topped the enlarged store with a wraparound rooftop sign that boasted, "The Largest Clothing House in America." Thanks to his genius for marketing and emphasis on customer service, Wanamaker had become one of the most successful merchants in Philadelphia by the early 1870s. It was only fitting that he be asked to join the Centennial Board of Finance for the 1876 Centennial.

Wanamaker's financial expertise and promotional talents served the Centennial in a variety of ways. In 1874, he took command of a Citizens'

The Centennial Finance Committee, which included some of Philadelphia's most influential and entrepreneurial men. John Wanamaker, at thirty-nine the youngest member, is at the center in the rear row.

Centennial Trade Committee, which encouraged financial support of the fair among Philadelphia businesses and industries. By 1875 Wanamaker had joined Welsh as a member of the inside "finance committee" that directed the activities of the larger Centennial Board of Finance. As chairman of the Bureau of Revenue, Wanamaker played a key role in the development and sale of the $10 million in Board of Finance stock certificates. He would later boast, "I wore all my shoes out getting the first million dollars subscribed" for the Centennial. Wanamaker's name appeared first in the Philadelphia subscription book, next to a substantial contribution of $17,500. In recognition of Wanamaker's efforts, Welsh asked him to chair the July 4 celebration at Independence Hall. In this capacity, Wanamaker introduced General Sherman and the other distinguished speakers.[9]

While Wanamaker was ensuring the Centennial's success, he was also developing the concept for a "new kind of store" that would serve as a larger stage for his revolutionary style of retailing. In 1874, Wanamaker spent $505,000 to purchase the dilapidated Pennsylvania Railroad freight depot and train shed at Thirteenth Street between Market and Juniper Streets. The abandoned terminal stood across the street from Penn Square, where the cornerstone had just been laid for Philadelphia's new public buildings or City Hall. By the spring of 1876, Wanamaker had transformed the empty

Opened shortly before the Centennial began, John Wanamaker's Grand Depot attracted so many world's fair visitors that it became known as the "Centennial Annex."

structures into a Moorish-Venetian-Gothic fantasy called the Grand Depot. Advertised as "the largest space in the world devoted to retail selling on a single floor," the Depot offered its customers two acres of merchandise, plus a restaurant. It opened on May 6, 1876, four days before the Centennial, and attracted so many world's fair visitors that it became known as the Centennial Annex. Just as the Centennial proclaimed that something new and exciting was happening in America, the Grand Depot announced that something revolutionary was occurring in Philadelphia.[10]

Economically, culturally, and spiritually, the Centennial was a transformational event for both the United States and Philadelphia. After the dual traumas of the Civil War and Lincoln's assassination, Americans had endured another decade of upheaval. They had seen Lincoln's successor, Andrew Johnson, tried for impeachment and acquitted by only one vote. They had watched the administration of Ulysses S. Grant disintegrate into an endless series of political scandals. The Panic of 1873 ushered in a depression that lasted the rest of the decade. In the eyes of the world, the stunted shaft of the Washington Monument was an apt symbol for the United States, born with high aspirations but arrested by political schism, corruption, and apathy. Begun in 1848, the obelisk remained half-finished in 1876, reminding Mark Twain of "a factory chimney with the top broken off."[11] Many Americans wondered if their country would ever again be a coherent entity. Inspired by the success of the Centennial, Congress appropriated $200,000 to resume construction on the Washington Monument.

If the Centennial was a revelation for Americans, it was a lightning bolt for Europeans. The Centennial showed them a United States bursting with optimism and energy, and anxious to assume its role as a world power. After viewing such wonders as the Corliss Engine, the Edison Quadruplex Telegraph, and the Westinghouse air brake, the London *Times* acknowledged that "the American invents as the Greek sculpted and the Italian painted; it is genius." British engineer John Roberts officially reported to Her Majesty's Government that "if we are to be judged by the comparison with Americans in 1876 . . . we are losing our former leadership and it is passing to the Americans." The French critic Louis Simonin wrote with alarm in the *Revue des Deux Mondes* that "even American wines are competing with ours. The connoisseur alone demands the wines of France."[12]

Soon after the Centennial showed the world what the United States was producing, America became a net exporter. In 1875 imports to the United States outpaced exports by approximately $34 million. In the Centennial year, the balance of trade flipped, and exports exceeded imports by $65 million. A year later, the United States showed a whopping $139 million in surplus exports. By the end of the decade, American exports outstripped total imports by nearly $265 million.[13]

The Centennial proved to be a windfall for its host city, Philadelphia. The U.S. Centennial Commission's final report estimated that each visitor had contributed $4.50 to the local economy, generating between $40 million and $50 million. Still a major port, Philadelphia's docks and piers along the Delaware River were jammed with ships bearing and removing exhibits throughout the Centennial. The city had been a manufacturing center since the beginning of the Industrial Revolution, but preparing for the Centennial forced many of its industries out of the slump initiated by the Panic of 1873. Iron manufacturing in Philadelphia jumped more than 30 percent between 1870 and 1876. During the same period, revenues of the building and construction industries nearly doubled. By 1880 Philadelphia ranked first among the country's largest industrial cities in six fields: bricks and tiles, drugs and chemicals, mixed textiles, woolens, dyeing and finishing, and shipbuilding. Thanks to William Cramp and Sons and other local shipyards, the city was known as "Clyde on the Delaware." Philadelphia's heyday as the "Workshop of the World" had arrived.[14]

The Centennial was also a windfall for Philadelphia in terms of its national and international reputation. Many American and foreign visitors had arrived in Philadelphia expecting to find a sleepy, provincial burg whose glory had passed. Instead, the Centennial Exposition exposed them to a Philadelphia that was a model of the modern American industrial city. Outsiders were amazed at the brisk efficiency and logistical genius the Centennial Commission (dominated by Welsh and other Philadelphians) had shown in erecting buildings on time, developing an effective transportation network, accommodating thousands of visitors, and ensuring low rates of crime and disease throughout the fair.

Visitors reported favorably on Philadelphia's vast enterprises, its broad boulevards and handsome mansions, its neat rows of workers' houses and high level of home ownership, its educational institutions, and its verdant suburbs. They admired the groundbreaking structures completed in time for the Centennial. Many of them traveled to the fair via the Girard Avenue Bridge, erected at a cost of more than $1 million and said to be the widest bridge in the world. Besides shopping at Wanamaker's Grand Depot, they visited the Masonic Temple at Broad and Filbert Streets; the Academy of Natural Sciences on Logan Square; and the Pennsylvania Academy of the Fine Arts on North Broad, designed by a young Philadelphia architect and Civil War hero named Frank Furness. Even Philadelphia's historic shrines received makeovers for the Centennial. Thousands of visitors flocked to Independence Hall, where the Assembly Room had been restored with some of its original furnishings.[15]

Fairmount Park, the Centennial site, came in for particular acclaim. Before the Civil War, the park had been limited to two estates comprising eighty acres on the east bank of the Schuylkill River. After the war, Philadelphia City Councils had expanded the park to the west bank in an effort to protect the city's water supply. By 1876 Fairmount Park encompassed 2,648 acres, making it the largest park in the United States and the fourth largest in the world. It was more than three times as large as New York's Central Park, completed in 1873. The idea of such a vast public retreat within walking distance of a major metropolis was a revelation to both American and foreign visitors. "The Philadelphians are proud of this immense garden," wrote one Centennial tourist, French composer Jacques Offenbach. "They are right, for it is most beautiful and picturesque."[16]

More observant commentators were aware that a den of serpents lurked within this Eden. By 1876 Philadelphia had become a one-party Republican machine town, with a new class of professional politician gaining control over City Hall. The machine was not yet all-powerful: it did not command either the City Councils or the Republican City Committee. Philadelphia's first real political boss, "King" James McManes, was an Irish immigrant who controlled the Gas Trust, the lucrative city-owned monopoly on illuminating gas. Despite his influence, the highest position McManes occupied at City Hall was prothonotary or chief clerk in the district court. But McManes's Republican cronies had taken control of the election board, flooding the polls at every election with repeat voters using fake names. Other illegal practices were on the rise, including intimidation of voters by machine-backed police, vote miscounts, and outright falsification of election returns. Philadelphia's independent voters were finding it increasingly difficult, if not dangerous, to cast their votes on Election Day.

At City Hall, politicians spent much of their time "shaking the plum tree," using a favorite phrase of state Republican boss Matthew Quay, to catch the rich fruit of patronage produced by a fast-growing city. In 1873 the city treasurer, Joseph P. Mercer, had been arrested for conspiracy to embezzle city funds in a traction company fraud run by a young Philadelphia banker, Charles T. Yerkes. Both Mercer and Yerkes were convicted and sentenced to Eastern State Penitentiary. There was increasing suspicion that Philadelphia's mayor, a former confectioner nicknamed "Sweet William" Stokley, was on the take, too, steering construction contracts for the new City Hall to those who would pay him the biggest bribes. In 1871 ground had been broken for the municipal building at Penn Square, where Broad and Market Streets intersected, with hopes that the magnificent new structure would be completed by 1876. Yet Centennial visitors to Penn Square saw little more than a large hole in the ground, where the cavernous foundations for City Hall were being excavated at a glacial pace.

Meanwhile, the municipal debt had topped $80 million, and the patrician Sydney George Fisher complained that Philadelphia streets were "dirty, ill lighted, and wretchedly paved," despite constant tax hikes.[17] Fisher's irritation was symptomatic of a growing schism between the city's political leaders and its social and economic elite. The Centennial had been the child of the latter group, who controlled anti-machine organizations like the Union League and the Reform Club. Many local Centennial commissioners, including Welsh, were instrumental in these organizations. During the 1870s, their financial power and social influence were strong enough to allow them to create the Centennial with minimal interference from the Republican machine. The politicians conceded the fair to the elite, focusing their attention instead on the lower-hanging plums of City Hall and the trolley system.[18]

Despite these snakes in their garden, Philadelphians realized that the year 1876 had been a watershed moment for their city. Going forward, Philadelphia would be known as the center of American manufacturing might, organizational capability, and entrepreneurial efficiency. The Centennial was irrefutable proof of this new status, not just to the rest of the world but to self-doubting Philadelphians themselves. As the Philadelphia *Press* proudly announced, "The Centennial is to ring the death knell of that non-enterprising, fearing-to-dare spirit which has so long ruled us." While Philadelphia was still the Second City of the United States after New York, the Centennial removed it from the lengthy shadow of its northern neighbor. Philadelphia might have been unable to compete directly with New York in terms of finance or population. But the Centennial proved that it was a worthy consort, possessing the physical breadth, variety of industries, historic heritage, and natural beauty that the skinny island of Manhattan lacked. Philadelphians knew how to get things done; they could take a million movable parts and assemble them into a steam locomotive, a Girard Avenue Bridge, or a Centennial Exhibition.

At the fair's closing ceremonies on November 10, 1876, the Honorable Daniel J. Morrell, chairman of the executive committee of the Centennial Commission, gazed into the future and saw the Quaker City hosting even more magnificent expositions in years to come. "The managers of future centennial celebrations to be held on these grounds," he said in concluding his address, "will see and do things more wonderful than our wildest dreams, and the remnants of our finest things may be exhibited by them as proofs of the rudeness of early days." His confidence, though far from Quaker in spirit, was justifiable. A city that could pull off the greatest world's fair ever seen in the face of economic depression, political opposition, and public apathy, could accomplish anything.[19]

NOTES

1. Norton, *Frank Leslie's Historical Register*, pp. 83–89; Maass, *The Glorious Enterprise*, pp. 66–67; Post, *1876*, pp. 103–159; Weymouth, *America in 1876*, p. 28.

2. Maass, *The Glorious Enterprise*, pp. 66–67; Post, *1876*, pp. 27–65; Cheney, "1876," pp. 22–24.

3. McCabe, *The Illustrated History*, pp. 173–186.

4. Meant to be a permanent ornament of Fairmount Park, Horticultural Hall was demolished by the Fairmount Park Commission in 1955. Keels, *Forgotten Philadelphia*, pp. 141–143; Maass, *The Glorious Enterprise*, pp. 60–65; Post, *1876*, pp. 68–73.

5. Maass, *The Glorious Enterprise*, pp. 44–59; McCabe, *The Illustrated History*, pp. 191–200.

6. McCabe, *The Illustrated History*, pp. 221–240; Post, *1876*, pp. 66–71.

7. David Sellin, quoted in Fairmount Park Art Association, *Sculpture of a City*, pp. 78–93.

8. McCabe, *The Illustrated History*, p. 242; John Maass, quoted in Post, *1876*, pp. 11; Keels, *Forgotten Philadelphia*, pp. 132–133; Rydell, Findling, and Pelle, *Fair America*, p. 17.

9. Pizor, "Preparations," p. 223; Gibbons, *John Wanamaker*, 1:158–160.

10. Arrigale and Keels, *Philadelphia's Golden Age of Retail*, pp. 10, 15–17; Keels, *Forgotten Philadelphia*, pp. 146–148; Giberti, *Designing the Centennial*, pp. 208–216.

11. Weymouth. *America in 1876,* p. 105.

12. Rydell, Findling, and Pelle, *Fair America*, pp. 16–17; "The Centennial Exhibition. What a Frenchman Thinks of Its Industrial and Commercial Aspects," *PI*, November 16, 1876, p. 8.

13. Rydell, Findling, and Pelle, *Fair America*, pp. 18–19; John Maass, quoted in Post, *1876*, p. 22; *Industrial Depressions*, U.S. Department of Labor, 1886, p. 73.

14. Rydell, Findling, and Pelle, *Fair America*, p. 42; Lorin Blodget, *The Industries of Philadelphia as Shown by the Manufacturing Census of 1870, Compared with 1860 and Estimates for 1875 and 1876*, pp. 3–33; Wolf, "The Origins of Philadelphia's Self-Deprecation," pp. 69–70; Hershberg, *Philadelphia*, p. 46.

15. Shinn, *A Century After*.

16. Maass, *The Glorious Enterprise*, p. 22.

17. Richardson, "Centennial City," p. 32.

18. Weigley, *Philadelphia*, pp. 419–470; Hodos, "The 1876 Centennial in Philadelphia"; Richardson, "Centennial City," pp. 26–32.

19. Richardson, "Centennial City," p. 17; Rosewater, *Notes on the Sesqui-Centennial*, VR/AJA, p. 1.

1

★ ★ ★

Philadelphia, 1916

AUGUST 5, 1916, was a typically steamy summer day in Philadelphia, with temperatures nearing ninety. On this hot Saturday, readers of Philadelphia's leading morning papers, the *Inquirer* and the *Public Ledger*, learned that German U-boats might be prowling the waters off the Jersey coast. While the United States was still at peace in August 1916, the conflict that had engulfed Europe for two bloody years lurked relentlessly at the edge of American consciousness. The front page of the August 5 *Inquirer* featured a photograph of British Tommies using shell craters as "a very comfortable bedroom," next to articles about French victories in the Battle of the Meuse and the Russian retreat from the Carpathians.[1]

On the national front, attention focused on the upcoming presidential election between Democratic incumbent Woodrow Wilson and his Republican challenger, former Supreme Court Justice Charles Evans Hughes. While the erudite and progressive Hughes was seen as a strong contender, Wilson's campaign slogan that "He Kept Us Out of War" was swaying many Americans desperate to remain at peace. On May 7, 1915, a German submarine had torpedoed the ocean liner *Lusitania*, killing 1,195 of the 1,959 on board, including 27 Philadelphians. Three days later, Wilson had addressed a capacity crowd of twenty thousand in Convention Hall at Broad Street and Allegheny Avenue in Philadelphia. The audience had applauded Wilson thunderously when he assured them, "There is such a thing as a man being too proud to fight. There is such a thing as a nation being so right that it does not need to convince others by force that it is right."[2]

Wilson had handled the crisis skillfully, forcing the German government to promise that it would halt unrestricted submarine warfare against nonmilitary vessels. America had remained at peace, and the economy had avoided a second war panic like the one that had paralyzed it in August 1914. While the stock market was still choppy, the Dow Jones Industrial Average had closed at 88.41 on August 4, 1916, up 62 percent from its close at the end of 1914. Philadelphia's factory workers were putting in double shifts to replace the materiel that kept disappearing into the mud of European battlegrounds. The industrial output of the "Workshop of the World" had jumped from $746 million in 1910 to an estimated $1 billion in 1916, while the number of workers employed in manufacturing had risen from 252,000 to roughly 300,000. The city's investment banks, led by Edward T. Stotesbury's Drexel and Company, were booking record profits from underwriting the conflict. In this uneasy calm before the storm, wages were rising, unemployment had dropped, and consumer spending was at an all-time high. Business had never been better at either the John Wanamaker Department Store or the half-dozen other large emporia lining East Market Street between City Hall and Independence Hall.[3]

The great palazzo that housed the Wanamaker Store did not open for business on August 5. Instead of working until 1:00 P.M. as was customary on summer Saturdays, John Wanamaker's employees had a full forty-eight hours to join the thousands crowding Atlantic City and other shore resorts. Despite his store being shuttered, John Wanamaker remained on the minds of his fellow Philadelphians thanks to his customary essay in the morning papers. On August 5, the elderly merchant took his readers on a sentimental journey back to 1848, when an eight-year-old Wanamaker "first walked up to the city through 'Long Lane,' then ending at 'Schuylkill-Sixth' and Pine Streets." While acknowledging the momentous changes that had happened to his hometown since then, Wanamaker took his fellow citizens to task for not "booming" Philadelphia as "a city of the first class":

> [We have] done nothing to put forward the city as a great city since the Centennial of 1876. We have stopped with the graves of our fathers. The growth of this city is a two-story-four-rooms-and-a-kitchen growth.
>
> Are we to wait for 1976 to show our hand again in another Centennial? Why not celebrate the century and a half in 1926, and begin to get ready now?
>
> Public sentiment for the 1876 exhibition began ten years before the time to get Government support and necessary legislation.

> Are there any sons left of those who toiled in old times to make the city head the list, willing to take off their coats and go to work for a great future of Philadelphia?[4]

At seventy-eight, the portly, white-haired merchant was still as energetic and progressive as when he was a thirty-nine-year-old wunderkind guaranteeing the financial success of the Centennial Exhibition. Over the past forty years, Wanamaker had established one of the country's great mercantile empires, making him a multimillionaire. Gone was the Moorish fantasy known as the Grand Depot that had delighted Centennial visitors. In its place stood a magnificent Roman-Doric palace designed by Daniel H. Burnham, Wizard of the White City at the 1893 World's Fair. The granite-and-steel structure occupied the entire city block bordered by Market, Chestnut, Thirteenth, and Juniper Streets. At its dedication on December 30, 1911, President William H. Taft had addressed a crowd of more than thirty-five thousand in a magnificent marble-lined Grand Court. In 1896 Wanamaker had expanded to New York City, acquiring the old A. T. Stewart store at Ninth Street and Broadway. With the possible exception of Chicago's Marshall Field, John Wanamaker was the face of twentieth-century American retailing.

By 1916, Wanamaker's Grand Depot had been replaced by this magnificent granite palazzo, designed by Daniel H. Burnham, Director of Works at the 1893 Columbian Exposition in Chicago.

Since 1876 Wanamaker had dabbled in politics, serving as the U.S. postmaster-general in the Benjamin Harrison administration. The Progressive Republican had run for the offices of mayor of Philadelphia, governor of Pennsylvania, and United States senator from Pennsylvania, losing each time to puppets of the state's corrupt Republican machine. A devout Presbyterian, Wanamaker had established the largest Sunday school in America, which had evolved into the Bethany Presbyterian Church at Twenty-Second and Bainbridge Streets. As he neared eighty, Wanamaker showed no signs of slowing down. The last surviving member of the 1876 Centennial Finance Committee was urging his fellow Philadelphians to mobilize for another great world's fair in a decade, celebrating 150 years of American independence. The August 5 editorial was only one of hundreds crafted by the semiretired Wanamaker since 1912 at the suggestion of his son Rodman, who managed the Philadelphia and New York stores. They allowed the Grand Old Man of Philadelphia a bully pulpit from which to scold his fellow citizens on their shortcomings.

It would have been easy for Philadelphians to dismiss Wanamaker's sermons as the disgruntled mutterings of a moralistic old crank. By any measure, Philadelphia in 1916 was a truly great city. Its 1.8 million inhabitants made it the third largest city in America, after New York, with nearly five million residents, and Chicago, with 2.2 million inhabitants. Philadelphia's pride had not recovered from being booted out of its position as Second City by Chicago in the 1890 Census, or by seeing its 1876 Centennial eclipsed by the Beaux-Arts magnificence of Chicago's 1893 Columbian Exposition. Despite this displacement, Philadelphians could still argue that no other American city manufactured as many different things, or employed as many people to make them, as the "Workshop of the World."

Philadelphia's hundreds of textile mills employed nearly three hundred thousand workers and manufactured more rugs and carpets than all of Great Britain and Ireland. Henry Disston and Sons was the largest manufacturer of saws in the world, while J.G. Brill & Company was the biggest maker of electric street cars in the world. The Baldwin Locomotive Works produced more steam locomotives than any other company: 1,989 in 1916 alone, most ordered by the Allied Powers. The factory of John B. Stetson and Company, maker of the famous ten-gallon cowboy hat, produced more than a million hats each year. With the European war dragging on indefinitely, Philadelphia's industrial growth showed no sign of abatement.[5]

A massive Second Empire structure stood at the junction of the city's main boulevards, Market and Broad Streets. This was the Philadelphia City Hall, home to the municipal government. Originally known as the Public

John Wanamaker in 1914, when the department store magnate, philanthropist, and former postmaster-general had been enthroned as Philadelphia's Grand Old Man.

Buildings, City Hall was meant to be the tallest structure in the world when its cornerstone was laid on July 4, 1874. The grandiose structure was also meant to epitomize the power and prestige of the Second City of the United States. Taking thirty years and costing nearly $25 million to complete, City Hall set a precedent for future civic projects in Philadelphia. They would inevitably be completed years behind schedule and millions of dollars over budget, thanks to the graft and corruption that had become endemic to the municipal government.

By the time City Hall was finally completed in 1901, its architecture was considered déclassé, its height had been surpassed by other structures, and Philadelphia had fallen behind Chicago in terms of population. Within a few years of its completion, urban planners were debating how they could modify the massive structure or demolish it completely. By this time, a loathing of City Hall was a prerequisite for progressive Philadelphians. Lawyer Francis Biddle castigated it as a "symbol of dishonesty and ugliness, squatting over the city's heart," while essayist Agnes Repplier called it "that perfect miracle of ugliness and inconvenience."[6]

For many Philadelphians, the unsightliness of City Hall reflected the evil that lurked within. In theory, Philadelphia was governed by its mayor and a bicameral legislative body, composed of a forty-eight-member Select Council and an eighty-three-member Common Council. In reality, Philadelphia in 1916 was run by a Republican machine known as the

Organization, controlled by a cabal of political bosses. Republicans occupied virtually every office, while the Democratic vote had withered from 39 percent in 1891 to less than 4 percent in 1915.

Most large American cities in the early twentieth century were ruled by machines, yet few achieved the degree of tyranny practiced in Philadelphia. "All our municipal governments are more or less bad, and all our people are optimists," journalist Lincoln Steffens conceded in 1904. "Philadelphia is simply the most corrupt and the most contented." Other major American cities, Steffens alleged, "no matter how bad their own condition may be, all point with scorn to Philadelphia as worse—'the worst-governed city in the country.'"[7]

Two blocs controlled by competing "contractor kings" battled for domination of the Republican Organization. State Senator James P. "Sunny Jim" McNichol, a big, handsome man with a ready smile and an affable manner, ran the northern half of the city. His Keystone State Construction Company had won the contracts for the Northeast Boulevard (later renamed the Roosevelt Boulevard after Theodore Roosevelt), the Market Street Subway, and water filtration plants throughout the city. Following the death of George Vare in 1908, the area below Market Street was ruled with an iron fist by his younger brothers Edwin and William Vare, the "Dukes of South Philadelphia." State Senator Edwin Vare ran the family construction, street cleaning, and trash collection businesses. Younger brother Bill was the U.S. congressman for the First Congressional District, which encompassed South Philadelphia. In theory, the McNichol and Vare blocs had agreed politely to divide the city at Market Street. In practice, the two camps were engaged in a bloody struggle for control of the Republican City Committee, composed of the leaders of the forty-eight wards that constituted the city's primary political territories.

The upper hand in the struggle between McNichol and the Vares was held by Boies Penrose, the Philadelphia aristocrat who had represented Pennsylvania in the United States Senate since 1897. With Pennsylvania's oil, steel, coal, and railroad interests behind him, Penrose was untouchable. A "magnificently coarse" giant of a man who weighed more than three hundred pounds, Penrose believed in power above all else. Watching a parade one day, "the Big Grizzly" told a friend that the only spectacle capable of exciting his admiration was "a well-drilled body of voters marching in perfect and obedient order to the polls."[8] Penrose maintained equilibrium between the McNichol and Vare blocs, favoring the former but allying with the latter when it suited his purpose.

A political cartoon depicting Philadelphia's ruling bloc: U.S. Senator Boies Penrose, banker and lawyer George H. Earle Jr., State Senator James P. McNichol, State Senator Edwin H. Vare, and U.S. Congressman William S. Vare.

In the city that had given birth to American independence, many voters no longer attempted to be heard. Despite the efforts of reform organizations like the Committee of Seventy, Philadelphia elections were a joke. "The Philadelphians do not vote; they are disenfranchised, and their disfranchisement is one anchor of the foundation of the Philadelphia organization,"[9] Steffens wrote. The Organization controlled the entire electoral process. Horror stories abounded of the frauds perpetrated by its bosses: 252 votes returned from a division with fewer than one hundred legal voters; registration lists padded with the names of children, dead men, and pets; a one-story house where forty-four voters were registered. While paid repeaters voted over and over again at twenty-five cents a vote, honest citizens trying to cast their single ballot were ignored, intimidated, or attacked.

As a result, Steffens observed, "many Philadelphians do not try to vote. They leave everything to the machine, and the machine casts their ballots for them. . . . Only in Philadelphia is 'to vote' a passive verb—people don't vote, they are voted." Most citizens accepted this state of affairs with little or no protest; hence Steffens' assertion that they were "contented." He acknowledged that "supine" or "asleep" might be more appropriate terms. The people of Philadelphia "seem to prefer to be ruled by a known thief than an ambitious reformer."[10]

With so many docile sheep to fleece, everyone in City Hall seemed to be on the take. Since most elected officials owed their positions to the machine bosses, they followed their patrons' dictates and ignored the will of the voters. Large, semiprivate utilities like the Philadelphia Electric Company (PECO), the United Gas Improvement Company (UGI), and the Philadelphia Rapid Transit Company (PRT) acted as monopolies, providing poor service at high rates thanks to long-term sweetheart contracts arranged by their City Hall allies.

Similarly, most of the city's nearly thirteen thousand civil servant jobs were held by machine appointees, who saw no reason to serve their fellow citizens for free. It was impossible to get anything processed at City Hall without slipping the clerk a bribe. The fire marshal took ten cents per gallon of capacity for every oil burner he inspected. Applicants for low-paying posts as public school teachers had to kick back most of their salaries for the first three months to local committeemen. Since 94 percent of all city employees were forced to pay between 1 and 4 percent of their salaries to the Republican Organization war chest, there might have been some excuse for their greed. These "voluntary contributions" pumped an estimated $3 million into the Organization treasury between 1903 and 1913.[11]

In 1911, a standoff between the McNichol and Vare factions had permitted the election of "Old Dutch Cleanser" Rudolph Blankenburg, a wealthy manufacturer turned reform politician. Mayor Blankenburg promised "a clean, progressive, constructive business administration, not for the profit and gain of the few, but for the benefit of all."[12] The Blankenburg administration was a stressful period for the McNichol and Vare camps. They had to watch municipal contracts that would have been handed directly to them in the old days go to the lowest bidder in an open competition. The Organization's treasury plunged as Blankenburg's technocrats inspected existing contracts, revealing widespread padding. Municipal fees paid to the Vares and other private garbage collectors dropped more than 50 percent between 1911 and 1913. Blankenburg's "Great Experiment" saved city taxpayers $5 million during his four years in office.

By 1915, the Vares and McNichol had learned their lesson and declared a truce, ensuring the election of reliable hack Thomas B. Smith as mayor. Smith made sure that most of Blankenburg's political reforms were scrapped early in his administration. Once again, city employees were forced to make "voluntary contributions" to the Organization in exchange for their jobs. Contracts for large public works projects, stalled by Blankenburg's resistance, were given the green light by a new mayor anxious to appease his contractor friends.[13]

Despite this reversion to the mean, the denizens of City Hall were doing more than accepting bribes in 1916. Philadelphia may have returned to being corrupt and contented, but it remained a dynamic, powerful, and fast-growing metropolis. To reduce reliance on the PRT's overcrowded trolleys, City Councils appropriated $63 million to build an integrated rapid transit system connecting every corner of the city. Expanding on the one existing line, an elevated subway that ran along Market Street from the Delaware River to Upper Darby, this system would include a Broad Street Subway running from Olney Avenue to League Island Park; elevated lines to Darby in the southwest, Roxborough in the northwest, and Holmesburg in the northeast; a surface line stretching to Byberry on the city's northern border; and a Center City subway loop.

The Councils approved a second loan package totaling $47.4 million to modernize the city's obsolete wharves and docks, and to pave the streets in rapidly developing areas like Oxford Circle, East Germantown, and Roxborough. Ordinances were signed authorizing the erection of a new central library and a new Convention Hall. A commission was formed to examine the feasibility of a Delaware River Bridge connecting the city with Camden. Councils also considered the possibility of a new municipal stadium. The city had just forfeited the Army-Navy football game, a Philadelphia fixture since 1899, because it lacked a fifty-thousand-seat stadium. The 1916 Army-Navy game would be played at the Polo Grounds in New York, rather than Franklin Field at the University of Pennsylvania. "Thus," mourned the *Inquirer*, "Philadelphia loses what has become the most spectacular athletic event in the world."[14]

Mayor Smith also revived the Fairmount Parkway project, which had stagnated during the Blankenburg years. First proposed in the 1880s, the mile-long boulevard would cut diagonally through the northwest quadrant of the city, connecting Center City Philadelphia with Fairmount Park. The Parkway would begin at City Hall, wrap around Logan Square, and terminate at the rocky bluff that contained the old Fairmount reservoir. An ordinance approving the "Park Boulevard" was signed in 1892, but little progress was made on the Parkway until Smith took office in 1916. He pushed through a $9 million construction loan, stepped up the condemnation of properties, and signed an ordinance to open the boulevard for its entire length. Within a year, "Sunny Jim" McNichol's construction company was awarded a $202,000 contract to complete the Parkway between Logan Square and Fairmount.[15]

Concurrently, the city's Art Jury approved the design for a new Museum of Art that would stand atop the Fairmount plateau. The joint design, by Horace Trumbauer and the firm of Borie and Zantzinger, envisioned a massive Greek temple overlooking Center City. Mayor Smith approved a $1 million loan to begin construction on the museum, which would replace the overcrowded and outmoded Memorial Hall in Fairmount Park. Completion of the museum was projected for 1920. Other magnificent structures would soon join it along the Parkway, including the new library, a Hall of Justice, and a magnificent Episcopal cathedral. By 1926, Philadelphia would boast a civic center equal to London's Mall or Berlin's Unter den Linden.[16]

This was the Philadelphia—corrupt and crass yet struggling to redeem itself—that John Wanamaker had tried to awaken on that steamy August morning when he asked his readers, "Are there any sons left of those who toiled in old times to make the city head the list, willing to take off their coats and go to work for a great future of Philadelphia?" Wanamaker believed that a Sesqui-Centennial would return his beloved Philadelphia to its core values of honesty, industry, and patriotism. At the same time, it would propel the increasingly arthritic burg into the twentieth century, bringing it up to speed with other great cities.[17]

Wanamaker's appeal attracted one important ally: Howard B. French, president of the Philadelphia Chamber of Commerce. By the end of August 1916, French announced that his organization fully supported Wanamaker's vision for a 1926 world's fair. By the end of October, the Chamber had appointed an executive committee to plan for "a Great International Exposition in Philadelphia in 1926." The committee urged the speedy completion of the Fairmount Parkway so that it could be the site of the 1926 fair. The Chamber also recommended that such proposed civic buildings as the Art Gallery, Free Library, and Convention Hall be erected on the Parkway as quickly as possible, to be utilized as exposition pavilions.[18]

The Franklin Institute of the State of Pennsylvania for the Promotion of the Mechanic Arts had been founded in 1824 to honor Benjamin Franklin and promote his inventions. Over the years, its mission had expanded to include the education of working men and the evaluation of new inventions.

The Fairmount Parkway as envisioned in 1911, lined with impressive civic structures from City Hall at one end to the new Museum of Art at the other.

The final model for the Museum of Art, approved by the Philadelphia Art Jury in 1916.

In 1870, the influential institute had been one of the first organizations to advocate an International Exhibition in Fairmount Park to commemorate the Centennial. On October 30, 1916, the board of managers of the Franklin Institute adopted a similar resolution, urging Mayor Thomas B. Smith to sponsor an international exhibition to be held in 1926. In January 1917, a resolution was introduced in the Pennsylvania House of Representatives calling for the governor to appoint a Sesqui-Centennial Commission, and appropriate $10,000 for preliminary expenses.[19]

That spring, John Wanamaker launched a new series of newspaper essays, each one detailing what had happened at the 1876 Centennial on that day. The first one on May 10 described the opening day ceremonies, when President Grant and Emperor Dom Pedro of Brazil had switched on the giant Corliss Steam Engine, which powered all of the other machines in Machinery Hall. Wanamaker's essay ended with another plug for the 1926 fair:

> No city is as well-qualified to hold a sesqui-centennial as Philadelphia, if it has the men of far vision to do it and start soon enough. Under existing conditions, nine years is not too long to get ready. What other nation can do it as well as the United States?[20]

By the time Wanamaker's essay appeared, the United States had far weightier matters on its mind. The state of grace in which the country had lived ended on April 6, 1917, when President Wilson signed a joint resolution of Congress declaring war on Germany. Faced with the announcement that Germany planned to resume unrestricted submarine warfare, and hounded by rumors of a German-backed revolution in Mexico, Wilson was forced to conclude that America was not too proud to fight.

Four days later, a mysterious explosion rocked the Eddystone Ammunition Corporation near Chester, part of the Baldwin Locomotive Works industrial complex south of Philadelphia. The Eddystone site was one of the largest munitions plants in America, responsible for manufacturing millions of rifles, cartridges, and artillery shells for the Allied governments. With the United States joining the fight against the Central Powers, Eddystone would play a crucial role in the war effort. The unexplained blast killed 121 workers and injured 300 more, most of them women. The force of the explosion mangled victims beyond recognition, and blew some bodies hundreds of yards into the Delaware River. The *Inquirer* predicted that "Philadelphia has been selected as the scene for the beginning of a new reign of terror."

A few days later, the Navy Department ordered all private wireless stations in the city dismantled. Rodman Wanamaker turned over control of the radio stations at the Wanamaker stores in Philadelphia and New York to the U.S. government. On April 29, the first two Philadelphians were killed in action when the American armed tanker *Vacuum* was torpedoed by a German submarine. On May 6, a civilian was shot and killed when he failed to heed the challenge of an army sentry on the Pennsylvania Railroad bridge at Thirty-Fourth Street and Girard Avenue. Suddenly, the European war seemed very close to home.

A week after Wanamaker's Centennial essay appeared, Congress approved the federal conscription of troops for armed services under the Selective Service Act. By July the first of fifty-three thousand servicemen from Philadelphia would be drafted. On May 21 the First Liberty Loan was launched, a campaign to sell $2 billion in bonds to finance the American war effort. By the end of the campaign on June 14, Philadelphians had bought $145,172,950 in bonds, beating their quota by more than $5 million. A few days later, Red Cross Week began, with Philadelphia's expected contribution set at $3 million. As the war effort gripped the Quaker City, it became clear that no time, money, or manpower could be spared for anything as frivolous as a world's fair. The 1926 Sesqui-Centennial International Exposition, with its dreams of universal peace and progress, would have to be postponed for the duration.[21]

NOTES

1. "Shell Holes Used as Sleeping Quarters by Tommies on the Western Front," *PI*, August 5, 1916; "French Win Double Victory in Furious Fight Along Meuse," *PI*, August 5, 1916; "Russians Driven from Village Taken at Bayonet Point," *PI*, August 5, 1916.

2. Cooper, *Woodrow Wilson: A Biography*.

3. Weigley, *Philadelphia*, p. 558.

4. "Wanamaker Store Is Closed This Saturday Holiday," *PI*, August 5, 1916, p. 7.

5. *Philadelphia: "The Work Shop of the World"*; Keels, *Forgotten Philadelphia*, pp. 104–105, 138–140; Miller et al., *Still Philadelphia*, pp. 73–80; "Baldwins to Build $500K Structure," *PI*, February 16, 1916.

6. Moss, *Historic Landmarks of Philadelphia*, pp. 180–185; Keels, *Forgotten Philadelphia*, pp. 271–273; McCaffery, *When Bosses Ruled Philadelphia*, pp. 22–27, 66–67; Biddle, *The Llanfear Pattern*, pp. 233–234.

7. Steffens, *The Shame of the Cities*, pp. 134–136.

8. Lukacs, *Philadelphia*, p. 62.

9. Steffens, *The Shame of the Cities*, p. 138.

10. Lukacs, *Philadelphia*, pp. 49–84; Steffens, *The Shame of the Cities*, pp. 134, 138–144, 158; Weigley, *Philadelphia*, p. 535.

11. Weigley, *Philadelphia*, pp. 540–543, 547–548; "The 'Reputation' of Philadelphia," editorial, *PI*, January 8, 1916; Warner, *The Private City*, p. 216; McCaffery, *When Bosses Ruled Philadelphia*, p. 93.

12. Blankenburg, *The Blankenburgs of Philadelphia*, p. 44.

13. Weigley, *Philadelphia*, pp. 553–557; Blankenburg, *The Blankenburgs of Philadelphia*, p. xx.

14. "Mayor Promises to Rush Parkway and Transit Work," *PI*, July 22, 1916; "Army-Navy Game Goes to New York; Lost to This City," *PI*, February 16, 1916.

15. "Speak for Park Plan," *PI*, December 3, 1916.

16. "Mayor Promises to Rush Parkway and Transit Work," *PI*, July 22, 1916; *Annual Report of the Department of City Transit of the City of Philadelphia for the Year Ending December 31, 1916*, pp. 1–15; Brownlee, *Building the City Beautiful*, pp. 13–30, 39–60; Blankenburg, *The Blankenburgs of Philadelphia*, pp. 89–90.

17. Joyce, *The Story of Philadelphia*, p. 314.

18. "World's Fair Here in 1926," *PB*, October 12, 1916; "World's Fair for 1926 Given Practical Start," *PPL*, October 13, 1916; "Seek Cooperation for 1926 Exhibit," *PI*, October 25, 1916; Rosewater, "Notes on the Sesqui-Centennial," VR/AJA, pp. 1–4.

19. Rosewater, "Notes on the Sesqui-Centennial," VR/AJA, p. 3; "World's Fair Plans Framed," *PI*, November 22, 1916; "Plan Philadelphia Expo in 1926," *PB*, January 23, 1917.

20. Advertisement, *PI*, May 10, 1917.

21. Philadelphia War History Committee, *Philadelphia in the World War*, pp. 29–31; Weigley, *Philadelphia*, pp. 558–561; "119 Killed, 150 Injured, Majority Women, by Explosion Laid to Plotters in Plant of Eddystone Ammunition Corporation," *PI*, April 11, 1917; "Shrapnel Volleys Wither Trapped Survivors of First Blast," *PI*, April 11, 1917; "Wanamaker Offers U.S. Two Wireless Plants," *PI*, April 11, 1917; "Order All Wireless Stations Dismantled," *PI*, April 11, 1917.

2

★ ★ ★

As Welcome as Jazz Music at a Funeral

AS THE 1920s DAWNED, Philadelphia was as shell-shocked as a veteran of the Battle of the Argonne Forest. Besides dealing with the loss of 1,399 Philadelphians in the Great War, the city was struggling with the aftermath of the Spanish influenza epidemic, which had killed nearly 13,000 citizens. A deepening postwar recession had idled many factories in the Workshop of the World, and ex-soldiers found themselves joining an army of unemployed. The onset of Prohibition aggravated the recession, shuttering dozens of Philadelphia breweries and throwing thousands more out of work. It also triggered a wave of crime as Philadelphians turned to bootleggers and gangsters to supply them with alcohol. Even the promise of civic reform with the election of a new mayor, J. Hampton Moore, and the adoption of a new City Charter could not distract the city from the postwar economic downturn and social malaise.[1]

Despite this grim atmosphere, plans persisted to hold a great world's fair in 1926. Moribund during the war, the Sesqui-Centennial International Exposition had returned to life thanks to the unrelenting efforts of John Wanamaker. When reporters gathered on July 11, 1919, to interview Wanamaker on his eighty-first birthday, Philadelphia's Grand Old Man had used the occasion to advance the cause of his beloved fair. In the wake of the most destructive war in history, he emphasized the Sesqui as a way for America to reconnect with the world while advancing its new primacy in international affairs. "No nation in the world has today such an opportunity to hold a sesqui-centennial in 1926," Wanamaker insisted, "which should cover not less than three hundred acres of [Fairmount] Park and make an astounding presentation of the capacity and productive power of the United States."[2]

Inspired by Wanamaker, other prominent Philadelphians renewed the call for a 1926 fair. The Franklin Institute and the Philadelphia Chamber of Commerce urged Mayor J. Hampton Moore to begin planning immediately. In May 1920 Congressman George P. Darrow of Philadelphia introduced a bill in the U.S. House of Representatives calling for governmental recognition of the Sesqui-Centennial, although he withdrew it until City Hall could present more concrete information. The *Bulletin* endorsed these efforts, noting that as the world moved away from "the war of 1917 and the agitations which have followed it . . . there will be a steadily increasing spirit of international amity." In such an atmosphere, the Sesqui-Centennial would assume the trappings of a "great Festival of Peace," promoting harmony among all nations.[3]

On November 4, 1920, Mayor Moore hosted a group of leading citizens to "prepare for the organization of a movement to celebrate in Philadelphia, in 1926, the Sesqui-Centennial of the signing of the Declaration of Independence." The well-attended meeting resulted in the formation of a Committee of 100 to develop plans for the celebration. The committee constituted a cross section of all segments of Philadelphia society, including industrialists, retailers, publishers, financiers, clergymen, academics, lawyers and magistrates, social leaders, and even a civil servant, Receiver of Taxes W. Freeland Kendrick.

At its first meeting on January 24, 1921, the Committee of 100 agreed that the Sesqui-Centennial celebration should take the form of an international exposition. In February the committee incorporated itself as the Sesqui-Centennial Exhibition Association (SCEA) and elected officers. Mayor Moore agreed to serve as president. While financier Edward T. Stotesbury resigned as treasurer after only a few days, he agreed to head the SCEA Finance Committee and to serve as one of the twenty-five directors of the association. The venerable John Wanamaker was named honorary chairman of the SCEA board.[4]

Soon after Philadelphians got their first glimpse of the Sesqui, the increasingly popular nickname for the upcoming fair. Architect Paul Philippe Cret, head of architecture at the University of Pennsylvania, unveiled his preliminary plans on January 13, 1921. Although not officially sanctioned, Cret's designs had been commissioned by the Fairmount Park Art Association. They centered on the newly finished Fairmount Parkway, incorporating the many civic monuments projected for the boulevard. Cret proposed a monumental entrance to the Sesqui fairgrounds at Logan Circle, the midpoint of the Parkway. By 1926 it was expected that this space would be surrounded by magnificent new structures, including the Free Library of Philadelphia, a Municipal Court, and Victory Hall, an auditorium honoring the city's war dead.[5]

The Parkway itself would become a gigantic pedestrian esplanade, lined with temporary exhibition buildings. At its northwestern end would stand the new homes of the Pennsylvania Academy of the Fine Arts (PAFA) and the Pennsylvania Museum School of Industrial Art (PMSIA). Beyond a monumental Court of Honor, a grand staircase would lead to the Greek temple housing the new Museum of Art atop the Fairmount Plateau. Visitors leaving the art museum through its rear entrance would stroll through gardens into Lemon Hill, the original section of Fairmount Park. A park drive adorned with sculpture would follow the east bank of the Schuylkill to a gigantic new stadium in Snyder's Woods. Next to the stadium, an old reservoir would be developed into an aviation field where spectators could thrill to air shows.

Cret's plan fulfilled his long-held desire to beautify both banks of the putrid and polluted Schuylkill River. A temporary bridge at Arch Street would shield fairgoers from the unsightly industrial landscape below Fairmount Park. The West Philadelphia stockyards and slaughterhouses that lined the river above Arch Street would be condemned by the city, and their land reclaimed for exhibition halls. The removal of these noxious enterprises would help purify the river's water, and make the fair a pleasure to smell as well as to see. The railroad tracks on both sides of the Schuylkill would be covered over and an amusement area built atop them. A permanent bridge, modeled after the Pont Alexandre III in Paris, would extend from the southwest side of the Art Museum complex, terminating in ornamental fountains on the west bank of the Schuylkill. A West River Parkway would be lined with state and foreign pavilions, leading fairgoers to the Zoological Gardens and the Centennial grounds. There, the two remaining buildings from the 1876 fair, Memorial Hall and Horticultural Hall, would serve as exhibit halls.

Cret's plan for the Sesqui accomplished a number of key objectives. The central fairgrounds would be accessible from Center City by foot, and within walking distance of all three train stations. Ten trolley lines would stop at various access points to the fair, while nearby parking lots would accommodate automobiles. Water taxis could transport visitors from points upriver, while the adventurous could arrive via airplane at the aviation field. This accessibility would not only maximize attendance, but would allow Center City business owners to reap the full economic benefit from fairgoers.

Cret's seemingly elaborate design was relatively economical. At 165 acres, the central fairgrounds would be less than one-third the size of the

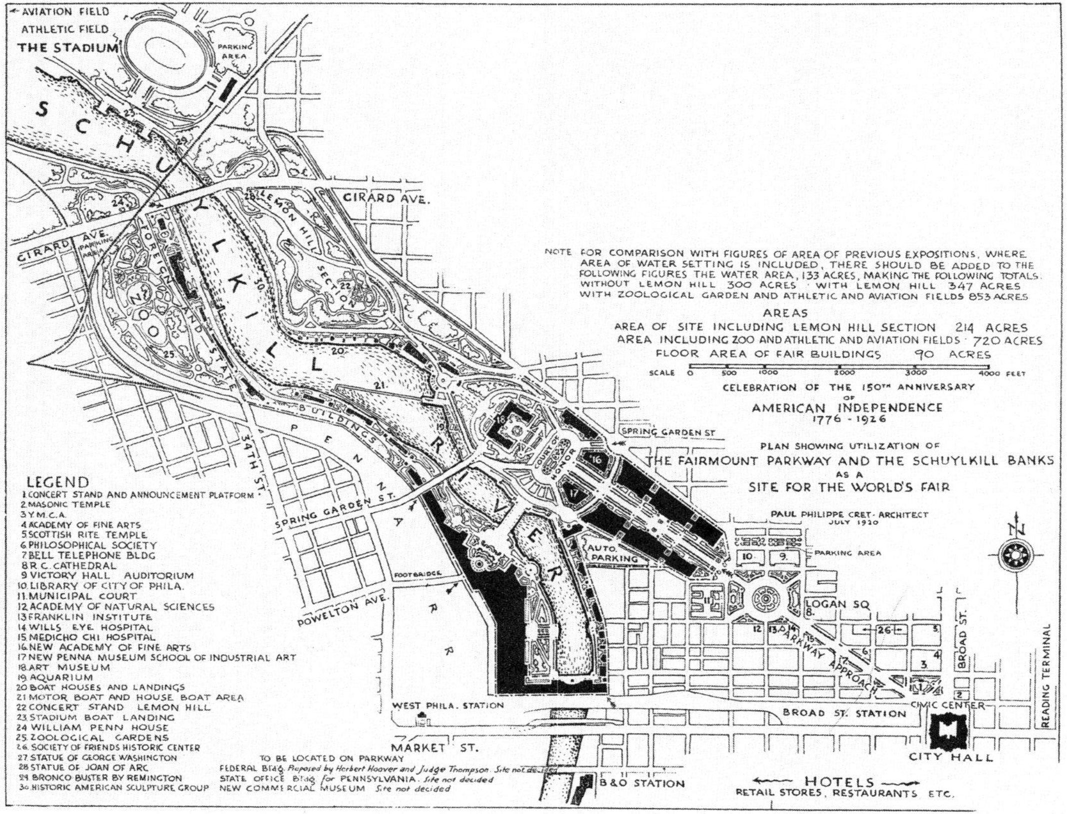

AVIATION FIELD
ATHLETIC FIELD
THE STADIUM
PARKING AREA
SCHUYLKILL RIVER
GIRARD AVE.
LEMON HILL SECTION
FOREIGN AND STATE BUILDINGS
ZOO
PENNA R R
34TH ST.
SPRING GARDEN ST.
POWELTON AVE.
FOOTBRIDGE
WEST PHILA. STATION
MARKET ST.
B&O STATION
COURT OF HONOR
AUTO. PARKING
LOGAN SQ
PARKWAY APPROACH
BROAD ST.
BROAD ST. STATION
CIVIC CENTER
CITY HALL
READING TERMINAL
HOTELS
RETAIL STORES, RESTAURANTS ETC.
NOTE FOR COMPARISON WITH FIGURES OF AREA OF PREVIOUS EXPOSITIONS, WHERE AREA OF WATER SETTING IS INCLUDED, THERE SHOULD BE ADDED TO THE FOLLOWING FIGURES THE WATER AREA, 133 ACRES, MAKING THE FOLLOWING TOTALS: WITHOUT LEMON HILL 300 ACRES · WITH LEMON HILL 347 ACRES WITH ZOOLOGICAL GARDEN AND ATHLETIC AND AVIATION FIELDS 853 ACRES
AREAS
AREA OF SITE INCLUDING LEMON HILL SECTION 214 ACRES
AREA INCLUDING ZOO AND ATHLETIC AND AVIATION FIELDS · 720 ACRES
FLOOR AREA OF FAIR BUILDINGS 90 ACRES
SCALE 0 500 1000 2000 3000 4000 FEET
CELEBRATION OF THE 150TH ANNIVERSARY OF AMERICAN INDEPENDENCE 1776 - 1926
PLAN SHOWING UTILIZATION OF THE FAIRMOUNT PARKWAY AND THE SCHUYLKILL BANKS AS A SITE FOR THE WORLD'S FAIR
PAUL PHILIPPE CRET · ARCHITECT JULY 1920
LEGEND
1 CONCERT STAND AND ANNOUNCEMENT PLATFORM
2 MASONIC TEMPLE
3 Y.M.C.A.
4 ACADEMY OF FINE ARTS
5 SCOTTISH RITE TEMPLE
6 PHILOSOPHICAL SOCIETY
7 BELL TELEPHONE BLDG
8 R.C. CATHEDRAL
9 VICTORY HALL AUDITORIUM
10 LIBRARY OF CITY OF PHILA.
11 MUNICIPAL COURT
12 ACADEMY OF NATURAL SCIENCES
13 FRANKLIN INSTITUTE
14 WILLS EYE HOSPITAL
15 MEDICHO CHI HOSPITAL
16 NEW ACADEMY OF FINE ARTS
17 NEW PENNA MUSEUM SCHOOL OF INDUSTRIAL ART
18 ART MUSEUM
19 AQUARIUM
20 BOAT HOUSES AND LANDINGS
21 MOTOR BOAT AND HOUSE BOAT AREA
22 CONCERT STAND LEMON HILL
23 STADIUM BOAT LANDING
24 WILLIAM PENN HOUSE
25 ZOOLOGICAL GARDENS
26 SOCIETY OF FRIENDS HISTORIC CENTER
27 STATUE OF GEORGE WASHINGTON
28 STATUE OF JOAN OF ARC
29 BRONCO BUSTER BY REMINGTON
30 HISTORIC AMERICAN SCULPTURE GROUP
TO BE LOCATED ON PARKWAY
FEDERAL Bldg. Proposed by Herbert Hoover and Judge Thompson. Site not decided
STATE OFFICE Bldg for PENNSYLVANIA. Site not decided
NEW COMMERCIAL MUSEUM Site not decided

1900 Paris Exposition, and even smaller than the 284-acre Centennial. Condemnation and purchase of properties would be limited, since most of the land belonged to the city, or was due to be acquired for the Parkway and Art Museum. Much of the fair would take place in permanent structures that were already in progress or scheduled for construction, such as the Museum of Art, Free Library, and Victory Hall. The 1926 deadline would ensure the timely completion of these projects, always an important consideration in Philadelphia.[6]

The Parkway plan won the endorsement of the Philadelphia Real Estate Board, the Fairmount Park Commission, the City Art Jury, and most of the city's leading newspapers. Envisioning the changes to the city that would be wrought by the Sesqui, the *Bulletin* imagined Philadelphia as a "City Beautiful, as a by-product of the Exposition, which will return dividends on the investment long after the great fair shall have passed into history."[7]

Other parties quickly protested the Parkway site. Foremost among them was Joseph Huston, the architect who had designed the grandiose Pennsylvania State Capitol at Harrisburg, and who had served six months in prison in 1911 for conspiring to defraud the Commonwealth during its construction. Huston felt that the Sesqui-Centennial should take place at League Island Park on the "South Philadelphia flats, where there could be reproduced the hanging gardens of Babylon and where the navies of the world could ride east at the gates." Other parties recommended locations in West Philadelphia, along the Roosevelt Boulevard in Northeast Philadelphia, or in rural Roxborough. To the surprise of the SCEA, Mayor Moore called the Parkway plan "beautiful but expensive" and "decidedly premature." While Moore insisted that he was of an "open mind" for a site, he expressed admiration for Huston's plan because of the permanent improvements it would provide for South Philadelphia.[8]

Meanwhile, political leaders battled over who would control the Sesqui. The 1921 elections had seen a resurgence of the Republican Organization, controlled by Ed and Bill Vare after the 1917 death of "Sunny Jim" McNichol. Mayor Moore, an independent Republican, found himself increasingly at loggerheads with a reorganized City Council filled with Vare puppets. Councilman Joseph C. Gaffney, a Vare man, protested that no council member had been appointed to the Committee of 100. After some discussion, Councilman Charles B. Hall, Vare floor leader, was named to the

---

FACING PAGE: Paul Philippe Cret's original plan for the Sesqui-Centennial, centered on the new Fairmount Parkway.

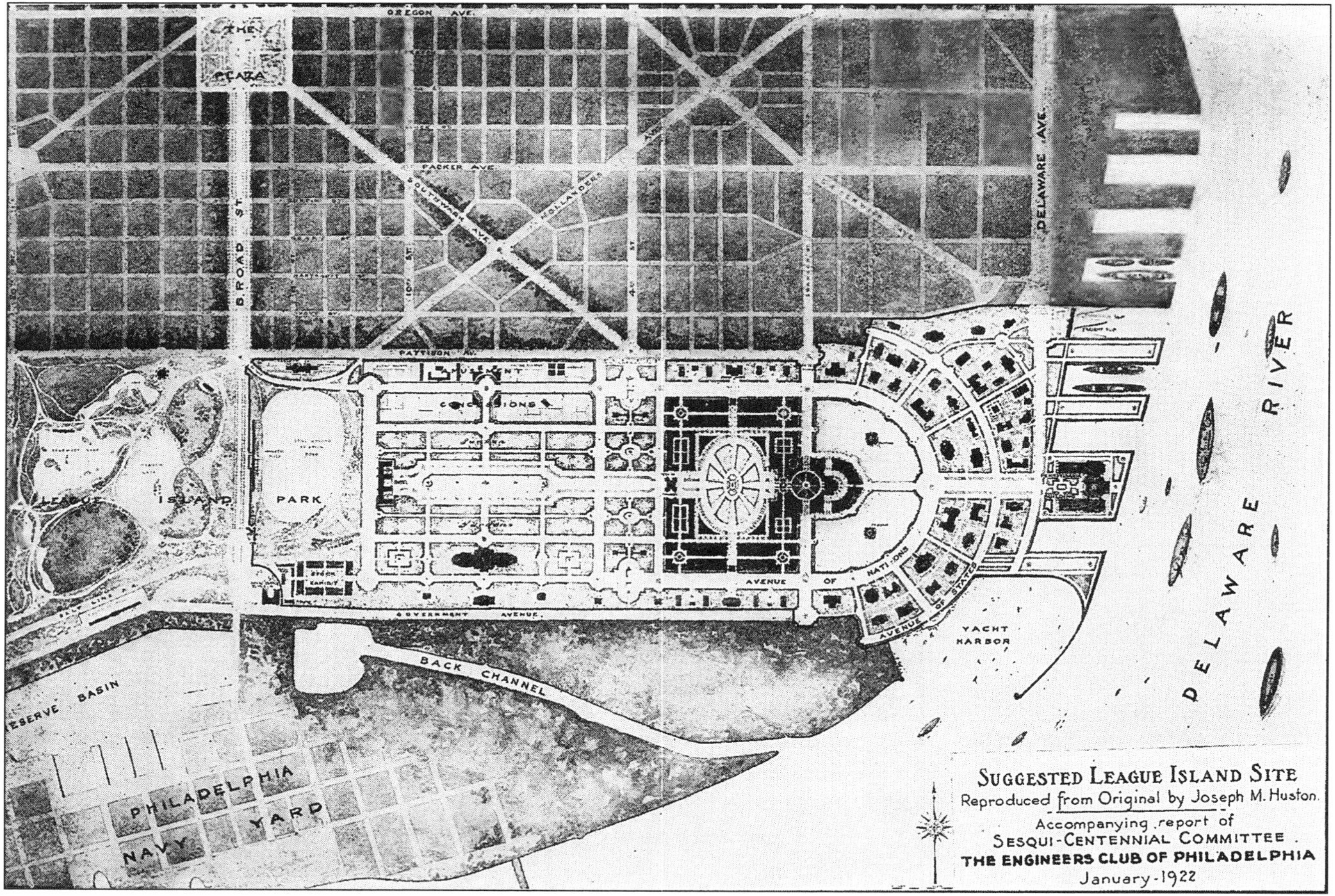
SUGGESTED LEAGUE ISLAND SITE
Reproduced from Original by Joseph M. Huston.
Accompanying report of
SESQUI-CENTENNIAL COMMITTEE.
THE ENGINEERS CLUB OF PHILADELPHIA
January-1922
OREGON AVE.
THE PLAZA
BROAD ST
PACKER AVE.
SOUTHWARK AVE.
10TH ST
4TH ST
DELAWARE AVE.
PATTISON AV.
CONCESSIONS
PARK
LEAGUE ISLAND
AVENUE OF NATIONS
AVENUE OF STATES
GOVERNMENT AVENUE
YACHT HARBOR
DELAWARE RIVER
BACK CHANNEL
RESERVE BASIN
PHILADELPHIA NAVY YARD

committee. Soon after, Mayor Moore requested that City Council allocate $50,000 to defray initial fair planning. Council earmarked that amount, but insisted that it control expenditures. After several months of wrangling, City Council grudgingly approved the $50,000 appropriation, to be administered jointly by the mayor and city treasurer.[9]

By mid-June, the Pennsylvania Legislature had passed a resolution pledging its support for the 1926 Sesqui-Centennial in Philadelphia. U.S. Congressman George P. Darrow had reintroduced his bill in the House of Representatives authorizing the federal government to recognize and sponsor the Sesqui. The SCEA had been incorporated, had received its state charter, and had drawn up its official bylaws. Yet the association had taken no concrete steps toward planning the fair, such as drafting the customary "plan and scope" agenda for the fair, selecting a site, or developing a budget. Until it did so, Congress could take no action on the Darrow Bill.[10]

As 1921 drew to a close, City Hall and the SCEA took their first tentative steps toward making the Sesqui-Centennial a reality. On December 30, after an impassioned plea from the executive committee of the SCEA, City Council pledged $2.5 million to the Sesqui. When Mayor Moore asked City Council to double its appropriation as a goodwill gesture, the council readily agreed to spend $5 million "or as much more as may be required." On the last day of 1921, the *Inquirer* published an editorial praising the armistice between Mayor Moore and City Council. "The happy situation as regards the Sesqui-Centennial shows what can be achieved when there is accord. Let politics be forgotten, therefore, and for 1922 let us have harmony."[11]

Within hours, Philadelphia had learned of the death of one of its most powerful citizens. As midnight neared on December 31, 1921, Boies Penrose, U.S. senator from Pennsylvania, died in his hotel suite in Washington, DC. Cancer had caused the "Big Grizzly" to shed half of his 350 pounds; both his flesh and his clothes hung limply from his once-massive frame. The *New York Times* called him "one of the last of the 'Old Guard' leaders," once so powerful in the affairs of the Republican Party. Few observers realized that Penrose's death marked the beginning of the end of Pennsylvania's dominance in American politics.[12]

FACING PAGE: The League Island Park site championed by architect Joseph Huston and South Philadelphia boosters. The Engineers' Club report gave this area low marks, citing the time and money needed to prepare it for construction.

One of the reasons behind the initial complacency and inertia of the SCEA might have been a belief that the powerful Penrose, the kingmaker who had been instrumental in putting Warren G. Harding in the White House, would be able to "sell" the Sesqui to the federal government at any time. Throughout 1921 the senator had promised to enlist the support of the president and Congress for the Sesqui-Centennial. With Penrose in charge of the Senate Finance Committee, obtaining a large federal appropriation would have been an easy matter. Now the most powerful voice representing Pennsylvania in Washington had been stilled, and the impact on the Sesqui had yet to be felt.[13]

Before Penrose had been buried, State Senator Ed Vare called on Governor William C. Sproul of Pennsylvania to demand that his younger brother Bill be appointed senator to fill out the remainder of Penrose's term. By 1921, Ed and Bill Vare had achieved complete political control of Philadelphia, except for the upper-class, reform-minded outposts of Germantown and Chestnut Hill in the northwest. Penrose's death seemed like the perfect occasion for fifty-four-year-old Bill Vare to move to the U.S. Senate after nearly a decade in the House of Representatives.

From an early age, Bill had been groomed to be the statesman of the family, despite his undiplomatic demeanor. Unlike his jovial older brother Ed, Bill was cold, taciturn, and an uninspiring speaker despite years of elocution lessons. Of medium height with a stocky boxer's build, he had a full face, a strong jaw, and a thick head of hair. Politically astute and an expert strategist, Bill possessed the sharpest mind of the Vare family. He could rattle off the key statistics for every one of Philadelphia's forty-eight wards and 1,566 political divisions. But his congressional record had been lackluster, while his clumsy efforts to acquire a patina of class only amused his better-born opponents. The Union League of Philadelphia refused to accept Bill as a member, even though he was sponsored by former Pennsylvania governor Edwin S. Stuart. Harvard-educated Boies Penrose dismissed Bill as an "ash-cart statesman" and took pleasure in sabotaging his 1911 mayoral campaign.[14]

Governor Sproul ignored Ed Vare's request and selected an old friend named George Wharton Pepper to succeed Penrose. Pepper was everything Vare was not: a member of two of Philadelphia's oldest and most distinguished families, a graduate of the University of Pennsylvania, a prominent lawyer, a member of the Union League, and a Progressive Republican. Pepper also had two powerful sponsors: Andrew W. Mellon, the Pittsburgh millionaire who served as Harding's treasury secretary; and Joseph R. Grundy, politically powerful president of the Pennsylvania Manufacturers

William S. Vare as he appeared at the outset of his campaign for the Republican nomination for the U.S. senator from Pennsylvania.

Association. Once again, the establishment had closed ranks to exclude the Vares.[15]

With the financial support of the Vare-controlled City Council secured, the SCEA attempted to settle the matter of the Sesqui site. In late 1921, the SCEA Executive Committee asked the Engineers' Club of Philadelphia

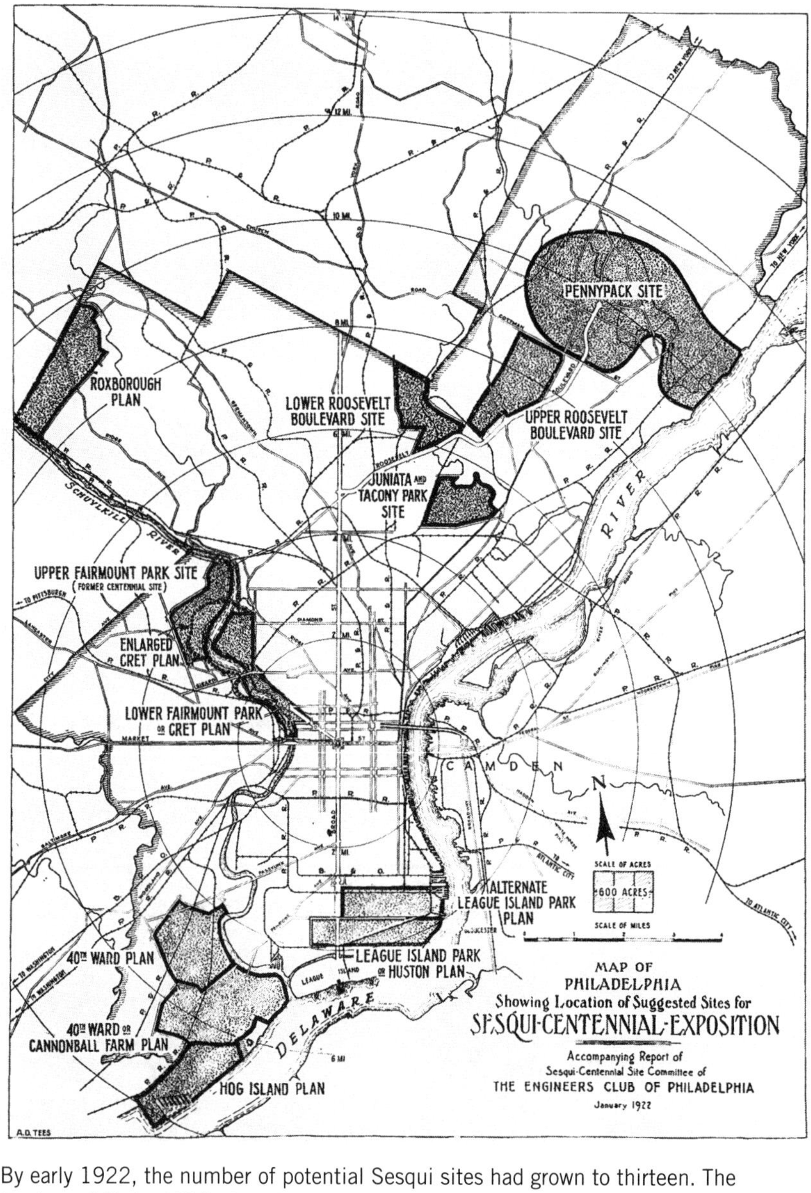

By early 1922, the number of potential Sesqui sites had grown to thirteen. The Engineers' Club of Philadelphia carefully evaluated the pros and cons of each location.

to evaluate thirteen potential locations, working with the Philadelphia Real Estate Board and the local chapter of the American Institute of Architects. In February 1922, the three organizations released their joint report. The *Report of the Sesqui-Centennial Committee of the Engineers' Club of Philadelphia on Sites* selected the Parkway and adjacent areas of Fairmount Park as the most desirable location for the Sesqui. This site offered unique advantages: its accessibility to Center City, its natural beauty, the utilization of such planned structures as the Art Museum and Free Library, and the prospects for construction of other buildings that would benefit Philadelphia permanently.

By contrast, the experts found that outlying locations in Roxborough, the Northeast, and South Philadelphia were sufficiently remote to reduce fair attendance. The several South Philadelphia sites evaluated, including League Island Park and Hog Island, received the lowest ratings. All of the South Philadelphia sites "would require large sums . . . to prepare them for the specific needs of the Exposition." They were also "not readily adapted to easy treatment from the aesthetic standpoint, because of their flat character, nor would they draw the attendance and income which would come to a site more centrally located, with better entrance from all parts of the City."[16] The report estimated that it would require $10 to $20 million to prepare these sites for construction, including drainage, laying water mains, filling and grading the marshy soil, eliminating mosquitoes, and driving thousands of piles for the massive fair buildings. The report recommended revising the Cret Plan to include much of West Fairmount Park, while dropping his proposal to transform the Schuylkill River below Spring Garden Street. This shift would eliminate the need to clean up the lower Schuylkill and its riverbanks, while reducing the city's condemnation and purchase of riverfront property. The report acknowledged that Cret's goal of redeeming the Schuylkill was worthy, but argued that neither the time nor the money was available to achieve this objective before 1926. As a concession to the outlying districts, the report suggested staging a marine exhibit in South Philadelphia and an agricultural exhibit in the Northeast.[17]

The recommendations of the Engineers' Club report were adopted unanimously by the SCEA Executive Committee. They were rejected by neighborhood organizations in the city's outlying areas, usually composed of middle-class businessmen with strong ties to the Republican Organization. Residents of South Philadelphia were especially vociferous in booming their district, despite the disadvantages delineated by the Engineers' Club report. Soon after the report was released in January 1922, South Philadelphians staged a meeting to promote League Island Park for the Sesqui. The meeting was chaired by City Councilman and Vare lieutenant Joseph P. Gaffney, who described the SCEA adoption of the Fairmount Park-Parkway site as "a big mistake."[18]

When Mayor Moore submitted a $3 million bill to City Council to condemn properties on the Schuylkill riverbanks for the Sesqui, Gaffney

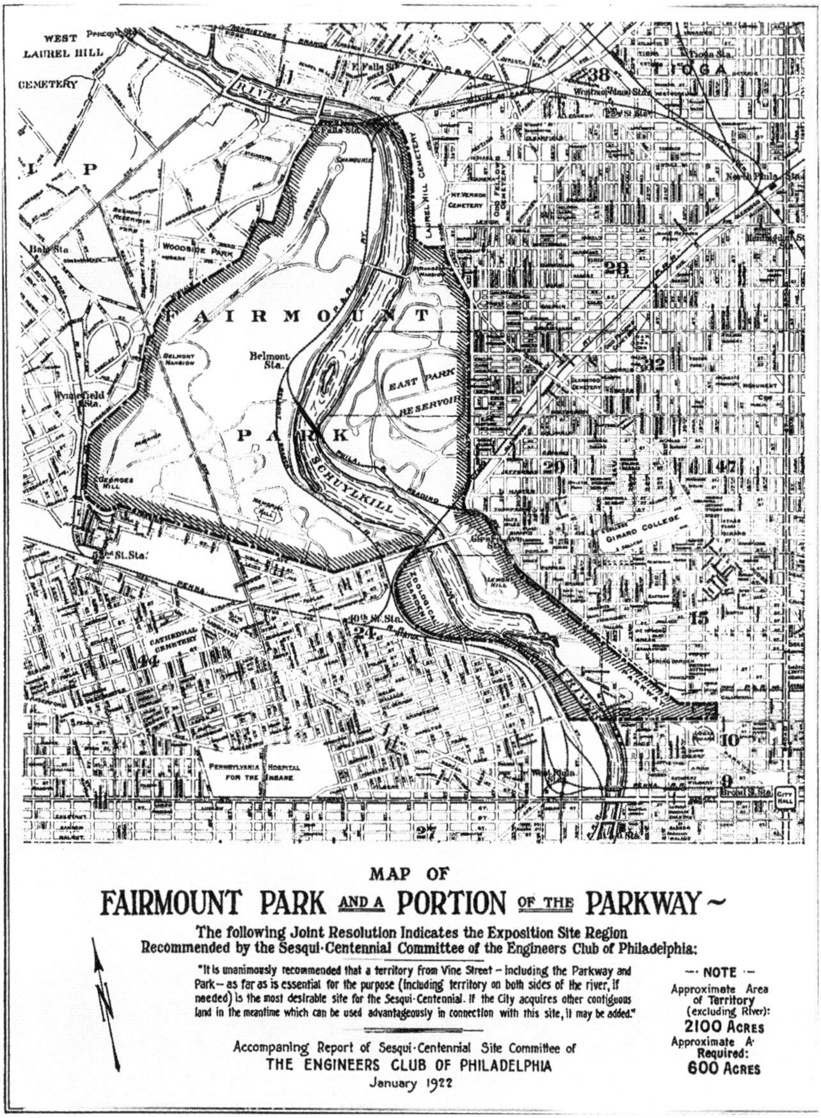

Fairmount Park and the Parkway, the site recommended by the Engineers' Club report as the optimal location for the Sesqui.

held up the bill on a technicality. Gaffney also organized a "Save the Stockyards" hearing at City Council, where owners of West Philadelphia stockyards and slaughterhouses protested Moore's plans to condemn their properties along the Schuylkill River. Such a move, they warned, would threaten Philadelphia's $20 million meat-processing industry, giving Chicago even greater supremacy in that field. Rumors circulated of a Gaffney-led, "anti-park" bloc in City Council that would freeze the entire $5 million Sesqui appropriation if the fair were to be held in Fairmount Park.[19]

Despite these protests, Moore and the SCEA held firm on their decision to stage the Sesqui in Fairmount Park and on the Parkway. With the fair site finalized, a $5 million commitment from the city, and a guarantee of support from the state of Pennsylvania, President Harding recommended that Congress officially recognize the Sesqui-Centennial. On March 24 Harding asked for enactment of legislation fixing 1926 as the time to commemorate the 150th anniversary of the Declaration of Independence, and designating Philadelphia as the site of an international exposition celebrating the event.

In April members of the Senate and House Committees on Industrial Arts and Expositions visited Philadelphia to inspect the Parkway and Fairmount Park. Mayor Moore promised the visitors that the Sesqui-Centennial Exposition would be "the biggest ever held in the world." The initial reaction of the congressmen was positive, but they stressed that no federal appropriation would be forthcoming until the SCEA had presented a detailed plan for the fair and put an experienced executive team in place. So far the SCEA had hired only one full-time employee: Victor Rosewater, a respected and well-connected author who had edited the *Omaha Bee* and served as chairman of the Republican National Committee. SCEA President Moore had hired Rosewater as publicity director without consulting his executive committee. When they protested over his presumption, Moore was forced to backtrack and demote Rosewater to assistant to the president.[20]

On May 3 Moore traveled to Washington to testify before the House of Representatives Committee on Industrial Arts and Expositions, accompanied by a small army of Philadelphia dignitaries. Moore assured the representatives that Philadelphia was "wholly for the Sesqui." City Council President Richard Weglein boasted that Philadelphia had sufficient resources to pay for "the greatest exposition in the history of the world."[21] Besides an official borrowing capacity of $60 million, Philadelphia could tap a councilmanic borrowing capacity of $14 million to sponsor the Sesqui. The equivalent of today's "walking around" or "street money," councilmanic loans were a renewable form of soft funding available to City Council members, enabling them to bankroll pet projects without the trouble of a loan approved by popular referendum.

The House Committee unanimously approved Resolution 170 for "the holding of a national and international exhibition in the city of Philadelphia in 1926." The committee added a phrase specifying that the Sesqui would be held "upon the Fairmount Park and Parkway site selected by the Sesqui-Centennial Exhibition Association and lands contiguous thereto which may be acquired for that purpose." On June 5, the entire House passed Resolution 170 by a unanimous vote. Representative Langham of Texas, the ranking Democrat on the House Committee, said that the bill's passage marked America's "return from war to peace." The resolution still carried no monetary appropriation for the Sesqui-Centennial. That would come after the SCEA had presented a detailed plan and scope document for the fair, and selected a director-general to run the show.[22]

The latter decision was seen as increasingly critical as the days until 1926 dwindled. The director-general would be the organizational wizard who would define the overall plan and scope of the fair, select and supervise the permanent staff, and coordinate the myriad logistics needed to make the Sesqui a reality. Representative Martin B. Madden, chairman of the House Appropriations Committee, told his fellow committee member William S. Vare that "not until a Director General of national reputation has been appointed . . . will Congress authorize any Federal financial aid to the Sesqui-Centennial Exposition." In Harrisburg, Governor Sproul also indicated that the selection of an executive head would be a prerequisite for state support.[23]

Unfortunately, the SCEA was having trouble filling this critical position. It spent months courting Secretary of Commerce Herbert Hoover, whose honesty, efficiency, and organizational genius made him the golden boy of the increasingly troubled Harding administration. Councilman Charles B. Hall suggested offering Hoover the astronomical salary of $100,000 a year, $25,000 more than President Harding earned. When Hoover rebuffed initial feelers from the SCEA, Curtis Publishing executive Edward W. Bok offered to pay Hoover $50,000 a year to direct the SCEA for a minimum of five years. Hoover declined again, citing Harding's wish that he remain in the Cabinet, and his own desire to complete the reorganization of the Commerce Department.[24]

Desperate to find a leader for the Sesqui, Edward Bok offered $50,000 a year for five years to Charles M. Schwab, president of Bethlehem Steel, who also declined the offer. Other prospects whose names were floated included General John J. Pershing, commander of American forces during the World War; Major General George W. Goethals, who supervised construction of the Panama Canal; and Matthew C. Brush, who had directed construction of the gigantic Hog Island Shipyard in South Philadelphia during the war. None of them expressed any interest in running the Sesqui.[25]

With no firm leadership in place, the SCEA was beginning to show signs of stress by mid-1922. Former Chamber of Commerce president Alba B. Johnson resigned from the SCEA board of directors. He was soon followed by ex-governor Edwin Stuart and William Potter, the former ambassador to Italy. City Council, asked to appoint five members to be advisory SCEA directors, flatly refused. A furious Mayor Moore ordered the SCEA to support itself financially, cutting off access to the remaining funds from the $50,000 city appropriation. Disgusted by the internecine politics of the SCEA board, John Frederick Lewis resigned as president.[26]

Senator George Wharton Pepper, trying to shepherd the resolution to grant federal approval for the Sesqui-Centennial through the Senate before it adjourned for the summer, bombarded the SCEA with increasingly frantic telegraphs seeking direction. He received little guidance. Told to hold up passage of the resolution in the Senate indefinitely, a frustrated Pepper told the press, "I do not know what the situation in Philadelphia is, but this uncertainty and delay tends to minimize the importance of the situation." Rumors began to circulate that the House would rescind its approval of the Sesqui. Rep. Oscar Bland wrote "Dear Friend Rosewater" about the "disquieting reports" he had heard of the Sesqui, asking the Nebraskan to slip down to Washington and enlighten him.[27]

By the end of July, most of the remaining directors of SCEA had left Philadelphia for their own extended summer vacations, leaving the Sesqui on hold until September. "So far, the Sesqui-Centennial has been a series of fishing excursions," one director said before departing for Maine. "Six months ago they were fishing in Florida, now they are fishing in Maine. One year ago they were also fishing. How anyone on earth thinks a great Exposition is to be evolved from fishing excursions is beyond my understanding." Despite this inactivity, Senator Pepper managed to push the Darrow Bill through the Senate before it adjourned.[28]

Just before the SCEA disintegrated completely, it acquired a new president who would serve as de facto director-general for the Sesqui: Colonel Franklin Woolman D'Olier. The World War army veteran appeared to have all the credentials that would enable him to bring the Sesqui to fruition. Tall and aristocratic, the Princeton graduate came from an old French Huguenot family. He was president of D'Olier and Company, a textile wholesaler located in Philadelphia. As a lieutenant colonel on the General Staff of the American Expeditionary Forces (AEF) during the war, D'Olier had won a Distinguished Service Medal for his organizational and management skills. He had been elected the first national commander of the newly formed

American Legion in 1919, representing the interests of the nearly two million men who had served in the AEF.

Directors of the cash-starved SCEA were thrilled that the wealthy D'Olier had agreed to serve without salary. The new president promised a policy of "full speed ahead" for the next four years. But he insisted that the people of Philadelphia must determine whether the Sesqui would be "a big international exposition, along the 'greatest-show-on-earth' lines," or "a subdued international cultural display." After accepting the presidency, D'Olier left on an automobile trip of New England, motoring to the various vacation homes of SCEA directors to gauge their opinions on how to proceed. A delighted John Wanamaker placed his imprimatur on the new president by donating $50,000 to the Sesqui treasury. His gift was quickly followed by a $25,000 pledge from Ellis A. Gimbel.[29]

As summer drew to a close, President Warren G. Harding signed Resolution 170 into law in the Oval Office of the White House on August 29, 1922. In doing so, he bestowed the approval of the federal government on "a national and international exhibition in the City of Philadelphia in 1926 upon the Fairmount Park and Parkway site selected by the Sesqui-Centennial Exhibition Association." He was observed by a smiling crowd of Philadelphia notables, including Franklin D'Olier, Senator George Wharton Pepper, Congressman William S. Vare, City Council President Richard Weglein, and Lucretia Blankenburg, SCEA director and widow of the late mayor.

After the ceremony, the smiles of the Sesqui supporters grew strained when reporters outside the White House showed them the afternoon newspapers from Philadelphia. Under the headline "A Protest" was an open letter to the SCEA from an organization called the North Philadelphia Manufacturers Association (NPMA). Headed by Samuel Vauclain, president of the Baldwin Locomotive Works, the group consisted of thirty large employers who opposed the Sesqui because of its negative impact on "the industrial and civic welfare of Philadelphia." Besides Baldwin, members included firms like the E. G. Budd Manufacturing Company and the Tasty Baking Company, maker of Philadelphia's iconic Tastykakes. Vauclain, one of the original Committee of 100 formed by Mayor Moore in 1920 to plan the Sesqui, had turned into an adamant opponent of the fair, concerned over its inflationary influence on taxes and workers' wages. "Sesqui-Centennial talk," he had announced in July 1922, "is about as welcome as jazz music at a funeral."[30]

The publication of the NPMA advertisements in every Philadelphia afternoon newspaper had been timed to coincide with the presidential approval of the Sesqui-Centennial resolution. It splashed cold water in the face of the SCEA during one of its few moments of triumph, and it exposed the divisions in Philadelphia society to the world. Reading the open letter, a tight-lipped Lucretia Blankenburg said sarcastically, "That is encouraging."[31]

The Sesqui remained moribund throughout the fall of 1922 as the SCEA struggled to mount a counteroffensive against Samuel Vauclain and the NPMA. In early October, Drexel and Company banker Edward T. Stotesbury and his wife, Eva, returned home on the liner *Majestic* after a two-month European tour. When the wealthiest man in Philadelphia was asked by reporters if he thought Philadelphia could raise the funds for a major world's fair, his answer was an emphatic no. Given the worldwide economic downturn, Stotesbury felt it "inadvisable" to mount an international exposition, instead recommending a small, local celebration.[32]

On December 11 the Sesqui-Centennial was dealt another decisive blow with the death of John Wanamaker. The merchant prince was eighty-four years old and had been in ill health for weeks, so his death from a heart attack should have been expected. Yet Wanamaker's passing shocked his hometown far more deeply than its residents could have anticipated. By 1922 most Philadelphians had never known a world without John Wanamaker, and few could imagine one without him. His magnificent store, filled with the riches of the globe, was a source of pride for the city. It proved that Philadelphia was still on the cutting edge of American life, capable of showing New York a thing or two about making money with style. Wanamaker himself had been a constant presence in Philadelphians' lives, inspiring them, badgering them, and occasionally irritating them. But he practiced what he preached. By his own example he urged his fellow citizens on to greater endeavors, offering them a vision of what their city could be if only they would exert themselves. He was, in the words of the *Inquirer*, a "creator of big things" in a city that seemed increasingly preoccupied with the petty.

With Wanamaker's death, a vacuum opened up in the communal life of Philadelphia, a sense that a vital force had vanished from its midst. The chances of a dynasty seemed remote. John's surviving son, Rodman, a semi-invalid prematurely aged from nephritis, showed little interest in local affairs. He seemed more at home in New York or in Paris, cloistered with his priceless collection of antique musical instruments. Rodman's son, John II, had already gained a reputation as an uncontrollable debauchee. A week before the death of his grandfather and namesake, John II had been fined nearly $13,000 by a New York court for passing one million francs' worth of bad checks to cover his baccarat losses in the casino at Deauville. After failing to pay the debt, he was sentenced to six months in a French prison.[33]

The day after Wanamaker's death, an article on page 6 of the *Inquirer* noted that the proposed 1926 Sesqui-Centennial celebration had been suggested by the late merchant. The December 12 article noted that none of the SCEA directors were willing to comment publicly on the future of the enterprise in the immediate aftermath of its champion's demise. Behind the directors' silence, the unspoken message was clear: the Sesqui-Centennial International Exposition was as dead as John Wanamaker himself.[34]

NOTES

1. Sharrar et al., "Some Aspects of the 1918–1919 Influenza Epidemic in Philadelphia and the United States," *Philadelphia Medicine*, n.d., pp. 454–462; Barry, "Epidemic!" *Philadelphia* Magazine, October 1998, pp. 81–199; Weigley, *Philadelphia: A 300-Year History*, pp. 567–568.

2. "Wanamaker Points Ways to Progress," *PI*, July 12, 1919, p. 2.

3. Rosewater, "Notes on the Sesqui-Centennial," VR/AJA, pp. 6–7; "The Sesqui-Centennial," editorial, *PB*, May 23, 1920.

4. "Mayor Asks $50K for 1926 Expo," *PB*, January 27, 1921; "Asks Philadelphia to Back 1926 Fair," *NYT*, January 28, 1921; Rosewater, "Notes on the Sesqui-Centennial," VR/AJA, pp. 9–11; Zwicker and Zwicker, *Whitemarsh Hall*, pp. 35–37.

5. Brownlee, *Building the City Beautiful*, pp. 95–99.

6. "Highlights of Dr. Cret's Plan for 1926 World's Fair," *PB*, January 13, 1921; "Tentative World's Fair Plans Provide City Improvements," *PI*, January 14, 1921; "Next Big World's Fair," *NYT*, January 30, 1921; "Tells of Exposition," *PI*, February 3, 1921.

7. "Random Jottings," *PB*, March 15, 1922.

8. Untitled newspaper article, *PB*, January 21, 1921; "Has New World Fair Plan," *PB*, January 27, 1921; "Fair Site Offered," *PI*, May 11, 1921; "Exposition Plans Early, Mayor Says," *PI*, March 4, 1921, p. 3; "Plan Offered to Hold 1926 Fair in South Philadelphia," *PB*, n.d.

9. "Will Seek Charter for 1926 Fair Body," *PI*, February 11, 1921, p.3; "Men and Things," *PB*, February 15, 1921; "Council Yields to Aid Big 1926 Expo," *PI*, April 8, 1921, p. 3; "Signs $50,000 Fair Bill," *PB*, April 19, 1921; Weigley, *Philadelphia*, pp. 567–568.

10. Pennsylvania Legislature Resolution on Sesqui-Centennial, VR/AJA, MS0503.021.021, p. 3; Adoption of Joint Resolution by Senate and House of Representatives of Pennsylvania to Arrange for Commission of Sesqui-Centennial, VR/AJA, MS0503.021.021, p. 4; "State Supports 1926 Fair," *PB*, April 29, 1921; "Charter for Exposition," *PI*, May 10, 1921; "Penrose to Press Wanamaker Plans for World's Fair," *PI*, June 8, 1921, p. 1; "Congress Has Bill for World's Fair," *PB*, June 13, 1921; "Darrow Bill for Sesqui-Centennial Is Comprehensive," *PI*, June 19, 1921, p. 1; "Chamber Plans Drive," *PI*, November 2, 1921, p. 10; Rosewater, "Notes on the Sesqui-Centennial," VR/AJA, pp. 15–16.

11. "To Present Sesqui Plan to Delegates," *PI*, November 23, 1921, p. 6; "Ask 3 Bodies to Name Sesqui-Centennial Site," *PI*, December 7, 1921, p. 14; "A Site for the Sesqui-Centennial," editorial, *PI*, December 11, 1921, p. 10; "Council Pledges $2,500,000 to Aid 1926 World's Fair," *PI*, December 30, 1921, p. 1; "Let Us Have Harmony in Philadelphia," editorial, *PI*, December 31, 1921, p. 12; "$5M for Fair Wanted of Council,"

January 4, 1922, *PB*; "Mayor to Request $5,000,000 Fund for Phila. World's Fair," *PI*, January 5, 1922, p. 1; "Council Pledges $5 Million or More to 1926 World Fair," *PB*, January 9, 1922.

12. "Senator Penrose Dies Suddenly in Washington," *NYT*, January 1, 1922; "Senator Boies Penrose Dies Suddenly in Washington after Illness from Cold," *PI*, January 1, 1922; "Body of Penrose Buried as Night Fades into Dawn," *PI*, January 6, 1922.

13. "Penrose to Press Wanamaker Plans for World's Fair," *PI*, June 8, 1921, p. 1.

14. Vare, *My Forty Years in Politics*, pp. 41–42.

15. "George Wharton Pepper Is Appointed to Senate to Fill Penrose Seat," *PI*, January 10, 1922; Pepper, *Philadelphia Lawyer*, pp. 138–142.

16. *Report of the Sesqui-Centennial Committee of Philadelphia on Sites*, p. 3.

17. "Public to Be Heard on Fair Site Choice, Mayor Moore Says," *PI*, January 8, 1922, p. 1; "Four Years to the Sesqui-Centennial," *PI*, January 8, 1922, p. 8; "Cret Plan Urged for World's Fair," *PI*, January 8, 1922, p. 18; "Parkway Fair Site Reported as Best by Three Expert Bodies," *PB*, February 2, 1922; "Parkway and Park Plot Recommended as Expo Site," *PI*, February 3, 1922, p. 1; "Park-Parkway Site Selected for Great Fair Set for 1926," *PPL*, March 15, 1922; "Park-Parkway Site Is Chosen for Fair as Foes Plan Fight," *PB*, March 15, 1922; "Park Site Is Chosen for 1926 Expo by Unanimous Vote," *PI*, March 15, 1922, p. 1; *Report of the Sesqui-Centennial Committee of the Engineers' Club of Philadelphia on Sites*, pp. 1–32.

18. "Will Urge Hog Island as Site for Exposition," *PI*, February 5, 1922, p. 18.

19. "Parkway and Park Plot Recommended as Expo Site," *PI*, February 3, 1922, p. 1; "Will Urge Hog Island as Site for Exposition," *PI*, February 5, 1922, p. 18; "Fair in Park Opposed," *PI*, February 7, 1922, p. 13; "Rosewater Named to Boom 1926 Fair," *PR*, March 4, 1922; "Gaffney Sees Hitch in Bill to Condemn Streets for Sesqui," *PI*, March 17, 1922, p. 1; "Organize against Park as Fair Site," *PB*, March 21, 1922; " 'Save Stockyards,' Council Is Begged at Sesqui Hearing," *PI*, April 14, 1922, p. 1; "Mayor Signs Act for Sesqui Land," *PI*, June 14, 1922, p. 3; "Mayor Signs Fair Measure," *PB*, June 14, 1922.

20. "The Sesquicentennial of the Declaration of Independence," Senate Document No. 173, 67th Congress, 2nd Session, VR/AJA, MS0503.021.021, P.1; "President Urges Congress Aid Fair," *PB*, March 24, 1922; "For Congress Sanction of Philadelphia Fair," *NYT*, March 25, 1922; "Sesqui Commended by 7 Congressmen Who Inspect Site," *PI*, April 25, 1922, p .1. "Editor from West Named for Sesqui Publicity Director," *PI*, March 4, 1922, p. 1; "Rosewater Named to Boom 1926 Fair," *PR*, March 4, 1922; "Victor Rosewater to Direct Publicity for the 1926 Fair," *PPL*, March 4, 1922; "Rosewater Plans Big Fair Campaign," *PB*, March 4, 1922; Rosewater, "Notes on the Sesqui-Centennial," VR/AJA, pp. 27–39.

21. *Hearing before the Committee on Industrial Arts and Expositions, House of Representatives, Sixty-Seventh Congress, Second Session on H.J. Resolution 170, Thursday, May 3, 1922*, VR/AJA, MS0503.021.021, p.14.

22. Ibid.

23. "Three Needs for the Fair," editorial, *PPL*, January 14, 1922; "Fair Director Urged by State," *PPL*, March 20, 1922.

24. "Bok Offers Hoover $50,000 to Head Fair," *PB*, February 17, 1922;"Bok Offers to Pay Hoover $50,000 a Year as Head of Sesqui-Centennial Exhibition," *NYT*, February 18, 1922; "Hoover to Refuse Sesqui Post Here," *PI*, March 10, 1922, p. 3; "Hoover Declines $50K Fair Post," *PB*, March 11, 1922; "Hoover Declines Again to Head Fair," *PPL*, May 5, 1922; "Hoover Declines $50,000 Office Offer," *NYT*, March 12, 1922.

25. "May Ask Goethals to Direct 1926 Fair," *PB*, April 16, 1922; "Director General for Fair Demanded," *PI*, April 17, 1922, p.1; "Seeks Schwab as Director," *NYT*, April 18, 1922; "Conflict Looms in Direction of Fair," *PB*, April 18, 1922; "National Celebrity for Fair Director Is Committee Plan," *PI*, April 20, 1922, p. 1; "Bok Denies Schwab Will Head Sesqui," *PI*, April 26, 1922, p. 3; "Weglein Suggests Receiver of Taxes to Direct Sesqui," *PI*, March 18, 1922, p. 1; untitled article, *PB*, March 18, 1922.

26. "Johnson and Potter Resign from Sesqui Board of Directors," *PI*, June 20, 1922, p. 1; "Council Balks at Joining Fair Body," *PB*, June 1922; "Council Votes Not to Name Directors for the Expo," *PI*, June 22, 1922, p. 1; "Moore Bids Board Pay Own Fair Bills," *PB*, June 23, 1922; "No More City Cash for Fair Salaries, Directors Are Told," *PI*, June 23 1922, p. 1; "Lewis Quits Post As Fair President; No Action on Date," *PI*, June 27, 1922, p. 1.

27. Rosewater, "Notes on the Sesqui-Centennial," VR/AJA, pp. 41–48; telegram from John Frederick Lewis to George Wharton Pepper, June 12, 1922, VR/AJA, MS0503.021.015, p. 16; telegram from George Wharton Pepper to John Frederick Lewis, June 13, 1922, VR/AJA, MS0503.021.015, p. 17; telegram from John Frederick Lewis to George Wharton Pepper, June 12, 1922, VR/AJA, MS0503.021.015, p. 21; Letter from Victor Rosewater to Edward W. Bok, June 29, 1922, VR/AJA, MS0503.021.015, pp. 19–21; telegram from George Wharton Pepper to John Frederick Lewis, July 7, 1922, VR/AJA, MS0503.021.015, p. 17; "Delays May Hurt Fair, Says Pepper," *PB*, July 7, 1922; "Congress Irritated by Delays over Fair; May Halt Approval," *PI*, July 8, 1922, p. 1; Letter from Rep. Oscar E. Bland to Victor Rosewater, July 8, 1922, VR/AJA, MS0503.022.004, p. 14.

28. "What about the Sesqui?" Philadelphia *Sunday Dispatch*, July 16, 1922; "Sesqui Officials All Busy—Fishing," *PI*, July 21, 1922, p. 5; "Still No Leader for World's Fair," *PB*, July 27, 1922.

29. "D'Olier Selected as President of Fair Association," *PB*, August 2, 1922; "Pick D'Olier to Head Fair," *NYT*, August 3, 1922; "Think D'Olier Will Serve as Fair Head without a Salary," *PB*, August 3, 1922; "D'Olier Unwillingly Takes Sesqui Post; Ready for Big Task," *PI*, August 4, 1922, p. 1; "Full Speed Ahead Is D'Olier Pledge," *PB*, August 4, 1922; "Wanamaker Gives $50,000 to Fair," *PB*, August 8, 1922; "E. A. Gimbel Gives $25,000 for Fair," *PPL*, August 10, 1922.

30. "'Success to Sesqui,' Harding's Message as He Signs Bill," *PI*, August 30, 1922, p. 1; Rosewater, "Notes on the Sesqui-Centennial," VR/AJA, pp. 62–64.

31. Rosewater, "Notes on the Sesqui-Centennial," VR/AJA, pp. 62–64.

32. "'Success to Sesqui,' Harding's Message as He Signs Bill," *PI*, August 30, 1922, p. 1; Rosewater, "Notes on the Sesqui-Centennial," VR/AJA, pp. 62–64.

33. "Enter Judgment against Wanamaker's Grandson," *Harrisburg Patriot*, December 5, 1922; "John Wanamaker Dies at Age of 84 from Heart Attack," *NYT*, December 13, 1922; "John Wanamaker Dies in Peaceful Passing from City He Loved," *PI*, December 13, 1922; "John Wanamaker, Great Citizen, Is Gone," editorial, *PI*, December 13, 1922; "Wanamaker Mourned as Best Son of City," *PI*, December 13, 1922.

34. "Sesqui Was Suggested by John Wanamaker," *PI*, December 13, 1922, p. 6.

3

★ ★ ★

The Sesqui Sinks

SHAKEN BY THE DEATH of John Wanamaker, the attacks of the North Philadelphia Manufacturers Association, and the resignation of many directors, the Sesqui-Centennial Exhibition Association struggled to regroup as 1922 ended. SCEA President Franklin D'Olier formed an advisory executive committee that he hoped would take more decisive actions to advance the Sesqui than the larger, more conservative executive committee. The new fourteen-man committee included the SCEA's most dedicated members, including D'Olier, Judge Eugene C. Bonniwell, department store owner Ellis Gimbel, Grand Exalted Ruler of the Elks Charles H. Grakelow, realtor Albert M. Greenfield, Logan Improvement Association President E. J. Lafferty, and theater magnate Jules Mastbaum. The committee was chaired by Ernest T. Trigg, a former president of the Philadelphia Chamber of Commerce. While D'Olier may have reinvigorated the SCEA, he had also delivered it into the hands of the Philadelphia Organization. Many of the advisory executive committee members, including Gimbel, Grakelow, Greenfield, Lafferty, and Mastbaum, were closely allied with William S. Vare.[1]

In the final days of 1922, the advisory committee labored over the Sesqui Plan and Scope, drafted by Victor Rosewater from input provided by SCEA directors and from advisers like Senator George Wharton Pepper. This document was meant to define the central theme and philosophy of the fair and provide a detailed description of its exhibits, grounds, and attractions. Essential to obtaining federal and state funding, the Plan and Scope was presented to City Council and the public on January 3, 1923.

"The Sesqui-Centennial Exhibition," read the document, "shall be a World Festival of Peace and Progress" with three distinct objectives: to mark the 150th anniversary of the signing of the Declaration of Independence; to portray world progress since 1876; and to foster international goodwill. The keynote theme of the Sesqui would be "to interpret the spirit of the Twentieth Century and to reflect it in beauty and happiness." Reflecting the slender SCEA budget, the Plan and Scope emphasized that the Sesqui would be "an Exhibition of quality rather than of quantity, depending upon ideas and ideals rather than upon the amount of money spent."

Again emphasizing economy, the Plan and Scope noted that "the distinguishing feature of the Sesqui-Centennial Exhibition will be its legacy of permanent buildings." The Fairmount Parkway would be transformed into a "Triumphal Way of the Republic," lined with "imposing, impressive and inspiring" structures that would "give to millions of Americans a striking and unforgettable impression of the majesty" of the United States. Besides the Free Library, Art Museum, Hall of Justice, and Victory Hall, these edifices would include a federal government building, a Pennsylvania State building, and "the most complete maternity and general hospital in the world," contributed by the women of Philadelphia.

The war-ravaged countries of Europe would be asked to cherry-pick the choicest treasures from their art galleries and deliver them to Philadelphia. The new Museum of Art atop Fairmount would house "the most magnificent loan art exhibit ever gathered together." Sesqui visitors could feast their eyes on the *Mona Lisa*, *Venus de Milo*, and *Winged Victory* from France; Raphael's *Sistine Madonna* from Germany; the Gobelin tapestries from Belgium; works by Turner, Reynolds, and Gainsborough from Great Britain; "the greatest Rembrandt from the Netherlands"; and "the most wonderful Velasquez from Spain." Displayed alongside these works of art would be the Magna Carta from England, shown alongside originals of the Declaration of Independence and the Constitution and Lincoln's draft of the Gettysburg Address.

The accomplishments of the past half century would be highlighted in a series of temporary pavilions, including an Automobile Hall, an Aeroplane Building, an Electrical Palace, and a Palace of the Press. An Exhibition of Scientific and Social Progress would describe recent advances in education, public health, medicine, and welfare. In the Motion Picture Palace, Hollywood stars would film an epic called "America," a panoramic depiction of the history of the United States. Foreign nations would contribute "unexampled offerings of good-will and cordiality." France would offer a Palace of Fashion, Belgium a House of Lace, and the Netherlands a Dutch Farm, complete with "Dutch cows, the country's cheeses, chocolates, etc., and the people in costume."

Sesqui buildings would be surrounded by lagoons and magnificent gardens filled with Dutch tulips, English rhododendrons, French fleur-de-lis, and Japanese flowering cherry trees. Its athletic facilities, including a new Stadium in Fairmount Park, would host exciting sports events: an American version of the Henley Regatta, a special edition of the Olympic Games, and world championships in baseball, football, tennis, and polo. At a nearby aerodrome, spectators could thrill to races for "navigation of the air by airplane, glider, helicopter, and dirigible."

The Plan and Scope estimated that the total cost of the fair would be $15 million. The City Council had already pledged $5 million. Public subscription would raise another $5 million, with the remainder to come from state and federal appropriations. Overall attendance would easily reach forty million during the fair's twenty-six weeks, enough to cover operating expenses and interest on Sesqui bonds. With receipts of $100,000 a day, based on an average daily attendance of two hundred thousand, the Sesqui-Centennial would realize at least $18 million between its opening on April 30 and its closing on November 13. On July 4 alone, when the president of the United States would officiate at the triple dedication of the Delaware River Bridge, Museum of Art, and Victory Hall, more than one million visitors would pack Philadelphia. Thanks to the Sesqui, the year 1926 would mark "the beginning of a new era, the inception of an even finer Philadelphia, foremost in everything worthwhile."[2]

The Plan and Scope was a superlative example of 1920s ballyhoo, drawing on Victor Rosewater's long career as an editor, writer, and publicist. Simultaneously with its publication, Rosewater circulated a press release to newspapers throughout the country. "Philadelphia, the mother city of the Republic," the document gushed, "invites the Nation and the world to join in a great demonstration of progress and amity at the Sesqui-Centennial Exhibition, by which the peace and prosperity of all peoples will be advanced and insured."[3]

While the Plan and Scope may have convinced the country that the Sesqui was still alive, it did little to encourage public support in its hometown. E. T. Stotesbury, who had already stepped down as SCEA finance chairman, quit the board of directors soon after the document's release. He was followed by former Pennsylvania Governor Edwin S. Stuart. At the recommendation of Jules Mastbaum, Stotesbury and Stuart were replaced by advisory executive committee members E. J. Lafferty and Charles H. Grakelow. Philadelphia's upper class was divorcing itself from the Sesqui, and the vacuum was being filled by middle-class professionals and entrepreneurs like Grakelow and Lafferty. These Organization men used their new influence to shape the Sesqui to benefit William S. Vare. During this period, Congressman Vare testified at a hearing in the mayor's office, urging the relocation of the fair to his congressional district in South Philadelphia.

This growing domination of the Sesqui by Vare allies may have forced Mayor J. Hampton Moore to step down completely from the SCEA board in February. Since Moore had not attended any board meetings in nearly a year, his official departure was barely noticed. With a mayoral election coming up in November, the advisory committee did its best to work around the lame duck Moore until a more reliable ally was in place. At Ernest Trigg's recommendation, Colonel John Price Jackson was appointed executive director of the SCEA to manage Sesqui operations. Jackson, an electrical engineer, had coauthored the site selection report that had recommended the Fairmount Park-Parkway site for the fair.[4]

Meanwhile, the growing chasm between Philadelphia's upper classes and the SCEA board created fresh complications. The Fairmount Park Commission, charged with overseeing one of the largest municipal parks in the world, had not given its final approval on whether the SCEA could use the Parkway and Fairmount Park for the Sesqui. Although the sixteen-member commission included the mayor and City Council president, the real power resided with its ten private citizen members, all unpaid and court appointed. Most of the latter group belonged to Philadelphia's social elite, including Commission President E. T. Stotesbury. They tended to be reform-minded, independent Republicans, who resented the Organization's ham-fisted rule of their city.

In March the Fairmount Park Commission gave its provisional approval to SCEA use of the Parkway-Park site, provided that the SCEA prove that it had the financial backing to stage the Sesqui. The commission also demanded a guarantee from the SCEA that all parklands would be completely restored after the fair. Before the adoption of the resolution, a letter was read from Stotesbury (wintering in Palm Beach) insisting that final permission to use parklands would depend on whether the public actually wanted the Sesqui, and if so, in Fairmount Park. Vice President Eli Kirk Price lectured SCEA representatives that final approval would wait "until we know that we are dealing with a responsible association." The Fairmount Park Commission's high-handed manner played into the hands of both opponents of the Sesqui, and opponents of the Parkway-Fairmount Park site. Ray Machen, representing a citizens' group called the Anti-Sesqui-Centennial League, declared that it would be impossible to hold a world's fair in the park "without accomplishing ruin to the greatest portion of this playground of the people." Those who favored a South Philadelphia fair cited the interference of the Fairmount Park Commission as another reason to remove the Sesqui from the Parkway.[5]

Given these schisms, attracting support for the Sesqui became increasingly difficult. A preliminary membership campaign in late 1922 had been a fiasco, netting $1,290. With Stotesbury's departure from the SCEA board of directors, the pocketbooks of Old Philadelphia snapped shut en masse. When Ernest Trigg attempted to raise $50,000 in early 1923 for a public relations campaign, he was rebuffed by former allies. Edward W. Bok, who had once offered to pay Herbert Hoover an astronomical $250,000 to run the fair for five years, replied that he would not provide any financial support "until the whole matter is taken out of its present nebulous state and put upon a firm foundation." Bok's father-in-law, Cyrus H. K. Curtis, sent a curt telegram in response to Trigg's solicitation: "Do not care to contribute until better leadership develops."[6]

In Harrisburg, the new governor, Gifford Pinchot, informed the SCEA that no state funds were available for the Sesqui. Pinchot's refusal to support the Sesqui-Centennial reflected both his contempt for the Philadelphia Organization and his fiscal conservatism. The Progressive Republican was vehemently opposed to Vare's boss politics, telling one reporter that "the gang-controlled majorities in the great cities is the most dangerous factor in American public life today." Pinchot's bare-bones inauguration in February 1923 had cost $3,015, compared with $28,000 for the previous governor. Once in office, Pinchot had initiated a rigid program to slash the state government's uncontrolled spending, enacting Pennsylvania's first executive budget. A bill in the Pennsylvania Senate approving a $5 million appropriation for the Sesqui was voted down by a narrow margin of twenty-three to twenty-two. The legislature adjourned shortly afterward, killing the possibility of state support until the end of 1923.[7]

City Council President Richard Weglein, who had boasted before a House Committee in 1922 that Philadelphia had the financial resources to pay for "the greatest exposition in the history of the world," refused to back a $1 million appropriation to condemn land near the Parkway for the Sesqui grounds. Weglein was backed by Councilman Charles B. Hall, who had once pronounced a proposed $2.5 million appropriation for the Sesqui "a small sum." By the end of March 1923, the SCEA books showed a net deficit of $944, with revenues of $12,760 and expenditures of $13,614.[8]

The Sesqui logo—a picture of the Liberty Bell with the slogan "Ring It Again!"—was appropriated by Ray Machen at the Anti-Sesqui-Centennial

League. Machen distributed a brochure bearing a cartoon of a disgruntled taxpayer squeezing his empty purse under the words “Wring It Again!” The Trenton *Times* opined, “It begins to look as if there would be no Sesqui-Centennial Exposition in Philadelphia in 1926,” adding that “even if the $15 million was in sight, it is doubtful whether the exposition can be organized and built in time for the celebration of the signing of the Declaration of Independence.” Meanwhile, the SCEA finance and campaign committees found themselves hopelessly divided on whether or not to sell bonds, a standard financing technique for world’s fairs since the Centennial. Some of the more conservative directors of the SCEA, such as Lucretia Blankenburg, thought that bonds were unpatriotic and smacked of usury. She was not assuaged when other directors suggested calling them “participating certificates” instead.[9]

The sudden death of President Warren G. Harding on August 2, 1923, added to the uncertainty. Harding, whose history of heart conditions had been concealed from the public, appeared to have died of a heart attack in San Francisco at the end of a grueling cross-country tour. Despite the personal and political scandals surrounding his administration, Harding had been a popular president, and Philadelphians mourned his passing along with the rest of the country. At the SCEA, workers wondered how his death would affect federal support of the Sesqui. Harding, whose presidency had been due to the efforts of the late Boies Penrose, had always supported the Philadelphia fair. The easygoing president, with his penchants for liquor,

This cartoon by the Anti-Sesqui-Centennial League put a new twist on the Sesqui slogan, “Ring it Again.”

poker, women, and backroom politics, had worked well with Congressmen Vare and other Organization men. Little was known about his replacement, former vice president Calvin Coolidge, except that the tight-lipped Vermont lawyer exuded the disapproving aura of a Puritan preacher. Philadelphia politicians wondered if they would be able to talk turkey with Coolidge as easily as they had with Harding and his cronies.[10]

At this crucial juncture, the campaign to resuscitate the Sesqui was further derailed by personality conflicts and missteps on the part of SCEA staff. Executive Director John Price Jackson demonstrated an uncanny ability to antagonize people, especially women. Several experienced female members of the SCEA clerical staff quit after Jackson berated them publicly, using "vehement language." Lucretia Blankenburg refused to deal with him, saying that the colonel "had no use for women." The usually patient Victor Rosewater, now working as SCEA corresponding secretary, called Jackson "a colossal disappointment."[11]

Rosewater charged that Jackson loaded the SCEA staff with friends and hangers-on, including his own son-in-law. The elderly father of a friend from the Chamber of Commerce was put on the payroll at one hundred dollars a month to paste press clippings into scrapbooks. With experienced workers deserting the SCEA and being replaced by Jackson's dubious choices, operations became almost chaotically disorganized. SCEA Director Edward W. Bok, whose eponymous autobiography was one of the best-selling books in America, complained that he regularly received letters addressed to "Edward V. Bock." Meanwhile, Rosewater complained that both SCEA President Franklin D'Olier and Advisory Committee Chairman Ernest T. Trigg shrank from the public spotlight, allowing the undiplomatic Jackson to act as sole spokesman for the SCEA.

By this point, even some of the Sesqui's former advocates appeared ready to pull the plug on the project. The *Public Ledger* newspaper, owned by Cyrus H. K. Curtis, had supported the fair initially. In October 1923, the *Ledger* published an editorial that could have been written by the Anti-Sesqui-Centennial League:

> It is time for Philadelphia to review the whole Sesqui-Centennial proposal, to take account of blunders, delays and mistakes and seek some solution. We are getting nowhere. For two years we have done nothing except step on our own feet and get in our own way. The whole business is still too vague and planless. This is October, 1923, and the Sesqui-Centennial is scheduled for 1926. . . . The whole idea is dead on its feet.

The writer went on to state that Philadelphia should turn its back on "extravagantly ambitious schemes" and plan a modest and dignified Sesqui-Centennial. This downsized fair would take place in the great buildings planned for the Parkway and historic structures like Independence Hall. This would eliminate the need to "disturb an acre of Fairmount Park" with "a group of flimsy structures to melt and crumble under the brief rains and suns of a single summer." The editorial also advocated limiting the length of the fair to one or two months, rather than a six-month celebration. "There must be a lopping-off of vague plans and a getting down to the very essence of a suitable commemoration," the article concluded.[12]

Postponed once and rescheduled for early November, a major SCEA fund-raising campaign was delayed yet again thanks to E. T. Stotesbury. By this stage, the former SCEA director appeared to be waging guerrilla warfare against the Sesqui. Although Stotesbury had severed his ties with the SCEA, his firm, Drexel and Company, continued to act as treasurer for the association. Just before the November campaign began, Drexel and Company asked to be relieved as treasurer and to act only as a depository for SCEA funds. The firm insisted that its name be removed immediately from all materials associated with the fund-raising campaign, except as a depository. Thanks to this last-minute change, hundreds of thousands of pieces of campaign literature, pledge cards, and financial forms had to be destroyed or revised.[13]

While SCEA workers crossed out the word *Treasurer* on countless documents, the voters of Philadelphia dutifully elected Receiver of Taxes W. Freeland Kendrick as their next mayor. As the *Record*, the city's only Democratic newspaper, pointed out, failure to do so would violate "the childish unreasoning belief that obsesses the average Philadelphian, that all governmental virtue reposes in the Republican Party." Kendrick's election was a repudiation of independent Republican J. Hampton Moore and his unsuccessful attempts at political reform. It was also a vivid demonstration that Bill Vare wielded complete control over both the Organization and Philadelphia, a year after the death of his brother Ed in October 1922. The popular Kendrick, an ally and protégé of Vare, had won by a plurality of 249,331 over his Democratic opponent, contractor A. Raymond Raff.

Organization-backed candidates also won nineteen of the twenty councilmanic seats up for grabs, ensuring political harmony between mayor and council for the next four years. The only independent Republican to emerge unscathed was Councilman William W. Roper of the Sixth District, popular coach of the Princeton University football team. In the same election, Philadelphia voters overwhelmingly approved two municipal loans totaling $71 million for municipal improvement projects, including four new

Mayor-elect W. Freeland Kendrick, who was named honorary president of the SCEA as 1923 drew to a close.

subway lines. Despite his ties to Vare and the Organization, Kendrick presented himself to the world as a reform candidate. He promised to wage war on bootleggers and corrupt cops by naming the incorruptible Smedley Darlington Butler, a brigadier general in the U.S. Marine Corps, as his director of public safety.[14]

Aside from Butler, most of the men in Kendrick's cabinet were loyal members of the Organization. Charles H. Grakelow, who besides ruling the

Elks was a fellow Shriner of both Kendrick and Vare, was named director of public welfare. Vare deputy Joseph P. Gaffney, advocate for moving the Sesqui to South Philadelphia, was appointed city solicitor. E. J. Lafferty became the new director of supplies. Harry A. Mackey, longtime Vare lieutenant and leader of the Forty-Sixth Ward, was elected city treasurer. Within City Council, Vare floor leader Charles B. Hall was named to replace Richard Weglein as the new council president, while Edwin R. Cox became chairman of the finance committee. One of the few non-Organization men in Kendrick's cabinet was Director of Public Works George H. Biles, former highway commissioner for the state of Pennsylvania. Biles would be responsible for overseeing the large public construction projects that had languished during the Moore administration, and that Kendrick hoped to reinstate as mayor.[15]

The SCEA finally kicked off its fund-raising campaign on November 19, just as the Christmas shopping season was getting under way. Twelve hundred workers fanned out across the city to solicit their fellow citizens for funds for the Sesqui. By this time, the entire SCEA campaign committee had resigned en masse. In their joint resignation letter, the four men expressed their disgust with the "perfectly apparent inadequacy" of the "Professional Staff of the Association." Both Lucretia Blankenburg and Governor William C. Sproul also resigned from the SCEA board of directors during this period.[16]

At this point, a disenchanted Mayor Moore launched a bombshell designed to discredit the SCEA and crush the Sesqui completely. Perhaps he hoped to deny Vare the juicy plums of an expensive world's fair that would provide hundreds of construction contracts and thousands of jobs. On November 22 Moore issued a public statement that called the Sesqui fund-raising campaign "a financial scheme which has not been approved by the President and Congress, or the Governor or General Assembly, or the Mayor or Council, or the Commissioners of Fairmount Park." He urged the immediate disbandment of the SCEA and the cessation of its fund-raising. Instead, he recommended that his successor fund a simple "inspirational demonstration," freeing the city from "the menace of ramshackle structures and cheap and gaudy entertainments, all of which would leave an aftermath of expense and embarrassment." Moore called for "an old-fashioned town meeting" at City Hall on November 30, the day after Thanksgiving, to determine "what the fair movement is to develop into and whether anything permanent is to come from this project."[17]

The SCEA issued a statement calling the mayor's attack "an attempt to injure a great patriotic and unselfish movement." It pointed out that Moore, as one of the incorporators of the original SCEA charter, should have known that the association was within its legal bounds in launching a fund-raising campaign without seeking approval from any federal, state, or municipal bodies. Noting that Moore had launched the Sesqui by summoning one hundred of the city's leading citizens to form a committee three years earlier, the SCEA concluded that "it is regretted that one who was originally a leader in this movement should now spurn his own child." At an emergency meeting, the SCEA board of directors elected Mayor-Elect Kendrick as honorary president of the organization. The directors refused to participate in the public meeting in the mayor's office. They also decided to terminate their fund-raising campaign, even though SCEA workers had collected more than $72,000 during its first week.[18]

On November 29, Thanksgiving Day, Philadelphia's feuding factions buried the hatchet for one afternoon to honor the late father of the Sesqui-Centennial. Mayor Moore, Senator Pepper, City Council President Weglein, E. T. Stotesbury, and other dignitaries gathered on the east side of City Hall to unveil a statue of John Wanamaker, crafted by sculptor J. Massey Rhind. They were joined by hundreds of employees from the Wanamaker Store across the street. The statue had been paid for by a popular subscription, mostly funded by members of Wanamaker's Bethany Presbyterian Church and children who attended the Bethany Sunday School.

After an oration by Senator Pepper, the statue was unveiled. Philadelphia Orchestra conductor Leopold Stokowski led the Police Band in "The Star-Spangled Banner." The pink granite base bore the simple inscription, "John Wanamaker—Citizen," with his birth and death dates. The statue depicted an elderly Wanamaker in his customary bowtie and three-piece suit, the wrinkled vest stretched across his paunch. He held his overcoat and crumpled fedora in his right arm, while the thumb of his left hand was hooked in his pants pocket. Thoughtful yet energetic, Wanamaker looked as if he were taking a moment to plot his strategy before dashing off to yet another committee meeting or fund-raising drive.[19]

Within twenty-four hours, the truce had ended. On November 30, more than five hundred men and women crowded the Mayor's Reception Room at City Hall to debate the merits of Wanamaker's beloved Sesqui-Centennial. With the SCEA refusing to participate, the mood was heavily anti-Sesqui. The two leading nemeses of the fair, E. T. Stotesbury and Samuel M. Vauclain, both declared that the Sesqui-Centennial was "doomed to fail." Instead of an international exposition, Stotesbury favored a more modest celebration "without too much expenditure of money."[20]

Vauclain concurred, saying that he was "not opposed to an appropriate old home week or two for which we can pay and have a reasonably good time without exhausting the resources of this grand old city." Both Stotesbury and Vauclain were enthusiastically applauded. Ray Machen, representing the Anti-Sesqui-Centennial League, insisted that more than fifteen thousand Philadelphia citizens had expressed their opposition to a world's fair in Philadelphia. Moore called for a proponent of the Sesqui-Centennial to plead the case for the fair, but no one stepped forward. When Moore asked for a voice vote for or against the Sesqui, a loud chorus of nos rang through the reception room, almost drowning out the few ayes. A hastily counted show of hands indicated that 304 of the attendees were against the Sesqui, while 43 brave souls were for it. Most of the latter were members of the West Philadelphia branch of the SCEA, who had evidently missed the communiqué from the board of directors to skip the meeting. The mayor then called for a vote as to whether the meeting favored a "celebration in the regular way, under the auspices of the city." This time, the vote was unanimously in favor.[21]

The SCEA made a feeble response to the City Hall rally, vowing that it would resume its fund-raising campaign. SCEA Publicity Director John B. Geraghty pointed out that only 403 persons could be found to oppose the Sesqui out of Philadelphia's 1,800,000 citizens. "What a sorry spectacle would have been presented if Mayor Moore had selected the Academy of Music for his mass meeting," Geraghty crowed. "His guests would have had elbow room in the orchestra pit!"[22]

Within a week, Geraghty was gone from SCEA headquarters. So were Colonel Jackson, the old man who pasted newspaper clippings in scrapbooks, and the other two dozen employees of the SCEA, all dismissed as the association struggled to regroup. The only workers left by December 7 were Victor Rosewater, now called the executive secretary, and two clerical assistants. An exasperated Franklin D'Olier was on the verge of quitting, expressing hope that Ernest Trigg would succeed him as president. The SCEA had $6,134.91 in its checking account. More than $150,000 had been spent on the fair to date, most of it, in Rosewater's words, "dissipated by reckless or misdirected outlay." Stotesbury, Vauclain, and Moore had good reason to believe that they had succeeded in slaying the Sesqui-Centennial. Aided by a feckless SCEA leadership and an incompetent SCEA administration, the most insular and conservative segment of Quaker City society had prevailed. The "greatest international exposition in the world" would be no more than a modest "inspirational demonstration," a humble, homespun, "home week," of Philadelphia, by Philadelphia, and for Philadelphia.[23]

As the dreary year of 1923 drew to a close, a faint glimmer of hope for the Sesqui emerged from the winter darkness. On December 13, Ernest T. Trigg received a brief note from City Hall:

My Dear Mr. Trigg:

Kindly convey to those interested in the success of the proposed Sesqui-Centennial my best wishes and appreciation of the work done in connection with their recent Campaign. May I impress upon them the necessity of keeping up the interest in this matter, so that some time after the first of the year we can all get together on a celebration that will fittingly commemorate the 150th Anniversary of the Declaration of Independence.

Very sincerely,

W. FREELAND KENDRICK[24]

CHAPTER 3

1. "New Sesqui Board 'Starts Something,'" *PI*, December 24, 1922, p. 2; Rosewater, "Notes on the Sesqui-Centennial," VR/AJA, pp. 59–60.

2. "Release of Initial Plan for the Sesquicentennial Exhibition," VR/AJA, MS0503.021.19, pp. 74–131; "Plans and Purposes of Philadelphia Fair," *NYT*, January 4, 1923.

3. "Hold Sesquicentennial Exhibit in Philadelphia," *Dallas Morning News*, January 10, 1923, p. 9.

4. "E. T. Stotesbury Quits Sesqui Body," *PB*, January 16, 1923; "World Fair Fund Launched," *PB*, February 6, 1923; "Mayor Resigns as Sesqui Director," *PB*, February 20, 1923; "Philadelphia Mayor Quits Fair Board," *NYT*, February 21, 1923; "Jackson Selected as Head of Sesqui," *PB*, March 20, 1923.

5. "E. T. Stotesbury Quits Sesqui Body," *PB*, January 16, 1923; "Fair Site Good but Approval Withheld," *PB*, March 14, 1923.

6. Rosewater, "Notes on the Sesqui-Centennial," VR/AJA, pp. 91–94.

7. McGeary, *Gifford Pinchot*, pp. 284, 291.

8. Telegram from Ernest T. Trigg to Edward W. Bok, February 13, 1923, VR/AJA, MS0503.022.004, p. 20; "Mayor Resigns as Sesqui Director," *PB*, February 20, 1923; Letter from John C. Martin to Ernest T. Trigg, March 5, 1923, VR/AJA, MS0503.022.004, p. 20; "No Funds for Fair Now, Says Pinchot," *PB*, April 13, 1923; "$1M for Fair Asked of Council," *PB*, April 19, 1923; Victor Rosewater notes on SCEA finances, VR/AJA, MS0503.022.004, p. 1.

9. "State Aid for Fair Killed in Senate," *PB*, June 12, 1923; "The Sesqui-Centennial," editorial, *TT*, June 18, 1923, p. 6.

10. "Independence Bell Tolls," *NYT*, August 11, 1923, p. 6.

11. Rosewater, "Notes on the Sesqui-Centennial," VR/AJA, pp. 91–94.

12. "Let's Have a Sesqui Everybody Will Want," editorial, *PPL*, October 5, 1923.

13. "Notes on Charles B. Crist," VR/AJA, MS0503.022.004, pp. 41–48; "Minutes of Executive Committee Meeting at 12:30 Noon, Wednesday, September 26, 1923," VR/AJA, MS0503.022.005, p. 10; Rosewater, "Notes on the Sequi-Centennial," VR/AJA, pp. 83–91; "Sproul Quits Sesqui Board," *PB*, October 2, 1923.

14. "Kendrick Promises 'Free Rein' to Butler," *NYT*, December 17, 1923, p. 24; "Quaker General Ready to Clean Up Philadelphia," *NYT*, December 23, 1923, p. 125.

15. "What's the Matter with Philadelphia," *PR*, September 28, 1923; "Kendrick Wins by 216,000," *NYT*, September 20, 1923; "Philadelphia Elects W. F. Kendrick Mayor," *NYT*, November 7, 1923; "To Reform Philadelphia," editorial, *NYT*, December 9, 1923; "Kendrick Fills Directorships," *PPL*, December 18, 1923; "The City Embraces Normalcy 1919–1929," in Weigley, *Philadelphia*, pp. 570–571.

16. "Drexel & Co. Only Sesqui 'Depository,'" *PNA*, November 20, 1923.

17. "Mayor Would Drop Fair," *NYT*, November 23, 1923.

18. "Mayor Would Drop Fair," *NYT*, November 23, 1923; "Sesqui Drive Nets $72,119 First Week," *PB*, November 26, 1923; Rosewater, "Notes on the Sesqui-Centennial," VR/AJA, pp. 91–94.

19. "Unveils Statue of John Wanamaker," *NYT*, November 30, 1923, p. 23.

20. "Proposed Sesqui Doomed to Fail, Says Stotesbury," *PB*, November 30, 1923.

21. "Proposed Sesqui Doomed to Fail, Says Stotesbury," *PB*, November 30, 1923; "Smaller Fair Is Urged," *NYT*, December 1, 1923.

22. "Sesqui Officials to Continue Drive," *PB*, December 1, 1923.

23. "Proposed Sesqui Doomed to Fail, Says Stotesbury," *PB*, November 30, 1923; "Smaller Fair Is Urged," *NYT*, December 1, 1923; "Sesqui Officials to Continue Drive," *PB*, December 1, 1923; "Col. Jackson Quits Sesqui," *PB*, December 7, 1923; Rosewater, "Notes on the Sesqui-Centennail," pp. 107–116.

24. "The Sesqui-Centennial," publicity flyer, Committee of 1926 Sesqui-Centennial Archives.

4

★ ★ ★

Call Me Freel

ALTHOUGH WILLIAM FREELAND KENDRICK was as tall and lean as George Follansbee Babbitt was short and stout, the new mayor of Philadelphia had much in common with the eponymous hero of Sinclair Lewis' best-selling novel of 1922.

Both the fictional realtor from Zenith and the real-life politico from Philadelphia were in their midforties when the 1920s dawned, entering the decade in their prime. Knowing the importance of a favorable first impression, the two men possessed a peacocklike pride in their attire. "The best-dressed man in Philadelphia" usually wore a bespoke suit, accessorized with spats, an elegant homburg, and a silver-headed cane. In summer, the homburg gave way to a straw boater, personalized with the silver initials "W. F. K." on its inside band. For important ceremonies, Kendrick wore full morning dress, with a tailcoat, striped trousers, and a top hat of the shiniest silk.[1]

Like Babbitt, Kendrick understood the value of making friends and influencing people: his easy manner and talent for public speaking had carried him from running a pawnshop to running the third-largest city in America. Both men were natural joiners, blossoming in the overheated bonhomie of all-male organizations like the Shriners and Masons. Like Babbitt, Kendrick was a boomer for his birthplace, delivering speeches extolling Philadelphia at the drop of a hat. Both men were bored and puzzled by high culture. Kendrick never attended a performance of the Philadelphia Orchestra; he preferred to make his own music on a harmonica.

Despite his philistinism and humble beginnings, Kendrick aspired to gracious living. As his fortunes increased, he favored such upscale pursuits

The mayor relaxes. Kendrick, who reputedly "toots a mean harmonica himself," in a publicity shot with boys selected from Philadelphia public schools to form a Harmonica Band to promote the Sesqui.

as golf, equestrianism, and breeding pedigreed bulldogs. He longed to fit in with Old Philadelphia; hence the moniker "W. Freeland Kendrick," which sounded more patrician than "William F. Kendrick." But he begged fraternal brothers and reporters to call him Freel. Like Babbitt, Kendrick's confident manner masked an almost desperate need to be recognized, appreciated, even loved. His City Hall office was crammed with photographs, trophies, and medals, including a Shriners' emblem depicted in diamonds, given to him by Buffalo Bill Cody in 1911. "I'd hate to be a man without friends," he once confided. "I like to think that I know people in all parts of the country, people in Maine and in Oregon, people I can call by their first names and people who will call me Freel." The Sesqui-Centennial would be Kendrick's chance to make the whole world call him Freel.[2]

Kendrick was born June 24, 1874, at 144 North Twenty-First Street, a respectable middle-class neighborhood "North of Market." His father William was a Civil War veteran, prominent Mason, and Democratic politician in an era when the party was being eclipsed by a burgeoning Republican machine. The family's primary means of support was a pawnshop. William died in 1889 at the age of fifty-one, leaving a widow, two sons, and two daughters. As the oldest son, William had to drop out of high school at fifteen and support his family by running the pawnshop. In 1899, he married Mabel Bernard, a childhood sweetheart whom he had once serenaded on his harmonica with "Two Little Girls in Blue." The couple would have no children during their fifty-three-year marriage.[3]

In 1896, the twenty-two-year-old Kendrick followed in his late father's footsteps by joining the Masons. Kendrick was particularly drawn to the Ancient Arabic Order of the Nobles of the Mystic Shrine, an offshoot of the Masons founded in 1870. Along with the traditional Masonic values, "Shriners" emphasized fun and fellowship, cloaked in a heady mélange of Egyptian and Oriental iconography. At their temples, Shriners donned elaborate costumes (including their signature red fezzes), participated in theatrical rituals, and enjoyed luxurious dinners. In 1901, Kendrick was initiated into the Lu Lu Temple of the Oasis of Philadelphia. Among its members were many of the Quaker City's rising businessmen and political figures, including Recorder of Deeds William S. Vare.

Elected to the Oriental Guard (the first rung on the ladder of Shrine offices) in 1904, the glib and gregarious Kendrick was named potentate or chief officer of the Lu Lu Temple in 1905. He would hold the position for thirteen years. The lanky Philadelphian with the engaging smile soon attracted notice in the Shriners' national organization. In 1910, Kendrick was elected to the Imperial Council at the national convention in New Orleans.[4]

The following year, Kendrick had the opportunity to help his fellow Noble, William S. Vare, during Vare's 1911 campaign for the Republican mayoral nomination. Even loyal Philadelphia Republicans seemed unenthusiastic about surly, taciturn William Vare as a mayoral prospect. For help, Vare turned to his charismatic potentate, W. Freeland Kendrick. Kendrick, now an insurance executive, formed the Business Men's Committee of One Hundred to "draft" the recorder of deeds for mayor.[5]

Although Bill Vare lost the Republican nomination, he remained grateful to Kendrick. In 1913, the Republican City Committee nominated Kendrick for receiver of taxes, responsible for the collection of tax revenues, license and permit fees, and rents from all public properties. Like the recorder of deeds position that Vare had held, the receiver of taxes was paid a hefty $10,000 a year. It was a plum patronage position, with hundreds of jobs to dole out to Organization men. Kendrick was elected receiver of taxes by a hefty margin, and easily won reelection in 1917 and 1921. He was one of the few men in City Hall who had not worked his way up through the neighborhood ward system. Under the Blankenburg, Smith, and Moore administrations, Kendrick gained a reputation as both an efficient and capable administrator, and a loyal servant to the Vare Organization. The well-spoken, urbane Kendrick emerged as a real "vote-getter," the friendly public face of an often vicious Organization.[6]

In June 1919 Kendrick reached the peak of his fraternal career when representatives of the nation's 363,744 Shriners elected him imperial potentate. When the new national leader of the Mystic Shrine returned to Philadelphia, he was welcomed at Broad Street Station by a committee of notables headed by Mayor Smith and Governor Sproul. A parade consisting of twenty-eight fraternal organizations and six bands escorted Kendrick around City Hall and up North Broad Street to the Lu Lu Temple. Kendrick, said to be a member of more lodges than any other Philadelphian, probably belonged to each of the twenty-eight organizations participating in the parade.[7]

At the Shriners' 1920 convention in Portland, Oregon, outgoing Imperial Potentate Kendrick proposed that the group establish hospitals in North America for the care and treatment of crippled children. The move enhanced Kendrick's national profile and cemented his reputation as a far-sighted philanthropist. The assembled Shriners adopted their Brother Kendrick's hospital proposal unanimously. The first Shriners' Hospital opened in 1922 in Shreveport, Louisiana; that same year, Lu Lu Temple purchased land near Roosevelt Boulevard for the Philadelphia Unit.[8]

By 1923 Kendrick's prominence was such that winning the Philadelphia mayoralty almost felt like a minor honor. He had led parades and delivered speeches around the country, and had been fêted at more banquets than he could remember. He had escorted a Caravan of Nobles to Washington, DC, in 1921 to witness the initiation of his fellow Noble, President-Elect Warren G. Harding. A Shriners' march had been dedicated to Kendrick; the

This 1920 song, "I'm in Love with a Mystic Shriner," was dedicated to Imperial Potentate Kendrick, seen in his robes and plumed headdress.

sheet music for a romantic ballad called "I'm in Love with a Mystic Shriner" featured a dashing photograph of the imperial potentate in his robes and plumed headdress. There was even a W. Freeland Kendrick rose, bred by Captain George C. Thomas Jr. of Philadelphia.

After four years of municipal gridlock between Mayor J. Hampton Moore and the Vare-controlled city council, Kendrick's mayoral inauguration on January 7, 1924, took on the air of a royal coronation. Months before Kendrick took office, an adoring council voted to raise the incoming mayor's salary from $12,000 to $18,000. They also authorized the purchase of a new mayoral motorcar, an $11,000 limousine. Kendrick had the car equipped with a distinctive siren that would send Philadelphia pedestrians scurrying for safety during the next four years.[9]

Under his administration slogan of "Cooperation and Action," Kendrick formed a unified political camp with the Vare-controlled city council. During his administration, the mayor would not veto a single legislative act, an achievement he would call a "wonderful record." Within weeks of Kendrick's inauguration, nearly every bureaucrat in City Hall was benefiting from his generosity. The Bureau of Surveys was given $8,500 to purchase thirteen new motor cars; city property chief Charles W. Neeld received $3,000 for

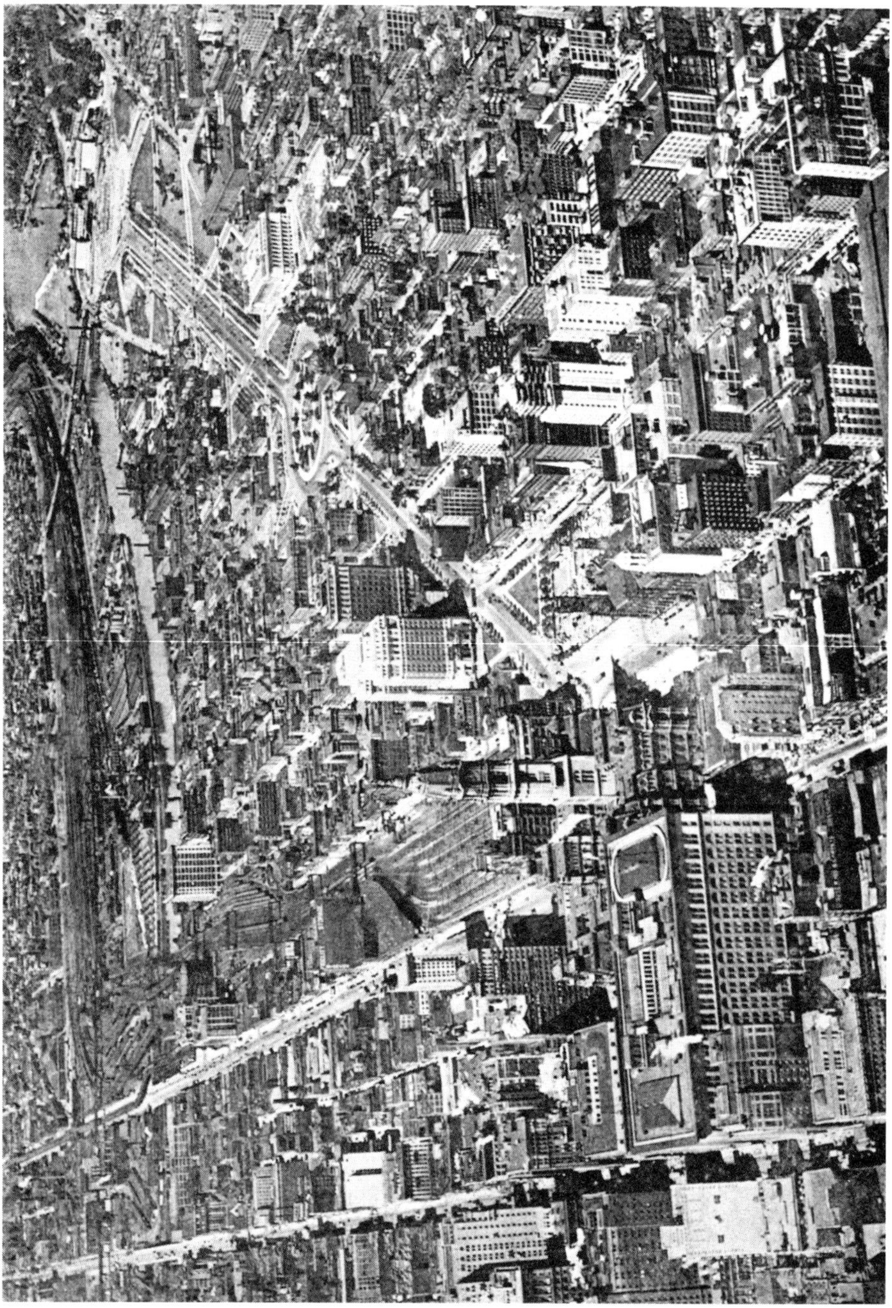

his own personal vehicle. Raises were proposed for all policemen, firemen, and Fairmount Park Guards.[10]

Money was no object to the Mayor Bountiful. Kendrick had the good luck to take office just as America was recovering from its postwar slump and entering the economic boom that would characterize the Roaring Twenties. In Philadelphia, Center City was being reshaped by the first new skyscrapers since prewar days: the Insurance Company of North America at the foot of the Parkway, the Packard Building at Fifteenth and Chestnut, and the Elverson Building on North Broad Street. At Logan Square (now reconfigured as Logan Circle), a magnificent Fountain of the Rivers, with heroic nude statues by Alexander Stirling Calder, was unveiled on July 23, 1924. Further afield, new neighborhoods sprang up overnight on the city's periphery, as speculators transformed acres of farmland into monotonous rows of Tudor and Spanish Mission cottages.[11]

Kendrick's first priority was to revive and expand the grandiose program of public works that had stagnated during the four-year feud between Moore and City Council. Using the $71 million municipal loan that had been approved in November 1923, Kendrick proposed a massive redevelopment of Philadelphia's infrastructure. His two main priorities were the modernization of its antiquated water and sewer systems, and the creation of an integrated transportation system. Soon after his inauguration, Kendrick endorsed a $100 million plan to redevelop Philadelphia's water supply system, drawing on the Perkiomen and Tohickon Creeks outside the city. He also proposed a $100 million transportation program, with a north–south Broad Street Subway to supplement the east–west line of the existing Market-Frankford Subway-Elevated.[12]

Kendrick accelerated work on postponed or delayed construction projects. He promised that the Delaware River Bridge, Free Library, and Museum of Art would be finished before the Sesqui-Centennial, although all were running over budget and behind schedule. Besides the Free Library, Logan Circle would soon be graced with the long-planned Palace of Justice and Victory Hall. A site would be chosen for a municipal Stadium, probably

---

FACING PAGE: Center City Philadelphia at the onset of the Kendrick administration. In the center of the photo, the Chinese Wall of the Pennsylvania Railroad bisects the city. This elevated viaduct connected Broad Street Station with the main tracks of the northeast corridor line in West Philadelphia. To the right, the Fairmount Parkway extends northwest from City Hall to Logan Circle, where the Free Library is under construction, and then to the Fairmount plateau, where the side wings of the new Museum of Art are near completion.

in East Fairmount Park. Plans were drawn up for a new Philadelphia General Hospital, Hospital for the Insane at Byberry, and City Hall Annex.[13]

Besides re-creating the Quaker City, Kendrick hoped to pacify it by staunching the flood of Prohibition-related crime that alarmed Philadelphians and blackened their city's national image. Despite stiff competition from New York, Chicago, and Detroit, Philadelphia was renowned as the wettest city in the wettest state in the Union. "The saloons in Philadelphia," chided Pennsylvania Governor Gifford Pinchot, a dedicated dry, "have been selling liquor more lawlessly and operating in more open defiance of the Federal and State laws than in any other city in the Commonwealth." Ignoring the Volstead Act's ban on the sale of alcohol, thirteen hundred legal saloons peddled "high-voltage beer and whiskey of character" instead of the soft drinks and near-beer they were supposed to offer. Another eight thousand "blind-tigers" or speakeasies operated outside the law, selling unimaginable varieties of chemical concoctions. In 1925, Philadelphia Coroner Charles Colgan estimated that a dozen city residents were dying each day from imbibing such lethal liquids as "Soda Pop Moon," derived from isopropyl alcohol. Many of the city's four thousand policemen turned a blind eye, paid off by gangsters like the Lanzetta Brothers of South Philadelphia and Max "Boo Boo" Hoff, the "King of the Philadelphia Bootleggers."[14]

To combat this lawlessness, Kendrick had hired Brigadier General Smedley Darlington Butler of the United States Marine Corps as his director of public safety, in charge of the police and fire departments. Scion and namesake of three venerable Quaker families, the West Chester native had seen action in the Philippines, France, Mexico, Haiti, and Central America, winning two Congressional Medals of Honor. Known by his troops as "Old Gimlet Eye," "The Fighting Quaker," and "Helldevil Butler," he had a reputation as a loose cannon who would step on anyone's toes to achieve his goals.

Kendrick had asked Butler to join his cabinet in December 1923. He sweetened the deal by offering an annual salary of $15,000, twice Butler's pay as the commanding general at the Quantico Marine Corps Base. Butler agreed on condition that Kendrick allow him to run his department without interference, and to resign at any time. President Coolidge agreed to release Butler from the Marine Corps for one year, with an option for renewal. Privately, Butler doubted he could dry up Philadelphia, telling a friend that his new position was "a terrible one and I will probably be cut to pieces."[15]

Despite his doubts, Butler came out swinging. Soon after Kendrick and Butler were inaugurated on January 7, 1924, all of Philadelphia's four thousand policemen were summoned in shifts to the Metropolitan Opera

Smedley D. Butler at a reenactment of the Battle of Gettysburg in 1922, when he was Commanding General of the Marine Corps Base at Quantico. (Prints and Photographs Division, Library of Congress.)

House on North Broad Street. Director of Public Safety Butler informed his new charges that they had forty-eight hours to get rid of vice in the city or else resign. Calling them "a joke," he promised to demand the resignation of corrupt policemen, and gave notice that he had spies ready to report any colleagues seen accepting bribes. Offering a promotion to the first cop to kill a criminal, he told the force: "I don't believe there is a single bandit notch on a policeman's gun in this city. Go out and get some."[16]

Within days, Butler had mounted his first forty-eight-hour raid on the city's saloons, speakeasies, brothels, and other dens of ill repute. Police estimated that 973 saloons selling illegal liquor had been padlocked. Butler toured the Tenderloin District, directing raids, making surprise visits to station houses, and suspending officers for shirking their duty. It made for dramatic newspaper stories, but when Butler mounted a second raid the following week, he found hundreds of places shut down the week before open for business again. The outraged director ordered a major shake-up of the police force. By Washington's birthday, "Old Gimlet Eye" boasted that his men had made fourteen thousand arrests, and had driven five thousand undesirables out of the city.[17]

With so much on the mayor's plate, the Sesqui-Centennial slid far down his list of priorities. On February 15, 1924, Kendrick was appointed the official president of the SCEA, as opposed to the honorary leadership offered him prior to his election. He replaced a disillusioned Franklin D'Olier, who had been announcing his desire to step down for months. Three weeks later, Kendrick stunned the association's executive committee by announcing that "the amount of money City Council can appropriate for a Sesqui-Centennial Exhibition necessarily must be small, because of the new water supply program and other large city programs." The SCEA was told to expect a municipal appropriation that would be significantly less than the $5 million or more promised in early 1922.[18]

Scrambling to respond to the mayor's budget cutting, SCEA Executive Secretary Victor Rosewater drafted a memorandum for "A Practical Sesqui-Centennial Program," with a price tag of $5,500,000. The barebones program projected a construction budget of $4,000,000 to cover not only such permanent structures as the new municipal Stadium but a temporary convention hall, music pavilion, journalism building, education and welfare building, aviation field, and a street of model homes illustrating modern decorative art. Other fair attractions would be housed in the Museum of Art and Free Library, or in structures financed by outside interests, like the automobile, electrical, and motion picture industries.[19]

In May 1924 the discredited Sesqui-Centennial Exhibition Association surrendered its charter to Mayor Kendrick prior to reorganization. Under the bylaws of the new association, Kendrick had more power than any previous SCEA president, including the ability to appoint directors. The new board of directors featured several holdovers from the previous association, like Albert M. Greenfield and Jules Mastbaum. But it now included most of Kendrick's mayoral cabinet, except for Director of Public Safety Butler. The rationale for their inclusion was that only the close involvement of city agencies would enable the city to prepare a celebration in the time remaining before 1926. Also on the new board were City Council President Charles B. Hall, Finance Committee Chairman Edwin R. Cox, and the councilmen representing districts that were Organization strongholds. The new board also featured several other friends of the Organization: Mrs. Blanche M. Bellak, politically powerful president of the local chapter of the National War Mothers of America; Thomas E. Mitten, chairman of the Philadelphia Rapid Transit Company; and Francis Shunk Brown, former state attorney general and one of Bill Vare's old elocution coaches. Aside from a few Old Philadelphians for window dressing, the new SCEA leadership was designed to rubber-stamp Bill Vare's orders.[20]

Kendrick unveiled plans for a modest, three-month celebration in 1926, lasting from Flag Day (June 14) until Constitution Day (September 17). A refurbished Independence Hall would be the focus of the celebration, with a series of athletic events scheduled for the new Stadium in Fairmount Park. Ever the booster, Kendrick believed that despite all the cut corners, "we can have a wonderful celebration—one of pageantry that would utilize all the permanent structures we are building, and make the affair representative of art, music, and literature."[21]

Given the narrow scope of the new Sesqui plans, SCEA Secretary Victor Rosewater felt it was time to return to Omaha. He had been brought on board two years earlier by then-Mayor J. Hampton Moore to secure recognition for "the greatest international exposition ever held." Rosewater sent a brief letter of resignation to Ernest T. Trigg, chairman of the SCEA Executive Committee. He was quickly replaced by Colonel George Washington Barnes Hicks, former director of contracts and statistics at City Hall. Hicks' annual salary was $15,000, twice what Rosewater had earned during his stormy tenure.

On June 28 a rally was held at Independence Square to show the world that the Sesqui-Centennial was alive and well. Mayor Kendrick asked the crowd of ten thousand to show their support for the fair with a "standing vote." According to the *Bulletin*, about one-fourth of those present stood, but "many of the remainder lifted their hands, signifying their approval." This was good enough for Kendrick, who announced "to the civilized world our purpose fittingly to observe the 150th anniversary of American independence in this historic city in 1926." He read a message from President Coolidge supporting the Sesqui, transmitted by radio from the dirigible *Shenandoah*, floating high above the square. At the climax of the ceremony, Mrs. Kendrick pulled a streamer on a tall white box, releasing forty-eight homing pigeons. Each bird had a message attached to its leg addressed to the governor of one of the forty-eight states, requesting their participation in the 1926 Sesqui. The birds fluttered off in all directions, each one supposedly headed for the capital of its designated state.[22]

Despite this promising kickoff, Kendrick failed to take any concrete actions to advance the Sesqui. Instead, he was distracted by an increasingly acrid feud with his renegade director of public safety. Butler, frustrated by the corrupt and ineffectual Philadelphia police, implemented a restructuring that put him on a collision course with the Organization. Traditionally, Philadelphia's forty-two police districts were paired almost identically with

At a June 28 rally in Independence Square, Mayor Kendrick attempted to revive public interest in the Sesqui. At the ceremony's climax, Kendrick read a message from President Coolidge that had been transmitted by radio from the dirigible *Shenandoah*, floating above the Square.

its forty-eight political wards, giving local bosses control over police in their neighborhood. Butler reduced the number of districts to twenty-two, each one with two lieutenants and one captain shipped in from a different part of the city. In the Vare stronghold of South Philadelphia, eleven stations were consolidated into four precincts manned by officers with no ties to local ward bosses. Butler became dictator of the city's police, effectively disenfranchising the Organization.

Not daring to oppose Butler directly, Kendrick subverted the director discreetly. When Butler requested $25,000 to upgrade the police communication system, he was refused. The Fighting Quaker accomplished the job himself, using workers from the Bureau of Electricity and secondhand materials. After this public embarrassment, Kendrick did not speak to Butler for three months. Instead, each man told his story to the newspapers. On the verge of pneumonia from eighteen-hour workdays, an ailing Butler complained that he "received no support in City Hall." In response Kendrick announced, "I had the guts to bring General Butler to Philadelphia and I have the guts to fire him." When asked his opinion of the Butler-Kendrick feud, a smiling Congressman William S. Vare replied, "I am not interested in General Butler."[23]

Despite his antipathy toward Butler, Kendrick knew that dismissing the director of public safety before his leave ended would be political suicide. In late September the mayor was presented with a petition signed by fifty thousand congregants of 150 Philadelphia churches, insisting that Butler be retained. In late September, more than four thousand Philadelphians packed the Academy of Music to show their support for the beleaguered Marine. Kendrick allowed several intermediaries to arrange a truce with Butler that reaffirmed the director's independent status. By October an uneasy peace had returned to City Hall.[24]

When City Council drafted its 1925 budget in November 1924, Finance Committee Chairman Edwin R. Cox announced that the Sesqui-Centennial would not receive any appropriations until every other municipal need was met. After much debate, city council finally voted a $500,000 appropriation for the Sesqui in 1925, taking the money from a proposed pay increase for policemen. Director Butler's budget for the coming year was being slashed by roughly $1 million, another attempt to punish the maverick Marine.[25]

On December 30 Kendrick addressed the city council to review his first year as mayor, which he modestly declared "the greatest year in the history of our City government." He noted that ground had been broken on the Broad Street Subway, and that "you and I, before the close of my administration, will be able to ride under Broad Street from Olney Avenue to Spruce Street." But given cost overruns on the subway, art museum, and other projects, the mayor felt that the $100 million plan to modernize Philadelphia's water system should be postponed indefinitely.

There was, the mayor noted, $2 million available for a new municipal Stadium. Kendrick urged that ground be broken for this new project as soon as possible. An exhaustive canvass of the entire city had uncovered only two suitable sites. One was the Burd Home, a historic property on the border of West Philadelphia and Delaware County. The other was League Island Park at the tip of South Philadelphia. City Solicitor Joseph Gaffney (who as councilman had boosted League Island Park for the Sesqui) had warned of possible litigation issues with the Burd Home site. Therefore, Kendrick felt that South Philadelphia was the only spot for the Stadium. League Island Park was "ample in size," with "tremendous possibilities for automobile storage." The "transportation facilities are excellent," taking only twenty minutes to reach by trolley from City Hall. Finally, "a natural depression exists at this place which can be taken advantage of in the building of the bowl," making League Island Park "a very desirable location for this structure." Without a pause, the mayor proceeded to discuss the Sesqui-Centennial, and the need to "build a permanent memorial of some shape which has not yet been determined."[26]

Some councilmen and reporters reacted with surprise on hearing of this hitherto unannounced city canvass. Other observers smiled knowingly. The proposed stadium site was nearly four miles south of Center City, in a remote location accessible via a single trolley line that ran along South Broad Street through isolated marshes to the Navy Yard. But the site was deep in the heart of the First Congressional District, or "Varesville." Mayor Kendrick, assisted by City Solicitor Joseph Gaffney, had just taken the first step toward delivering the municipal stadium, and by extension the Sesqui-Centennial, into the personal fiefdom of his political mentor, William S. Vare.

NOTES

1. "Former Mayor Kendrick Dies Suddenly at 78," *PB*, March 20, 1953.
2. Ferris, "Freel Kendrick of Philadelphia," *Plain Talk*, November 1927, pp. 87–93.
3. "William D. Kendrick," *PI*, October 15, 1889; "Philadelphia at War over General Butler," *NYT*, July 27, 1924; "Mayor Practices on Mouth Organ to 'Show 'Em' during Boys' Week," *PPL*, April 12, 1924.
4. Harry Speth, "The History of the Shrine and Lu Lu"; "W.F. Kendrick Wins High Shrine Honor," *PP*, April 15, 1910; "Shriners Hail Freeland Kendrick," *PB*, May 16, 1910.
5. "Reformers Again Hail Contractor Campaign Issue," *PI*, July 21, 1911, p. 1; "Vare in Fight for Mayor and Says 'To Finish,'" *PI*, August 8, 1911, p. 1.
6. "Mystic Shriners at Big Meeting Extol Kendrick," *PI*, October 28, 1913, p. 1; "Rotan Elected, Has at Least 25,000 Plurality," *PI*, November 5, 1913.
7. "Mayoralty Possibilities," *PP*, July 17, 1919; "Kendrick Heads Shriners," *PB*, June 18, 1919; "Welcome for Kendrick," *PB*, June 20, 1919.
8. "Shriners for Kendrick Plan," *PB*, June 16, 1921.
9. "Mayor Signs Rise in Successor's Pay." *PB*, October 24, 1923; "Mayor to Have New Motor," *PB*, December 26, 1923; Ferris, "Freel Kendrick of Philadelphia."
10. *Address by Mayor W. Freeland Kendrick to Members of City Council, Tuesday, December 30, 1924, Together with a Review of the Activities of the City Departments during the Year 1924, and as Far as Possible Departmental Plans for 1925*; "Kendrick Wants $2K Pay

Boost for 2 Directors," *PPL*, January 24, 1924; "Reach Agreement on Police Pay Rise," *PB*, March 10, 1924.

11. Glazer, *Philadelphia Theaters*, pp. 33–40; Fairmount Park Art Association, *Sculpture of a City*, pp. 231–238; Miller, *Still Philadelphia*, pp. 175–190; Miller et al., *Philadelphia Stories*, pp. 5–6.

12. "Philadelphia Elects W. F. Kendrick Mayor," *NYT*, November 7, 1923; "Mayor Says He Favors $100,000,000 Water Plan," *PR*, February 12, 1924; *Annual Message of W. Freeland Kendrick, Mayor of Philadelphia for 1926*, p. 49.

13. Beers, *Pennsylvania Politics Today and Yesterday*, p. 62; "Mayor Shocked to Hear Museum Cost Will Be $13,700,000," *PB*, April 17, 1924; "Victory Hall Work Must Wait a Year," *PB*, November 27, 1924.

14. "Personal Glimpses: How Wet Is Philadelphia?" *Literary Digest*, November 10, 1923, pp. 34–46; "Says Liquor Kills 12 Daily," *NYT*, February 10, 1925; Okrent, *Last Call*, p. 215.

15. Schmidt, *Maverick Marine*, p. 129.

16. "Police Get 48 Hours to Rid Philadelphia of Vice or Quit Jobs," *NYT*, January 7, 1924.

17. Schmidt, *Maverick Marine*; "Philadelphia at War over General Butler," *NYT*, July 27, 1924; "Philadelphia Bares a Bootleg Kingdom," *NYT*, September 2, 1928.

18. "Can't Give Sesqui Much, Mayor Says," *PB*, March 8, 1924.

19. "A Practical Sesqui-Centennial Program," memorandum, VR/AJA, ms0503.022.004, p. 148.

20. Austin and Hauser, *The Sesqui-Centennial International Exposition*, pp. 35–42, 462–463; "Rosewater Resigns from Sesqui Post," undated newspaper article, VR/AJA, ms0503.022.005, p. 44.

21. "Sesqui Will Open in June 1926 at Independence Hall," *PB*, May 23, 1924.

22. "10,000 Back Sesqui as Mayor Assures Observance in 1926," *PB*, June 28, 1924.

23. Schmidt, *Maverick Marine*, 153; "Mayor Deluged by Pleas to Keep Butler in Post," *PB*, July 21, 1924; "Doubt Mayor Will Drop Butler Now," *PB*, July 22, 1924.

24. "Kendrick-Butler at Breaking Point; May Last Out Year," *PB*, September 20, 1924; "Kendrick Yields to Gang to Save 'Protected' Joints," *PNA*, September 21, 1924; "Butler Must Quit Is Kendrick's Hint to Clergy Callers," *PB*, September 23, 1924; "Mayor Won't Act on Butler until General Returns," *PB*, September 29, 1924.

25. "Fair Comes Last on Budget List," *PB*, November 27, 1924; "Butler's Budget Cut over 1 Million; $500k to Sesqui," *PB*, December 2, 1924.

26. "Kendrick Is Given Plans for Sesqui," *PB*, December 3, 1924; "Mayor and Price Confer on Sesqui," *PB*, December 4, 1924; "Mayor May Drop Gigantic Water Supply Project," *PR*, December 27, 1924; "Mayor Advises Further Delay in Water Plan," *PR*, December 31, 1924; *Address by Mayor W. Freeland Kendrick to Members of City Council, Tuesday, December 30, 1924, Together with a Review of the Activities of the City Departments during the Year 1924, and as Far as Possible Departmental Plans for 1925*, Philadelphia, January 10, 1925.

5

★ ★ ★

The Sesqui Moves South

WITH THE SESQUI-CENTENNIAL showing renewed signs of life, Mayor Kendrick gave it a shot of adrenaline by appointing Colonel David Charles Collier as director-general in February 1925. Collier, a lawyer and real estate developer, had been the driving force behind the small but successful Panama-California Exposition held in San Diego in 1915 and 1916. Although overshadowed by the San Francisco Panama-Pacific International Exposition held at the same time, the popular San Diego fair turned a profit and provided its host city with permanent improvements. With his flowing cravat, cowboy hat, and wavy gray hair cresting in a pompadour, the irrepressible Collier looked like the owner of a successful Wild West Show.[1]

Although Kendrick still insisted that the Sesqui would be "dignified, economical, and effective," he signed a nineteen-month contract with Collier at the lofty salary of $25,000 a year. Collier hired A. L. Sutton, a Los Angeles resident with extensive experience in international expositions, as his executive assistant. Captain Asher C. Baker, a seventy-five-year-old retired naval officer who had handled American displays at several world's fairs, was named chief of exhibits, at an annual salary of $15,000. Baker began to prepare for a lengthy trip abroad to persuade European nations to participate in the Sesqui.[2]

Within a week of signing his contract, Collier released preliminary plans for an international exposition to be held on three hundred acres in and around League Island Park, across Broad Street from the new stadium site. While the park would serve as the main fairground, exhibitions and events would be scattered throughout the city. The Commercial Museum in West Philadelphia would house foreign displays, while the Museum of Art, Free Library, and Independence Hall would also host exhibits. Agricultural shows would be staged near the City Poor Farms, nineteen miles north of League Island Park. The Collier plan was the first confirmation that the Sesqui had been shifted from Center City to South Philadelphia. This relocation had been assumed since Kendrick's decree that the new Stadium would be located in the League Island Park athletic fields east of Broad Street. Given the crucial role the Stadium would play in Sesqui events, it followed that the fair would have to be adjacent.[3]

League Island Park stood above the Navy Yard at the southernmost tip of Philadelphia, near the confluence of the Delaware and Schuylkill Rivers. It consisted of roughly 300 acres of marshy land on both sides of Broad Street below Pattison Avenue, stretching east to Eleventh Street and west to Twentieth Street. In 1912, the Olmsted Brothers had laid out the park, with athletic fields east of Broad Street and a more natural, picturesque landscape on the west. There, a drainage system funneled numerous creeks into two large bodies of water, Meadow Lake and Edgewood Lake. The neglected park was part of a grandiose development scheme called the South Philadelphia Improvements, championed by Ed and Bill Vare, which had been abandoned during the World War.[4]

Collier's proposals for the Sesqui-Centennial at League Island Park were quickly given unanimous approval by the SCEA Executive Committee, and forwarded to Mayor Kendrick for his signature. Critics protested that the act signed by President Harding in 1922 had specified federal recognition of a world's fair held "upon the Fairmount Park and Parkway site." Others recalled the site selection report compiled by the city's top engineers and architects for the SCEA in January 1922, which had ranked League Island Park as one of the least desirable fair sites. Citing the large sums of money required to fill and grade the area, the report had also given South Philadelphia low marks in terms of aesthetics, accessibility, and healthfulness. Experts had warned that a South Philadelphia site would add $12 million to the cost of the fair, in the form of water conduits, grading, pile driving, and pest control.[5]

Little had changed in the neighborhood known as the Neck since the 1922 site report. The undeveloped region was still occupied primarily by truck farms and trash dumps, although an industrial rail loop had brought in freight yards and oil refineries. In some places, the swampy ground stood eighteen feet below Broad Street. Outside League Island Park, all land was privately owned, increasing the need to condemn, lease, or buy property needed for the Sesqui. Among the local landowners was William S. Vare, who owned two plots adjacent to Broad Street, assessed at $77,000. Announcing that he was "willing to be of whatever assistance I can to further the Sesqui-Centennial," Vare promised to lease the property to the SCEA for a reasonable fee.[6]

None of these drawbacks mattered to either the SCEA or City Hall. On April 3, 1925, Mayor Kendrick received a confidential report prepared by City Consulting Engineer Solomon M. Swaab, Director of Public Works George Biles, SCEA Executive Committee Chairman Ernest Trigg, and Director-General David Collier. Their report contradicted the 1922 Engineers' Club Report and sang the praises of League Island Park. Draining and leveling the ground would not be a problem: "apparently there is sufficient ground at the high level for at least 40 acres of Exposition-Exhibition Buildings." The report concluded that "the site and the plan of development possess innumerable advantages over all of the others that have been suggested in the fact that the accomplishment of the Exposition project can be brought about in much less time, with a whole lot less effort, at considerably less expense than any of the others."[7]

Now packed with Vare puppets and allies, the SCEA Executive Committee agreed that any another location would require the expenditure of a "vast amount of time and millions of money . . . in order to get it into the acceptable condition of an Exposition site that League Island Park was at the time of its selection." The committee praised the "accessible rail and water transportation advantage" of the site, ignoring the fact that only the Broad Street trolley line ran south of Oregon Avenue at the time. Concerns over the cost of filling and grading were also dismissed: trash collectors would dump their ashes in the lowlands, and the Army Corps of Engineers, then dredging the Delaware River, would deposit debris from the river bottom there as well.[8]

Mayor Kendrick insisted that the Sesqui and the City Stadium were the keys that would unlock the virgin territory of South Philadelphia for expansion:

> For many years I have had an eye on that great undeveloped area of South Philadelphia with its possibilities of civic improvement. I made up my mind that if I had the opportunity something would be done to make that great district fit for homes, industries, and port developments on a grand scale. The Sesqui-Centennial is giving South Philadelphia that opportunity. When the site of the stadium was located in the eastern section of League Island Park it settled that matter.[9]

No concrete evidence ties the decision to relocate the Sesqui directly to Congressman William S. Vare. But the money trail indicates that Vare and his Organization were the primary beneficiaries of the move to League Island Park. Vare's stranglehold on Philadelphia was acknowledged nationally: the *New York Times* charged that "the whole [Sesqui-Centennial] enterprise is no more than a gigantic real estate scheme to boost realty values in South Philadelphia, a lagging realty section which has been for many years and which still is the stronghold of the Vare Republican machine." As a property holder in the Neck, Vare stood to benefit personally from deals made to obtain land for the Sesqui. His contracting firm would receive lucrative contracts for Sesqui construction, while other companies that wished to be considered would have to pay him to play the Sesqui game. One historian has estimated that more than four hunded Sesqui contracts were channeled through the Organization, with Vare's men skimming a cut off each deal.[10]

For Congressman Vare, the acclaim that the Sesqui would elicit from his constituents was more valuable than any financial gain. South Philadelphia residents would cheer him as the beneficent leader who had transformed their region from a backwater into a model suburb with paved streets, sewers, lighting, and plentiful jobs. A South Philadelphia Sesqui would be the consummate illustration of "Service," the motto and mission of Vare's political machine. The entire country would see, as Vare insisted, that "the Philadelphia Organization is in fact one of the greatest welfare organizations in the United States." Finally, the national attention fixed on Philadelphia during the Sesqui would generate tremendous publicity for Vare as he planned the next step in his political career. He hoped to run for U.S. senator from Pennsylvania in 1926, challenging incumbent George Wharton Pepper and winning the prize that had been snatched from him in 1922.[11]

On February 14 Mayor Kendrick and Director-General Collier visited the White House, accompanied by Senator George W. Pepper and Congressman George P. Darrow. After reviewing their plans, President Coolidge officially approved the Sesqui-Centennial, dispelling fears that the site change might jeopardize federal support. Coolidge assured the delegation that "the full machinery of the Department of State and Department of Commerce would be thrown behind the Sesqui to make it one of the greatest exhibitions of its kind ever held." Finally, he advised Congress to favor Kendrick's request for federal participation in the fair, without naming a specific amount. As he left the White House, a jubilant Kendrick assured reporters that the Sesqui would remain an economical celebration. "I don't

The Sesqui-Centennial executive committee visits the White House. Among the delegation were Director-General Charles D. Collier (second from left), Mayor Kendrick (fourth from left), Senator George W. Pepper (fifth from right), and Congressman George P. Darrow (third from right). Also present were Secretary of State Frank B. Kellogg (third from left) and Secretary of Commerce Herbert Hoover (behind President Coolidge). (Prints and Photograph Division, Library of Congress.)

intend to be the goat," he told the assembled scribes. "I am opposed to any plans mortgaging the future of the city. . . . I will not consent to any schemes that we can't pay for."[12]

Upon returning to Philadelphia, Kendrick and Collier sent telegrams to the governors of all forty-eight states, assuring them that the Sesqui-Centennial was on. The State Department would immediately notify the nations of the world that the U.S. Government supported the fair, "and we have every assurance that foreign participation will be on a large scale." Kendrick and Collier urged each governor to arrange for an appropriate building at "the first great exposition to be held in the eastern center of population since 1876." The telegrams ignored the fact that it was already a year late for many state legislatures to allocate funds for a Sesqui pavilion in 1926.[13]

Shortly after, the House Committee on Industrial Arts and Expositions and the Senate Committee on Libraries approved the revised Sesqui-Centennial plans. Elsewhere on Capitol Hill, the Senate passed a resolution creating a National Sesqui-Centennial Exposition Commission to be appointed by President Coolidge, consisting of two members from every state and territory. Secretary of State Kellogg and Secretary of Commerce Hoover would serve as directors of the commission. Unfortunately, Congress adjourned before allocating funds for the new body. Coolidge would not appoint commissioners until the fall of 1925, further hindering state participation in the Sesqui.[14]

Without a guaranteed federal appropriation, Kendrick continued to emphasize economy. He announced that key members of his cabinet who served on the SCEA Executive Committee would assume Sesqui responsibilities in addition to their municipal jobs, at no extra pay. George H. Biles, director of public works, would be responsible for all Sesqui engineering and construction. The Bureau of Highways would supervise street construction at the Sesqui, while the Bureau of Public Transit would coordinate transportation of the millions of anticipated visitors. City Architect John Molitor found that his $6,000-a-year position now entailed building design and site layout for the Sesqui. Molitor would be assisted by his small staff, including a young draftsman named Louis I. Kahn, a former student of Paul Cret at the University of Pennsylvania.[15]

One important position not assigned to a cabinet member was the Sesqui director of concessions. This officer would be responsible for awarding hundreds of lucrative concessions to hot dog vendors, soda pop manufacturers, and other companies whose fees would bankroll the Sesqui. This prize plum went to William S. Abrahams, a manufacturer of military uniforms and personal friend of Mayor Kendrick. Besides furnishing Philadelphia policemen and firemen, Abrahams provided "Oriental Uniforms" to fraternal organizations like Kendrick's Lu Lu Shriners. Abrahams, who had agreed to fulfill his duties without pay, insisted that favoritism would play no role in Sesqui concessions: "Privileges on the exposition grounds will be granted to the highest and most responsible bidder."[16]

On February 26 City Council gave final approval to Mayor Kendrick's bill designating the South Philadelphia site for the Municipal Stadium, and authorized construction to begin at Broad Street and Pattison Avenue. The $2 million structure, designed by architect brothers Grant M. Simon and Edward P. Simon, would have a seating capacity of 100,000, and standing room for another 150,000. The U-shaped structure, 710 feet wide and 1,020 feet long, would open to the north. Its arms would cradle a

A preliminary sketch for the new Municipal Stadium. Once it was moved to South Philadelphia, the fate of the rest of the Sesqui was sealed.

300,000-square-foot playing field with room for a football gridiron, baseball field, and quarter-mile track. The "Sesqui Stadium" would be the heart of the fair, hosting athletic competitions, patriotic pageants, music festivals, and military parades.[17]

In mid-March Director-General Collier unveiled his detailed plans for the Sesqui-Centennial, now scheduled to run from June 1 to December 1, 1926. The scale of Collier's Sesqui was significantly larger than the economical celebration Kendrick had described. Seven large exhibition palaces would be built, while hundreds of smaller pavilions would house exhibits from foreign governments, states, and private organizations. An elaborate Gladway would entertain fairgoers with "amusements of a high type." The entire fairground would be surrounded by a picturesque moat rather than an unsightly fence, broken at intervals by bridges leading to the entrance gates.[18]

On March 30, 1925, construction work began with the driving of the first pile for the new Stadium. By this time, the SCEA Executive Committee had announced plans to extend the fair site northward to Packer Avenue, both to take advantage of the higher, drier ground north of Pattison Avenue and to accommodate the forty million to fifty million expected visitors. This move would more than double the size of the fairgrounds, from three hundred to nearly seven hundred acres, and would increase the need to purchase or lease privately owned land.[19]

Buoyed by this expansion of the fairgrounds, federal recognition of the fair, and soaring municipal expenditures, a Sesqui boom erupted in Philadelphia. Land parcels in the Neck, previously assessed at $1,000 to $10,000 an acre depending on their proximity to Broad Street, now sold for $16,000 to $28,000 an acre. Residential development in South Philadelphia, which had barely dipped below Bigler Street, thundered southward to the front door of League Island Park. Developers announced plans to build on Packer Avenue and even on Pattison Avenue, directly across from the Sesqui entrance.[20]

In Harrisburg, Governor Gifford Pinchot threw cold water on the Sesqui wildfire. With a bill on his desk that would allocate $1 million to a state Sesqui-Centennial Commission, he announced that there were no state funds available for the fair. A stunned Collier warned that most states would look to Pennsylvania before deciding if they would participate in the Sesqui. Pinchot held firm. By refusing to grant state funds for what he considered an Organization boondoggle, Pinchot fired the latest salvo in his ongoing feud with William Vare. After desperate pleading by SCEA officers, Pinchot signed a bill guaranteeing Pennsylvania's participation in the Sesqui. He cut the proposed appropriation from $1 million to $750,000, and recommended that the entire amount be used to construct a Pennsylvania State Building.[21]

With thirteen months to go before opening day, Sesqui planners had a grand total of $1.25 million firmly committed to the fair: $500,000 from the Philadelphia City Council, and $750,000 from the Commonwealth of Pennsylvania. At this point, Kendrick received an independent engineers' report that estimated it would cost $14 million to prepare the Sesqui site before any buildings were erected. Of this amount, $6 million would be required to fill in and grade the fairgrounds. Another $7 million would cover transportation projects that would connect the Sesqui with the rest of Philadelphia by routes other than South Broad Street. It would include the extension of Tenth, Eleventh, and Twentieth Streets south to Pattison Avenue; improvements to Delaware Avenue from the new Delaware River Bridge to Pattison Avenue; and the development of Oregon Avenue from Delaware Avenue to Broad Street.[22]

Before adjourning for the summer, City Council passed two bills authorizing $4,686,000 for streets and grounds in the Sesqui district. Separately, the city negotiated leases with twenty owners of property on the proposed Sesqui site, including Congressman Vare. In exchange for use of the land, the city would pay landowners $1, suspend property taxes for two

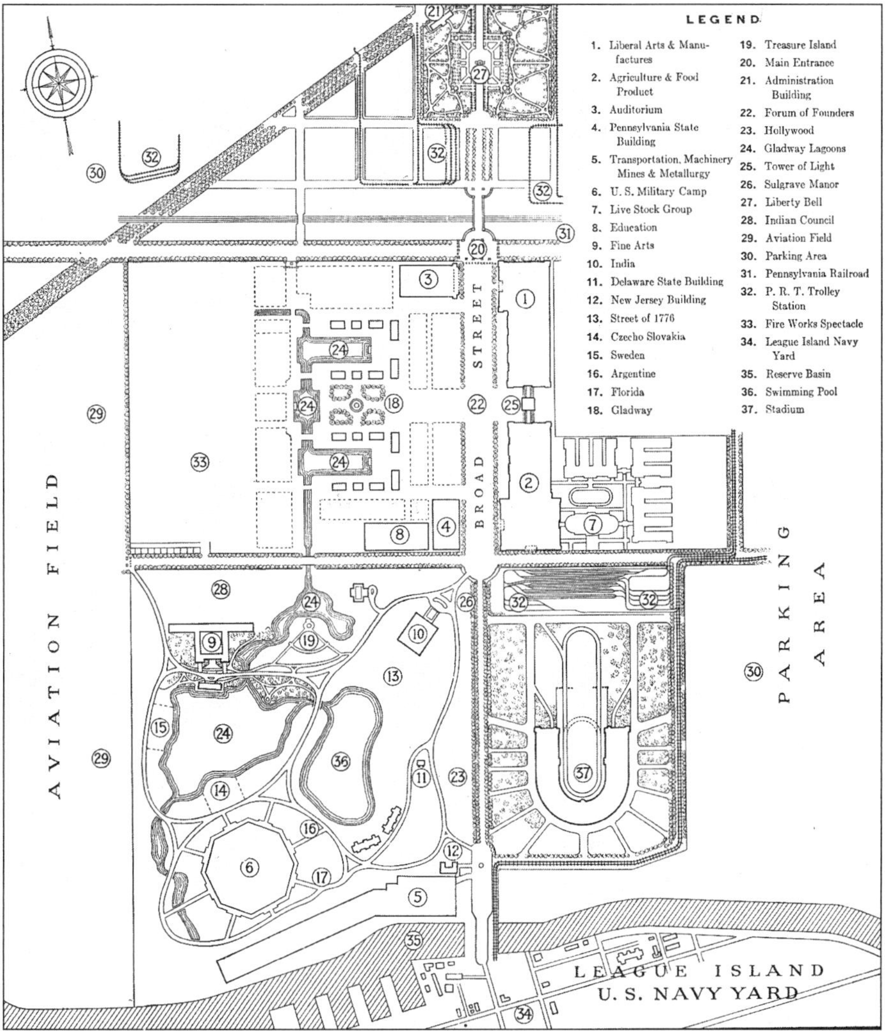

A map of the Sesqui-Centennial grounds.

years, and make improvements. At this point, all of the work in the Sesqui district—property acquisition, filling and leveling grounds, laying sewers, cutting new streets, and stadium construction—was covered by the City Treasury rather than the SCEA, under the designation of "South Philadelphia Improvements."[23]

Chief Sesqui designer and City Architect John Molitor increased his staff to more than twenty draftsmen, under the supervision of principal assistant W. J. Sutphen. These designers began to produce designs for the seven large palaces, which would cover a total of 3.8 million square feet and cost an estimated $7,148,000. All were in a vaguely Modernist style referred to

A designer's sketch of one of the central towers for the main exhibit halls.

as "Aztec-Mayan," symbolic of America's aboriginal culture. The two main exhibit halls were huge oblong boxes, their facades broken by a colossal central entrance. Their primary ornamentation was the corner towers, covered with Art Deco sunbursts and topped by gilded statues of naked heralds surrounding a jewellike electric beacon. To prevent the steel-and-stucco structures from looking too austere, their rough surfaces would be daubed in pink, yellow, and salmon. At night, multicolored lights would play upon their walls, giving the fair the soubriquet of "The Rainbow City."[24]

On September 30 Philadelphia's elite attended a banquet at the Bellevue-Stratford Hotel, marking the inauguration of a campaign planned by SCEA Finance Chairman Albert M. Greenfield to sell $3 million in Sesqui bonds. These "certificates of participation," to be sold in denominations ranging from $50 to $1,000, would be redeemable within six months of the exposition's close in December 1926, repaying principal plus 5 percent interest. The proceeds from the sale would, according to Mayor Kendrick, allow the SCEA to create a world's fair "without parallel in comparison to other expositions."[25]

More than $1.5 million in certificates were pledged by the time dessert was served. Most were snapped up by big local concerns that would benefit from a successful world's fair, and that had already pledged their financial support. The Pennsylvania Railroad, Philadelphia Electric Company, Philadelphia Rapid Transit Company, United Gas Improvement Company, and Bell Telephone of Pennsylvania subscribed $100,000 apiece. The big five department stores on East Market Street—Wanamaker's, Strawbridge and Clothier, Gimbel Brothers, Lit Brothers, and Snellenburg's—each purchased $50,000. Edward T. Stotesbury pledged $50,000 on behalf of Drexel and Company. The elderly banker explained his change of mind about the Sesqui by saying, "Two years ago I was opposed to it because I had been told it would require thirty or forty million dollars. When Mayor Kendrick told me that the celebration would be a sane and sensible one, I changed my mind and told him I would do everything to help." The next morning, more than fifteen hundred volunteers fanned out across the city to sell the remaining certificates to the public.[26]

The success of the fund drive was overshadowed by a fresh crisis. In August City Architect Molitor had solicited bids from six construction companies for Building No. 1, the Palace of Liberal Arts and Manufactures, with a budgeted cost of $600,000. The 375,000-square-foot structure near the fairground entrance would house industrial and commercial exhibits, the meat and potatoes of world's fairs. With major manufacturers paying five dollars per square foot for large display areas, Building No. 1 would be a cash cow for the fair.

When Molitor opened the six contractors' bids, however, the lowest figure he saw was $374,000 over his estimate. Michael Melody and Sons, a local contractor with strong ties to the Organization, submitted the low bid of $974,000, with the next lowest offers at $1,149,900 and $1,240,000. Mayor Kendrick rejected all six bids and insisted that the specifications for Building

No. 1 be modified to reduce its cost. Its size was reduced from 375,000 to 338,000 square feet. Instead of a fireproof gypsum concrete roof, a wooden roof would be used; wood lath and plaster stucco would replace metal lath and cement stucco for the walls; a concrete slab floor, likely to crack and settle, would be laid directly on the ground. An angry Molitor refused to accept responsibility if Building No. 1 was constructed along the revised lines.

Molitor was ignored, and the contract for Building No. 1 was awarded to Austin and Company for $758,000. Although this figure was still significantly above Molitor's original estimate, it was $216,000 less than the Michael Melody bid. Austin and Company, a Cleveland-based specialist in large-scale industrial construction, did not bid on the project. The firm was selected without competition by the Sesqui Building Committee, which included Finance Committee Chairman Albert M. Greenfield, Director of Concessions William S. Abrahams, and Kendrick's Director of Supplies E. J. Lafferty.[27]

As more contractors' bids were received, it became clear that Building No. 1 was the first of many miscalculations made by Molitor. His original estimate of $7,148,000 for construction of the seven main exhibition buildings was at least $5 million too low. The city architect was relieved of his Sesqui duties, and future architectural decisions were handled by a five-man board of design.[28]

Another tempest was brewing around William Abrahams, Kendrick's handpicked director of concessions. A *Bulletin* columnist cited the activities of Abrahams, "the Mayor's personal friend," as one of the key reasons that the Sesqui lacked credibility, and why "such a side show may be abandoned altogether." In September several food suppliers accused Abrahams of practicing the old Philadelphia tradition of "pay to play." Abrahams and an assistant city solicitor named Frank W. Melvin had allegedly offered concessions to these firms in exchange for bribes disguised as advertising in a Sesqui publication. Melvin, ex-president of the South Philadelphia Business Men's Association, had worked closely with former Councilman Gaffney to have the Sesqui moved south. When Gaffney was appointed city solicitor, he hired Melvin to work in his office.[29]

Hires root beer, developed by Philadelphia pharmacist Charles E. Hires and popularized at the 1876 Centennial, should have been a natural to sell to thirsty Sesqui visitors. But in September 1925 Hires's two sons announced that the Charles E. Hires Company would not sell its root beer at the Sesqui. They told reporters they had been approached by Melvin, acting as Abrahams's representative, who assured him them Hires would get the exclusive root beer concession at the Sesqui "for a proper consideration."[30] The Hires

By the end of October, beleaguered City Architect John Molitor had been relieved of his duties as chief architect for the Sesqui, thanks to his miscalculations on building costs.

brothers would have to buy $15,000 in advertising in the *Daily Sesqui-Centennial Exposition Magazine*, published by Abrahams and Melvin. They would also have to pay Abrahams and Melvin 5 percent of the gross profits on all root beer sold at the Sesqui. To sweeten the deal, Hires was promised a gold medal at the end of the fair, as part of the competition among commercial exhibitors. The Hires brothers declined to either pay or play.

Chicago-based William Wrigley Jr. Company, and Philadelphia chocolatier H. O. Wilbur and Sons Inc. also alleged that Melvin and Abrahams had demanded they advertise in a daily Sesqui program in exchange for the chewing gum and chocolate concessions at the fair. Other companies charged that Abrahams had instructed them to use certain suppliers, or to provide kickbacks, in order to win Sesqui concessions. When confronted, Abrahams refuted all allegations.[31]

A reluctant Kendrick ordered an audit of Abraham's records and the eighty-five contracts awarded to date, but refused to dismiss his friend as director of concessions. Meanwhile, the SCEA insisted that it had never heard of the *Daily Sesqui-Centennial Exposition Magazine*, and City Solicitor Gaffney began to investigate Melvin independently. Finally, the SCEA Executive Committee went over Kendrick's head and fired the beleaguered director. The stubborn Abrahams would not resign until the end of November, when he was replaced by W. E. Cash, who had supervised concessions at the Chicago, St. Louis, and Buffalo fairs. By this time, the Sesqui was losing between six and twelve concessions a week.[32]

Despite the Molitor and Abrahams debacles, progress inched forward on the Sesqui-Centennial. President Coolidge accepted an invitation to visit Philadelphia over the Independence Day weekend. Sardonically, the president told reporters that he was "booked to be one of the exhibits" at the fair. By October 12 the $3 million participation certificate campaign was oversubscribed, with a total of $3,005,840 pledged. By the end of November, ground had been broken for the Palace of Liberal Arts and Manufactures (Building No. 1) and the Palace of Agriculture and Foreign Exhibits (Building No. 2), as well as on a ten-thousand-seat Auditorium.[33]

Outside organizations cast votes of confidence in the Sesqui by announcing plans for their own buildings. In New York City, textile and apparel executives unveiled designs for a Temple of Fashion that would feature a ten-thousand-seat amphitheater and a circular stage for daily fashion shows. The futuristic, octagonal structure was designed by Louis I. Kahn (moonlighting from his job in the city architect's office, much to Molitor's displeasure), in conjunction with Stewart Culin, described by *Women's Wear Daily* as "the ultimate fashion dictator of America." Archaeologist J. W. Kelchner announced plans to re-create Solomon's Temple in Jerusalem, a ziggurat towering three hundred feet. On the final day of the Sesqui, huge blasts of steam from hidden pipes would simulate the destruction of the temple in 587 B.C.E.[34]

Emboldened by the success of the certificate drive, Director-General Collier announced in October that the Sesqui budget would be $23 million: $11.5 million for construction, $7.5 million for management and operating expenses, $2 million for pageantry and entertainment, and $2 million for contingencies. These expenses would be covered by $19 million in exhibitors' fees, $3 million in concession fees, and $19 million in admissions, for total receipts of $35 million to $40 million. There would be sufficient profits to repay both the city and certificate holders with interest.[35]

Collier bombarded newspapers across the country with hyperbolic press releases. He assured Americans that the opening of the Sesqui-Centennial on June 1, 1926, would "give to the entire world one of the greatest exhibitions ever created." Despite the fair's remote location, visitors could reach it easily via three hundred daily trains to a new Union Station on the fairgrounds, two hundred double-decker buses being added to the PRT South Broad Street line, or the new harbor capable of handling one million waterborne passengers each month. Those traveling by car would be welcomed by "triumphal welcoming arches of artistic design" on all major highways into Philadelphia.[36]

These exaggerated descriptions were derided by local critics who could see how little actual progress was being made in South Philadelphia. A *Bulletin* columnist noted that "the Sesqui balloon is finally being brought down to earth" under the weight of Collier's exaggerations. The director-general's exaggerations appeared to act as a reality check on his boss. Within days of Collier's announcements, Kendrick proclaimed that a $23 million budget was "impossible." The mayor decreed that the $3 million already raised would have to cover all building costs, limiting construction to those structures already under way. Such a drastically truncated program was not only fiscally prudent, Kendrick insisted, but it was also the only way that the Sesqui would open on its scheduled date of June 1, 1926.[37]

Addressing the Philadelphia press corps at the end of October, Kendrick performed a deft volte-face from master showman (a role Collier had usurped all too well) to civic custodian, protecting the purses of Philadelphia taxpayers. "It is up to the Mayor to sit tight," Kendrick told reporters, "and I intend to do so":

> We must construct buildings and arrange an affair that will be as attractive as possible in the limited time that is left to us. With the administration building, two exhibition buildings, the Stadium and an Auditorium we will have a very good start. With the Commercial Museum, the Art Museum and the new library we have a background against which we can build an affair that will be interesting to those who come here next year.[38]

Kendrick's panicked response had been provoked by preparation of the 1926 budget for the City and County of Philadelphia, which he submitted to City Council on October 15, 1925. Behind its apparent prosperity, the Workshop of the World was sinking in a sea of red ink. During the first nine months of 1925, the city had borrowed more than $52 million, compared with $14 million for all of 1924. The money allocated to service the city's indebtedness had grown by nearly $6 million since 1924. Philadelphia was piling on debt despite a rise in the assessed value of the city's taxable real estate of nearly $194 million in the past year, to $2.94 billion.

At least $18 million more would be required on top of the millions already spent to finish the Broad Street Subway, the showpiece of Kendrick's administration. The Museum of Art was proving to be exceptionally costly.

In October a shocked Kendrick learned that the cost of the building shell alone, estimated at $8.5 million in 1922, would top $14 million. Other projects, like the Delaware River Bridge and the Free Library, were also running well over budget. The mayor realized that he had to rein in Colonel Collier's elaborate plans for the "Big Show" in South Philadelphia, even if Collier had been following his lead.[39]

At a meeting of the SCEA on October 27, the board of directors unanimously approved Kendrick's plan to scale back the Sesqui. They also conceded that the Sesqui would no longer be an international exposition. Only ten countries had agreed to participate in the Sesqui; one of the largest, Brazil, would soon drop out. The following day, both Director-General David C. Collier and Ernest T. Trigg, chairman of the SCEA Executive Committee, submitted their resignations. Trigg wrote Kendrick, "I feel that the celebration can better be carried out by members of your official family." Despite a contract valid until January 1, 1927, Collier offered to leave at the end of 1925, serving in an advisory capacity until then. Until an appropriate successor to Colonel Collier was found, Controller E. L. Austin and Acting Assistant Director-General A. L. Sutton were assigned to handle daily operations.[40]

The announcement of the reduced Sesqui and the dual resignations of its leaders threw the SCEA into chaos. Under Collier's direction, a team of salesmen had scoured the country, selling exhibition space to businesses. Suddenly, the 1.8 million square feet of space already sold was more than twice what could be accommodated by the sixteen acres available in the two remaining palaces. The sales force was ordered to abandon its efforts and return home at once, probably to be fired. Exhibitors and concessionaires besieged SCEA headquarters, questioning the status of their contracts and, in many cases, canceling them. Legal experts debated the validity of the sale of $3 million in participation certificates, given the radical change in the size and scope of the Sesqui. Kendrick slashed the SCEA staff, which under Collier had inched back up to 120 employees earning a monthly total of $20,000. Director of Exhibits Baker, recalled from his European trip, was another strong candidate for dismissal.[41]

Across the Delaware River in Camden, Mayor Victor King suggested merging the troubled Sesqui-Centennial with his city's fair. The South Jersey Exposition was on schedule to open July 5, 1926, the day when President Coolidge would dedicate the new Delaware River Bridge. Graciously, King even offered to change the name of the celebration to the "Sesqui-Centennial Exposition of Philadelphia and Camden." Kendrick declined King's offer, insisting that the birthplace of the Declaration of Independence was the only proper site to celebrate its 150th anniversary.[42]

By this point, Kendrick's actions began to appear wildly erratic. After shrinking the Sesqui, he proposed doubling the size of its fairgrounds. On October 31 the City Council Committee on City Property and Service, acting at Kendrick's bequest, recommended that 627 additional acres in South Philadelphia be acquired for the Sesqui-Centennial. The move would extend the eastern boundary of the fairgrounds from Seventh Street to Second Street while pushing it west five blocks, from Twentieth Street to Twenty-Fifth Street. The new property, most of which was privately owned, would be leased by the city until 1928, during which time it would be exempt from municipal taxes. The direct cost was estimated at $370,000, not counting the thousands of dollars of taxes the city would sacrifice. Once again, the outlay would be covered not by the SCEA, but by the City Treasury as another "South Philadelphia Improvement."

The initial reaction from City Council was silence. Why did the smaller fair need 627 more acres? More important, as Council President Charles B. Hall demanded, "Where's the money coming from?" The answer given was that additional space was needed for automobile parking. Given the size of the average 1925 car, 627 acres could have accommodated between 400,000 and 450,000 cars, or twice the number registered in Philadelphia at the time. When City Council was informed that both Mayor Kendrick and City Solicitor Gaffney had approved the bill, it was passed unanimously and without further debate. The Organization had spoken, and its servants had obeyed. "We're going to have the Sesqui, and we have to do everything to make it a success," announced President Hall. "The ground is needed, and I'll move for a favorable recommendation."[43]

Repercussions from the Abrahams concessions scandal, the Kendrick retrenchment, and the Collier-Trigg resignations began to be felt around the country. Under an editorial titled "Frost on the Sesqui-Centennial," the Trenton *Times* sighed that "the celebration of the 150th anniversary of the birth of the Nation deserved a more fitting observance than it is like to get at the hands of the city of Philadelphia." New York's *Commercial and Financial Chronicle* sniffed, "It is hard to conceive of a more complete fiasco." Other newspapers from the Cleveland *Plain Dealer* to the New Orleans *Times-Picayune* expressed fears about the fair, with many recommending that it be postponed or canceled.[44]

Rumors circulated that the federal government planned to recall its invitations to foreign countries to participate in the Sesqui-Centennial, or even withdraw federal sanction for the fair. While the U.S. Government denied plans to take either step, its official disappointment was clear. "It is up to Philadelphia to decide what kind of Sesqui it wants," said a White House spokesman, "whether it is to cost $50,000 or $50 million." Secretary of State Kellogg noted that foreign governments "may be depended upon to use their own eyes and form their own conclusions, cutting their participation to the bone or eliminating it altogether."[45]

This universal criticism made Kendrick realize that he had overreacted. By condensing the Sesqui-Centennial so radically, he had jeopardized the exposition itself, as well as Philadelphia's reputation and his own political future. He needed to come up with a new program that might repair the damage without breaking the municipal budget. On November 23 Kendrick boarded a train to Washington, along with the Sesqui's new director-general, former Exhibits Director Asher C. Baker. There, they would meet with Secretary of State Kellogg and Secretary of Commerce Hoover, cochairs of the National Sesqui-Centennial Exhibition Commission, to discuss federal support of the fair.

Simultaneously, the Mayor's office issued a revised Plan and Scope statement outlining the latest Sesqui-Centennial program. Over the past two weeks, Kendrick had brainstormed on these plans with his cabinet and the remaining SCEA staff. It was a Hail Mary pass to salvage the Sesqui, a feverishly mixed cocktail of the 1920s virtues of booming and ballyhoo. The statement began with a defense of Kendrick's recent actions, noting that when the Mayor took "direct charge" after Collier's resignation (Kendrick had been the active president of the SCEA for over a year), he found "an extravagant program impossible of fulfillment in 1926, and he revised that program down to common sense."[46]

After nearly starving the Sesqui to death with his crash diet, Kendrick force-fed it back into fatness. The fairground had now ballooned to two thousand acres, including the one-thousand-acre Philadelphia Navy Yard. On this huge tract would be built not two but three main palaces with exhibition space of well over 1.5 million square feet. Besides the three great halls, the Sesqui would offer the Stadium, the Auditorium, and an administration building. At Oregon Avenue, a giant Liberty Bell, "the height of a six-story building and containing 20,000 incandescent lamps," would span Broad Street. Along with the six Sesqui structures, at least twenty other exhibits would fill the fairgrounds, all illustrating the "spiritual, scientific, economic, artistic and industrial progress that has been made in America and the world" since 1876.[47]

It was a bold and desperate bid for survival, and it worked. After the conference, a smiling Kendrick told reporters, "We had a very satisfactory and a very encouraging hour with Secretary Kellogg and Secretary Hoover,

Sketches for the gigantic Liberty Bell that would mark the entrance to the Sesqui began to appear in 1925, just as the fair's financial situation was cratering.

and they assured us of their co-operation and assistance in every possible way." While the meeting ensured continued federal support for the fair, the substance of this support was still left unspecified. "One of the first questions [Hoover] asked was what we wanted from the Federal Government," Kendrick explained. "I told him nothing at present except whole-hearted co-operation in the present plan. We agreed to leave the matter of direct Federal participation for a later conference."[48]

On his return to Philadelphia, Kendrick attempted to pull together a new management team for the SCEA. Besides Director-General Baker, there was the new director of concessions, W. E. Cash, who had to recoup lost business. Dr. Herbert J. Tily, chairman of the Sesqui Music Committee, was appointed to the executive committee and asked to oversee the fair's artistic activities. Lewis R. Meisenhelter replaced Baker as director of exhibits, while R .J. Pearse was brought on as director of the division of works. John Trask, a former manager of the Pennsylvania Academy of the Fine Arts, was appointed director of fine arts and told to prepare plans for yet another palace to house paintings and sculpture. To build the $250,000 Palace of Fine Arts, money would be shifted from the $1 million budget for Building No. 3, the Palace of Machinery, Mines, Metallurgy, and Transportation.[49]

Unfortunately for Kendrick, the end of 1925 saw the total collapse of his truce with Director of Public Safety Smedley Darlington Butler. Throughout 1925, Butler's attempts to dry out the city had grown more aggressive, heightening the tensions between the director and "wet" Philadelphia. Raids on speakeasies and private parties were stepped up, including one at the Hotel Stenton that netted the president of a chemical company and several members of the prestigious Racquet Club. Announcing, "I am going to go to war," Butler launched another reorganization of the police department. He was going to stop "men taking money to protect gambling houses and rum sellers if I have to turn the department inside out to do it."[50]

Kendrick did not confront his director of public safety directly, as he had in 1924. He waited for Butler's leave of absence to end on January 1, 1926, when he would be rid of the meddlesome Marine. In September 1925, Kendrick even announced his desire to have Butler stay on, saying, "I am going to go to the limit to keep General Butler." This announcement was savvy politicking, since Coolidge had insisted that Butler return to the Marines come January. But it made Kendrick look good to the nearly fifteen hundred churches and Sunday schools demanding that Butler be retained. Kendrick and Senator Pepper even made a well-publicized trip to the White House, unsuccessfully trying to persuade President Coolidge to let them keep Butler until 1928.

By this time, Butler was ready to flee Philadelphia and take command of the Marine base at San Diego, confiding to a friend that he was "completely worn out and am unable to see how I fit into the scheme of things in any way." But the maverick Marine kept fighting. In mid-November, he staged a series of raids on Philadelphia's large hotels on South Broad Street: the Bellevue-Stratford, Ritz-Carlton, and Walton. Despite evidence that the hotels had violated the Volstead Act by selling liquor to their high-toned customers, Kendrick refused to padlock the establishments. Butler alleged that the mayor told him to "lay off the big places," warning him that the city needed the big hotels for the Sesqui-Centennial. At that point, he decided that he couldn't abandon Philadelphia. With his household already packed for San Diego, Butler resigned from the Marines and announced his intention to remain as director of public safety.[51]

An infuriated Kendrick insisted that Butler step down as planned. When Butler refused, Kendrick fired him on December 23, telling him that he "did not have a proper appreciation of the obligations which you hold to the Mayor as your superior officer." Kendrick issued a public statement in which he committed himself to enforcing law and order without the assistance of Butler. He asked his fellow Philadelphians to join him during the Sesqui-Centennial year in showing America that "Philadelphia is a safe, sound, patriotic American city, and that its citizens respect the laws and those enforcing them." Many Philadelphians were unconvinced by Kendrick's statement. Mrs. Joseph M. Gazzam, chairman of the Women's Committee for Law Enforcement, called Butler's replacement, Charles Elliott, a straw man. With Butler gone, Mrs. Gazzam charged, the Vare Organization would force Kendrick to "open up" the city for liquor, vice, and gambling during the Sesqui.[52]

At 12:30 P.M. on December 23, Butler dictated his final report to the mayor prior to his departure. The letter, which Butler distributed to the press, accused Kendrick of "balking" at taking action against the big hotels, which "are controlled by your friends." Butler surrendered the blue-steel army Colt .45 pistol that Kendrick, an avid gun collector, had given him in January 1924. "Give [Kendrick] the letter and the pistol," he told his assistant. "He can publish the letter and do what he pleases with the gun." Remembering that he had been paid in advance for the month, Butler wrote a check for $333.33 to the city treasurer, representing his salary for the last week of December. "You know," he mused as he glanced at his checkbook, "I have less money in the bank today than when I first came here." Butler climbed in a U.S. Marine Corps automobile and departed City Hall to the cheers of a waiting crowd.[53]

On December 27 Brigadier-General Butler stood on a stage in Soldiers' Memorial Hall in Pittsburgh, wearing a Marine Corps uniform. An audience of three thousand Prohibitionists, led by Governor Gifford Pinchot, cheered Butler as he announced, "You have a cesspool in Philadelphia, and if necessary you should pass laws taking their government away from them if they don't know how to run it." Butler estimated that the "vice interests" in Philadelphia had $5 million to $6 million at their disposal to corrupt the police, and that only about two hundred policemen out of four thousand he had commanded were honest. He characterized Kendrick as a puppet in thrall to the Vare gang. "I should have pulled his nose," Butler sneered.[54]

"Make no mistake," Governor Pinchot intoned at the end of the meeting, "This was a happy Christmas for the crooks in Philadelphia because Smedley Butler had been driven out, and for the politicians who protected them. But it was a sad day for Philadelphia, Pennsylvania, and the United States." The governor had already scheduled a meeting with the state attorney general to discuss criminal proceedings against the Philadelphia hotels accused by Butler of violating the liquor laws.[55]

The harsh winds from central Pennsylvania had chilled Philadelphia to the bone by New Year's Eve. Anxious to prove that he was no straw man,

An exhausted looking Smedley Darlington Butler (second from left) and his family prepare to depart New York for Butler's new post as Commandant of the San Diego Marine base in early 1926.

Director of Public Safety George W. Elliott had staged forty raids on saloons over Christmas. Most revelers avoided Center City, preferring the privacy of suburban country clubs, or the more wide-open venues of New York or Atlantic City. The Walton Hotel was nearly deserted, having decided not to accept any New Year's Eve bookings. Only two of the Bellevue-Stratford's five dining rooms were open. Uniformed policemen patrolled the speakeasy district along Twelfth and Thirteenth Streets, forcing the usually raucous crowds there to exercise restraint.[56]

Thousands of other Philadelphians had loftier thoughts on their minds as they trudged through the frosty night. They were headed toward Independence Hall for the gala ceremonies to welcome 1926. More than one hundred thousand people crowded Independence Square and the surrounding streets. Inside, in the lavishly decorated Supreme Court Chamber,

Mayor Kendrick and his party greeted the distinguished guests who had fought their way through the crowd outside.

Fourteen young women in powdered wigs and eighteenth-century gowns floated among the crowd like colonial phantoms. Descendants of signers of the Declaration of Independence, some were garbed in carefully preserved outfits worn by their female ancestors when the Continental Congress met at the State House. Fifty-two members of the Philadelphia Consistory of the Ancient and Accepted Scottish Rite of Free Masonry, in tailcoats and knee britches, impersonated the signers themselves. After greeting Mayor Kendrick, they withdrew to the Assembly Room to reenact the debate preceding the adoption of the Declaration. In the vestibule, radio technicians from WIP, the Gimbels' Department Store station, surrounded the Liberty Bell. They positioned microphones at the base of the historic relic, put on their headphones, and warmed up their equipment. Thanks to hook-ups with radio stations across America, nearly all of the country's 116 million inhabitants would be able to hear Philadelphia welcome 1926.[57]

The broadcast began at 11:30 P.M. City Council President Charles B. Hall enumerated the many projects that would be completed by the end of the Kendrick administration: the Broad Street Subway, Museum of Art, Free Library, Delaware River Bridge, and, of course, the Sesqui-Centennial. All of this development would not come cheaply. More than $80 million of loan money had been spent on permanent improvements in 1925, Hall boasted, the most expended in one year. The municipal budget for 1926 would the largest in the city's history: $73,733,063.91.

After a few remarks by Mrs. Kendrick, introduced as "the first lady of the first capital of the United States," Mayor Kendrick stepped forward. He asked the people of Philadelphia to "act as trustees for the nation" in 1926, "and see to it that the solemn event upon whose threshold we stand is fittingly observed." He assured his listeners that "not anything stands in the way of success now and we will succeed. . . now that we have a thoroughly practicable plan, adequately financed and expertly administered." Kendrick invited all Americans to join Philadelphia in celebrating a new epoch in the history of both the United States and the world, "which will have for its purpose the peace and happiness of the people of this universe, without distinction."[58]

It was almost midnight. Richard Gimbel, son of department store magnate Ellis Gimbel, handed Mrs. Kendrick a delicate gold hammer with a rubber-tipped head. The stately matron approached the Liberty Bell. As the State House bell began to chime in the tower overhead, Mrs. Kendrick tapped the historic relic gently: once, then nine times, then twice, and then

As midnight approaches on December 31, 1925, Mrs. W. Freeland Kendrick prepares to welcome in the Sesqui-Centennial year by tapping the Liberty Bell with a golden hammer.

six times (*1–9–2–6*). A microphone transmitted the hollow sound of the cracked bell to millions of homes across America. As the last reverberation died away, the airwaves were filled with the cheers of the throng in Independence Square.

The Sesqui-Centennial Year had begun.[59]

NOTES

1. Amero, "Colonel D. C. Collier"; Amero, "The Making of the Panama-California Exposition."

2. "Capt. Baker Gets $15,000 Sesqui Job," *PPL*, May 8, 1925.

3. "Col. Collier Named Director of Sesqui," *PB*, February 3, 1925; "Foreign Nations Will Join in Sesqui," *PB*, February 4, 1925; "Tentative Plan for Sesqui-Centennial Exposition at League Island Park, Drawn for D. C. Collier, Director General," *PB*, February 16, 1925. "Sesqui Plans Now Await Mayor's O.K.," *PB*, February 10, 1925; "Sesqui Farm Show Sites Inspected," *PB*, March 2, 1925.

4. Sports Complex Special Services District, *Looking Back & Moving Forward*, p. 44; "Disgraceful Conditions at League Island Beach," *PI*, n.d. 1925.

5. *Report of the Sesqui-Centennial Committee of the Engineers' Club of Philadelphia on Sites*, pp. 3, 12, 26; "Gigantic Undertaking to Transform the South Philadelphia Lowlands," *PB*, April 17, 1925.

6. "Land Values on the Sesqui Site Are Now a Question of Importance," *PB*, March 27, 1925; "Vare Owns Part of Sesqui Site," *PB*, April 29, 1925; Warner, *The Private City*, pp. 183–184.

7. "Subject: Report Sesqui-Centennial International Exposition," April 1925, PCA/SCEA, Folder 49.

8. Memorandum from the Sesqui-Centennial Association Executive Committee, February 1925, PCA/SCEA, F1, 10.2, 1.3.1; "Coolidge Gives His Official Approval to Sesqui Project," *PB*, February 14, 1925.

9. "Mayor Promises 'Practical' Sesqui," *PB*, April 30, 1925.

10. "Philadelphia Fair Appears Assured," *NYT*, December 9, 1925; Evensen, "Saving the City's Reputation: Philadelphia's Struggle over Self-Identity, Sabbath-Breaking and Boxing in America's Sesquicentennial Year," *Pennsylvania History* 60, no. 1 (January 1993):10–11.

11. Vare, *My Forty Years in Politics*, p. 45; "Philadelphia Fair Appears Assured," *NYT*, December 9, 1925.

12. "Coolidge Gives his Official Approval to Sesqui Project," *PB*, Feb. 14, 1925.

13. "Biles Named Head of Sesqui Building," *PB*, February 16, 1925.

14. "$1M State Aid Sought for Sesqui; Congress to Help," *PB*, February 18, 1925; "Sesqui Resolution Passed by Senate," *PB*, February 19, 1925; "Sesqui Shy $25K Expected of U.S.," *PB*, June 27, 1925.

15. "Biles Named Head of Sesqui Building," *PB*, February 16, 1925; Lewis, "Kahn's Graphic Modernism," p. 2.

16. "Abrahams Starts Work," *PB*, March 6, 1925; "No Favoritism in Sesqui," *PB*, April 6, 1925.

17. "Stadium Site Foes Fail to Halt Bill," *PB*, February 20, 1925; "Philadelphia Council Votes for $2M Stadium," *NYT*, February 27, 1925; "City Moves to Get Sesqui Park Site," *PB*, March 11, 1925.

18. "Abrahams Starts Work," *PB*, March 6, 1925; "Plan Advance Sale of Sesqui Tickets," *PB*, March 16, 1925; "Expo Plans for 1926 Are Ready," *NYT*, March 1925; "Announce Stadium Plans," *PB*, March 16, 1925.

19. "Drive First Stadium Pile," *PB*, April 3, 1925.

20. "Land Values on the Sesqui Site Are Now a Question of Importance," *PB*, March 27, 1925; "Erect Sign at Sesqui Site," *PB*, March 1925.

21. "No Sesqui Funds, Pinchot Asserts, Intimating Veto," *PB*, April 11, 1925; McGeary, *Gifford Pinchot*, pp. 284, 291.

22. "Plan Street Work Costing $7M," *PB*, April 21, 1925; "Sesqui Site Work to Cost $14M," *PB*, April 23, 1925.

23. "Council Passed 13 Bills, Ends Sesqui Legislation," *PB*, 1une 16, 1925; "Land Owners Sign Leases for Sesqui," *PB*, June 17, 1925; "Sesqui Site Loan Ready," *PB*, June 24, 1925; "Ordinances Approved for Sesqui Street Work," *PB*, June 25, 1925; "Mayor Kendrick Holds the Reins for Sesqui-Centennial Expenditures," *PB*, August 1, 1925.

24. The nickname "Rainbow City" had also been used for the 1901 Pan-American Exposition in Buffalo, New York. Molitor, "How the Sesqui-Centennial Was Designed," *American Architect*, November 5, 1926, pp. 377–382; Austin and Hauser, *The Sesqui-Centennial International Exposition*, pp. 60–61; Lewis, "Kahn's Graphic Modernism," p. 5; "Mayor and Sesqui Heads Differ on Building Costs," *PB*, October 22, 1925; letter to David C. Collier from Percival Gallagher of Olmsted Brothers, August 11, 1925, HSP/AMG.

25. "Sesqui $3,000,000 Drive Must Win, Mayor Says," *PPL*, September 30, 1925.

26. "Over Half of Fund for Sesqui Gained," *PB*, October 1, 1925; "Sesqui $3,000,000 Drive Must Win, Mayor Says," *PPL*, September 30, 1925.

27. "Sesqui Building Bids $300,000 High," *PB*, August 14, 1925; "Mayor Rejects Sesqui Bids," *PB*, August 14, 1925; "Sesqui Building Contract Awarded," *PB*, August 20, 1925; "Kendrick Hears Molitor on Plans," *PB*, August 24, 1925; letter from John Molitor to Albert M. Greenfield, August 21, 1925, HSP/AMG; letter from John Molitor to Albert M. Greenfield, August 27, 1925, HSP/AMG.

28. "Will Free Molitor of Sesqui Planning," *PB*, October 12, 1925; "Fix Sesqui Building Cost at $12M," *PB*, October 19, 1925; "Sesqui Building Cost Up $5,000,000," *PB*, October 20, 1925; "Mayor and Sesqui Heads Differ on Building Costs," *PB*, October 22, 1925.

29. "Kendrick Holds Up Concessions Board," *PB*, September 28, 1925; "Sesqui-Centennial Dreams Are Due for a Rude Awakening before Long," *PB*, n.d.

30. "Hires Charged Ads Were Demanded to Get Sesqui Favors," *PB*, September 30, 1925.

31. Letter from Charles E. Hires to Ernest T. Trigg, August 1, 1923, HSP/AMG; "Hires Charged Ads Were Demanded to Get Sesqui Favors," *PB*, September 30, 1925; "To Probe Sesqui Concession Books," *PB*, October 1, 1925; "Says Abrahams 'Suggested' Deal," *PB*, October 15, 1925.

32. "To Probe Sesqui Concession Books," *PB*, October 1, 1925; "Kendrick-Collier Split Is Reported," *PB*, October 2, 1925;"Abrahams to Stay, Mayor Indicates," *PB*, October 4, 1925; "Presbyterian Ministers Praise Concession Probe," *PB*, October 5, 1925; "Abrahams Still Boss, He Declares," *PB*, October 13, 1925; "Prepare for Fresh Start on Sesqui Concessions," *PB*, December 1, 1925; "Matters to Be Reported to Mayor Kendrick, November 6, 1925," PCA/SCEA, Folder 44.

33. "President Will Visit Philadelphia in July," *NYT*, October 15, 1925; "Coolidge Says He Is 'Booked' as Philadelphia Fair 'Exhibit,'" *NYT*, December 19, 1925; "Sesqui

Success Now Assured," *PR*, October 13, 1925; letter to E. L. Austin from Albert M. Greenfield, October 19, 1925, HSP/AMG; Hauser and Odell, pp. 64–65; "Plans Taking Shape for Philadelphia Exposition," *Architect and Engineer* 8 (August 1925): 110.

34. "Exposition to Have Temple of Fashion," *NYT*, October 21, 1925; Leach, *Land of Desire*, pp. 324–325; "Solomon's Temple Sesqui-Centennial Exhibit Feature," *Jewish Chronicle*, November 13, 1925, p. 9; Sky and Stone, *Unbuilt America*, p. 128.

35. "Sesqui Heads Plan on $12M Fair," *PB*, October 24, 1925.

36. *Sesquicentennial News Bulletin* 40, October 14, 1925; *Sesquicentennial News Bulletin* 41, October 21, 1925; "Philadelphia Invites World to Come to Expo Next Year," *Daily News*, August 31, 1925, p. 3.

37. "Sesqui-Centennial Dreams Are Due for a Rude Awakening before Long," *PB*, n.d., 1925. "Mayor Would Cut Sesqui Expenses," *PB*, October 21, 1925; "Mayor and Sesqui Heads Differ on Buildings Costs," *PB*, October 22, 1925; "Kendrick's Ire Roused by New Sesqui Figure," *PPL*, October 22, 1925; "Sesqui Heads Plan on $12M Fair," *PB*, October 24, 1925.

38. "City Has Ample Time to Finish Work on Sesqui, Mayor Declares," *PPL*, September 25, 1925; "Sesqui's Scope Cut Down for Lack of Time," *PPL*, October 28, 1925; "Limited Sesqui Plan Approved," *PB*, October 28, 1925.

39. "Philadelphia Values Grow," *NYT*, September 27, 1925; "Mayor Reassured on Art Museum," *PB*, October 15, 1925; "To Sell Municipal Issues," *NYT*, November 1, 1925; *Message of Mayor W. Freeland Kendrick Transmitting to City Council of Philadelphia Budget Requests of City and County Departments for the Year 1926*, Philadelphia, October 15, 1925; Brownlee, *Making a Modern Classic*, pp. 80–82; Rydell, *World of Fairs*, p. 66.

40. "Sesqui's Scope Cut Down for Lack of Time," *PPL*, October 28, 1925; "Limited Sesqui Plan Approved," *PB*, October 28, 1925. "Mayor Drops Hope for World Sesqui," *PB*, November 2, 1925; "Kendrick-Collier Split Is Reported," *PB*, October 2, 1925.

41. "Council Praised Mayor on Sesqui as Collier Quits," *PB*, October 29, 1925; "To Push Sesqui Plans," *PB*, October 31, 1925; "Pageantry Will Feature in Sesqui," *PB*, November 3, 1925.

42. "Proposes Moving Sesqui to Camden," *PB*, n.d., 1925; "Sesqui Merger Declined," *PB*, November 3, 1925.

43. "Favor 627 Acres More for Sesqui," *PB*, October 31, 1925. "Trigg Resigns; Collier Also to Quit the Sesqui," *PPL*, October 29, 1925; "Collier to Resign; Trigg Quits Sesqui Executive Board," *PB*, October 29, 1925; "Muddling Through," *PB*, October 29, 1925; "A New Sesqui Crisis," *PI*, October 29, 1925.

44. "Frost on Sesqui-Centennial," *TT*, November 3, 1925; "The Coming World Exposition at Philadelphia—Trifling with A Great Project," *Commercial and Financial Chronicle*, October 31, 1925, pp. 9–17. "The Sesqui-Centennial," *Times-Picayune*, November 5, 1925; "The Sesqui-Centennial," *CPD*, November 14, 1925.

45. "U.S. May Recall Its Invitations to the Sesqui," *PPL*, November 9, 1925; "U.S. Puts Sesqui upon Probation," *PPL*, November 10, 1925; "U.S. Won't Recall Sesqui Invitations," *PB*, November 10, 1925.

46. "Mayor Pictures Splendid Sesqui in New Plans," *PB*, November 23, 1925.

47. "Mayor Pictures Splendid Sesqui in New Plans," *PB*, November 23, 1925; "Philadelphia Fair Outlined by Mayor," *NYT*, November 23, 1925; "Sesqui Has Ample Exhibition Space," *TT*, November 23, 1925; "Takes Collier's Place as Sesqui Head," *PR*, November 24, 1925.

48. "Coolidge Picking U.S. Sesqui Board," *PB*, November 23, 1925; "Philadelphia Fair Accord," *NYT*, November 24, 1925.

49. "Capt. Baker Named Director of Sesqui," *PPL*, November 23, 1925; "Prepare for Fresh Start on Sesqui Concessions," *PB*, December 1, 1925; "W. C. Cash New Concessions Director," *PR*, December 2, 1925; "Dr. Tily on Sesqui Board," *PB*, December 2, 1925; "Heads Sesqui Committee," *PB*, December 3, 1925; "Philadelphia Fair Appears Assured," *NYT*, December 9, 1925; "Will Direct Sesqui Art," *PB*, December 29, 1925.

50. "9 Arrests after Party," *NYT*, February 22, 1925; "Butler Opens 'War to Finish,' on Crime in Philadelphia," *NYT*, June 24, 1925.

51. Schmidt, *Maverick Marine*, pp. 154–158.

52. "Philadelphia Arid as Butler Left It," *NYT*, December 29, 1925.

53. Ibid.; "Mayor Promises to Push Crime War," *PPL*, December 23, 1925; "Butler Harpoons Kendrick as He Accepts Dismissal," *PI*, December 24, 1925; "Butler in Quitting Fires Shot at Mayor," *NYT*, December 24, 1925; "Philadelphia Arid as Butler Left It," *NYT*, December 29, 1925.

54. "Butler's Last Shots Hit Philadelphia, Its Mayor and 'Gang,'" *NYT*, December 28, 1925, p. 1,

55. "Butler's Last Shots Hit Philadelphia, Its Mayor and 'Gang,'" *NYT*, December 28, 1925, p. 1; "Pinchot and Woodruff to Confer on Policy in Ritz-Carlton Case," *PI*, December 29, 1925.

56. "40 Christmas Raids Made in Philadelphia," *NYT*, December 26, 1925; "Hotels Expecting Subdued New Year," *PB*, December 29, 1925; "Street Crowds Gay, but Dry Edict Is Blow to Hotels," *PI*, January 1, 1926.

57. "Liberty Bell to Ring in 1926 via Radio," *PI*, December 31, 1925.

58. *1925 Report of W. Freeland Kendrick, Mayor City of Philadelphia, Sesqui-Centennial Edition 1926, Philadelphia, PA: City of Philadelphia, 1926,* pp. 189–193.

59. "Sesqui Year Rung in by Liberty Bell," *PPL*, January 1, 1926; "Liberty Bell Welcomes 1926," *PB*, January 1, 1926; "Thousands Greet Sesqui Year at Cradle of Liberty," *PI*, January 1, 1926; "Liberty Bell Rings in 1926 in Philadelphia, While Historic 1776 Scenes Are Re-Enacted," *NYT*, January 1, 1926.

6

★ ★ ★

Philadelphia Progressive

THE NEW YEAR OF 1926 brought the promise of continued stability and prosperity to millions of Americans, and a fresh crisis to Mayor Kendrick and the Sesqui-Centennial Exhibition Association. As the first week of January ended, Senator George Wharton Pepper delivered gloomy news from Washington: the Sesqui would receive no financial support from the U.S. Government unless it was postponed a year. Congressmen who had visited Philadelphia were aghast at the lack of progress made on the world's fair scheduled to open in six months. Aside from the half-finished Stadium, the Sesqui grounds were a barren plain, interrupted by gaping foundations for the main structures and mounds of landfill trucked in to bolster the waterlogged soil.

Based on this information, the chairmen of the Senate and House Appropriations Committees announced that they would refuse to recommend any support unless the Sesqui was delayed until 1927. Otherwise, they felt, it would be doomed to failure. A "high official in Washington" anonymously told the *Bulletin*: "If the Sesqui-Centennial is held this year, I do not see how Philadelphia can expect more than a $500,000 to $800,000 appropriation from Congress. If it is postponed until next year, I am convinced that nothing short of a $5 million appropriation will be forthcoming, with a very strong possibility of that being increased."[1]

James M. Beck, the former U.S. Solicitor General who had just been named Chairman of the National Sesqui-Centennial Advisory Commission, agreed that a year's delay was advisable. Pennsylvania's junior senator, David A. Reed, cited the 1893 Chicago fair and 1904 St. Louis fair, both of which had been delayed for a year. Director-General Asher C. Baker told the SCEA Board of Directors that the Washington diplomatic corps had serious doubts about a 1926 fair, and were advising their governments accordingly. The engineer sent by the Japanese government to survey the Sesqui site had reported that it would be impossible to prepare an adequate exposition that year. France refused to participate if the fair took place in 1926, while Great Britain was on the verge of canceling its exhibition space.

Many of Kendrick's closest advisers agreed that the Sesqui should be delayed. The Sesqui-Centennial Women's Committee passed a resolution urging the board of directors to postpone the exposition until 1927. A smaller fair in 1926, they suggested, would serve as a "historical prologue," filled with tableaux, pageants, and educational displays. SCEA Finance Chairman Albert M. Greenfield concurred that such a program would mollify the army of conventioneers expected that year. In New York, the Textile and Apparel Exhibit Association cancelled their plans for the Temple of Fashion. Word also came from New York that the gold-and-white towers of Solomon's Temple would not rise above the Gladway, another victim of insufficient time and funds.[2]

Ignoring all critics, Kendrick pressed even more vigorously for a 1926 fair. "We could have the exposition this year if the Government would stand by us in a courageous way," he lectured the SCEA directors. After a contentious meeting with James Beck and Asher C. Baker, a petulant Kendrick told reporters, "If there is to be any postponement, it will have to be done by someone else. . . . If there is to be a postponement, I would suggest that it be put over until about 1930. That would give ample time to finance a large undertaking."[3]

Kendrick was confident that he would prevail at the upcoming conference of the National Sesqui-Centennial Advisory Committee, to be held in Philadelphia on January 20 to review the status of the fair. The verdict of the committee's ninety-six members (two from each state), would be a critical factor in determining whether or not the federal government would support the Sesqui, and to what extent. It would also decide whether the fair would be held in 1926 or in 1927. After convening at Independence Hall in the morning, the assembly would take a tour of the Sesqui grounds. Afterward, they would return to Independence Hall and render their decision. That evening, the SCEA would host a banquet in honor of the state commissioners in the ballroom of Albert M. Greenfield's Benjamin Franklin Hotel.[4]

Kendrick's cavalier behavior at the conference did not endear him to his visitors. The meeting began at in the Assembly Room at Independence Hall at 10:00 A.M., with forty-five committee members present representing thirty-four of the forty-eight states. Delayed by municipal business, the mayor did not appear until 11:20 A.M., when he made a grand entrance followed by his cabinet. Shortly afterward, the delegates boarded Philadelphia Rapid Transit Company buses, forming the tail end of a procession led by six motorcycle police and eighteen motorcars holding the mayor and his party. The lengthy motorcade headed south on Broad Street toward League Island Park. As usual, the mayoral limousine sped ahead, its siren blaring. The mayor's party soon became separated from the lumbering buses holding the delegates, caught in traffic on Broad Street.

On reaching League Island Park, the mayor and his party stopped at a spot near Edgewood Lake, with most of the PRT buses nowhere to be seen. Standing with the scaffold-shrouded Stadium behind him, Kendrick shouted to make his voice heard over the roar of construction: "I don't see how we can celebrate the anniversary of the signing of the Declaration of Independence one, two, or three years after that date. Personally, I have taken the stand for the exposition to be held in 1926. I believe there is still sufficient time to complete what I have outlined to you."[5]

While the mayor orated, buses carrying half of the delegates were searching for him. The laggard vehicles had driven through the Sesqui

The landscape that greeted the members of the National Sesqui-Centennial Advisory Committee on their visit to Philadelphia in January 1926. Many members of the Congressional committee could not imagine how the Sesqui would be ready to open in five months.

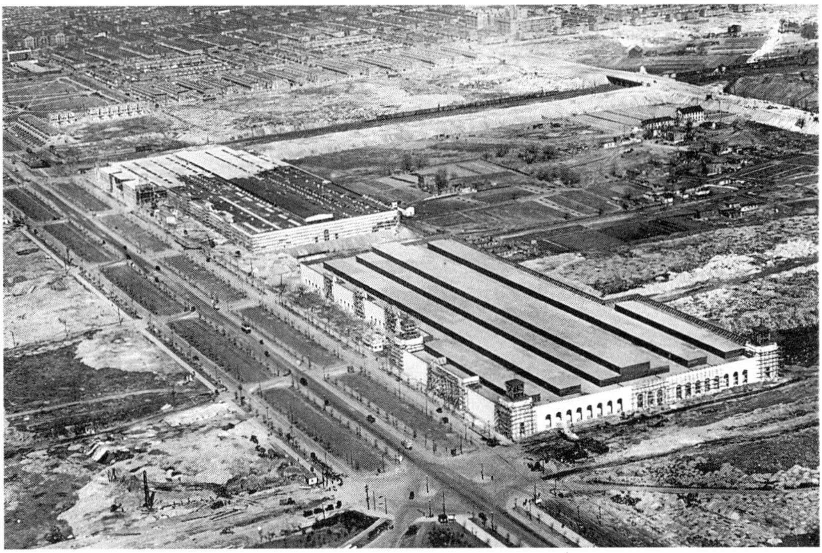

grounds into the Navy Yard and were heading back up Broad Street when a policeman stopped them and guided them to the mayor, who was finishing his talk. Reunited, the committee members inspected the fairgrounds and then returned to town for luncheon. The overwhelming consensus was that the fair should be delayed until 1927, given its rudimentary state. Minnesota commissioners Francis A. Gross and Charles R. Adams announced jointly that "a 1926 exposition is an impossibility."

Despite this negative reaction, several hours of concentrated lobbying by a host of local dignitaries, including Congressman Vare, Senator Pepper, and ex-Governor Sproul, convinced the delegates to have faith. The afternoon session at Independence Hall ended with all forty-five commissioners voting to approve a 1926 Sesqui-Centennial. Their doubts were allayed somewhat by the news that, while they were slogging through League Island Park, City Council Finance Committee Chairman Edwin R. Cox had proposed an additional $1 million councilmanic loan for the Sesqui.

That evening, Mayor Kendrick acted as toastmaster at a celebratory banquet at the Benjamin Franklin Hotel, entertaining the delegates he had abandoned earlier that day. Kendrick, "in a more jovial frame of mind than he had been at Sesqui meetings for some weeks," introduced a series of speakers, including Secretary of State Herbert Hoover. A jubilant Kendrick announced that "from now on, the Sesqui-Centennial will drive forward. . . . Philadelphia and the nation have never failed in any mighty effort when they are in accord." Hoover struck a more neutral tone:

> There has been some discussion as to whether there is now sufficient time to prepare for an Exposition this year, but that is a matter solely for the determination of Philadelphia. The Federal Government will not fail to meet the situation with whatever resources are provided.[6]

Having secured the nominal support of the National Sesqui-Centennial Advisory Committee, the SCEA moved to obtain concrete funding from the federal government. James M. Beck and Herbert Hoover both appeared before the House Committee on Industrial Arts and Expositions, which approved their request for a federal appropriation of $4,186,500 for the Sesqui. Before the committee recommendation could be forwarded to the full House, it ran afoul of President Coolidge's notorious parsimony. Wryly terming the $4.2 million appropriation "quite a little sum,"[7] Coolidge announced that he would approve no more than $2.5 million for the Sesqui. After much negotiation, Congressman Vare and Senator Pepper agreed to cut $1 million from the amount approved by the House Committee.

On February 11, 1926, a bill appropriating $3,186,500 in federal funds for the Sesqui-Centennial was forwarded by the Committee on Rules to the House of Representatives. The powerful Rules Committee, of which Philadelphia Congressman Harry Ransley was a ranking member, recommended "immediate action": the House should pass the bill quickly and without debate. Instead, the bill was nearly torpedoed by Democratic Congressmen in an onslaught that took its Republican supporters by surprise. House Republicans had been confident of the bill's passage, given their majority (247 to the Democrats' 183) and the number of Pennsylvania congressmen in positions of authority. Besides William Vare, the second most senior member of the House Appropriations Committee, these included George A. Welsh, chairman of the House Committee on Industrial Arts and Expositions and the bill's author, and George P. Darrow of the House Steering Committee.

Vare, whose presence might have ensured a smooth passage, had left Washington unexpectedly the night before. He was en route to St. Lucie, Florida, to confer with other members of the Organization on his candidacy later that year for the U.S. Senate seat held by George W. Pepper.

Taking advantage of the absence of Vare and other Republicans, House Democrats mounted a major attack on the appropriations bill. Clifton A. Woodrum (D-Virginia) tried to kill it by referring it back to the House Committee on Industrial Arts and Expositions. When that failed, he offered other amendments: first to remove authority for the Sesqui from Philadelphia officials and place it with Secretaries Hoover and Kellogg, and then to strike out the entire authorization for buildings. "Here's a picture showing what kind of an exposition we are being asked to subsidize," Woodrum sneered, displaying a photo of the unfinished grounds. "If I had my way, the exposition wouldn't get a nickel."[8]

As Republican congressmen scrambled to save the bill, Thomas L. Blanton (D-Texas) suggested slashing the government appropriation to a measly $186,500. The fiery Blanton compared the absent Vare to the Fascist Mussolini, charging that "there is not in Italy today a dictator with more power in his bailiwick than our distinguished colleague from Pennsylvania now exerts in his home city of Philadelphia." Blanton's attack grew so vitriolic that both Democrats and Republicans demanded that he be called to order. After further debate, a compromise was reached by reducing the appropriation by $1 million, to $2,186,500. The amended bill was approved by the House by a vote of 226 to 121. While a respectable majority, the final vote was hardly the stamp of national approval the Sesqui needed.[9]

On February 26 President Coolidge approved the resolution authorizing $2,186,500 in federal appropriations for the Sesqui-Centennial. The bill was approved by the Senate, forty-three to twenty-nine, and signed by Coolidge on March 4. Senate Republicans managed to restore the slashed $1 million in a separate appropriation that would finance two additional structures: the Palace of Fine Arts, and the U.S. Government, Machinery, and Transportation Palace.[10]

In Philadelphia, the SCEA and the city government struggled to cope with the shortfall of federal support. Including the recent $1 million councilmanic loan, the city had pledged $8,720,000 directly to the Sesqui, not counting the $2 million allocated for the Sesqui Stadium and the millions dedicated to infrastructure under "South Philadelphia Improvements." There was also the $3 million raised through selling participation certificates. Even including the recent federal appropriation, available funds for the Sesqui totaled less than $14 million, far short of the fair's latest budget of $20.4 million.

Construction and development costs had jumped to $13.1 million, thanks to the increasingly tight schedule. Another $7.3 million would be needed for operation and maintenance. The gap of more than $6 million would have to be covered by exhibition space rental, concession fees, and admissions. After the debacles of 1925, however, the first two categories were running far below expectations. As of mid-February, fewer than sixty concessionaires had signed on for the Gladway, while only 60,000 out of an estimated 1.1 million square feet of exhibit space had been rented.[11]

While a nervous City Council debated ways to slash Sesqui costs further, a separate drama was playing out on the local political stage. After conferring with other Organization bigwigs in Florida, Bill Vare had thrown his hat into the ring for the upcoming race for U.S. senator from Pennsylvania. The actual election in November was of minor interest; in the staunchly Republican Keystone State, excitement centered on the party primary, scheduled for May 18. Vare had been undecided until Governor Gifford Pinchot declared that he would run against the incumbent Pepper in the primary. Sensing that Pinchot and Pepper would split the dry vote, Vare announced his candidacy the day after Pinchot entered the race. His primary campaign platform was Modification. Rather than try to kill Prohibition (a political impossibility at the time, given the strength of dry lobbies), Vare sought to modify the law to allow the sale of beer and nonfortified wine.[12]

Vare was the underdog. Pepper had the Mellon millions backing him and the support of most major newspapers and banks, as well as Joseph P. Grundy and the Pennsylvania Manufacturers Association. Pinchot controlled fifty thousand state jobs, was endorsed by the United Mine Workers, and could draw on his own private fortune. But Vare had the substantial war chest of the Organization at his disposal, plus the sheer number of voters controlled by his machine in the state's largest city. He also had Harry A. Mackey, Philadelphia city treasurer, lawyer, and longtime leader of the Forty-Sixth Ward, as his campaign manager. A master strategist, Mackey had assembled a network of powerful special interest groups to back Vare, including veterans, war mothers, and lawyers.

The three-way fight soon turned vicious. After assigning a dozen detectives to investigate the Vare campaign, Governor Pinchot charged his opponent with fraud. He proved that the congressman's petitions contained hundreds of fake signatures, many written in the same hand. Vare workers explained that they were simply helping semiliterate voters by writing down their names for them during their door-to-door polling. "Perjury and forgery!" Pinchot thundered. "This is the Vare machine in action." Senator Pepper laid the blame for the struggling Sesqui at Vare's feet. "When at Washington and through the country people are skeptical about the Sesqui-Centennial," he declared, "it will be fine to be able to assure them that we are going to celebrate our independence by pitching Vare into the river."[13]

Oblivious to the barrage of mud, Mayor Kendrick continued to plan the Sesqui as if he were Flo Ziegfeld mounting the latest edition of the *Follies*. He took to riding around the fairgrounds on a white stallion, supervising construction and looking like a plantation overseer. At the beginning of April, Kendrick shocked fair planners by announcing that the Sesqui would open one day earlier than planned, on Monday, May 31. His official explanation for shortening an already truncated schedule was his wish to inaugurate the exposition on Memorial Day. The move would also allow Kendrick to accommodate his brother Shriners, who were descending on Philadelphia to celebrate their Fifty-Second Imperial Council Session, or annual convention. Although the session would begin on Tuesday, June 1, most of the 250,000 Shriners expected would arrive in Philadelphia on Sunday, May 30, rather than on Memorial Day. Opening the Sesqui twenty-four hours earlier would enable Past Imperial Potentate Kendrick to welcome his fellow Nobles in grand style, and to incorporate their Oriental pageantry into what threatened to be a lackluster debut.[14]

As federal funds became available, Kendrick and his team mounted around-the-clock work crews. The unhurried pace that had dumbfounded committee delegates in January was replaced by feverish, nonstop activity. "Overalled men dash about like characters in a rapid-motion movie film," wrote one reporter. "Hammers beat a tattoo like machine gun fire. Saws buzz. Foremen swear. Men shout. Steam shovels hiss and groan under capacity loads—it's only two months 'til Sesqui time!" Sailors and Marines at

The Forum of the Founders in early 1926, looking south. To the left are the two main exhibit halls, the Palace of Liberal Arts and Manufactures, and the Palace of Agriculture and Foreign Exhibits.

the Navy Yard suffered sleep deprivation, thanks to the glare of spotlights and the roar of machinery engaged in night work on the monumental U.S. Government Palace, going up just north of the yard's gates.[15]

In a studio on the Sesqui grounds, dozens of sculptors labored like assembly-line workers, crafting hundreds of statues and decorations out of reinforced plaster that would masquerade as marble during the fair. Sculptor Samuel Murray had created the model for a massive statuary group called *Philadelphia Progressive*. This work would occupy a commanding position in the Court of Honor, the grand plaza between the two main palaces. Murray's design depicted two gigantic figures on horseback advancing amidst an army of banner-wielding celebrants, symbolizing the city's perpetual progress toward enlightenment. Using pointing machines that expanded the dimensions of the plaster model to the actual size of the final sculpture, an army of artisans broke the model into twenty-eight components and created giant molds for each part. Nearby, other allegorical works by Isidore Konti and J. Otto Schweizer underwent a similar process of deconstruction and expansion.[16]

By mid-April exterior construction was complete or nearly finished on the Stadium, the Palace of Liberal Arts and Manufactures, and the

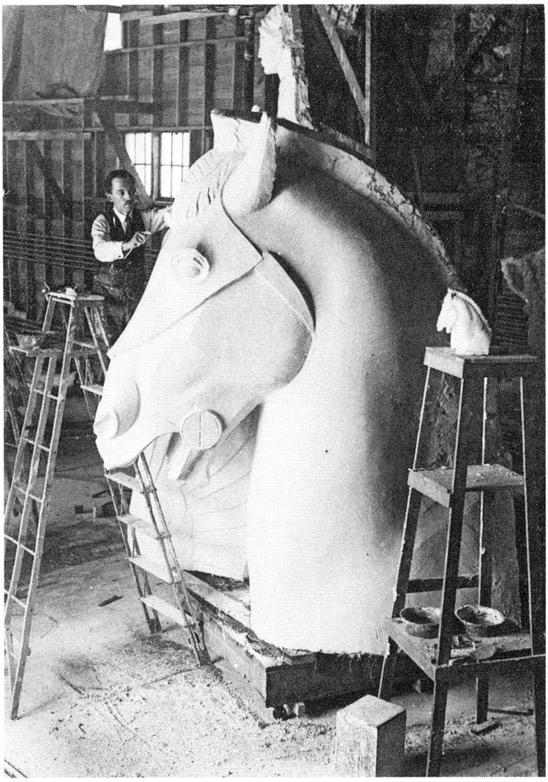

Elemilio Angelo, one of an army of sculptors employed by the Sesqui, works on a giant horse head for the *Philadelphia Progressive* statue in May 1926.

Palace of Agriculture and Foreign Exhibits. Work was progressing on the ten-thousand-seat Auditorium, the 650-ton steel frame of which had been erected in a record six weeks. Ground had been broken for the two structures paid for by federal largesse: the Palace of Fine Arts, and the Palace of United States Government, Machinery, and Transportation. City Council scraped together another $250,000 to pay for a sixth exhibition hall, the Palace of Education and Social Economy. At Oregon Plaza, welders began to rivet copper plates over the steel skeleton of the eighty-foot-high Liberty Bell.[17]

More than fifty sports events had been scheduled for the Sesqui, most of them to take place in the new Stadium. Among the competitions were the Davis Cup International tennis championship, the National Archery Association championship, an American Henley regatta on the Schuylkill River, and a marathon bicycle race between New York and Philadelphia. In April the Stadium's crowded calendar looked like it might be wiped clean overnight. The Amateur Athletic Union of the United States, sponsor of many sports events, raised doubts about the safety and stability of the

By the end of April, the skeleton of the giant Liberty Bell at Oregon Plaza was complete and workmen had begun to attach its copper skin.

structure. Judge Eugene C. Bonniwell, an AAU officer, reported defects and "preliminary settling" in the huge brick-and-concrete horseshoe. Each of its sections, built separately to speed up construction, had a varying weight and was sinking into the soft soil at a different rate of speed. Bonniwell's concerns were denied strenuously by a city administration desperate not to lose one of the few Sesqui structures that would be complete on Opening Day.[18]

With this day less than a month away, Sesqui planners turned their attention to handling the tens of millions of visitors they were still confident would come. The Philadelphia Rapid Transit Company began to lay trolley tracks to the fairground on Seventh, Tenth, and Eleventh Streets. In yet another sweetheart deal for the powerful PRT, City Council agreed to cover all costs related to draining, paving, and grading the affected roadways before tracks were laid. The accommodating councilmen also gave PRT and its bus subsidiary exclusive use to Sesqui terminal facilities, denying competing bus lines access to the fair. Besides the vast parking lots adjacent to the Sesqui grounds, eight motor camps were set up in suburban areas ringing the city to reduce the thousands of motorcars expected to jam city streets.[19]

The Municipal or "Sesqui" Stadium under construction. As Opening Day approached, the Stadium appeared to be the only Sesqui-related structure close to completion.

Anxious to dispel rumors that he was running a "wide-open" city, Kendrick established a separate police force of three hundred men to patrol the Sesqui. He also created an eighteen-man fire department to keep the fair's flimsy, wood-roofed structures from going up in flames during the hot Philadelphia summer. Director of Public Safety Elliott ordered one hundred police detectives to sweep Philadelphia each night, rounding up hundreds of known miscreants until "the city is in fit condition to receive and protect the thousands of exposition visitors." By the end of May, Elliott would beat Butler's arrest record for the first five months of 1924 by more than seven thousand, padlocking over seventeen hundred speakeasies in his zeal to clean up the city before the Big Show.[20]

New Jersey, New York, and Delaware all announced that they would support the Sesqui by replicating historic structures. Otherwise, "the number of buildings to be erected by States and foreign governments is disappointingly low," the *New York Times* noted. In March, an ailing Director-General Baker sailed for Europe again in a last-ditch effort to secure foreign participation in the Sesqui. In early April, he scored his first bagatelle: an $800,000 replica of Bernini's Fountain of the Sea Horses at the Villa Borghese, a promised gift of the Italian government to the Sesqui.

(The fountain would arrive after the fair closed and would be erected behind the Museum of Art.)

Spanish President Miguel Primo de Rivera promised a Spanish pavilion, making his country the only Western European power to contribute its own building to the Sesqui. King Alfonso XIII offered to lend priceless works of art from the royal collection, including selections from the Quixote collection of eight hundred tapestries. Sesqui managers expressed their gratitude for the art but passed on a private exhibitor's offer to give each adult visitor a free glass of Spanish wine, on the grounds that the pavilion would enjoy an independent ambassadorial status. Taking no chances, federal Prohibition officials decreed that foreign governments displaying alcoholic products as part of their exhibits had to keep them sealed, stamped, and safeguarded.[21]

Other countries—not major powers but foreign nations all the same—announced plans to build pavilions, including Argentina, Cuba, and Czechoslovakia. These coups were offset by the revelation that Captain Baker's agent in Germany was a fraud who had absconded with thousands of marks representing fees from potential exhibitors throughout the country. Demanding that the Sesqui reimburse its members, the Reichsverband—the national association of German business and industry—boycotted the Philadelphia fair. Soon after this exposure, Baker's health failed, and he was confined to bed in a Rome hotel. Management of the fair was once again assumed by Controller Austin, assisted by A. L. Sutton, now the director of special events and domestic participation.[22]

A further embarrassment for Philadelphia erupted at the same time, thanks to Mayor Kendrick's nemesis, Smedley Darlington Butler. After assuming command of the Marine base in San Diego, Butler had dictated his memoirs of life as director of public safety to Philadelphia journalist E. Z. Dimitman. The thirty-part series, "Smashing Crime and Vice," was syndicated to more than one hundred newspapers nationally, including Philadelphia's venerable *Bulletin*. As the city tried to put its best foot forward for the Sesqui in April and May, millions of Americans read each day of Butler's valiant yet doomed effort to keep integrity from drowning in the stinking sewer of Philadelphia politics. While Butler blasted Vare and the Organization, he saved his strongest attacks for his former boss. The series ended days before the Sesqui opened with a description of Kendrick's refusal to padlock the big hotels that served liquor, his deference to their wealthy owners and patrons, and his efforts to get rid of Butler. Kendrick, Butler concluded, had "bunked" not just his director of public safety, but the people of Philadelphia.[23]

Despite Butler's mudslinging, Sesqui-Centennial fever began to spread throughout the country as May drew to a close. When the new two-cent Liberty Bell stamp commemorating the Sesqui-Centennial went on sale on the morning of May 10 in Philadelphia, Boston, and Washington, all one million copies were sold out by noon. A week before Opening Day, the normally aloof *New York Times* printed a gushing, full-page article headlined "Sesquicentennial Fair Shows Our Progress." The author, Steuart M. Emery, had not visited the site and relied on outdated press material, listing the canceled Palace of Fashion among the fair's buildings. But his lengthy description of a "magnificent Rainbow City . . . of shining towers and huge edifices," betrayed America's secret hope that the Sesqui would truly be the greatest of all world's fairs.[24]

Meanwhile, the staid streets of Philadelphia swelled with exotic strangers: not just military men assigned to the Navy Yard and the Sesqui Army and Marine camps but Italian officers in dazzling uniforms, mustached Cossacks in sky-blue blouses and astrakhan hats, Indians in brightly colored turbans, and fez-topped Persians. Dozens of battleships were en route to the Navy Yard from around the world. So were the frigate *Constellation*, built in 1797 as the first warship of the new nation, and the *Olympia*, Admiral Dewey's flagship at the Battle of Manila Bay in 1898. Four Norwegian sailors were braving sixty-four hundred miles of sea aboard the *Leif Erickson*, a forty-two-foot replica of the craft that brought the tenth-century Norse explorer to America. Meanwhile, two hundred federal Prohibition agents arrived at the city's railroad stations, to make sure that the city was "as arid as a desert" during the Sesqui.[25]

South of City Hall, workmen struggled to turn Broad Street into the Temple at Karnak, raising dozens of pseudo-Egyptian columns to welcome the Shriners. At the old Centennial grounds in Fairmount Park, Japanese Ambassador Tsuneo Matsudaira presented a birthday gift from his country to America: sixteen hundred flowering cherry, crab apple, peach, and plum trees to be planted throughout the park. Noting that the study of American history is "the delight of schoolboys in Japan," the ambassador gracefully described the gift as "carrying with it the good will and friendship which the Japanese Nation has long entertained for you."[26]

The construction vehicles and delivery wagons that jammed Broad Street during the week were replaced by motorcars every Sunday, as pleasure trippers flocked to see how their Sesqui was progressing. Traffic grew so heavy that the SCEA barred automobiles on the fairgrounds on Sunday, and charged fifty cents admission on other days. But the crowds kept coming, and pedestrians were allowed free access to the grounds until shortly before

A close-up of the corner tower of the Palace of Liberal Arts and Manufactures, one of the few eruptions of ornament on the otherwise spartan structure.

Opening Day. The *Bulletin* recommended visiting the fair at sunset, when the dying light made it "a city of dreams done in rose and turquoise. . . . an endless chain of fantastic palaces equaled in grandeur only by those of legendary Spain." Twilight visitors were allowed to linger on the grounds after dark, when the Sesqui became Philadelphia's biggest Lovers' Lane. At dawn the enchanted dreamland gave way to an increasingly crazed whirl of activity that reminded one reporter of "a great, disturbed anthill. Men, trucks, horses, tractors, lumber, rope, mortar and mud are mingled in the greatest construction stew ever seen in this city!"[27]

During the last week of May, long lines of men and women stood outside the Administration Building at Oregon Plaza, in the shadow of the Liberty Bell. They were waiting to be interviewed for more than one thousand openings as Sesqui policemen, gate attendants, clerks, cashiers, and janitors, in one of the greatest employment windfalls ever to strike South Philadelphia. Once hired, they were measured for the fair's blue-and-yellow uniforms and trained in Sesqui procedures and equipment, including the fifty new ticketless turnstiles, operated by foot pedals when visitors deposited their fifty-cent admission in a slot.

With their freshly laid concrete floors finally dry, the two main palaces were invaded by an army of porters carrying thousands of crates. In the Palace of Agriculture and Foreign Exhibits, representatives from foreign countries rushed to assemble their exhibits, shouting directions in a dozen languages. The Japanese contingent fascinated their American hosts as thoroughly in 1926 as they had at the Centennial fifty years before. Trading Western clothing for "queer flowing robes," they dashed about quietly and deftly, "plying quaint tools, skipping nimbly among the boxes, lumber and glass as they put together the parts of their display." Nearby, William Arup of Copenhagen grumbled about American logistics as he unpacked Danish porcelain and pewter. "We of Denmark know that you are fast workers over here but we can't see how they can fill this big building up by Monday. . . . Why, because you know you can build a skyscraper in a fortnight, do you waste the first week?"[28]

Across Broad Street in the Gladway, a second army of workers rushed to construct the Nuremberg Market, Battle of Gettysburg, Trip through the Orient, and other amusements. A third mass of men tried to transform the acres of barren, tracked soil into a verdant landscape, planting hundreds of trees and shrubs and stuffing the beds around the buildings with thousands of flowers. Vast flatbeds transported huge poplars and evergreens, uprooted from other sections of League Island Park, to be planted along Broad Street. Luckily nature was cooperating. Philadelphia was enjoying an extended spell of dry, sunny weather that allowed the workmen to labor nonstop on "the greatest exposition ever attempted in so short a time." One reporter noted that some rain would be "a blessing in Sesqui-town," since it would wash away the thick dust coating everything.[29]

As Philadelphia struggled to whip the Sesqui into shape, its former director-general was carried off the *Berengaria* on a stretcher to a waiting ambulance at the Hudson River piers in New York. Captain Baker was near death, suffering from a complete physical collapse and internal hemorrhaging brought on by the strain of his work for the Sesqui. The seventy-five-year-old invalid had been brought home by his daughter after three previous sailing dates had been canceled because of his ill health. The ambulance took Baker directly to the Memorial Hospital in Morristown, New Jersey, where he would die a week later. With Baker's death, Controller Austin officially became the final director-general of the Sesqui-Centennial.[30]

On Saturday, May 29, the Sesqui-Centennial received its first official visitors when Governor Gifford Pinchot and his party arrived from Harrisburg to dedicate the Pennsylvania State Building. Designed by Modernist architect Ralph B. Bencker, the stylish structure was so striking that Mayor Kendrick, no friend of the governor, labeled it "the Gem of the Exposition." The rectangular structure of rose-tinted stucco was built around a central courtyard, visible through a thirteen-bay colonnade fronting Broad Street. Still empty, the entire building would be filled with works by Pennsylvania's leading artists, including Violet Oakley, Daniel Garber, and Alexander Stirling Calder. The interior courtyard evoked the original pristine state of Penn's Woods with native plants and trees arranged around a keystone-shaped reflecting pool.[31]

Like much of the Sesqui, the Pennsylvania State Building was still under construction at its dedication. As Pinchot and other state dignitaries delivered speeches in the central courtyard, plasterers high up on scaffolds put the finishing touches on the exterior. When Governor Pinchot raised the state flag on a flagpole near the entrance, a trowel of plaster missed its mark and splattered the chief executive. The workmen were asked to take a break until the ceremony was finished.

After the dedication, Governor Pinchot told Mayor Kendrick that he would not be present at the Opening Day ceremonies, saying simply, "You know why." Kendrick replied, "I am sorry." Pinchot was furious that he had not been asked to give a speech along with Secretary of State Kellogg and Secretary of Commerce Hoover. His bitterness extended well beyond the Sesqui. On May 18, the governor had lost the Republican primary for the U.S. Senate nomination to William S. Vare. Vare won only two counties out of sixty-seven in Pennsylvania, but still received 597,000 votes, versus 339,000 for Pinchot and 516,000 for George W. Pepper. In Philadelphia alone, Vare won 337,944 votes, compared with fewer than 27,000 for Pinchot. Pinchot's banishment from the speakers' roster was Vare's heavy-handed way of adding insult to the injury of his rival's loss. A few days before dedicating the Pennsylvania State Building, Pinchot wrote his nephew that "the man who won [the primary] is a wet gangster who represents everything that is bad in Pennsylvania."[32]

The dedication of the Pennsylvania State Building on May 29, 1926.

As the Sesqui's opening loomed, its new director-general, E. L. Austin, announced that he anticipated a record attendance of thirty million, generating $12 million in admissions. He was pleased to announce that nineteen nations were represented at the Sesqui through their governments and/or private exhibits, ranging from Japan's $1 million extravaganza to Haiti's $2,500 effort. In addition, thirteen states and three cities would have a presence at the fair. The fair, 70 percent finished at its opening, would be 100 percent complete by July

4, which was now considered its "original opening day." A cautious Kendrick said he was sure the Sesqui would compare favorably with any past exposition.[33]

On Saturday, May 29, Philadelphia seethed with activity. Its three train stations were packed with an ever-growing mob of arrivals, savoring the sunny, warm weather and the festival atmosphere. They thronged Market Street, where hundreds of American flags flapped in the breeze, suspended from the skyscrapers lining the wide avenue. They studied the elaborate displays in department store windows, like Strawbridge and Clothier's model of the new Delaware River Bridge, constructed from more than 250,000 pearl beads. They joined the lines waiting to enter Independence Hall and see the Liberty Bell, guarded by two handsome but unsmiling Marines. And they thought about all the wonders they would see in forty-eight hours, when the Big Show opened.[34]

Among the arrivals was James C. Burger, a Denver banker who was Kendrick's successor as imperial potentate of the Shriners. Reporters were waiting to interview him when he stepped off the Broadway Limited at Broad Street Station on Saturday afternoon. The "stocky, pleasant-faced man with a square jaw and brown hair tinged with gray"[35] was in the vanguard of the quarter-million Nobles who were starting to fill every hotel in town, and whose Pullman coaches had begun to crowd railroad sidings around the city. Even the municipal piers were experiencing traffic jams, since many temples had rented steamboats to serve as floating dormitories.

The moment he stepped off the train, the imperial potentate began to heap praise on his host city, its mayor, and its fair. Burger assured the local press that he and his fellow Shriners did not expect the Sesqui to be 100 percent complete, but that "most of them, including myself, are astounded at the progress made. It was a splendid achievement, which reflects credit on the members of the Sesqui-Centennial Association, the Mayor and the entire city administration." Burger had not actually been to the fair, he admitted, but he anticipated seeing it with the greatest pleasure. Like a true boomer and booster in the Golden Age of Ballyhoo, Burger also anticipated what he and his fellow Shriners could do for the struggling Sesqui:

> I believe the Shriners' session will be the best possible thing for the Sesqui. I feel sure their nation-wide praise of the Sesqui will make the best possible advertising. . . . Every Shriner who comes to Philadelphia will be a living advertisement for the Sesqui-Centennial.[36]

What more could a Shriner do to support his friend and Brother Noble "Freel"?

NOTES

1. "No U.S. Money to Be Given Sesqui If Held This Year," *PB*, January 7, 1926.

2. " No Sesqui Fashion Temple," *NYT*, January 7, 1926; "Solomon's Temple Will Not Be Built in Philadelphia," *JDB*, April 4, 1926; "Will Delay Part of Sesqui a Year," *PB*, January 16, 1926; "Kendrick Confers on Fair," *NYT*, January 17, 1926; "Arrange for Pageants," *PB*, January 20, 1926; Mrs. Wilmer Krusen, "Story of the Women's Committee of the Sesqui-Centennial: Secretary's Report," COM1926/SCA, p. 2.

3. "Mayor Still Hopes for Sesqui in 1926," *PB*, January 8, 1926.

4. "Mayor Still Hopes for Sesqui in 1926," *PB*, January 8, 1926; "Kendrick Hits U.S. Apathy on Sesqui," *PB*, January 12, 1926; "Attacks U.S. Plea for Sesqui Delay," *PB*, January 13, 1926.

5. "Delegates Back Scope of Sesqui," *PB*, January 20, 1926.

6. "Delegates Back Scope of Sesqui," *PB*, January 20, 1926; "Council Gets Bill for Sesqui Loan," *PB*, January 21, 1926.

7. "Sesqui Heads Hope for Larger U.S. Aid," *PB*, Feb. 6, 1926.

8. "Senate Approves $2,186,500 to Sesqui," *PB*, Feb. 17, 1926.

9. "Favor $3,186,500 for Sesquicentennial," *NYT*, February 11, 1926; "Senate Approves $2,186,500 to Sesqui," *PB*, February 17, 1926; "Votes Celebration Funds," *Richmond Times-Dispatch*, February 18, 1926; Salter, *The People's Choice*, p. 60.

10. "Senate Approves $2,186,500 to Sesqui," *PB*, February 17, 1926; "President Signs Sesqui Measure," *PB*, February 26, 1926; "Sesqui Fund Goes Through," *PB*, March 2, 1926; "Signs Sesqui Appropriation," *PB*, March 4, 1926.

11. "Sesqui Loan Bill," *PB*, February 18, 1926; "Sesqui Offers Cut Cost $1M," *PB*, February 19, 1926; "Criticizes Working of Expo Plan," *NYT*, February 28, 1926.

12. Pepper, *Philadelphia Lawyer*, p. 211.

13. "Criminal Action Looms in Pinchot's Vare Fraud Charge," *PPL*, April 9, 1926; "Admits He Wrote Vare Nomination Paper Signatures," *PB*, April 9, 1926; "Dozen County Detectives Probing Vare Petitions," *PB*, April 13, 1926; Salter, *The People's Choice*, p. 78.

14. "$800K Fountain Italy's Sesqui Gift," *PPL*, April 2, 1926; *Lu Lu Temple Official Program, June 1, 2, 3, 1926.*

15. "Hustling to Finish High St. for Sesqui," *PB*, April 6, 1926.

16. "Sculptors Speeding Designs for Sesqui," *PI*, May 9, 1926.

17. Austin and Hauser, *The Sesqui-Centennial International Exposition*, pp. 64–65; "Sesqui Auditorium Rushed," *PB*, March 15, 1926.

18. "50 Sports Events for Philadelphia," *NYT*, March 28, 1926; Rydell, *Fair America*, p. 75; "New Philadelphia Stadium Called Unsafe," *NYT*, April 19, 1926; "Sesqui Stadium Will Open Officially Saturday, May 1," *Sesqui-Centennial News Release*, April 26, 1926.

19. "Pick Motor Camps for Sesqui Visitors," *PB*, March 23, 1926; "Authorize Sesqui Transit Extension," *PB*, May 6, 1926; "Council Gives P.R.T. Sesqui Car Sites," *PB*, May 13, 1926.

20. "Sesqui Roundup of Crooks Begun," *PB*, April 2, 1926; "Sesqui Has Fire Company," *PB*, May 13, 1926; "Philadelphia Arrests Rise," *NYT*, June 10, 1926.

21. "Favor $150K Grant for Sesqui-Centennial," *NYT*, March 20, 1926; "If Permitted," *Times-Picayune*, December 17, 1925; "Look-On Liquor," *Daily Republic*, December 9, 1925.

22. "Alfonzo to Send Royal Tapestries to Sesqui," *PPL*, April 13, 1926; "Sesqui Agent in Berlin Denounced as Unreliable by Manufacturers," *PPL*, April 16, 1926; "Italy to Send Replica of Famous Fountain Here as Sesqui Gift," *PR*, June 1, 1926.

23. "Butler Describes His Battle Here on Vice and Crime," *PB*, April 7, 1926; "Butler Declares Politicians Tried to Pick His Aides," *PB*, April 9, 1926; "Smashing Crime and Vice: Chapter 25," *PB*, May 5, 1926; Schmidt, *Maverick Marine*, pp. 161–162.

24. "Merchants Endorse Sesquicentennial," *NYT*, March 14, 1926; "Sesqui Stamps Go Quickly," *PB*, May 10, 1926; Steaurt Emery, "Sesquicentennial Fair Shows Our Progress," *NYT*, May 23, 1926.

25. "Sesqui Cossacks Arrive," *PB*, May 12, 1926; "Sesqui Aliens Arriving," *PB*, May 17, 1926; "Order Troops to Sesqui," *PB*, May 12, 1926; "Oldest Navy Ship on Way," *PB*, May 13, 1926; "Constellation Sails to Sesquicentennial," *NYT*, May 14, 1926; "To Dry Up Philadelphia," *NYT*, May 27, 1926.

26. "Parades Will Set New City Record," *PB*, May 25, 1926; "Dedicate Japanese Flowering Trees," *PB*, May 21, 1926; "Native Trees Given by Japan to Sesqui," *PI*, May 22, 1926; Dilliplane, *Phila-Nipponica*, pp. 33–34.

27. "Sesqui Bans Sunday Cars," *PB*, May 15, 1926; "Sunset Ideal Time for Visiting Sesqui," *PB*, May 20, 1926.

28. "5 Main Buildings Ready for Sesqui," *PB*, May 25, 1926.

29. "5 Main Buildings Ready for Sesqui," *PB*, May 25, 1926; "Sesqui Exhibitors Race against Time," *PB*, May 26, 1926; "Rush Hiring of 1,000 Sesqui Employees," *PB*, May 27, 1926; "To Dedicate Penna. Building," *PB*, May 27, 1926.

30. "Capt. Baker Back, Carried Off Ship," *PB*, May 28, 1926; "Capt. Asher Baker, Sesqui Head, Dies," *PB*, June 5, 1926.

31. Ralph Bencker, "The Pennsylvania State Building at the Sesqui-Centennial International Exposition," *The American Architect*, Volume 130, CXXX, 1926, p. 384; *Report of the Sesqui-Centennial Commission of the Commonwealth of Pennsylvania*, pp. 9–13, 54; "Penn Spring Water Used in Sesqui Rite," *PI*, May 22, 1926; "To Dedicate Penna. Building," *PB*, May 27, 1926.

32. "Vare's Machine Prospers by Its Kindness," *NYT*, June 27, 1926; "State Dedicates Sesqui Building," *PB*, May 29, 1926; "Pinchot Avoids Sesqui," *PB*, May 31, 1926; Salter, *The People's Choice*, p. 42; Beers, *Pennsylvania Politics Today and Yesterday*, p. 65; McGeary, *Gifford Pinchot*, pp. 318–319.

33. "Predicts 30M Will Visit Sesqui," *PB*, May 28, 1926.

34. Anonymous, "Our Decorations for the Sesqui Centennial Year," *Strawbridge and Clothier Store Chat* 19, nos. 7–8 (July–August 1926): 12–14.

35. "Shrine Head Here, Amazed by Sesqui," *PB*, May 28, 1926.

36. Ibid.

7

★ ★ ★

Kendrick's Karnival

AS DAWN BROKE ON Monday, May 31, it became clear that the prayers of the reporter who wrote that "rain would be a blessing in Sesqui-town" had been heard by the Almighty. A torrential downpour hammered Philadelphia, turning the Sesqui fairgrounds into an ocean of mud and washing out banks of freshly planted shrubs and flowers. The deluge chased away many visitors waiting at the main entrance at Packer Avenue for the great fair to begin.

When the gates opened at 9:00 A.M., Jacob J. Henderson plunked down two quarters and strutted through the turnstiles "with the gait of an emperor." Shaking the water from his derby as he paused under a red-and-gold pergola, he proudly told waiting reporters: "Well, I opened the Sesqui!" The sixty-year-old resident of Woodbury, New Jersey, had visited the 1876 Centennial with his parents, deciding then and there that he wanted to be the first person to pass through the gates of another world's fair. A half century later, soaked to the skin but elated, Henderson had achieved his dream. His only regret was that he didn't have a ticket stub to memorialize his status, owing to the automatic turnstiles. Henderson was first only because the morning storm had chased away less resolute fairgoers who had arrived before him. Fewer than 250 people entered the Sesqui during its first hour of operation.[1]

Three and a half miles north, the weather was not a concern in the Mayor's Reception Room on the second floor of City Hall, although thunder rumbled outside the double-length windows overlooking North Broad Street. The high-ceilinged chamber, awash in marble and mahogany paneling, looked especially sumptuous in its new blue-and-gold decorations and draperies. Beneath an eight-foot gilt-bronze chandelier, Mayor and Mrs. Kendrick greeted the largest gathering of foreign and domestic potentates ever assembled in the hall.

The dazzling attire of the elite throng—"the polychromatic display of Army and Navy uniforms, the regalia of Oriental potentates, and the dress costumes of diplomats of a score and more of nations"—heightened the glamour of the occasion. Among the crowd were Secretary of State Kellogg and Secretary of Commerce Hoover; Rear Admiral Archibald H. Scales, commandant of the Philadelphia Navy Yard; and Major General Douglas MacArthur. As commander of the Third Army Corps, MacArthur was responsible for all War Department activities at the Sesqui; he was also the husband of Eva Stotesbury's daughter, Henrietta Louise. The British, Spanish, Italian, and Japanese ambassadors rubbed shoulders with the diplomatic representatives of thirty other nations, as well as the city's political, business, cultural, and social elite.[2]

The only missing entity was the Commonwealth of Pennsylvania. Governor Pinchot, still miffed over his loss to William Vare and his exclusion from the opening ceremonies, had declined to send a state representative. Although represented by Hoover and Kellogg, Calvin Coolidge was also notable in his absence. It was a telling sign that Coolidge had omitted to make the token gesture of sending a congratulatory telegram to read at the opening exercises. His secretary, Everett Sanders, explained that "Silent Cal" had nothing to say at present and would confine his remarks to the address he gave during his Independence Day visit.[3]

At 11:00 A.M., the dignitaries left City Hall and were ushered into seventy-four black limousines lined up around Penn Square. The rain had stopped, and the sun struggled to break through the leaden skies. The crowds lining Penn Square and South Broad Street cheered as the long cavalcade began its trek south. At its head was a troop of mounted police, followed by four cavalry troops: Troop G of the Third U.S. Cavalry, known as the "President's Own," and Troops A, B, and C of the Pennsylvania National Guard. Heads craned upward as a squadron of airplanes appeared over the Delaware River Bridge and flew southwest to escort the procession to League Island Park. The planes' drone was punctuated by a dull boom every thirty seconds, as six 75mm field cannon commenced a 150-gun salute at the Navy Yard.

The sunlight revealed how the drab squares of Philadelphia had been transformed into a colorful carnival. The four blocks of South Broad Street between Chestnut and Spruce Streets had become an Oriental wonderland called "The Arabian Way" in honor of the Shriners, lined with dozens of sphinx-topped columns covered with mock hieroglyphics. Below Spruce, the Arabian Way became the "Avenue of the Nations," decorated with the flags and shields of the twenty-four countries participating in the Sesqui. The skyscrapers of Center City gave way to churches and row houses. The cheering crowds lining the curbs became mostly black as the parade passed the African American ghetto around South Street, then Italian in the district below Washington Avenue. With every passing block, the cannons' roar grew more deafening.

At Oregon Avenue, the parade arrived at the grand entrance to the Sesqui-Centennial, the gigantic Liberty Bell that straddled Broad Street. Its massive stanchions were still hidden behind scaffolding. As the procession passed beneath the mouth of the bell, day turned to night for the dignitaries, who looked up to see an azure sky dotted with countless gold stars. The string of limousines passed the main entrance at Packer Avenue, receiving

The inaugural parade passes beneath the Liberty Bell at Oregon Plaza on May 31, 1926. Although the bell itself had been completed in time for Opening Day, its supporting stanchions were still shrouded in scaffolding.

a nineteen-gun salute from Battery "C," Sixth Field Artillery. It proceeded along the unfinished expanse that would become the Forum of the Founders and the Court of Honor, the main artery and central plaza of the Sesqui. The barren state of this area was masked by thousands of uniformed servicemen, joined by Shriners in their Oriental costumes, who lined the Forum and Court as the procession proceeded to the Sesqui Stadium.

With fewer than twenty thousand observers spread among its one hundred thousand seats (five thousand of whom were members of the Sesqui-Centennial Chorus), the cavernous Stadium appeared nearly empty. One reporter noted that "the only congestion is caused by hot dog, sandwich and pennant salesman,"[4] and that there seemed to be ten Boy Scouts ushering each arrival to his seat. As the sun grew stronger, spectators' rain gear and umbrellas disappeared, revealing women's spring dresses and cloche hats and the red fezzes of numerous Shriners.

At precisely 12:30 P.M., the procession entered the Stadium, where Hoover and Kellogg received a national salute of twenty-one guns each. The Stadium's amplifying system magnified and distorted the gunfire painfully, making it sound like "a thousand saws pulled over nails."[5] While troops of cavalry assembled on the central field, the long line of limousines circled the Stadium, allowing their occupants to acknowledge the crowd's scattered applause. The cars drew to a halt before a large canopied platform on the eastern side of the Stadium, where the distinguished guests were escorted to their boxes.

The only rousing ovation was for Congressman William S. Vare, triumphant Republican nominee for U.S. Senator, who waved his top hat as he entered the stand with his two pretty daughters, Beatrice and Mildred. Within Pennsylvania, most newspapers viewed Vare's victory as a triumph of one political machine over another: his Philadelphia Organization against the Pittsburgh-based Pepper-Mellon-Grundy combine, with both sides rejecting Pinchot's bone-dry Progressivism. Wets and drys alike agreed that Pinchot had enabled his enemy to win by splitting the Prohibitionist vote.

Outside Pennsylvania, pundits were calling Vare's victory the first litmus test as to whether Prohibition and the Volstead Act would remain intact, or would be modified to permit the sale of beer and light wine. Wayne B. Wheeler, the power behind the Anti-Saloon League, predicted that "the large majority of the Senate will still be dry." But the New York *Herald Tribune* called Vare's victory "a concrete and substantial advance for the wets." Vare himself called his win a victory for Pennsylvania voters, who viewed him as "an agency for the expression of their will and desire for a return of personal liberty and further non-interference with American rights."[6]

At 1:00 P.M., the crowd in the Stadium rose and sang "America," augmented by the five-thousand-voice chorus. Following a benediction by the Episcopal bishop of Pennsylvania, the audience stood for a minute of silence in memory of the roughly 117,000 Americans who had died in the Great War. The dozens of flags of all nations, fluttering atop the Stadium walls, were lowered to half-mast. The quiet was broken by a low hum of a single plane, glittering in the sunlight as it flew high overhead. Its aviator thrust a bundle over the side that exploded in midair, scattering three thousand white roses over the Stadium in tribute to the noble dead.

For the next ninety minutes, under an increasingly hot sun, the audience listened to a series of speeches alternated with patriotic and religious anthems sung by the chorus. Mayor Kendrick, the opening orator, wished "a cheerful greeting and a hearty handclasp to the men, women, and children of this glorious nation and of foreign countries assembled here." At 1:30 P.M., he officially opened the Sesqui-Centennial International Exposition to the world.

Kendrick was followed by keynote speakers Kellogg and Hoover. Both men cast the Sesqui-Centennial as a purifying ritual that could help the United States forsake its current state of frivolous prosperity and contempt for the law and regain its prewar paradise of obedience, sobriety, faith, and patriotism. Kellogg called the fair "an achievement of a virile and versatile people," and "a rededication of the nation to American ideals, a fresh acceptance of Americans' burdens and a renewed gratitude for the bounty of America's blessings."[7] During his speech, a lively black dog strayed onto the Stadium field, where it was chased by a number of bored policemen and scouts.

After Kellogg, Hoover delivered a detailed account of America's physical progress since 1876. In 1926, he warned, the country's greatest danger was neither economic nor foreign, but lay in the "possible submergence of the moral and spiritual by our great material success." The United States had "suffered a national misfortune in the growing disrespect for law," which meant that there was much to do "if we would make America the land of contentment and happiness, of service to the world and God." The United States, Hoover concluded, "stands in need of a moral and spiritual re-awakening if it is to maintain its position in the world."[8]

The final speech was given by Asa Philip Randolph, one of the country's most prominent African American political leaders. Besides being editor of the socialist newspaper the *Messenger*, Randolph was president of the

Mayor Kendrick officially opens the Sesqui-Centennial on May 31. To his left stand the federal representatives to the fair, Secretary of State Frank B. Kellogg and Secretary of Commerce Herbert Hoover. An alienated Governor Pinchot refused to send a state representative.

Brotherhood of Sleeping Car Porters, the first African American labor union. Only a week before the Sesqui opened, Kendrick had invited Randolph to speak as "Orator of the Negro Race of the World," after a group of "representative colored citizens" had insisted that an African American be included in the opening ceremonies. Given his radical background and outspoken demands for racial equality, Randolph was a startling addition to the roster of conservative Republicans. Evidently Kendrick's invitation had been issued after the Opening Day program was printed, for Randolph's name was missing from the schedule of events. Most of the predominantly white audience had no idea who Randolph was, even after Kendrick's brief introduction.

Randolph traced the history of the Negro in America, focusing on Aframerican (his term for African American) contributions to its history. Randolph pointed out that cheap Negro labor was the backbone of America's much-vaunted supremacy, and that the country's unwillingness to compensate the Negro fairly negated its greatness. Rejecting the then-accepted policy of "separate but equal," he demanded complete parity, integration, and justice

The Sesqui Stadium during Opening Day ceremonies, looking south. This aerial view shows how lightly attended the opening ceremonies were, except for the crowds of invited guests above the speakers' podium on the west side. The large stage at the Stadium's open end was where the massive pageant *Freedom* was staged.

for his race, including "the abolition of disfranchisement, segregation, and the Jim Crow car." Otherwise, America would lose its claim to primacy among nations. Despite some catcalls and racial epithets, the audience listened to Randolph in respectful if puzzled silence, applauding politely at the end.[9]

A delicate moment occurred when Japanese Ambassador Tsuneo Matsudaira, whose nation represented the largest foreign presence at the Sesqui, realized that the Japanese flag was missing from the ring of banners fluttering atop the Stadium. "It was an unfortunate affair," noted the man who had recently given Philadelphia sixteen hundred blossoming fruit trees, "but, in considering the haste with which the Sesqui-Centennial was engineered and the many details to be attended to, it is a very excusable blunder." The ceremonies ended at 3:00 P.M. with the singing of "The Star-Spangled Banner," after which the dignitaries in the mayor's party were chauffeured to a luncheon in the Auditorium. Many spectators remained in the Stadium for a band concert and a daylight fireworks display. The rest joined the Opening Day crowd, now numbering nearly one hundred thousand, to explore the Sesqui.[10]

Unfortunately, there was little to see. An advance SCEA press release boasted of "exhibition palaces just teeming with interesting exhibits from

An artist's conception of the Tower of Light, which was meant to occupy pride of place on the Forum of the Founders, between the two main palaces and behind *Philadelphia Progressive*.

many parts of the globe."[11] In reality, the two massive edifices facing the Forum of the Founders—the Palace of Liberal Arts and Manufactures and the Palace of Agriculture and Foreign Exhibits—were empty shells. Visitors venturing within the cavernous halls were forced to navigate an army of workmen building booths and unpacking crates. The other three palaces—Education, Fine Arts, and U.S. Government—were still closed for construction, as were most of the other structures on the fairground.

The cover of the Sesqui-Centennial Daily Program featured a soaring Art Deco spire, shooting beams of light in all directions. It was the Tower of Light, a majestic, 175-foot-tall pillar meant to be the tallest structure at the fair. Its blinding beams were generated by the "Light of Independence," the world's largest and most powerful searchlight, capable of producing a beam visible seventy miles away. When visitors asked Sesqui police where they could find this wonder, they were directed to five large holes dug for its foundation between the two main palaces.

Since few sidewalks had been paved, visitors were forced to crowd onto the handful of gravel paths, or sink up to their ankles in mud as they searched the one-thousand-acre fairgrounds for entertainment. Giving up, many drivers slogged back to the Sesqui parking lots, only to find their automobiles mired in mud as well. As evening approached, lines formed outside the unfinished trolley terminals, while competition for taxis was fierce outside the Packer Avenue entrance. The two comments heard most often on May 31 were, "Isn't the mud terrible?" and "It's a pity they did not have a few more weeks to complete things."[12]

The only moment of the day to capture the public's imagination occurred after dark, with the illumination of the giant Liberty Bell at Oregon Plaza. Shortly before 10:00 P.M., the familiar wail of the siren on the mayor's automobile became audible to the thousands of spectators gathered at the plaza, growing louder as the car sped down Broad Street. Both Mayor and Mrs. Kendrick received warm applause as they stepped from their car. At 10:05 P.M., Mrs. Kendrick threw the switch. Thousands of spectators gasped and cheered as twenty-six thousand bulbs exploded in a dazzling mosaic of amber lights, tinged with ivory and rose, making the eighty-foot bell glow like molten metal. The inscription from Leviticus around the top of the bell, "Proclaim Liberty throughout All the Land unto All the Inhabitants Thereof," sparkled in white against a golden-brown background. The spectacle was visible nearly four miles north, where crowds cheered as City Hall also burst forth in a kaleidoscope of colors. For one glorious moment, the Sesqui delivered on its promise of being the greatest world's fair of all time.[13]

Flanked by her husband, Mrs. W. Freeland Kendrick throws the switch illuminating the giant Liberty Bell at the Sesqui entrance as Opening Day draws to a close.

After the lighting, the Kendricks and their party proceeded to the Auditorium for the Sesqui inaugural ball, which also honored the Shriners' Imperial Potentate James C. Burger. A fez-wearing Kendrick joined two thousand guests swaying to the music of the Meyer Davis Orchestra on the vast temporary floor, which was promptly nicknamed "Philadelphia's first quarter-mile dance hall." Those not honored with an invitation to the ball watched fireworks until 11:00 P.M. As the last visitors departed, crews of construction workers swarmed through the grounds, continuing their frenzied efforts to finish the fair by July 4.[14]

The next morning, E. L. Austin announced that seventy-five thousand people paid to enter the Sesqui on Opening Day, with twenty-five thousand more admitted on complimentary passes. He expressed confidence that his preliminary estimate of thirty million visitors to the Sesqui would still hold. Kendrick declared himself delighted with the fair opening: "Those tremendous crowds, and the evidence of the enthusiasm and courtesy of the people of Philadelphia who are the hosts to the world—these, to me, were the biggest thrills of the opening."[15]

After the whirlwind of activity for the opening, day two was a chance for the staff to catch its breath before continuing the gargantuan task of completing the fair by July 4. A few thousand visitors roamed the fairgrounds, searching for something to do. At the Model Post Office, they could mail a letter to themselves, watch postal employees process and cancel it, and then retrieve it at the general delivery window. Visitors could pay twenty-five cents to enter Sulgrave Manor, a replica of the ancestral Washington family home in England, erected by the National Society of the Colonial Dames of America. In the Palace of Agriculture, they could pay another quarter to study "Titania's Palace," a miniature treasure house imported from England and filled with exquisitely executed artwork and furniture. Once they had done all these things, they could watch workmen lay sidewalks, remove scaffolding, and open crates.[16]

On June 2 attention was diverted from the Sesqui's lack of substance by the arrival of its first royal guests: Crown Prince Gustaf Adolf of Sweden, and his consort, Princess Louise. Philadelphia was the couple's third American stop, after New York and Washington, on a world tour to promote their country's business interests. The royals' visit came shortly before Swedish Day on June 6, the three hundredth anniversary of the signing of the charter of the South Company by King Gustavus Adolphus, establishing the first Swedish colonies in the New World. Americans were charmed by the Crown Prince, who at forty-four retained a youthful athleticism and exuberance. While Princess Louise was described as charming, she was also high-strung and almost pathologically shy, at one point practically running away from cameramen.

After a morning visit to Independence Hall, the royal party motored to the Sesqui-Centennial, where they were greeted by a twenty-one-gun salute. Gustaf Adolf presided at two ceremonies meant to emphasize the role played by Swedish immigrants in the Delaware Valley and in American history. While Swedes had settled in the Philadelphia region six decades before William Penn's arrival, their presence had been overshadowed by the British, who supplanted them. To counter this, the prince dedicated a replica of the Wicaco Block House, a one-story log fort built by Swedish settlers around 1666 on the site of the present-day Old Swedes' (Gloria Dei) Church in Queen Village. Gustaf Adolf also laid the cornerstone for the John Morton Memorial Building. Named after a signer of the Declaration of Independence, the memorial was to be funded by various Swedish American groups to broadcast the contributions of their nationality to their adopted country. That afternoon, the royals returned to New York and the next leg of their transcontinental journey.[17]

With the Swedish visitors gone, attention returned to the Shriners, who grew increasingly bemused to find themselves both the guests of honor and the primary entertainers at the Sesqui. On Wednesday, June 2, the Nobles staged a Mammoth Shrine Night Parade, generating the worst traffic jam in Philadelphia history. As dusk fell, all southbound roads were backed up for miles, as more than one hundred thousand Shriners struggled to reach the Sesqui grounds in overcrowded trolleys and buses. When the parade kicked off at 10:00 P.M., two hours late, hundreds of participants were still stuck in traffic. Several hours later, the nightmare was repeated in reverse as Shriners and spectators tried to get home after the parade. Dawn found dozens of Shriners, their silk finery sweat-soaked and muddy, trudging up Broad Street toward Center City. "The situation," the *Bulletin* observed, "could be blamed only on there being too few streets leading to the Exposition grounds, and the narrowness of the thoroughfares."

The following evening, the Stadium hosted a Shriner-sponsored Pyrotechnical Exhibition and Congress of Electrical Novelties. Among its features were electrical displays of Shrine emblems, fireworks, and huge illuminated portraits of past and current Imperial Potentates Kendrick and Burger. Attendance was far lower than it had been the previous night. Many Shriners were playing it safe in Center City, where they could dance and drink on the Arabian Way and then stagger back to their nearby hotels in minutes.[18]

On Friday, June 4, after a Water Carnival at Edgewater Lake, the quarter-million Shriners departed Philadelphia for their homes across the United States and Canada. Once there, many of them advised their friends and neighbors not to bother with the fiasco that became known in Shriner circles as "Kendrick's Karnival." Their negative word of mouth would later be cited as a principal reason for the fair's failure. Even the official history of the Sesqui, which used only the rosiest colors to paint its story, acknowledged that "all seemed confusion" during the Sesqui's first days, with the result that the Shriners "went back to their home towns, and word spread [that] the exposition could not be made ready for many months."[19]

As the Shriners were departing on June 4, a *Bulletin* reporter accompanied some fresh arrivals around the Sesqui: a family of five named McHenry who had driven from Iowa to Philadelphia, camping out along the way. The McHenrys, who paid $1.75 for admission, spent less than thirty minutes in the two main palaces, where fewer than 5 percent of the exhibits were in place. It took them under an hour to see the few attractions that were complete, like the Model Post Office and Sulgrave Manor. After another two hours touring Camp Anthony Wayne and the Navy Yard, the family was ready to leave by early afternoon. As he loaded his family into their Model T, Mr. McHenry gave the reporter his assessment of the Sesqui:

> This thing reminds me of a guy I knew in Ioway [*sic*]. He invited a raft of friends and family to a big birthday dinner and surprise party one time. He got so darned excited about how many he was going to have, invitations, his speech of welcome, and the program of entertainment, he plumb forgot to order any grub. When he thought of it, everybody was there, the stores closed, and he in a heck of a fix! But the fellow had a sense of humor. 'Come around next birthday and we'll have something to eat,' he said.[20]

Stung by criticism surrounding the Sesqui opening, Kendrick redoubled the city's efforts to complete the fair before the month was out. An exhausted Director of Public Works George Biles had promised Kendrick that all roads to and through the fairgrounds would be completed by mid-June. In the weeks before May 31, Biles's crews had paved an average of ten thousand square yards of road a day. Kendrick ordered Biles to transfer as many of the city's seven thousand Public Works Department employees as possible to the Sesqui construction detail. The fair was to be totally finished by the time of the Coolidges' visit on July 4, regardless of expense.[21]

In a special session on June 10, the City Council Finance Committee approved a new $3 million councilmanic loan for the Sesqui requested by Kendrick: $1 million would pay off an earlier appropriation, while $2 million would cover the mountain of debts accruing from the rush construction work. Kendrick assured City Council that the loan would be paid back once more exhibit space was leased, and once the expected thirty million visitors materialized. He promised that not one cent of the loan would be used for operating expenses, even though the Sesqui was devouring cash. In its first week, the fair had cost $300,000 to run but had collected only

$50,000. Admissions for the 250,000 Shriners had been included in their session fees, so the Sesqui derived little profit from them beyond out-of-pocket expenses. But since "the auspicious opening of the celebration and exposition is now a matter of history," Kendrick rationalized, "we must carry on."[22] Once again, a loyal council backed its mayor unanimously, raising the city's total commitment to the Sesqui to nearly $11 million.

Kendrick added that the official dedication of the Sesqui-Centennial would now take place on Monday, July 5. Originally, the mayor had selected Independence Day for the fair's inauguration, marking the point when the entire Sesqui would be fully operational. Unfortunately, President Coolidge had informed Kendrick that he would not travel to Philadelphia on Independence Day. Besides being his birthday, July 4 was also a Sunday. The politically savvy president had no intention of offending Sabbatarians, the millions of conservative Christians who considered it sacrilegious to open the Sesqui on Sundays, even for a momentous event like the nation's 150th birthday. While the fair's first Opening Day had been moved forward twenty-four hours to accommodate the Shriners, its second was being pushed back twenty-four hours to accommodate President Coolidge and his devout constituents.[23]

Falling on Monday, June 14, Flag Day, was meant to be a dress rehearsal for Independence Day. The governors of the thirteen original states had been invited to participate in special ceremonies marking the "Flag Day of the Nation." Throughout the fairgrounds, rough edges were smoothed and finishing touches applied. At Oregon Plaza, four statues of bald eagles now graced the stanchions of the gigantic Liberty Bell. At the Packer Avenue entrance, winged figures representing "Heralds of the Dawn" were placed atop the pylons above the turnstiles. The Women's Committee hurried to make sure that their High Street of 1776 would be ready to welcome the governors. The stretch of dirt road lined with replicas of historic Philadelphia houses, including President Washington's mansion and Benjamin Franklin's print shop, would serve as an important backdrop for Flag Day and other patriotic celebrations.[24]

On June 14 Mayor Kendrick welcomed the governors of Connecticut, Delaware, Maryland, New Jersey, New York, North Carolina, Pennsylvania, South Carolina, and Virginia; the lieutenant governors of Massachusetts and Rhode Island; the secretary of state of New Hampshire; and the adjutant-general of Georgia to Flag Day ceremonies at the Sesqui-Centennial. The state executives and their parties were treated to luncheon at the Union League, the political club on South Broad Street that had accommodated Philadelphia's Republican elite since the Civil War. Afterward, the dignitaries repaired to the League's front balcony to review a parade of five thousand members of the Centennial Legion, an organization of historic military commands from the original thirteen states. As each state's units approached the Union League in their colorful uniforms, the executive for that state left the balcony, entered a waiting limousine, and led his contingent down Broad Street to the Sesqui. The procession was led by the U.S. Marine Band, playing "The Sesqui-Centennial March," a new composition by John Philip Sousa. Sousa himself occupied a position of honor, riding in the car directly behind Mayor Kendrick's near the head of the parade.[25]

Despite an oppressively hot day, nearly four hundred thousand spectators lined the streets of Philadelphia to welcome the visiting dignitaries. The loudest accolades greeted New York Governor Alfred E. Smith, the Irish Catholic politician who had competed unsuccessfully for the Democratic presidential nomination in 1924. Like Bill Vare, "Al" Smith was a prominent wet who had recently proposed a state referendum to decide whether New York should modify Prohibition to permit wine and beer sales. As the temperature neared ninety degrees, a number of Centennial Legionnaires wearing heavy wool uniforms were overcome by heat on the trek to the Sesqui. Luckily, several hospitals were located on or near South Broad Street, and the victims were rushed to Children's, Methodist, or Saint Agnes, depending on where they fell.[26]

At the Sesqui grounds, the parade stopped at the Forum of the Founders, now lined with thirteen ornamental columns representing the original colonies. Each governor paused at his state's column to unveil a bronze tablet bearing the names of its signers of the Declaration of Independence, while the state flag was raised on a nearby flagpole. Then they proceeded to the Stadium, where the governors and Mayor Kendrick reviewed the parade of military units as they marched around the track. Noting that he had opened the Sesqui-Centennial two weeks before, Kendrick now formally dedicated the exposition and presented it to the people of America and the world in the name of more than two million Philadelphians.

Hundreds of schoolchildren in red, white, and blue uniforms marched onto the field, forming a gigantic U.S. shield and other American icons. As the youngsters went through their paces in the broiling sun, one little girl fell to the ground, senseless. Soon, she was joined by dozens of other children who dropped in their tracks, overcome by the heat. Boy Scouts with stretchers raced back and forth to fetch more than forty victims and convey them to the Sesqui hospital. The state executives in the reviewing stand were forced to smile for the cameras as the spectacle before them assumed the appearance of the Massacre of the Innocents.

Governor Albert C. Ritchie of Maryland unveils his state's column on the Forum of the Founders during Flag Day ceremonies.

Rumbles of thunder brought the dedication ceremonies to a rapid close as storm clouds gathered overhead. Spectators, schoolchildren, and military marchers scattered for shelter when a fierce windstorm whipped the Stadium, followed by lashing rain. As the downpour subsided, Governor Smith and his party scurried across Broad Street to the site where the two New York buildings were under construction. Smith turned a spadeful of dirt to dedicate the replicas of Federal Hall and Washington's Headquarters,

State executives of some of the thirteen original colonies enjoy Flag Day ceremonies at the Sesqui Stadium on June 14, 1926. From left to right are New Hampshire Secretary of State Hobart Pillsbury; Massachusetts Lieutenant-Governor Frank G. Allen; Pennsylvania Governor Gifford Pinchot; Connecticut Governor John H. Turnbull; New York Governor Alfred E. Smith; Delaware Governor Robert P. Robinson; Maryland Governor Albert C. Ritchie; New Jersey Governor A. Harry Moore; North Carolina Governor Angus W. McLean; and South Carolina Governor Thomas G. McLeod.

telling reporters, "I hope eleven million people from New York will visit the exposition by December." Soon afterward, the string of limousines returned the state executives to the Bellevue-Stratford Hotel for a much-needed rest and an evening banquet.[27]

By this time, national attention had turned from the Big Show in League Island Park to the Big Show in Washington, DC, where William S. Vare's campaign for the U.S. Senate was facing intense scrutiny. On May 17 the Senate adopted a resolution introduced by Senator James A. Reed (D-Missouri) to investigate reports of campaign fraud and excessive expenditures in both the Pennsylvania and the Illinois Republican senatorial primaries. On May 19, the day after Vare's primary victory, the U.S. Senate appointed a special committee of three Republican and two

Democratic senators, with Senator Reed as its chairman, to conduct the investigation.[28]

Just before the Sesqui opened, the Reed committee began to hear testimony from key figures in the Pennsylvania primary. In doing so, they revealed the byzantine machinations of the Philadelphia Organization to an American public still shocked by recent revelations of the Teapot Dome, Veterans' Bureau, and other Harding administration scandals. Vare himself testified before the Senate committee on June 15. He astonished his future colleagues by acknowledging nonchalantly that he had cosigned a note with financier Albert M. Greenfield for $100,000 to cover campaign expenses. It was quite an accomplishment for two boys who had grown up poor in South Philadelphia.

The star witness of the June 15 hearing was Vare's campaign manager, City Treasurer Harry A. Mackey. The plainspoken Mackey had his interrogators in stitches with his sarcastic attacks on Vare's leading opponent, Senator George W. Pepper. Calling Pepper a double-dealing hypocrite who had gotten into the good graces of "a few highbrows and a few social climbers among the women," Mackey claimed that Vare was supported by "decent people who wanted Modification" while Pepper "had the support of the bootleggers and the breweries and the people who are thriving under" Prohibition. Mackey's "ready wit" and "pungent answers" contrasted sharply with the "ponderous and sometimes pointless responses of his chief," making committee members wonder why the City Treasurer wasn't running for the Senate instead of Vare.[29]

Mackey denied that Vare had spent excessively on the primary campaign: the smooth precision of the Organization meant that the votes of an entire division could be guaranteed for fifty dollars. Besides, voters in the "first twenty" wards of Philadelphia—the river wards where one-third of the city lived, including most of its poor and immigrant population—required minimal outlay. "If you ask them the party they will vote for," Mackey explained, "they will name the [Republican] division leader."[30]

Appalled, Senator William H. King (D-Utah) asked, "Then one-third of the voters in Philadelphia have no knowledge of American institutions, but just follow their leader?" Mackey's cynical response provoked a wave of laughter in the Senate chamber:

> There are certain ignorant people; we have them out in our residential district. The most ignorant voter in the world is he who thinks he knows how to vote. We have got them out there who wear the

high hat and white front; they are too proud to ask how to mark their ballots, and they spoil them every time.[31]

On July 1 Senator Pepper retaliated for Mackey's jibes by charging that Vare and Greenfield had tried to bribe a South Philadelphia judge named Francis X. O'Connor to support their campaign for $150,000. Called before the committee, a sickly O'Connor testified that he had spoken with Greenfield and Vare, but refused to specify the topic. Asked if he had tried to entice O'Connor, Vare huffed that the matter "is so ridiculous that I will not dignify it by discussing it."[32]

Within twenty-four hours, Senator Matthew Neely (D-West Virginia) called for passage of a resolution for "disqualification of slush-fund Senators-elect." To prevent any punitive legislation from being enacted on the last day before the Senate adjourned for the summer, David A. Reed, the junior senator from Pennsylvania, broke ranks with his colleague George W.

William S. Vare (r.) and his campaign manager, Harry Mackey (l.), leave the United States Capitol after testifying before a Senate committee investigating Vare's campaign expenditures on June 9, 1926. (Prints and Photographs Division, Library of Congress.)

Pepper and organized a filibuster. On a hot and humid July 3, the pro-Vare forces staged a performance that one reporter called "as indefensible and disgusting an exhibition of the legalized system of time-killing as ever took place under Senate rules." Statesman after statesman monopolized the Senate floor, discoursing on irrelevant topics as the session crept to a close. The star was Senator Ralph H. Cameron (R-Arizona), a "weather-beaten old Western trailblazer" who droned on about the selection of dam sites while his colleagues yelled at him to be a "damn sight" quieter. At 3:00 P.M., Cameron fell silent when Vice President Dawes banged his gavel and adjourned the Senate until November 10, 1926, safely past Election Day. Until then, William Vare's future career as a United States Senator appeared intact.[33]

After such an exposure of corruption—prompting one Democratic congressman to call Pennsylvania "the open shame of this Republic"—President Calvin Coolidge could have been excused for wanting to avoid the City of Brotherly Love. Coolidge, the epitome of New England rectitude, had labored to distance himself from the numerous sins of his predecessor's administration. He was not about to condone the vanity project of an Organization whose venality had just been vivisected in detail before the eyes of America. Plans for a three-day presidential visit seemed like a distant dream when White House officials informed Philadelphia officials that they would have President and Mrs. Coolidge for four hours on the afternoon of July 5. And even during that brief period, Philadelphia would have to share the president with Camden, where Coolidge would inaugurate the South Jersey Exposition.[34]

On June 29 a new commemorative half-dollar coin went on sale at the Sesqui-Centennial, showing the profiles of George Washington and Calvin Coolidge on the obverse side, and the Liberty Bell on the reverse. It was the first and only time a living president would be featured on American currency, and it immediately attracted criticism. Government officials defended the decision to depict Coolidge. Since the Sesqui celebrated both America's past and present, they argued, the pairing of its first and thirtieth presidents was appropriate. Sold for one dollar at the Sesqui, the commemorative half-dollar (along with a $2.50 gold coin depicting the Goddess of Liberty, sold for $3.50) would prove to be one of the fair's few moneymakers.[35]

Two days later, dignitaries gathered near the foot of Race Street in Philadelphia and the foot of Pearl Street in Camden to celebrate the much-awaited opening of the Delaware River Bridge. Completed after nearly five years of construction, the bridge realized a dream to connect the two states that had first been proposed in 1818. The 1.82-mile-long span, designed by architect Paul Philippe Cret and engineers Ralph Modjeski and Leon Moisseiff, won renown as "the World's Greatest Suspension Bridge," since the 1,750-foot span between its two towers was the longest in the world at that time. It was also the largest toll bridge in operation, part of an effort to recoup its construction costs of nearly $40 million. Still, the magnificent Modernist edifice made a spectacular entrance to the Sesqui-Centennial City.[36]

July 4, 1926, was a typical summer day in Philadelphia: hot and muggy, with intermittent showers. It was also the first Sunday that the Sesqui was open to the public. When the SCEA Executive Committee voted, thirty-eight to one, to open the financially troubled fair on Sundays to boost attendance, many Protestant churchmen protested that they were defiling the Sabbath. Bishop Joseph F. Berry of the Methodist Episcopal Church resigned from the SCEA, and local religious groups asked Governor Pinchot to enjoin the Sesqui from opening. Pinchot, while admitting that he had no legal right to shut the fair, lectured the SCEA that they had violated "an obligation of honor" by opening the gates on Sunday. "Philadelphia," intoned one Philadelphia pastor, "stands indicted before God and Christian-thinking men."[37]

Despite dozens of anti-Sesqui sermons preached throughout the city and increasingly heavy rains, more than fifty thousand visitors paid to attend the Sesqui on July 4. By now most of its major attractions were open. To mollify church leaders, the SCEA had arranged an impressive religious

A stormy sky highlights the *Philadelphia Progressive* statue. By July, the unusually rainy weather had become a major problem for Sesqui managers.

service in the Auditorium featuring Metropolitan Opera Company diva Anna Case. In his invocation, the Reverend John W. Stockwell said that "so many good citizens were apparently trying to do good by staying away from the Sesqui-Centennial on Sunday,"[38] that he felt he could do more good by actually being at the fair.

In what some offended Christians viewed as an act of God, a violent rainstorm damaged many of the hastily constructed buildings at the Sesqui, with numerous leaks damaging their exhibits. The Palace of Agriculture and Foreign Exhibits was especially hard-hit. With its inadequate gutters and rainspouts overwhelmed, several tons of water collected on its flimsy wooden roof, raising fears of a collapse among fair engineers. Finally, workmen cut holes in the roof, releasing cascades that destroyed the Maryland state display.[39]

The rain had abated on Monday, July 5, when the special express from Washington pulled into Broad Street Station at 11:00 A.M. A crowd of several thousand spectators cheered as the Coolidges detrained, the president dapper in silk hat and morning dress, the first lady chic in a white suit and feathered bonnet. They were accompanied by Attorney General John G. Sargent, presidential secretary Everett Sanders, and Frank W. Stearns, the Boston tycoon who had financed Coolidge's political career. On hand to greet them were the mayor, Mrs. Kendrick, and a small reception committee. The presidential party was led to limousines outside the station, and the trek to the Sesqui grounds began.

If Philadelphians felt slighted by the brevity of the Coolidges' visit, they hid it well. More than two hundred thousand spectators lined South Broad Street from City Hall to the fairgrounds, while thousands more cheered from nearby windows and rooftops. The vivacious First Lady waved her handkerchief to acknowledge the crowd's cheers. Even her reticent husband seemed pleased with his reception, smiling broadly and tipping his hat to the crowd. As the procession reached the Liberty Bell, the Coolidges were greeted with a presidential twenty-one-gun salute from a nearby battery of 75mm tank guns. The cannon fire reverberated through the air, causing plaster to cascade in sheets from the exterior of the recently finished Auditorium. The ornate state columns lining the Forum of the Founders vibrated as the guns continued to roar. Suddenly, some of them seemed to explode, their decorative plaster shells shattered by the repercussions.

The presidential couple made a brief tour of the exposition grounds, remaining in their car while Kendrick pointed out key attractions. By now it was raining again, but a crowd of thirty-five thousand spectators roared with applause when the Coolidges entered the Stadium. A pandemonium

President Calvin Coolidge, in the right foreground, prepares to deliver his July 5 speech at the Sesqui Stadium. Coolidge is flanked by Attorney General John G. Sargent (at far right), First Lady Grace Coolidge, Mrs. Kendrick, Mayor Kendrick, and Pennsylvania Governor Pinchot.

of activity greeted their arrival: cannons at the Navy Yard boomed out another salute, three airplanes spun in trick maneuvers overhead, and the Navy Band struck up "The Star-Spangled Banner." An army of newsreel cameramen and newspaper photographers captured the Kendricks and the presidential party as they mounted a covered platform, joining the temporarily cordial trio of Governor Pinchot, Senator Pepper, and Congressman Vare. Mayor Kendrick stepped before the battery of radio microphones that was carrying the program to more than one hundred million people nationwide and introduced the president.[40]

For the first time, the whirlwind of activity that had characterized the presidential visit ground to a halt as Coolidge stepped forward and began his forty-minute speech. The carefully researched, scholarly address seemed better suited to a college classroom than to a huge public celebration. It appeared calculated to defy those members of the intelligentsia who had dismissed the Amherst graduate as a "frugal little man" whose ideal day was one "on which nothing whatever happens."[41] The *New York Times* would later call it "the most notable speech on a patriotic theme [Coolidge] has made in his Administration." In it, Coolidge laid a detailed spiritual and philosophical basis for political and social conservatism. Tracing the heritage of the Declaration of Independence, the Vermont native attributed its genesis not to Thomas Jefferson and French philosophers but to New England preachers like John Wise. These Puritans were inspired in turn by the seventeenth-century German political scientists von Chemnitz and Pufendorf, who challenged the divine power of the Holy Roman Empire and the Hapsburgs.[42]

By redirecting the lineage of the Declaration, Coolidge could posit that its principles were "the result of religious teachings," rather than deriving from Jefferson's unorthodox deist philosophy. Quoting Wise, Coolidge stated, "Democracy is Christ's government in Church and State." It was natural, then, that the Declaration of Independence should open with a reference to God, and close with an appeal to "the Supreme Judge of the world and an assertion of a firm reliance on Divine Providence." From there, Coolidge went on to state that "unless the faith of the American people in these religious convictions is to endure, the principles of our Declaration will perish."[43]

Given this spiritual grounding, Coolidge warned of the dangers not only of disobeying the law but of trying to improve on basic governmental institutions. "It is not the enactment, but the observance of laws," he stated, "that creates the character of a nation. About the Declaration there is a finality that is exceedingly restful." Even though the representatives of the government may sometimes go astray, "that is not a reason for criticizing the principles of our institutions." While those who wished to reform the government were often sincere, he acknowledged, many were also misinformed. "In my opinion very little of just criticism can attach to the theories and principles of our institutions. There is far more danger of harm than there is hope of good in any radical changes."[44]

Concluding, Coolidge noted the increasing material progress and prosperity of the current age with approval. But like Herbert Hoover on May 31, he warned against sinking into a "pagan materialism" without the spirituality and piety that inspired American forefathers to create the Declaration:

> We live in an age of science and of abounding accumulation of material things. These did not create our Declaration. Our Declaration created them. The things of the spirit come first. Unless we cling to that, all our material prosperity, overwhelming though it may appear, will turn to a barren scepter in our grasp.[45]

Once Coolidge finished speaking, the maelstrom of motion quickened again. Before the applause had died down, the presidential party was speeding back to Center City for a hurried luncheon at the Bellevue-Stratford Hotel and a flying tour of Independence Hall and Christ Church. There was no time to stop at the Betsy Ross House, but the Coolidges caught a glimpse of it as their car sped toward the Delaware River Bridge. Although it was pouring rain, heavy crowds still cheered the first couple as their limousine wove through Old City.

The procession crossed the bridge, lined on both sides with Pennsylvania National Guardsmen until the middle of the span, where they gave way to the National Guard of New Jersey. The Coolidges stopped at the Camden end of the bridge, where they were welcomed by New Jersey Senator Walter Edge and Camden Mayor Victor King, and cheered by a crowd of ten thousand. Donning a black slicker, President Coolidge left the shelter of his limousine to plant a Vermont maple tree, while rain beat a tattoo on his ruined silk hat. In doing so, the president officially opened the South Jersey Exposition, Camden's challenge to Philadelphia's Sesqui-Centennial.

The presidential party sped back across the bridge and up Market Street to the Broad Street Station. At 4:14 P.M., President and Mrs. Coolidge boarded the train that would return them to Washington, DC. Before getting on, the president shook hands with Mayor Kendrick and told him, "I've had a fine time. Enjoyed it very much."[46] As if to compensate for her husband's reticence, Mrs. Coolidge tore off her hat as the train pulled away, waving it frantically at the farewell party on the platform.

The Coolidges were gone. The *Bulletin* tried to treat their abbreviated visit as an outstanding example of scientific time management, praising the "dispatch that was both amazing and a tribute to the efficiency of the federal authorities who had the program in charge." More cynical observers noted that the President of the United States had paid the most minimal tribute that he could to the first world's fair held in his country since 1915, other than to ignore it completely.[47]

The Sesqui-Centennial International Exposition had now been opened (twice), dedicated, acknowledged by state and national leaders, ballyhooed and boomed, and for all practical purposes completed. During its first five weeks of existence, it had attracted fewer than 250,000 visitors. From now on, there could be no more excuses, no way of promising disappointed visitors that everything would be so much better if they came back in a month. The Sesqui was open for business, and it had fewer than five months to attract thirty million visitors, pay for itself, and vindicate its existence.

NOTES

1. "Woodbury Man First at Sesqui," *PB*, May 31, 1926.

2. "Kellogg, Hoover and Mayor Speak at New Stadium," *PB*, May 31, 1926; "Many Notables Accompany Mayor at Sesqui Opening," *PB*, May 31, 1926; "Sesquicentennial Opens as Sun Shines; 100K Pass Gates," *NYT*, June 1, 1926.

3. "Sesqui Gates to Open to World Monday," *PB*, May 29, 1926; "Coolidge Asks Support of Sesquicentennial," *NYT*, May 31, 1926.

4. "Centennial Visitor Early at Stadium," *PB*, May 31, 1926.

5. Ibid.

6. "Congressmen Hail Vare at Capitol," *PB*, May 19, 1926; "Wheeler Thought Vare Would Win," *PB*, May 19, 1926; "Vare Victory Puts Wet Issue Ahead," *PB*, May 20, 1926; "Call Vare Victory Dry Law Protest," *PB*, May 24, 1926; "The 'Vare and Beer' Victory as a National Portent," *Literary Digest* 89, no. 39 (May 1926): 5–9.

7. "Kellogg, Hoover and Mayor Speak at New Stadium," *PB*, May 31, 1926.

8. "Kellogg, Hoover and Mayor Speak at New Stadium," *PB*, May 31, 1926.

9. "Sesqui-Centennial Opening Attended by Thousands of Visitors to Quaker City," *PT*, June 5, 1926; Wintz, *African American Political Thought 1890–1930*, pp. 309–331; Rydell, *World of Fairs*, pp. 161–163; Rydell, Findling, and Pelle, *Fair America*, p. 74.

10. "Philadelphia Opens Sesquicentennial Today," *NYT*, May 31, 1926; "Coolidge Asks Support of Sesquicentennial," *NYT*, May 31, 1926; "Kellogg, Hoover and Mayor Speak at New Stadium," *PB*, May 31, 1926; "Whirring Planes and Guns Greet Inaugural Guests," *PB*, May 31, 1926; "Many Notables Accompany Mayor at Sesqui Opening," *PB*, May 31, 1926; "Japanese Regret Flag Is Missing," *PB*, May 31, 1926; "Pinchot Avoids Sesqui," *PB*, May 31, 1926; "Sesquicentennial Opens as Sun Shines," *NYT*, June 1, 1926; "Sesqui-Centennial Opening Attended by Thousands of Visitors to Quaker City," *PT*, June 5, 1926; Austin and Hauser, *The Sesqui-Centennial International Exposition*, pp. 190–193.

11. "Sesqui-Centennial Opens," SCEA press release, May 31, 1926.

12. Ibid.

13. "Sesqui Bell Is a Blaze of Lights," *PR*, May 31, 1926.

14. "2K Dance at Sesqui Ball," *PB*, June 1, 1926.

15. "First U.S. Exhibit Opens at Sesqui," *PB*, June 1, 1926.

16. "Titania's Palace Leaves England on Way to Sesqui," *PPL*, May 23, 1926; "First U.S. Exhibit Opens at Sesqui," *PB*, June 1, 1926.

17. Austin and Hauser, *The Sesqui-Centennial International Exposition*, pp. 193, 369, 377; "Gustaf Adolf Visits Independence Hall," *NYT*, June 3, 1926.

18. "Shrine Will Show Secrets in Giant Sesqui Pageants," *PPL*, May 8, 1926; "Parades Will Set New City Record," *PB*, May 25, 1926; "Stadium Trek Jams Whole South Philadelphia," *PB*, June 3, 1926; *Lu Lu Temple Official Program, June 1, 2, 3, 1926.*

19. Austin and Hauser, *The Sesqui-Centennial International Exposition*, pp. 48–49.

20. "Sesqui Buildings Have Few Exhibits," *PB*, June 4, 1926.

21. "First U.S. Exhibit Opens at Sesqui," *PB*, June 1, 1926; "City Employees Aid Expo Work," *PB*, June 8, 1926.

22. "Committee Votes 3 Million Loan for Sesqui Budget," *PB*, June 10, 1926.

23. "Mayor Will Ask for New Funds on Sesqui," *PB*, June 9, 1926; "Committee Votes 3 Million Loan for Sesqui Budget," *PB*, June 10, 1926.

24. "High Street Ready for Big Flag Day," *PPL*, June 10, 1926; "Dedication June 14 of Sesquicentennial," *NYT*, June 11, 1926.

25. Besides Governor Gifford Pinchot of Pennsylvania, the state executives present on Flag Day were Governor John H. Trumbull of Connecticut; Governor Robert P. Robinson of Delaware; Adjutant-General Charles H. Cox of Georgia; Governor Albert C. Ritchie of Maryland; Lieutenant Governor Frank G. Allen of Massachusetts; Secretary of State Hobart Pillsbury of New Hampshire; Governor A. Harry Moore of New Jersey; Governor Alfred E. Smith of New York; Governor Angus W. McLean of North Carolina; Secretary of State (and former governor) Charles Dean Kimball of Rhode Island; Governor Thomas G. McLeod of South Carolina; and Governor Harry Flood Byrd of Virginia.

26. "Alfred E. Smith Dies Here at 70; 4 Times Governor," *NYT*, October 4, 1944.

27. "High Street Ready for Big Flag Day," *PPL*, June 10, 1926; "Dedication June 14 of Sesquicentennial," *NYT*, June 11, 1926; "Mayor, Dedicating Sesqui, Reviews History of Flag," *PB*, June 14, 1926; "Planes Drop Flags While 13 Columns Are Dedicated," *PB*, June 14, 1926; "Scores Overcome by Heat at Sesqui," *PB*, June 14, 1926; "13 Governors Meet at Big Fair Today," *NYT*, June 14, 1926; "Gov. Smith Dedicates New York Buildings at Sesquicentennial," *NYT*, June 15, 1926.

28. "The 'Vare and Beer' Victory as a National Portent," p. 9; Astorino, "The Contested Senate Election of William Scott Vare."

29. "Inquirers Turn to Vare 'Machine,' More Funds Found," *NYT*, June 16, 1926.

30. Ibid.

31. "Inquirers Turn to Vare 'Machine,' More Funds Found," *NYT*, June 16, 1926, p. 1; "Vare Admits at Inquiry He Signed Notes for $150,000," *NYT*, June 16, 1926; Salter, *The People's Choice*, p. 62.

32. "Vare Ridicules 'Bid' to O'Connor," *PPL*, July 2, 1926.

33. "Says Pepper Was Told Vare Rumors," *PB*, July 1, 1926; "Testifies O'Connor Told Him of Offer," *PB*, July 2, 1926; "Vare Ridicules 'Bid' to O'Connor," *PPL*, July 2, 1926; "Filibuster Saves Vare and O'Connor from Senate's Ire," *PR*, July 4, 1926.

34. "Sesqui Shows $79,179 Loss for First Fifteen Days," *PB*, June 22, 1926;

35. "Put Coolidge and Washington Portraits on the New Sesquicentennial Half-Dollar," *NYT*, June 30, 1926; "Sesqui Coin Defended," *PB*, June 30, 1926.

36. Petroski, "The Benjamin Franklin Bridge": 406–410.

37. "Denounce Fair on Sunday," *NYT*, June 28, 1926.

38. "Philadelphia Fair Is Damaged by Rain," *NYT*, July 5, 1926.

39. Ibid..

40. "Coolidge Invokes Founders' Ideals as Guide to Nation," *NYT*, July 6, 1926.

41. Greenberg, citing Walter Lippmann and H. L. Mencken, *The American Presidents*, p. 3.

42. Ibid.

43. "Text of Coolidge's Speech at Sesquicentennial," *NYT*, July 5, 1926.

44. Ibid.

45. Ibid.

46. "Throngs Defy Rain as Coolidge Leads Celebration Here," *PB*, July 6, 1926.

47. "President Coolidge on Radio over 22 Stations Tomorrow," *NYT*, July 4, 1926; "Coolidge Invokes Founders' Ideals as Guide to Nation," *NYT*, July 6, 1926; "Throngs Defy Rain as Coolidge Leads Celebration Here," *PB*, July 6, 1926; Austin and Hauser, *The Sesqui-Centennial International Exposition*, pp. 197–199.

8

★ ★ ★

A Fine Thing to Show the Nation

WITH THE PRESIDENTIAL VISIT behind it, the Sesqui-Centennial could proceed with the business of being a bona fide world's fair. To the surprise of many observers after its chaotic debut, it succeeded fairly well. By the end of July, the fair was almost complete, and ready to welcome the tens of millions of Americans it still hoped to attract. With the onset of the summer vacation season, visitors' books at various attractions began to swell with signatures from New England, the South, the Midwest, and even a few from sunny California. If the McHenrys had motored back from Iowa to Philadelphia in July, they would have needed much longer than a single morning to take in the fair. According to the *New York Times*, a Sesqui visitor could now "put in weeks admiring its wonders."[1]

On a hot, sunny morning in late July, a steady stream of visitors strode past the pylons supporting the Heralds of the Dawn at Packer Avenue. They paid their fifty-cent admission, pushed through the turnstiles, and hurried into the Sesqui fairgrounds. Most turned left and headed toward Building No. 1, the Palace of Liberal Arts and Manufactures. With nearly two hundred exhibits sponsored by the country's leading manufacturers, this vast warehouse embodied the cult of the new that had gripped America. Building No. 1 celebrated the innovation that had propelled the United States to industrial and technological supremacy, and blessed its citizens with prosperity unimaginable a generation earlier.

By 1926 the American businessman had become a hero, venerated with almost pious devotion for his role in spreading the gospel of success. Writers of the period conflated faith and finance: Moses became "one of

The USS *Los Angeles*, one of the giant dirigibles used by the United States Navy during the 1920s, hovers over the *Philadelphia Progressive* statue during a visit to the Sesqui in late July 1926.

the greatest salesmen and real-estate promoters that ever lived," as well as "ad-writer for the Deity." In the best-selling *The Man Nobody Knows*, Bruce Barton praised Jesus Christ as "the founder of modern business," who "picked up twelve men from the bottom ranks . . . and forged them into an organization that conquered the world." It was fitting that many of the booths in Building No. 1 resembled temples, displaying the miraculous tools that enabled American businessmen to part the Red Sea of world commerce. Beneath a classical portico, the International Business Machines Corporation demonstrated its cutting-edge tabulating technology, including a sorter capable of cataloging 360 punch cards a minute. But IBM also displayed the prosaic meat choppers and cheese cutters that had been its stock in trade since the merger that created the company in 1911.[2]

Looking across the Forum of the Founders toward the Palace of Liberal Arts and Manufactures (Building No. 1).

At the Underwood Typewriter Company booth, a large transparent globe rotated around a typewriter, illustrating the firm's slogan, "More than 3,000,000 Underwoods now speed the World's Business." The Edison Company featured an eighteen-foot-tall model of the Ediphone, one of the first dictating machines. Alongside a replica of the original telephone introduced at the 1876 Centennial, AT&T used the new technology of talking pictures to bring to life the telephone switchboard of 1926, where female operators fielded thousands of calls every minute. Automatic Electric demonstrated a telephone with a rotary dial that allowed users to place a call directly and bypass the central switchboard. Photo-radio receivers and transmitters, primitive versions of the fax machine, proved that radio waves could transmit images as well as sounds.[3]

Most visitors were drawn by the lavish arrays of housing materials, furnishings, and consumer goods. Americans were on a spending spree in 1926, propelled by easy credit and low interest rates. Housing starts had doubled in the past decade, while automobile registrations had jumped from eight million to nineteen million in only six years. Between 1922 and 1925, the number of radio sets in America grew from roughly one million to more than five million. With more than two-thirds of American homes wired for electricity, consumers were snapping up electrical appliances like clothes washers, vacuum cleaners, toasters, and refrigerators. The centerpiece of the Frigidaire Company, housed in a green-and-gold Art Deco palace, was a statue of "The Modern Iceman," hefting an electrical refrigeration unit upon his brawny shoulder.[4]

Color was everywhere: thanks to advances in enamel and lacquer composition, every appliance and fixture in the American home was available in a rainbow of hues by 1926. The Associated Tile Manufacturers erected Casa Bonita, the House of Tiles, a bungalow decorated floor to ceiling in sanitary, colorful ceramic. Nearby the Wall Paper House suggested an alternative way to decorate one's home, with more than one hundred varieties of coverings. The Crane Company offered the deluxe Vitrolite bathroom, with a black-and-white checkerboard floor, gray-and-silver walls, and a white ceiling with touches of blue and green.[5]

Leaving Building No. 1, visitors continued south on the Forum of the Founders, a 250-foot-wide boulevard. On the west side stood the colonnade of pylons representing the thirteen colonies, freshly repaired after being shattered by the cannons welcoming President Coolidge on July 5 (since then, all cannon salutes had been shifted to the safe distance of the Navy Yard). At the central Court of Honor stood Samuel Murray's *Philadelphia Progressive*, its base already discolored and flaking from moisture.

Behind *Philadelphia Progressive* a metal skeleton bearing a strong resemblance to a prison watchtower rose 175 feet above the Model Post Office. This was the majestic Tower of Light, the Sesqui symbol that still shone from the cover of the fair's daily program. Until the city could scrape together enough money, the elaborate Art Deco exterior seen on the cover drawing would have to wait. Fair managers still hoped to have the sixty-two-inch-lens Light of Independence mounted atop the structure within the next two weeks. This powerful beacon would be "of such searing intensity that it would instantly ruin any human eye accidentally touched by it at close range and would burn the skin far worse than any tropical sun." For the time being, fairgoers' sight and skin were safe: at night, a small searchlight shone feebly from atop the naked metal shaft.[6]

The next stop was Building No. 2, the Palace of Agriculture and Foreign Exhibits, which housed the exhibits of the country's leading agribusiness firms and food manufacturers. Dozens of lavishly decorated booths for companies like Best Foods, Jell-O, and Maxwell House revealed the extent to which processed convenience foods had infiltrated the American kitchen. The Royal Baking Powder Company held court in a miniature French Renaissance castle, where costumed maidens distributed samples of its new

One of the few postcards to show the unfinished Tower of Light. The skeletal structure would cast a long shadow over the Sesqui, becoming a symbol of its unfulfilled promise.

The Court of Honor, looking southeast toward the Palace of Agriculture and Foreign Exhibits. In the foreground, a PRT PaRTyCar travels past the *Philadelphia Progressive* statuary group.

Royal Gelatin. The Great Atlantic and Pacific Tea Company installed a working model of one of its A&P grocery stores in a brick cottage with flower-filled window boxes. This cozy facade masked the ruthless efficiency with which the chain's fourteen thousand outlets (up from four hundred in 1912) were wiping out mom-and-pop shops across the country.[7]

Building No. 2 also held most of the Sesqui's international exhibits in its eight acres. Americans' growing fascination with foreign cultures was illustrated by the crowds around the booths of seventeen nations. Besides erecting pavilions elsewhere on the fairgrounds, four countries had mounted displays in the palace: Cuba, Czechoslovakia, Japan, and Spain. They were joined by official or private exhibits from Austria, Algeria, China, Denmark, Egypt, France, Germany, Great Britain, Haiti, Holland, Hungary, Palestine, and Sweden.

The largest and most elaborate exhibit was sponsored by Imperial Japan, using the Sesqui as a diplomatic gesture to relieve heightening political and trade tensions with the United States. Westerners admired an extraordinary selection of fine arts in lacquer, cloisonné, ceramic, and ivory, all suffused in the scent of fine incense. ("The Orientals sure like their perfume," groused an employee at the neighboring Los Angeles exhibit.) The Mikimoto Pearl Farms displayed a miniature pagoda decorated with 48,500 cultured pearls, valued at $500,000. The Raw Silk Association of Japan traced the manufacture of silk from worms to hand-embroidered screens by artists like Nishimura Sozaemon and Tanaka Rishichi. Also on display were products from the Japanese colonies of Korea and Formosa (Taiwan), as well as the Japanese-controlled South Manchuria Railway Zone in China.[8]

Leaving Building No. 2, visitors could cross Pattison Avenue and continue south on Broad Street toward the Sesqui Stadium. Every day, the giant arena hosted a variety of events: one day, the Women's National Track and Field Championship; the next, a rodeo full of "bucking broncos, snorting steers, and stubborn calves," subdued by "brawny boys from the 'wild and wooly' west." On June 17, Philadelphia boxing fans cheered when Philadelphia's own Tommy Loughran defeated former world light-heavyweight champion Georges Carpentier in the tenth round.[9]

At the foot of Broad Street stood the Philadelphia Navy Yard, where historic American vessels floated alongside the latest generation of naval battleships in the Reserve Basin. On July 7, Hawaii Day, ukuleles played and girls in grass skirts danced the hula on the deck of the frigate *Constellation*, which in 1843 had thwarted a British attempt to seize control of the kingdom of Hawaii (now an American territory). But the future of America's armed forces was also on display. On July 16 Philadelphians

The central tower of the gargantuan Palace of United States Government, Machinery, and Transportation.

thrilled as the U.S. Army's largest dirigible, the 180-foot-long TC-5, soared over City Hall and South Broad Street before coming to earth at the Navy Yard. While the TC-5 was equipped as a bomber and aircraft carrier, many observers dreamed of the day when it might serve as an airborne ocean liner, transporting them to Europe in seventy-two hours.[10]

Turning back up Broad Street, visitors could enter the Palace of United States Government, Machinery, and Transportation, or Building No. 5. About one-half of the building's 321,800 square feet was devoted to various federal departments and bureaus. Despite the stated goal of the Republican administration to reduce the scope of central government, the palace proved how omnipresent and necessary that government had become in Americans' lives since the Centennial. According to the *Bulletin*, this "million-dollar show window" transformed the vast army of federal employees, "more numerous than Santa Claus' helpers," into "a group of experts in all lines of human endeavor, all working toward one supreme end—to make America a better place in which to live."[11]

At the Bureau of the Census booth, a large electric chart tracked births, deaths, immigration, and emigration in the United States, while a row of changing numbers showed the steady rise of the population above 117 million. The Children's Bureau celebrated how improvements in diet, medicine, and sanitation had reduced child mortality by nearly two-thirds since 1900. The Women's Bureau, with a banner reading, "America Will Be as Strong as Her Women," offered an exhibit entitled, "The Home Maker as Wage Earner: A Problem Play in 4 Acts." The Veterans' Bureau, still scarred by recent revelations about graft and misappropriation, emphasized its solicitous care of disabled veterans.

The role of the federal government in transforming the national landscape was also explored. Panoramas of the Grand Canyon, Old Faithful, and Hawaii's Lake of Fire demonstrated the far-flung range of the National Park Service a decade after its establishment in 1916. Models of dams and irrigation systems illustrated how the Bureau of Reclamation had transformed more than 1.4 million acres of arid desert into productive farmland since its founding in 1902. An illuminated map highlighted the national system of interconnected highways being constructed by the Bureau of Public Roads in partnership with local and state governments. Thanks to the Federal-Aid Highway Acts of 1916 and 1921, drivers could travel from Philadelphia as far west as Kansas on paved roads, a distance of more than eleven hundred miles.[12]

Besides government exhibits, Building No. 5 was filled with titanic testaments to America's industrial supremacy. Aisle after aisle of airplanes, trolley cars, trucks, steam locomotives, and other heavy machinery made this palace a giant toy shop to delight small boys and their fathers. Industrial Philadelphia was well represented: the Baldwin Locomotive Works showed its evolution from the original "Old Ironsides" built in 1831 to the 350-ton Santa Fe locomotive of 1926. The Atlantic Refining Company displayed a model of its vast refinery at Point Breeze, less than a mile from the fairgrounds. The J. G. Brill Company, America's largest manufacturer of streetcars and motor buses, mounted photographs of its vehicles being used by transportation systems worldwide.[13]

North of Building No. 5 stood the model military camps, home to nearly two thousand armed forces: Anthony Wayne for the U. S. Army, and Samuel Nicholas for the Marine Corps. Every day, fascinated observers watched

Changing of the Guard: Marines in the uniforms of 1776 and 1926 in front of the replica of Philadelphia's Tun Tavern, where the first recruitment drive for U.S. Marines was held in 1775.

soldiers and Marines conduct their drills, parades, and mock battles. Visitors could hunker inside the latest armored tank, weighing forty-two tons and costing $100,000. Afterward, they could relax at a replica of the Tun Tavern on Water Street, where innkeeper Samuel Nicholas recruited the first Marines in 1775. Not everyone was thrilled with the military presence: by mid-July, municipal court judges had heard six cases involving soldiers plying young girls with liquor and committing other offenses.[14]

To the north of the military camps were the two large bodies of water created when League Island Park was laid out in 1912: Edgewood Lake, renamed Edgewater Lake when the surrounding woods were cut down for the Sesqui; and Meadow Lake, transformed into a huge, concrete-lined swimming pool. At Meadow Lake, the Sesqui hosted a series of swim meets, including one where Arne Borg of Sweden broke two world's records and stole the show from American Olympic champion Johnny Weissmuller. When the pool wasn't the site of competitions, it was packed with hundreds of swimmers escaping the summer heat, despite having to pay a whole dollar to rent a bathing suit and locker.[15]

Stretched along the eastern shore of Meadow Lake were the pavilions of the six states besides Pennsylvania to erect their own buildings:

The Modernistic Illinois State Pavilion, designed by Chicago architect Andrew Rebori.

Connecticut, Delaware, Illinois, New Jersey, New York, and Ohio. Most were replicas of historic structures within each state: New York reproduced Federal Hall in New York City and Washington's Headquarters at Newburgh-on-the-Hudson; New Jersey recreated the Hessian Barracks at Trenton; and Connecticut's building was a replica of Charles Bulfinch's Old State House in Hartford. The modern Illinois pavilion, designed by Andrew Rebori, featured a large open courtyard with a cast of the Saint-Gaudens statue of Lincoln located in Chicago's Lincoln Park.[16]

Scattered around Edgewater Lake were the handful of foreign pavilions that allowed the Sesqui to maintain its dubious status as an international exposition. Most were in the early stages of construction, and would not open until the autumn. Through nests of scaffolding, one could discern the onion dome of the Persian pavilion, modeled on an ancient palace in Persepolis; the clean lines of the Modernist Cuban building; the elegant glass roof of the Beaux-Arts Argentine pavilion; and the baroque detailing of the Spanish pavilion. Congress had vetoed Sesqui participation by the Soviet Union, which it would not recognize diplomatically until 1933. But visitors could still savor Slavic fare at the Russian Tea House (the repurposed League Island Park boathouse), sipping tall glasses of tea while musicians in silk tunics strummed balalaikas.

The main entrance to the Palace of Fine Arts, where Beatrice Fenton's playful *Seaweed Girl Fountain* greeted visitors.

North of the Russia Tea House stood the Palace of Fine Arts (Building No. 9), where nearly twelve thousand works of art were on display by the end of July. Built on a tight budget, the T-shaped building was severely simple, except for a sculptural frieze by Raphael Sabatini on its central facade. Visitors approached the front entrance through ornamental gardens, passing a pool decorated with Beatrice Fenton's *Seaweed Girl Fountain*, a playful sprite atop a giant sea turtle. The building's sixty-eight thousand square feet were divided into forty-eight galleries, providing more than a mile of display space.

Works by American artists filled nearly half of the galleries, focusing on artists who had emerged in the half century since the Centennial. Along with established figures like Winslow Homer and Charles Ryder, the "advanced school" of American art was represented with works by Charles Demuth, Robert Henri, and Arthur B. Davies. Despite a sprinkling of Modernists, the majority of works shown were traditional and representational. The Palace of Fine Arts did correct one major oversight: Thomas Eakins, whose graphic and groundbreaking *Gross Clinic* had been banished from the Gallery of Art at the Centennial, was honored with a gallery of his own in 1926. The fourteen Eakins works on display included *John Biglin in a Single Scull*, *Salutat*, *Mending the Net*, and studies for *The Gross Clinic*.

Gallery 25 was filled with more than one hundred works by Auguste Rodin in various media, reflecting the newfound passion of SCEA Director Jules Mastbaum for the French sculptor. On a trip to Paris in 1923, the theatrical magnate had been captivated by a small bronze hand by Rodin he glimpsed in a shop window. Within three years, Mastbaum had acquired more than two hundred sculptures and more than six hundred drawings by the artist, and he had commissioned casts of such unrealized works as *The Gates of Hell.* Mastbaum had commissioned Paul Philippe Cret and Jacques Gréber to design a neoclassical museum for the Fairmount Parkway that would house his collection. Gallery 25 gave Sesqui visitors a preview of the future museum, including such major works as *The Thinker*, *The Three Graces*, and studies for *The Burghers of Calais*. Three other Rodin masterpieces—*Adam*, *Eve*, and *The Shadow*—graced the front entrance of the Palace of Fine Arts.[17]

After savoring this beauty, visitors could witness a traditional tea ceremony at the Japanese pavilion, a few paces east of the Palace of Fine Arts. Built in traditional style, with curved roofs and sliding rice-paper panels, this complex of buildings contained both a Japanese tea pavilion and a Formosa teahouse. To the east rose the white onion dome of the "Taj Mahal," a pavilion sponsored by a private Anglo-Indian consortium. For ten cents, visitors could tour an ersatz bazaar, where attendants in native garb peddled Kashmir shawls, Benares brasses, and Mughal carpets. Other attractions included a fakir named Amir Bux (official magician of the city of Cawnpore), a replica of an Indian jungle, and the Famous India restaurant, where Americans could sample curries and other exotic delicacies.[18]

Halfway between the Palace of Fine Arts and the Indian pavilion, the Treasure Island attraction served as the southern entrance to the Gladway amusement area. Rising from a man-made lagoon, Treasure Island had been imported from the 1924–1925 British Empire Exposition at Wembley. Its mountainous landscape was meant to represent the Canadian Rockies; a miniature Canadian Pacific train ferried passengers between shrunken versions of landmarks like Quebec's Château Frontenac. Elsewhere on the island, an enchanted village was populated with actors portraying beloved characters from children's literature, like Peter Pan and Long John Silver.[19]

Despite being recycled from Wembley, Treasure Island was one of the fresher attractions on the Gladway, a complex of lagoons, canals, and ornamental gardens north of Pattison Avenue. The scandals that had rocked the Concessions Department had caused many reputable amusement owners to steer clear of the Sesqui. As a result, many of the Gladway's cobwebbed concessions were familiar to veteran fairgoers. At the 1904 St. Louis

Treasure Island, one of the most popular attractions on the Sesqui Gladway.

"A Bit of Old Venice at the Exposition": On the fair's rare sunny days, a gondola ride through the Gladway lagoons was a good way to stay cool. In the background are the Lookout gazebo and the Japanese Tea Pavilion.

World's Fair, Colonel Frederick T. Cummins' Wild West Indian Congress and Rough Riders of the World had boasted more than 850 cowboys and Indians. By 1926, Cummins' threadbare troupe had been reduced to one hundred Indian performers, who entertained sparse crowds with tribal dances. "Fire and Flame," which recreated a conflagration on New York's Bowery, had been one of the big hits at the 1893 Chicago Fair. The Battle of Gettysburg cyclorama, a 360-degree painting of Pickett's Charge, had been touring the country since 1883. Besides these attractions, there was the usual assortment of carnival rides, as well as gondolas steered by genuine Venetian gondoliers. But overall, the Gladway was so barren of fresh amusements that one of its most popular attractions was the Louis Mark Model Shoe Factory.[20]

As with past world's fairs, foreign "villages" attempted to capture the exoticism and romance of primitive countries, presenting natives as living exhibits in a supposedly educational setting. Ensconced in a white, high-walled Kasbah, the Tunisian Village, an official exhibit of the French protectorate, scored high marks for authenticity. About eighty Arabs, Moors, and other "dusky-skinned tribesmen" peddled their wares in a souk, or served visitors authentic Tunisian cuisine, including a staple called *kouskous*. Three times a day, a muezzin climbed to the top of the mosque minaret, calling the faithful to worship with "Allah Akbar." At the other extreme, the Chinese Village was "an amusement concession making no claim to authenticity of atmosphere." Most of the Chinese villagers were "troupers," hawking cheap parasols and lacquer souvenirs. When a reporter interviewed "Princess Mong Fang" in the "Night in the Streets of Canton" revue, the princess responded in flawless English. She and the other dancers had grown up in New York City.[21]

At the southwest corner of the Gladway, the Palace of Education and Social Economy (Building No. 8) and the Pennsylvania State Building huddled together in an oasis of respectability. At only 101,684 square feet, the Palace of Education and Social Economy was the smallest of the five main palaces. It was an attempt to show the developments in education, social work, and public welfare that were moving humanity toward perfection, despite the giant step backward of the recent World War. At the heart of the building was a non-denominational, nonsectarian Meditation Chapel, with stained glass windows and a jewel-encrusted altar designed by Louis C. Tiffany. In the Auditorium, films were shown daily on such topics as international school systems, educating immigrant children, and innovative hygiene techniques.[22]

Dozens of booths profiled the achievements of academic institutions, educational associations, governmental agencies, and religious organizations.

The Palace of Education and Social Economy.

On August 18 the Episcopal Diocese of Pennsylvania unveiled a model of historic Christ Church that had been displayed at the 1876 Centennial. By then it was one of the few religious exhibits left in the palace. To protest the decision to operate the fair on Sundays, most of the major Protestant denominations—including the Baptists, Lutherans, Methodists, and Presbyterians—had withdrawn their displays, as had the Philadelphia Bible Association and the Woman's Christian Temperance Union.[23]

The Pennsylvania State Building featured numerous works of art by Pennsylvania artists. Among the installations were Daniel Garber's twenty-two-foot lunette-shaped depiction of the Delaware Water Gap, *A Wooded Watershed*, and murals by Violet Oakley that would be installed in the Supreme Court Room of the State Capitol at Harrisburg later that year. Also on display were six historic liberty bells that had been rung at the first reading of the Declaration of Independence on July 8, 1776, in the towns of Allentown, Chester, Easton, Lancaster, Reading, and York.[24]

Just below the Sesqui entrance stood the 113,000-square-foot Auditorium (Building No. 3), site of weekly concerts by Leopold Stokowski's Philadelphia Orchestra. Many programs were accompanied by the "Organists' Organ," a $150,000, eleven-thousand-pipe instrument designed by a committee of leading Philadelphia organists. But while a normal concert audience of two thousand would fill the Academy of Music, it appeared lost when scattered among the Auditorium's ten thousand seats. Even the most *fortissimo* movements evaporated quickly within the cavernous space. Soundproof curtains had to be installed that could block off the rear half of

The ten-thousand-seat Auditorium, home to the eleven-thousand-pipe Austin Opus 1416 Organ, known as the "Organists' Organ."

The Sesqui at night, when illuminated fountains and colored lighting turned it into a magical Rainbow City.

the Auditorium to improve acoustics, and camouflage the spotty attendance at many events.[25]

With the fair now operating on Sundays and its palaces open until 9:00 P.M. every night, Philadelphians packed the trolleys to League Island Park. On balmy summer nights, a complex system of ornamental lighting transformed the Sesqui into a magical Rainbow City. The Forum of the

Founders was crowded with dancers who basked in a golden glow from amber floodlights lining the vast plaza. Every night, one lucky couple won a silver cup in the Charleston contests organized by the Women's Committee. Tinted floodlights danced on the walls of the two main palaces, while brilliant beacons illuminated the golden trumpeters on their corner perches. On the west side of the Forum, a ruby light radiated through the ornate grillwork above the entrance of the Pennsylvania State Building, while a pale moonlight glow emanated from the blue pendants lining its arcades. In the center of the Gladway, the jets of an illuminated fountain magically changed color, while the reflection from hundreds of Venetian lanterns sparkled on the surface of the lagoons.[26]

In mid-August, the *New York Times* gave the Sesqui its official seal of approval:

> The Sesqui-Centennial is complete. It appears now to have lived down its hoodoo and to have begun at last to take the place that properly belongs to it as one of the great American international expositions. And it is now giving the best show for 50 cents admission that is to be had in the United States, in the judgment of the thousands who are at last pouring into the grounds from all quarters of the country. . . . even the most stiff-backed of Philadelphians, who have seemed surprisingly reluctant to admit that they have a fine thing to display to the nation, are waking up to the fact that the Sesqui really is a great exposition.[27]

While attendance increased steadily throughout the summer, revenues did not begin to meet the operating costs of the sprawling spectacle. The millionth visitor did not pass through the Sesqui turnstiles until August 7, more than two months after its opening. Every day, it cost roughly $30,000 to run the Sesqui while income hovered around $25,000, for an average daily deficit of $5,000. Mayor Kendrick announced that the fair required another $3.7 million to pay construction bills, plus $637,653 simply to keep its doors open. Publicly, Kendrick declared that the mounting debt was "not a serious situation. A world's fair is expensive. A celebration like this is cheap at any price." Behind closed doors, a frantic mayor snarled at City Council President Charles B. Hall and City Solicitor Joseph P. Gaffney, "You people have got me into this fix, now get me out of it!" But City Hall could not spend its way out of this situation. Its borrowing capacity had shrunk from $60 million at the start of 1926 to under $3 million by the end of July, thanks to its numerous construction and improvement projects.[28]

After hasty negotiation, an emergency bond issue was arranged to bail out the Sesqui. Only one financial company expressed interest in purchasing these bonds at public auction, a clear indication of the low opinion bankers held of the fair's creditworthiness. With its back against the wall, the city pressured its Sinking Fund Commission, the watchdog agency supposed to safeguard money set aside for the repayment of long-term municipal debt, to purchase $2 million of the Sesqui bonds. The Sinking Fund Commission consisted of Mayor Kendrick, SCEA Director Edward T. Stotesbury, the oddly named City Controller WillB Hadley, and Second Deputy Controller John J. Leyburn.[29]

Politicians scrambled to find a more permanent solution to funding the Sesqui. They pored over municipal plans, looking for an uninitiated project that could be killed, and its budgetary allocation transferred to the Sesqui. Of the city's total funded debt of $501 million, more than $139 million had not actually been issued, but had been earmarked for civic improvements still in the planning stages. Among them was Victory Hall, the monument to the noble war dead that had been on the books for years. Its $5.3 million allocation would cover the Sesqui bill handily. Also vulnerable was the proposed Parkway subway-Roxborough elevated line, with a price tag of $7.5 million. But a public referendum would be required to approve the transfer of appropriations from one project to another, and such a referendum would have to wait until the fall.[30]

With the emergency bond issue providing a temporary trickle of liquidity to the Sesqui, Mayor Kendrick was able to resume his normally cocksure stance. "Although we are faced with a deficit of $3,750,000, I am not discouraged. In fact, I do not know what the word means," he told hundreds of local businessmen at a luncheon. "There are big things coming down at the Sesqui," he assured reporters. "The gate receipts are increasing every day, and I believe that on Labor Day there will be gathered the biggest crowd in the history of expositions."[31]

Despite Kendrick's reassurances, ripples from the funding crisis shook the Sesqui. A minor recession hit South Philadelphia when several thousand jobs were slashed from the Sesqui work force, reducing the weekly payroll by nearly $10,000. Construction ceased immediately on the Tower of Light, its naked skeleton still looming over the Court of Honor. A black-and-white drawing of the finished Tower in its Art Deco glory would appear on the daily program until early September, when it was replaced with a photograph of the Liberty Bell at Oregon Plaza.[32]

Meanwhile, Sesqui concessionaires struggled to cope with low attendance and revenues. In late July the Ober-Bayern Restaurant, a Bavarian eatery on the Gladway, closed its doors. Anticipating more than thirty million customers, its managers had spent $180,000 to build a five-thousand-seat restaurant in a hangar-like reproduction of a building on the Nuremburg Hauptmarkt. Anxious for authenticity, they imported 150 Bavarians to act as servers and entertainers. Unable to sustain their daily overhead of $9,000, the managers vanished, leaving their staff penniless in Philadelphia. The local German American community organized a team to feed and house the stranded Bavarians until they could raise the funds to return them to Germany. Rather than tolerate a huge shuttered building in the midst of the Gladway, the SCEA reopened the restaurant as the Alpine Haus, re-employing some of the Bavarians. By the end of summer, the SCEA would be operating a score of other bankrupted concessions.[33]

Hoping to avoid a similar fate, some concessionaires turned litigious. The owner of the "Through the Orient" attraction sued Sesqui management for violating the exclusivity clause of his contract by allowing another "Oriental" concession, the Tunisian Village, to operate nearby. Employing the wisdom of Solomon, the presiding judge ruled, "Tunis is of the Occident, but camel riding, snake charming, fortune telling and gyrating dancing girls are distinctly of the Orient." Therefore, such activities were barred at the Tunisian Village. The normally genteel neighborhood of the High Street of 1776 threatened to turn ugly when Beatrix Sherman, who had traced the profiles of Theodore Roosevelt and Woodrow Wilson, brought suit against competing silhouette artist Le Baron Henri Scotford, operator of the Snip Sketch Studio, insisting that her contract gave her the exclusive right to execute and sell "shadow portraits" at the Sesqui.[34]

Irritating as these petty lawsuits were to the SCEA, they paled next to the larger legal challenge to operating the fair on Sundays. The growing crowds on Sunday were one of the few bright spots at the Sesqui: attendance jumped from fifty-four thousand on July 4, the first open Sunday, to nearly one hundred thousand on July 25. For many Philadelphians who still worked six days a week, Sunday was their only chance to visit the fair. For most concessionaires, Sunday crowds were their only chance to stay solvent. This perceived violation of the Sabbath offended religious leaders and conservative Pennsylvanians, and gave Governor Gifford Pinchot ammunition against the Sesqui and its Organization sponsors. Prompted by Pinchot, the state attorney general charged that the Sesqui-Centennial was violating its state charter and breaking the Pennsylvania Blue Laws of 1794, which banned most amusements and commercial activities on the Sabbath.

Director-General Austin was hauled into court and fined for violation of the Blue Laws by allowing concessionaires to charge fees on Sunday.

Sesqui management responded by suspending all Sunday amusement and concession fees; the fifty-cent general admission would give visitors access to every Gladway attraction for free. This decision forced the SCEA to reimburse concessionaires for lost revenues, draining $10,000 from their coffers each week. Church groups hired undercover detectives to prowl the Gladway on Sundays, trying to provoke a legal challenge by persuading concessionaires to sell them a hot dog or a Liberty Belle dolly.

In early August Common Pleas Court Judge Edwin O. Lewis ruled that it was illegal for the Sesqui to charge any admission fee on Sunday, or to operate any amusements, free or not. This ruling could have cost the Sesqui more than $1 million, spelling ruin for the already-struggling fair. An enraged Mayor Kendrick proposed shutting Philadelphia down completely to give it "a real closed Sunday under the Blue Laws of 1794," with no trolleys or taxis allowed to run. Despite the court order, the SCEA continued to operate the fair on Sundays with the regular fifty-cent admission intact. The legal battle between the Sesqui and the city of Philadelphia versus the Sabbatarians and the Commonwealth of Pennsylvania would drag on throughout the fall, with SCEA officials being summoned to court on a regular basis.[35]

On top of its other plagues, the Sesqui had the misfortune to coincide with one of the worst summers ever to hit Philadelphia, meteorologically speaking. A deadly heat wave smothered much of the United States during July and August. Philadelphia suffered through a string of days where the temperature soared above 90, hitting an all-time record of 101 degrees in late July. Anyone who could afford to leave on vacation fled to the mountains or the shore, while the rest of the city dragged itself through the suffocating air. Fairmount Park resembled a refugee camp at night, filled with Philadelphians who had fled their oven-hot row houses and dragged their bedding to the relative cool of the woods. While the unbearable heat produced record crowds at the Meadow Lake swimming pool, it was another reason for Americans to avoid Philadelphia that summer.[36]

The heat wave was punctuated by a series of ferocious storms that washed away newly replanted landscapes and freshly repaved roads at the Sesqui, and battered the shoddily built structures. Following the July 4 storm, another deluge on July 15 dropped several inches of rain on the city in less than twenty-four hours, flooding the Broad Street Subway. At the Sesqui, most of the palaces were damaged, along with many Gladway attractions.[37]

A major casualty of the July 15 storm was *Freedom*, a massive theatrical spectacle at the Sesqui Stadium that had to be halted in mid-performance when fierce winds nearly blew actors off the stage. It was the seventh of eight scheduled presentations to be postponed or interrupted by weather. Unlike other pageants that relied on unpaid volunteers, *Freedom* was a professional enterprise, mounted by New York impresario R. H. Burnside. Billed as "the largest show of its kind ever produced," it employed 4,347 people, including 75 principals, 1,500 extras, a 1,000-voice chorus, a ballet troupe of 250, an orchestra of 125, and a menagerie of elephants, camels, horses, and papier-mâché dinosaurs. Performances took place on a 200-by-300 foot stage erected at the open end of the Stadium. The first performance was scheduled for Saturday, July 3, with the pageant to be presented three times a week until the first week of October.

The scenario for *Freedom* traced man's quest for liberty through the ages in fifty tableaux. Beginning in prehistory, when cavemen battled for independence from "the icthyosaurui" and "the tyrannosaurui," the pageant followed a convoluted path to the present day. Historical vignettes depicted critical moments, including the assassination of Caesar, Columbus discovering America, and the signing of the Declaration of Independence.

Oscar Ragland, as General George Washington, and Sarah Edwards, as Betsy Ross, discuss the fine points of flag making in *Freedom*. The rainy weather of the summer of 1926 would doom the expensive spectacle.

Between the vignettes, the mood was lightened by ballets, acrobatics, and four performing elephants. The show concluded with a spectacular "Ballet of the Cities," celebrating the New Declaration of World Peace of 1926, set to music by John Philip Sousa.[38]

Burnside, a veteran producer, had taken out a $150,000 rain insurance policy. But the policy paid off only if rain began before the curtain rose, forcing a complete cancellation. With almost diabolical timing, the first drops inevitably fell once the show was under way. By mid-August the show had been stopped by rain eleven times, and Burnside was $170,000 in the hole. The star, DeWolf Hopper, declared *Freedom* to be the "raining success" of the Sesqui. Its performers grew adept at dashing over to the usually dark Auditorium and staging an impromptu cabaret once the weather stopped their outdoor pageant. Hopper performed Gilbert and Sullivan ditties, the four elephants danced a shimmy, and female lead Belle Story brought down the house with her rousing rendition of "Philadelphia, My Home Town."[39]

In early September Burnside threw in the towel and announced that *Freedom* would close after its September 11 performance. Although the show had been scheduled to run for another three weeks, its producer was nearly bankrupt after seeing eighteen out of twenty-eight scheduled performances washed away. Staying true to form, the final performance of *Freedom* was also called on account of rain.[40]

Within forty-eight hours, Burnside's vast stage was being demolished in preparation for the next big show. While workers carted away cardboard chariots and papier-mâché dinosaurs, carpenters began to erect twenty-two thousand additional seats across the open end of the Stadium. Three weeks earlier, boxing promoter Tex Rickard had electrified Philadelphia by announcing that the next world heavyweight championship bout would take place at Sesqui Stadium. On September 23 champion Jack Dempsey, the "Manassa Mauler," would defend his title against challenger Gene Tunney, the "Fighting Marine." Now, the Stadium was being turned into a giant boxing ring, capable of hosting 150,000 spectators for "the Fight of the Century."[41]

As September began, Kendrick had some grounds to be cautiously optimistic about the Sesqui. City Council, meeting for the first time since July, had unanimously resolved to honor its earlier pledge to provide "at least five million dollars, and so much more as may be required," to carry the Sesqui to a successful conclusion. The city's unreserved willingness to back the Sesqui placated its major creditors for the time being. While the fair was still drowning in debt, it appeared to be benefitting the local economy. The latest National City Bank monthly review of finance and trade had noted a healthy increase in economic activity in the Philadelphia district, "doubtless reflecting the effects on business of the Sesqui-Centennial Exposition."[42]

With September would come autumn and cooler weather, perhaps persuading hesitant travelers to flock to Philadelphia in 1926 as they had come after the brutal summer of 1876. A lengthy article on the Sesqui was due to appear in the September 11 edition of the *Saturday Evening Post*, read by nearly three million Americans every week. The five-day National Air Races would attract armies of aviation enthusiasts in mid-September, when the Navy dirigible *Los Angeles* would float above the fairgrounds. After that would come the much-anticipated Dempsey-Tunney fight. There were dozens of conventions slated for Philadelphia during the fall, helping to swell Sesqui attendance over the next ninety days.[43]

During its first three months, only 1,638,084 people had attended the Sesqui-Centennial, a shamefully low number for a so-called international exposition. But they had come in greater numbers every month: 271,593 in June; 562,183 in July; and 804,308 in August. Now that the Sesqui had survived its initial trials by fire and water, would the gods finally smile and allow it to attract thirty million visitors in its remaining three months?[44]

NOTES

1. "Tourist Influx Begins at Sesqui," *PB*, July 8, 1926; "Sesquicentennial Is Now Complete," *NYT*, August 22, 1926.

2. Allen, *Only Yesterday*, p. 180; Leuchtenburg, *The Perils of Prosperity 1914–32*, pp. 188–189.

3. Austin and Hauser, *The Sesqui-Centennial International Exposition*, pp. 306–338; Cardinell, *A Pictorial Record of the Sesqui-Centennial International Exposition*, 1926.

4. Leuchtenburg, *The Perils of Prosperity 1914–32*, pp. 193–94, 200. White, "The Great American Real Estate Bubble of the 1920s: Causes and Consequences," Rutgers University Department of Economics; Rudel, *Hello, Everybody!* pp. 47, 105, 231.

5. Blaszczyk, *The Color Revolution*, pp. 1, 16, 24; Leuchtenburg, *The Perils of Prosperity 1914–32*, p. 182.

6. "Huge Sesqui Light Nears Completion," *PB*, July 19, 1926.

7. Leuchtenburg, *The Perils of Prosperity 1914–32*, pp. 180–181, 192; Austin and Hauser, *The Sesqui-Centennial International Exposition*, pp. 81, 94–96, 339–354.

8. "Sesqui Army Show Recalls War Time," *PB*, July 10, 1926; "Sesquicentennial Is Now Complete," *NYT*, August 22, 1926.

9. "Rodeo Full of Thrills," *PB*, July 13, 1926.

10. Austin and Hauser, *The Sesqui-Centennial International Exposition*, pp. 187–188; "Hawaiians Dance and Sing at Sesqui," *PB*, July 7, 1926; "Chief Surprises Sesqui Aviators," *PI*, July 10, 1926; "Army Airship Here as Sesqui Exhibit," *PB*, July 16, 1926.

11. "Uncle Sam's Work on View at Sesqui," *PB*, August 5, 1926.

12. Austin and Hauser, *The Sesqui-Centennial International Exposition*, pp. 104–121; "Uncle Sam's Work on View at Sesqui," *PB*, August 5, 1926; "Irrigation 'Magic' Bared at Exhibit," *PB*, August 27, 1926; Leuchtenburg, *The Perils of Prosperity 1914–32*, p. 185.

13. Austin and Hauser, *The Sesqui-Centennial International Exposition*, pp. 355–364.

14. Ibid., pp. 183–189; "Sesqui Army Show Recalls War Time," *PB*, July 10, 1926; "Three Soldiers Guilty," *NYT*, July 13, 1926; "Court Warns Soldiers as Sixth Is Acquitted," *PB*, July 14, 1926.

15. "Fee for Sesqui Bathing," *PB*, July 6, 1926.

16. *Report of the Illinois Commission of the Sesqui-Centennial International Exposition Philadelphia 1926*; Austin and Hauser, *The Sesqui-Centennial International Exposition*, pp. 122–127.

17. *Paintings, Sculpture and Prints in the Department of Fine Arts, Sesqui-Centennial International Exposition*, Philadelphia 1926, pp. 96–98; Austin and Hauser, *The Sesqui-Centennial International Exposition*, p. 96; Thomas H. Keels, "Rodin Museum Reopens to the Public," *PhiladelphiaStyle*, Fall 2012, pp. 130–133.

18. Austin and Hauser, *The Sesqui-Centennial International Exposition*, pp. 93–94; "A King's Ransom in Jewels at Sesqui," *PI*, August 1, 1926; "Sesquicentennial Is Now Complete," *NYT*, August 22, 1926.

19. Austin and Hauser, *The Sesqui-Centennial International Exposition*, p. 373; "Philadelphia Fair a Mecca for Women," NYT, August 29, 1926.

20. Austin and Hauser, *The Sesqui-Centennial International Exposition*, pp. 372–375.

21. "Tunisian Village Real Desert Camp," *PB*, July 22, 1926; Austin and Hauser, *The Sesqui-Centennial International Exposition*, p. 374; "Chinese Village Real Melting Pot," *PB*, August 9, 1926.

22. Leuchtenburg, *The Perils of Prosperity 1914–32*, pp. 201–202.

23. Austin and Hauser, *The Sesqui-Centennial International Exposition*, pp. 249–270; "Presbyterians Quit Sesquicentennial," *NYT*, July 7, 1926; "Lutherans Attack Sunday Expo," *NYT*, July 8, 1926; "W.C.T.U. Quits Big Fair," *NYT*, July 16, 1926; "Sunday Hosts Visit Philadelphia Fair," *NYT*, July 26, 1926; "Episcopal Exhibit Opens," *PB*, August 18, 1926.

24. Austin and Hauser, *The Sesqui-Centennial International Exposition*, pp. 130–146.

25. Ibid., pp. 365–367; "Tourist Influx Begins at Sesqui," *PB*, July 8, 1926; "The Sesqui Orchestra," *PB*, July 29, 1926.

26. Austin and Hauser, *The Sesqui-Centennial International Exposition*, pp. 68–69.

27. "Sunday Hosts Visit Philadelphia Fair," *NYT*, July 26, 1926; "Sesqui Hours Extended," *PB*, July 27, 1926; "Sesquicentennial Is Now Complete," *NYT*, August 22, 1926.

28. "Sesqui Financing Fixed, Mayor Hints," PB, July 28, 1926.

29. "Sinking Fund Gets Philadelphia Issue," *NYT*, July 8, 1926; "Mayor Hopes for Sesqui Solution," *PB*, July 26, 1926; "Sesqui Requires $3.7M More, Says Kendrick," *PB*, July 27, 1926; "Only Two Bidders for Sesqui Emergency Loan," *PB*, July 28, 1926; "Sesqui Financing Fixed, Mayor Hints," *PB*, July 28, 1926.

30. "Kendrick Administration is Hunting the Garret for an Unused $5M," *PB*, August 11, 1926.

31. "Mayor Says Sesqui Finances Arranged," *PB*, August 7, 1926; "Sunday Sesqui Crowds Break Record with 68,500," *PB*, August 9, 1926; "Declares Sesqui 'Over Sick Period,'" *PB*, August 18, 1926.

32. "Tower of Light Awaits Finances," *PB*, July 31, 1926; "Sesqui Wages Cut $9,689.32 per Week," *PB*, August 9, 1926.

33. Austin and Hauser, *The Sesqui-Centennial International Exposition*, p. 375; "Bavarian Restaurant at Sesqui Has Failed," *PB*, July 28, 1926; "Sesqui Bavarians Stranded in City," *PB*, August 4, 1926; "Plan Move to Aid 75 Stranded Girls," *PB*, August 5, 1926; "See Plan to Run Sesqui Next Year," *PB*, August 26, 1926.

34. "Sesqui Officials Sued by Exhibitor," *PB*, August 6, 1926; "Court to Define Limits of Orient," *PB*, August 10, 1926; "Court Restrains Tunisian Village," *PB*, August 17, 1926; "Silhouette Fight Reopens," *PB*, August 4, 1926; "Sues to Oust 'Squatters,'" *PB*, August 10, 1926.

35. "Pennsylvania Acts to Curb Sunday Fair," *NYT*, July 18, 1926; "Sunday Sesqui Crowds Break Record with 68,500," *PB*, August 9, 1926; "Fair Director Fined in Philadelphia," *NYT*, July 25, 1926; "Sunday Opening of Sesquicentennial Banned by Judge If Admission Fees Are Charged," *NYT*, August 11, 1926; "Sunday Sesqui Ban Might Cost Million," *PB*, August 12, 1926.

36. "Sizzling Heat in Capital," *NYT*, July 11, 1926; "Water Runs Low as City Sizzles on Its Hottest August 3 on Record," *PPL*, August 4, 1926; "Heat Overcomes 23; Relief Is Promised," *NYT*, August 5, 1926; "Think It's Hot Now? Worst Is Yet to Come," *PI*, July 19, 2011.

37. "Sesqui Hit Hard by Heavy Rain," *PB*, July 16, 1926.

38. "To Direct Pageant," *PB*, April 8, 1926; "A Spectacle of Freedom," *PB*, July 3, 1926; "'Freedom' Pageant Stirs Big Throng," *PR*, July 4, 1926; "The Sesqui Pageant," *PB*, July 6, 1926; "Freedom" program.

39. "Rain Policy on 'Freedom,'" *PB*, June 23, 1926; "'Freedom' Loses $100K by Rain," *PPL*, July 16, 1926; "160K See 'Freedom,'" *NYT*, July 26, 1926; "New Revue at Sesqui," *PB*, August 9, 1926; "Sesqui Pageant Hit by Storms," *PB*, August 19, 1926.

40. "'Freedom' Closes Saturday," *PB*, 8 September 1926; "Chester Day Concert," *PB*, 11 September 1926.

41. "Dempsey Title Bout Suddenly Shifted to Philadelphia," *NYT*, 19 August 1926.

42. "Record Fall Trade Foreseen by Bank," *NYT*, 2 September 1926; "Council Pledges Funds for Sesqui," *PB*, 3 September 1926; "Railroads Prepare for Record Holiday Travel," *NYT*, 4 September 1926; "Title Bout Site Will Be Enlarged," *NYT*, 5 September 1926.

43. Frazer, "1776-1926 at the Sesqui-Centennial," *The Saturday Evening Post*, 11 September 1926, pp. 50–56.

44. "Paid Attendance at Sesqui 4,622,211," *PB*, 1 December 1926.

9

★ ★ ★

We're All Good Americans Now

THE PALACE OF Education and Social Economy was one of the more sedate spots at the Sesqui-Centennial, dedicated to the "betterment, advancement, and enhancement of humanity." The humble building on the north side of Pattison Avenue seemed bathed in a nostalgic haze, as if the mass slaughter of 1914–1918 had never occurred. Inside the palace, the early twentieth-century Progressive vision of a steady and earnest march toward human perfection was still an engaging reality, and not a pointless lockstep toward "an intolerable utopia of dull citizens," in the words of author Malcolm Cowley.[1]

A nine-thousand-square-foot exhibit demonstrated every aspect of a modern American public school from kindergarten to senior high. Under a seal depicting a giant pair of scissors, the Needlework Guild of America showed photographs of its sewing circles at work, and the distribution of its handiwork to the deserving poor. To entertain visitors, Miss Martha Washington, great-great-grandniece of the first president, sang ballads while accompanying herself on an antique banjo.[2]

Compared with these staid attractions, the booth of the American Eugenics Society (AES) stood out like one of Jules Mastbaum's movie palaces, with bright red lights flashing at varying speeds. One light signaled that an American was born every sixteen seconds. A bulb that blinked every forty-eight seconds heralded the birth of one "who will never grow up beyond the mental age of 8," joining the growing army of Americans who "are born to be a burden on the rest." Another beacon indicated that "every 15 seconds $100 of your money goes to the care of persons with bad heredity such as

AMERICAN EUGENICS SOCIETY
SOME PEOPLE ARE BORN TO BE A BURDEN ON THE REST.
LEARN ABOUT HEREDITY YOU CAN HELP TO CORRECT THESE CONDITIONS.
AMERICA NEEDS
LESS OF THESE
MORE OF THESE
DOES INHERITANCE COUNT?
NUMBER OF DESCENDANTS IN 1911
MENDEL'S THEATRE
GOOD HEREDITY
See how your family record compares with the NATIONAL EUGENIC STANDARDS
INHERITANCE OF COLOR
Everybody knows that like produces like
But this is true only when the parents are pure-blooded
LOOK AT THESE GUINEA PIGS for INSTANCE
Mendel discovered that each trait has two determiners
The animal or plant gets one from each parent
Pure White
4 Pure White
Pure Black
4 Pure Black
Hybrid Black
PRESSMEN AND ASSIST
NORTH AMERICA

the insane, feeble-minded, criminals and other defectives." Meanwhile, one light flickered only once every seven and a half minutes. That was how often "a high grade person" was born in America, a dynamo who would "have ability to do creative work and be fit for leadership." Only 4 percent of America's population fell into this class. "How long are we Americans to be so careful for the pedigree of our pigs and chickens and cattle," demanded the accompanying placard, "and then leave the ancestry of our children to chance or to 'blind' sentiment?"

Thanks to the three-year-old AES, hope was at hand to deal with this predicament. Sesqui visitors could read "A Eugenics Catechism," an AES pamphlet defining eugenics as "the study of those agencies under social control which may improve or impair the inborn qualities of future generations of man either physically or mentally." According to the "Catechism," eugenics was the application of long-accepted principles of animal husbandry to the human race, refined by advances in the field of Mendelian genetics. Like cattle, superior human stock should be encouraged to breed as often as possible to create a continually improving progeny. Meanwhile, genetically challenged humans should be dissuaded from reproduction, by whatever means necessary. In this way, eugenics would eliminate not only mental retardation but its attendant evils: poverty, crime, sloth, and immorality.[3]

The message spelled out by the flashing lights of the AES was painfully clear. America—the old-line America composed of superior northern European stock, or "Nordics" in eugenics-speak—was under siege from the immigrating hordes of "Alpines" (southern Europeans) and "Mediterraneans" (eastern Europeans), not to mention the armies of American Negroes moving north to the great industrial cities. These geo-racial terms had been popularized by Madison Grant in his 1916 polemic, *The Passing of the Great Race*. Grant claimed that the Nordic caste ("the white man par excellence") was being polluted by Alpines ("submissive peasants") and Mediterraneans ("inferior in bodily stamina").[4]

This genetic mongrelization would lead inevitably to the collapse of Western civilization, a fear that haunted many Americans even as their country reached new heights of power. "The advanced races of mankind are going backward," Albert Edward Wiggam had warned in his 1922 best seller, *The New Decalogue of Science*. "The civilized races of the world are

---

FACING PAGE: Part of the American Eugenics Society display in the Palace of Education and Social Economy. By 1926, the three-year-old AES was becoming a powerful force in American social policy and planning. (Courtesy of the American Philosophical Society.)

biologically plunging downward." Wiggam told his readers to forget about the Biblical Golden Rule of "Do unto others as you would have them do unto you." The new "biological Golden Rule" commanded them to "do unto both the born and the unborn as you would have both the born and the unborn do unto you."[5]

Similarly, Americans would have to reconsider their uncritical acceptance of Europe's "teeming masses yearning to be set free." Charles B. Davenport, Harvard professor and America's foremost eugenicist, announced that "the idea of a 'melting pot' belongs to a pre-Mendelian age."[6] Unless Americans obeyed the new commandments of eugenics, they would be overwhelmed by fecund, foreign-born hordes of morons, idiots, and imbeciles. Just as a dictatorial degree of governmental control had helped the United States win the Great World War in 1918, authoritarian oversight of procreation would win the Great Eugenics War. Nothing less would keep America's citizenry intelligent and productive, its asylums and prisons empty, and its treasury full.[7]

These arguments, ridiculous as they may sound today, were absorbed with intense interest by visitors to the AES booth at the Sesqui-Centennial. In 1926 the AES had the financial backing of J. P. Morgan and John D. Rockefeller, the intellectual endorsement of Harvard University president Charles W. Eliot, and the political support of Pennsylvania Governor Gifford Pinchot. Birth control pioneer Margaret Sanger embraced eugenics, since "the chief issue of birth control" was "more children from the fit, less from the unfit." At the Sesqui, the booth for her American Birth Control League (precursor to Planned Parenthood) stood next to the AES exhibit.[8]

AES lobbying, led by society cofounder Dr. Harry Laughlin (who served as Expert Eugenics Agent for Congress), had ensured the passage of the American Immigration Restriction Act of 1924, also known as the Johnson-Reed Act. This law sharply reduced the number of foreign-born immigrants from such "inferior" regions as southern and eastern Europe, which had provided most of the roughly fifteen million immigrants to America between 1900 and 1915. On May 26, 1924, the immigration bill was signed into law by President Calvin Coolidge. As vice president, Coolidge had written in *Good Housekeeping* that "America must be kept American. Biological laws show that Nordics deteriorate when mixed with other races."[9]

At about the time of the Sesqui, the AES began to shift its strategy from such relatively benign events as Fitter Families Contests to the involuntary sterilization of those deemed mentally and morally deficient. Not long after the fair closed, AES expert testimony would persuade the U.S. Supreme Court to rule that compulsory sterilization was constitutional in

Buck v. Bell (274 U.S. 200 1927). This ruling authorized the Commonwealth of Virginia to sterilize Carrie Buck, an eighteen-year-old single mother whom the state had labeled a "moral imbecile." *Buck v. Bell* would invest the medical procedure of involuntary sterilization with national legitimacy. The number of states with sterilization laws, which had grown from six in 1911 to sixteen by 1917, would rise to twenty-eight by 1931. Between 1907 and 1928, fewer than nine thousand Americans were subjected to eugenic sterilization. By 1941 the number of sterilized Americans would rise to nearly thirty-six thousand, with an average of twenty-seven hundred procedures taking place each year during the 1930s.[10]

On January 1, 1934, the obedient cabinet of German Chancellor Adolf Hitler would enact the Law for the Prevention of Hereditarily Diseased Offspring, the opening act in Nazi Germany's march toward genocide. The law, which would force 225,000 people to be involuntarily sterilized within three years, would use American sterilization laws as its model. Throughout the 1930s, testimony by AES cofounder Harry Laughlin would back congressional decisions to prevent European Jews seeking to escape the growing Holocaust from entering the United States. In 1936, Heidelberg University would confer an honorary doctorate of medicine upon Laughlin for his contributions to the science of "race hygiene." This award would illustrate how far Laughlin and the AES had traveled during the decade that began so innocuously with the flashing lights and hand-lettered placards at the Philadelphia Sesqui.[11]

The hysterical xenophobia of the AES, cloaked in patriotism and pseudoscience, was only one indication of the fault lines throbbing beneath the prosperous, optimistic surface of the United States in the mid-1920s. Many Americans, basking in the Goldilocks economy of 1926, had adopted a double vision in their outlook. They supported the innate conservatism of the government and big business, and often expressed a desire to see the country revert to its traditional values of patriotism and piety. Yet they were growing more tolerant of modernity and cosmopolitanism. Middle-class Americans accepted their wives' bobbed hair and knee-high skirts; expected their daughters as well as sons to go to college and work afterward; enjoyed recordings by "race musicians" like Louis Armstrong and Jelly Roll Morton; watched films produced by Jews like Adolph Zukor and Louis B. Mayer; skipped church on Sunday for golf at the country club; and flagrantly flouted the law by drinking liquor.

In 1926 the Jewish songwriting team of Richard Rodgers and Lorenz Hart penned a tune called "Bugle Blow" for the Ziegfeld extravaganza *Betsy*, a paean to a polyglot America unified by popular culture. Hart's clever lyrics described how "a race that used to be gypped by the Pharaohs down in Egypt" had blended with other races thanks to jazz. The happy result was that "we're all good Americans now!"[12]

Despite the rosy picture painted by Rodgers and Hart of a diverse and accepting America, millions of their countrymen defined "good American" much more strictly than they did. During the 1920s, according to historian Robert Moats Miller, "an outraged citizenry participated in a gigantic police line-up to identify the enemies of society, with each 'good' American fingering a different suspect: uppity Negro, conspiratorial Catholic, avaricious Jew, dirty Mexican, wily Oriental, bloody-handed Bolshevik, scabrous bootlegger." In 1926, Philadelphia and the Sesqui-Centennial became an unwitting battlefield for the warring factions who sought to dictate who did and did not belong in the United States.[13]

Among those with an extremely narrow definition of a good American were industrialist Henry Ford, publisher of the weekly newspaper, the *Dearborn Independent*; his editor, Ernest Gustav Liebold; and *Independent* writer William A. M'Garry. For most of the 1920s, the *Independent* served as the primary envoy for the resurgent anti-Semitism poisoning American society, starting with an article entitled, "The International Jew: The World's Problem" on May 22, 1920. Every week for ninety weeks, the *Independent* enlightened Americans about the growing Jewish stranglehold on international finance, commerce, mass media, and sports. During this period, its circulation soared from seventy thousand to nine hundred thousand, making it one of the most widely read publications in America. Among its foreign readers was Nazi leader Adolf Hitler, who incorporated ideas from the *Independent* and other writings by Ford into *Mein Kampf*.[14]

Beginning in 1923, the *Dearborn Independent* began to pay attention to the floundering Sesqui-Centennial, and the efforts of certain Philadelphians to keep it afloat. The newspaper focused on three Philadelphia Jews whose actions guaranteed the survival of the Sesqui: department store magnate Ellis A. Gimbel, financier and realtor Albert M. Greenfield, and theater owner Jules E. Mastbaum. Gimbel, Greenfield, and Mastbaum were among Philadelphia's wealthiest and most prominent businessmen in the 1920s. By 1926 Gimbel Brothers boasted six stores and twenty-three thousand employees in four cities, along with Saks and Company in New York. Besides owning the real estate firm of Mastbaum and Fleisher, Jules Mastbaum controlled the Stanley Company of America, which operated 257 theaters and was valued at more than $46 million. Greenfield, Philadelphia's largest realtor, was assembling a financial empire that would encompass commercial banking, mortgage financing, and insurance. Greenfield was

Ellis Gimbel, department store magnate, philanthropist, and SCEA director, in May 1926. (Prints and Photographs Division, Library of Congress.)

also emerging as a political power broker, thanks to his financial support of the Organization and his friendship with William S. Vare.[15]

Besides their interest in the Sesqui, the three men were united by overlapping ties of family, friendship, and commerce. Mastbaum was a Gimbel brother-in-law twice over: his sister Minnie was the wife of Ellis Gimbel, while his sister Julia married Louis Gimbel, president of the New York store. Greenfield called Mastbaum "my closest friend," and collaborated with him on numerous deals. Gimbel had been a partner in the syndicate led by Greenfield to finance the Benjamin Franklin Hotel, across the street from his department store. All three men were prominent in Philadelphia philanthropy, especially the Federation of Jewish Charities. In 1922, at the height of the postwar recession, the Federation raised $1,250,000 in a ten-day drive, with Greenfield as campaign chairman and Gimbel and Mastbaum as his deputies.[16]

Gimbel, Greenfield, and Mastbaum stepped into the Sesqui power vacuum that emerged during the early 1920s, when many of Philadelphia's prominent Gentiles were abandoning the fair. Named directors of the Sesqui-Centennial Exhibition Association in 1921, Gimbel and Mastbaum were appointed to the SCEA Advisory Executive Committee in 1922. The following year, they were joined by Greenfield. All three men threw their considerable energies into salvaging the struggling Sesqui. As finance chairman of the SCEA, Greenfield masterminded the sale of $3 million of "participating certificates" to the public in 1925, enabling the SCEA to begin construction. Both Gimbel and Mastbaum were major supporters of this campaign, purchasing large blocks of certificates through their businesses.[17]

Mayor W. Freeland Kendrick and Jules Mastbaum greet Mayor James J. Walker of New York City, a friend and protégé of Mastbaum, at Broad Street Station in January 1926.

For their efforts, the three men were vilified by the *Dearborn Independent*, beginning with a March 1923 article entitled, "Philadelphia, Victim of Land Speculators, Sees Independence Fair Plans Fade Away." Writer William A. M'Garry laid the failure of the Sesqui at the feet of Philadelphia's "clique of Jewish speculators," who had hijacked John Wanamaker's patriotic dream and poisoned it with their greed. M'Garry fully expected these speculators to deny his charges, for "the inability of the Hebrew to admit that he has overreached himself is the fatal weakness of the race even in its own chosen fields of barter and finance."

M'Garry described how homes near the proposed Sesqui site on the Parkway, priced at $2,000 to $3,000 before the war, were now going for $4,000 to $5,000. Greenfield, "recognized as the most active of the real estate speculators in Philadelphia," had one Arch Street property priced at $45,000 that jumped to $65,000 on the day the Parkway site was recommended. But M'Garry also fingered Gimbel and Mastbaum as two other Jewish "speculators" responsible for the Sesqui's failure. M'Garry characterized the election of Mastbaum, "head of the so-called motion picture trust," to the SCEA Board of Directors as "the last straw," marking the "complete disappearance of circumspection on the part of the real estate speculators." Thanks to the unrelenting greed of Jewish realtors, M'Garry charged, the Sesqui was beyond salvation.[18]

Albert M. Greenfield, financial angel of the Sesqui, during his Senate testimony on his role in backing William Vare's Senate campaign. One newspaper described Greenfield as "so rich he can't count his money."

M'Garry continued his attack in the next issue of the *Independent*. Greenfield had taken out advertisements in Philadelphia newspapers, promising that "the Sesqui-Centennial will be worth every penny that it costs, no matter what it will cost." M'Garry alleged that, despite his ballyhooing, Greenfield had yet to fulfill his own $10,000 pledge to the SCEA. "The pressure that has been brought to bear by the frantic money seekers has not been without amusing side lights," M'Garry sneered. "Unquestionably, many speculators who went into the business of inflating real estate prices are doomed to bankruptcy." At least, M'Garry implied, the experience was providing a few chuckles for Philadelphia's Gentiles: "Many leading citizens who have not taken a stand openly against the exposition for business reasons are nevertheless making no secret of their amusement at the frantic efforts of the speculators to get something done."[19]

As the Sesqui stumbled toward its opening, it continued to attract the censure of the *Dearborn Independent*. In the wake of the William Abrahams concession scandal, the *Independent* published an article in April 1926 entitled, "Jews Grab Sesqui-Centennial Plums," which charged that the former director of concessions had granted many of the Sesqui's key concessions to his coreligionists. As proof, the article included a list of the names of sixty-two concessionaires, "22 of whom are apparently Jews." The article concluded with the sarcastic note that of the Sesqui's original supporters, "all are out except

Albert M. Greenfield . . . the Mastbaums and the Gimbels and other patriotic Americans." The *Independent*'s moral was clear: Jews had commandeered the Sesqui-Centennial at every level and at every stage, prostituting the celebration of American independence for their own enrichment.[20]

Along with Henry Ford and the staff of the *Dearborn Independent*, the estimated five million members of the Ku Klux Klan also held a much stricter definition of what constituted a good American. Reborn on a Georgia mountaintop on Thanksgiving 1915, the KKK saw its membership thrive throughout the country during the early 1920s. Much of the growth had occurred in industrial states like Pennsylvania, where native-born Americans felt threatened by the growing presence of Jews and Catholics. These immigrants or their offspring were seen as usurping jobs and infiltrating neighborhoods that had been the exclusive preserve of "Nordic" Protestants. The Klansman of 1926 was as likely to be a Pittsburgh steel worker or a Manayunk shopkeeper as he was to be a Mississippi cotton farmer.

The Klan had reinvented itself under Imperial Wizard William Joseph Simmons and his successor, Hiram Wesley Evans. The new Klan prided itself on being modern and efficient, with a corporate structure, million-dollar treasury, membership fees, image consultants, factory-manufactured costumes, women's and children's auxiliaries, charitable associations, and a business league that urged consumers to "TWK (Trade With Klansmen)." As an indication of the Klan's tolerant nature, its Krusaders Unit even accepted foreign-born members, as long as they were naturalized citizens and Protestants. On occasion, the KKK would harass, torture, and murder its usual targets, "the Jew, the Jug, and the Jesuit," along with new victims like "loose" women, "immoral" youth, political radicals, and bootleggers. Increasingly, this violence was concealed behind the frosted glass door of a modern office suite.

Shortly before the Sesqui opened, Imperial Wizard Evans penned an article for the *North American Review* entitled, "The Klan's Fight for Americanism." As the modern Klan moved into its second decade, Evans celebrated its "power to reform and cleanse itself from within." By civilizing itself, the Klan could focus on its central goal: "preserving and developing America first and chiefly for the benefit of the pioneers who made America." Using the language of eugenics, Evans described how "Nordic Americans of the pioneer stock" found themselves besieged by the forces of "radicalism, cosmopolitanism, and alienism." He then spelled out the challenges posed by Nordic America's three main threats: the Negro, the Catholic, and the Jew.[21]

Evans dismissed African Americans, traditional targets of the old Klan, in a single paragraph. The status quo of institutionalized racism and segregation in place throughout most of the United States in the 1920s was quite satisfactory to the new Klan. Condescendingly, Evans considered the Negro to be "a special duty and problem of the white American." While the Klan would offer the Negro its "full protection and opportunity," it would not coddle him: "we will not permit him to gain sufficient power to control our civilization. Neither will we delude him with promises of social equality which we know can never be realized."[22]

Turning to Catholics, Evans insisted that the Klan's argument with them was not religious but political. The Klan objected to the "autocratic structure of the Catholic Church organization, and its suppression of free conscience or free decision." It opposed the Church's acting as a political ombudsman for a large bloc of aliens, which it kept unassimilated through institutions like parochial schools. Evans insisted that the Catholic Church sought to dominate American politics through such corrupt machines as New York's Tammany and Boston's Curley Gang. Protestantism, with its traditions of individual freedom and undivided patriotism, had to reign supreme: "Rome shall not rule America."[23]

The Jew posed a particularly complex problem to the Klan, Evans explained, and thus to all true Americans. Besides rejecting Jesus Christ—the one link connecting all Christians—Jews were inherently alien and inassimilable. Evans noted that the term *melting pot* had been coined by "a member of one of the races—the Jews—which most determinedly refuses to melt." He admitted that the "Western Jew" (of German extraction) "contributes much to any country where he lives." With luck, these Jews would "disintegrate and amalgamate" within Christian society. But Eastern Jews of recent immigration showed little chance of assimilation, and presented "the most menacing and most difficult problem facing America today." Evans himself had no idea how to handle them: "We can neither expel, exterminate, nor enslave these low-standard aliens, yet their continued presence on the present basis means our doom."[24]

To defeat these internal enemies, the new Klan would prevail through purely democratic means, rather than the backwoods terrorism of old. To achieve its ends, the new Klan would send its millions of new members to the polls. By electing Klan-endorsed candidates and passing Klan-backed measures, the Klan would legally and peacefully make its slogan a reality: "Native, white, Protestant supremacy."[25]

By 1926 the new Klan had grown into a formidable political force, although it would soon succumb to political infighting, financial malfeasance, and scandal. In 1924 Klan member Edward Jackson was elected governor of Indiana; two years later, Bibb Graves became governor of Alabama with

Klan support. The Klan wielded influence over the governors of Georgia and Oregon, while in Oklahoma it had arranged the impeachment of a hostile governor. Throughout the United States, hundreds of other political leaders did the Klan's bidding, either as willing allies or as intimidated victims.

The 1925 KKK Klonvokation, or annual convention, in Washington, DC, offered stunning proof that the Klan was now a truly American institution. On August 8 tens of thousands of KKK members from around the country marched down Pennsylvania Avenue, their white robes and hoods fluttering in the summer breeze as the white dome of the Capitol shimmered in the background. While emphasizing the Klan's influence, the 1925 Klonvokation also made it look normal and acceptable, just another fraternal organization marching down Main Street in funny costumes. Klansmen were like the Shriners, except with white hoods instead of silk fezzes.[26]

After the Klan's triumphant progress in Washington in 1925, Philadelphia was the most logical site to celebrate its next Klonvokation in September 1926. The American media would be focused on the city during the Sesqui summer, and the Klan's image could only benefit from its association with such a revered patriotic celebration. Both Philadelphia and Pennsylvania were hubs of KKK activity, a striking illustration of the organization's growing presence in the mid-Atlantic. The Keystone State was the most important realm in the Klan's Northeastern domain, with membership estimated at 250,000.

In 1926 Philadelphia was home to more than twenty klaverns, or Klan chapters, with fourteen boasting more than three hundred members. Most were in the industrial neighborhoods ringing Center City that had experienced an influx of "Alpines" and "Mediterraneans" since 1900. The Robert Morris Klavern in Germantown boasted more than twelve hundred members, making it the tenth-largest klavern in Pennsylvania. The Klan had also made significant inroads in Philadelphia's suburbs. The shipbuilding center of Chester, in Delaware County, was home to the second-largest klavern in the state, with 2,155 members. The Montgomery County steel town of Conshohocken had Pennsylvania's third-largest chapter, with 1,831 members.[27]

The Philadelphia Klan was run by Paul Meres Winter, a self-described "journalist and organizer" born in Wilkes-Barre in 1895. The young World War veteran appeared to be the epitome of suburban respectability, living with his wife and two children on Anthwyn Road in the Main Line community of Narberth. His biography in the 1926 *Who's Who in Philadelphia* lists him as belonging to the Lutheran Church, the Masons, the American Legion, and the Veterans of Foreign Wars. It also notes that he was "appointed Field Representative of Philadelphia KKK August 1, 1924." Winter parroted Imperial

Paul Meres Winter, head of the Ku Klux Klan in New Jersey and eastern Pennsylvania.

Wizard Evans's call for a moderate, professional Klan, saying that his men would always conduct themselves in a "solemn, businesslike way." At heart, Winter was a violent, dictatorial man even by Klan standards. He formed his own personal bodyguard and law enforcement squad known as the Super-Secret Society, or SSS. Backed by his "Black-Robed Gang," Winter tried to bully anyone who stood in his way, including the mayor of Philadelphia.[28]

When W. Freeland Kendrick was elected mayor in 1923, the local Klan had rejoiced over the election of a true Protestant. (Evidently Kendrick's Scotch-Irish Presbyterian roots trumped those of his German Lutheran opponent, A. Raymond Raff.) Kendrick was obliged to deny that the Lu Lu Temple, home of his Shriners, was a hotbed of Klan activity. He refuted a local minister's criticism that 75 percent of Lu Lu Nobles belonged to the Klan, protesting that "not five per cent of that Temple's membership are [*sic*] of the KKK." In the early days of his administration, Kendrick had denounced the Klan frequently, especially before Jewish and African American audiences. In June 1924, Kendrick told the fifteenth annual conference of the NAACP that "one of the dangers that confronts the future of this republic is propaganda put out in various communities, regarding race and religious prejudice. A man who is prejudiced is not a desirable citizen."[29]

Despite Kendrick's noble language, plans were being made for the Klan to convene at the Sesqui as early as August 1925. A. L. Sutton, the director of domestic participation and special events and acting assistant director-general for the Sesqui, made it clear that the Klan would be warmly welcomed. Rumors abounded that the Southern-born Sutton, if not a Klansman himself, was a strong sympathizer with the Invisible Empire. After protests from African American, Catholic, and Jewish leaders, the SCEA appeared to distance itself from the Klan. But in May 1926, the New York *Jewish Daily Bulletin* noticed that the weekend of September 9–11 was still earmarked for the 1926 Klonvokation. On Saturday, September 11, an estimated one hundred thousand Klansmen—twice the number who filled Pennsylvania Avenue in 1925—would march down Broad Street from City Hall to the Sesqui. After a ceremony in the Stadium, the Klansmen would proceed to Edgewater Lake, where they would burn a giant cross.

When asked about the Klonvokation on a visit to Baltimore two weeks later, Mayor Kendrick treated the KKK as if it was just one of the many fraternal organizations visiting the fair that year:

> The Klan came to the exposition officials and asked that a day be set aside for them. When asked, they said they did not intend to wear hoods and carry burning crosses and other such symbols of their organization. The parade will be larger, according to the officials, than any previously held, including the one which took place in Washington nearly a year ago. The marchers will go unmasked.[30]

The *Baltimore Sun* slammed Kendrick's announcement as a "mockery of the Declaration of Independence. To permit [the Klan] to spread the poison of bigotry and intolerance is to make a mockery of the anniversary Philadelphia is commemorating." Accompanying the *Sun* editorial was a cartoon, "Sitting Pretty for the Sesqui-Centennial." It showed a bespectacled, balding man in his KKK robe, but with the hood thrown back, revealing his frowning face as he perched atop a massive Liberty Bell.[31]

On June 11 Paul Winter provided further details of the National Klonvokation. Winter announced that "Senators, Governors, and other civic and patriotic leaders from all over the country" would address the KKK, and would join in the grand parade down Broad Street. The Grand Kleagle promised that the Klan's perfect discipline would be an inspiration to an increasingly lax America: "During the march, not a man, woman or child in the ranks will be allowed to speak. The marchers will look straight ahead and it is my confident expectation that the country will be surprised and enlightened at the real meaning of our organization." Confirming Winter's plans, A. L. Sutton announced, "The Klan, like the Shriners or any other civic or patriotic group, will receive the same courtesies during their convention that we accord to all."[32]

For Philadelphia Jews, members of the second-largest Jewish community in America, the official equivocation over the Klan was a vicious slap in the face. The Sesqui would not have taken place had it not been for the financial support and personal involvement of the city's Jewish community. At the Palace of Education and Social Economy, an exhibit mounted by the Synagogue Council of America emphasized Jews who had made outstanding contributions to American history, including Philadelphia financier Haym Salomon, who lent the Continental Congress his personal fortune of $200,000 during the Revolution.[33]

When Mayor Kendrick and the SCEA took no action to ban the Klan, Philadelphia's Rabbi Louis Wolsey took it upon himself to shame Kendrick publicly. The forty-nine-year-old Wolsey had moved from Cleveland in 1925 to become senior rabbi of Rodeph Shalom, the oldest Ashkenazic synagogue in the Western hemisphere. Wolsey was a figure of national importance in American Judaism, serving as president of the Central Conference of American Rabbis and a director of the Union of American Hebrew Congregations. In mid-June, Wolsey's open letter to Kendrick appeared in the *Jewish Daily Bulletin* and other Jewish publications, and was quickly picked up by the national press. After asking Kendrick if he had indeed approved a Klan Day at the Sesqui, Wolsey respectfully asked the mayor to review the lack of logic in his thinking:

> The Ku Klux Klan is very definitely opposed to all those who are not native, or white, or Protestant; and that it believes in excluding this group from the rights of American citizenship; and that they are the only one hundred percent Americans. I presume it is just as clear to you as it is to me that this position of the Ku Klux Klan is counter to the principles of the Declaration of Independence. If this organization is given the privilege of celebrating its thought at an exposition which commemorates the publication of the Declaration of Independence, I should say that there was a glaring inconsistency.

With impeccable courtesy, the rabbi concluded by assuming that a sensible man like Kendrick would not allow any organization "which preaches religious or racial hatred to participate in the joy of our Sesqui Centennial."[34]

Soon after, Isaac Landman, editor of the *American Hebrew*, also challenged Kendrick publicly. He took issue with Kendrick's excuse that the assembled Klansmen did not intend to wear hoods or carry crosses. "Whether masked or unmasked," Landman wrote, "the principles proclaimed by the Klan are deemed un-American by a large proportion of

Rabbi Louis Wolsey of Philadelphia's Congregation Rodeph Shalom, who publicly shamed Mayor Kendrick into banning the Ku Klux Klan from the Sesqui.

our citizenry and on the very face of them nullify the Declaration of Independence and the principles therein proclaimed upon which American democracy has been founded."[35]

At this point, Kendrick caved. On June 22 his office issued a statement announcing that "the organization known as the Ku Klux Klan will not be permitted to parade and will not be permitted to assemble as a body within the Sesqui-Centennial grounds." He also revoked all police permits to hold a Klan pageant on the Parkway and South Broad Street, and ordered that all events scheduled in connection with the September Klonvokation be struck from the official program. Kendrick explained that until the recent protests of Wolsey and Landman had reached him, he had been "unaware that the Klan conclave and pageant were on the Sesqui program."[36]

Sutton, lacking Kendrick's political legerdemain, openly contradicted his boss. Several days after the mayor's ban, Sutton continued to insist that the KKK would convene at the Sesqui. "Of course the Klan will hold its session in the Sesqui Auditorium, just like any other organization would," Sutton assured the press. "We had no right to refuse it, even if we had so desired."[37]

Kendrick's sudden attack of principles was widely hailed in the Jewish press. "Mayor Kendrick," wrote *Der Tog*, "has rendered a real service in this matter to the American people." The *Jewish Morning Journal* stated that the barring of the Klan would be welcomed by the vast majority of public opinion in America, which the paper felt sure "is opposed to the

Klan." The *Jewish Daily News* agreed, asserting that Americans were "beginning to be ashamed" of the Klan. Within ten days of his capitulation, Kendrick was reveling in his new role as protector of all faiths. "I will not allow any group of men hooded and masked to dictate to me," he boasted, as he stood before the annual convention of the Daughters of the Revolution on July 3. "Fearlessly and with determination I will solve these problems of the city, state and nation, remembering the duty I owe to the nation, in view of the many people who are coming here to participate in the Sesqui-Centennial."[38]

As could be expected, the Ku Klux Klan felt differently, as witnessed by Paul Winter's prediction that Kendrick "will pay in the long run, all right." Yet after an initial outburst of threats, cross burnings, and poison-pen letters to the mayor and his wife, cooler heads prevailed. "We must remember that Mayor Kendrick is the highest executive in this city," cautioned Charles B. Lewis, a local leader, at a Klan meeting in Cobbs Creek, "and that he was elected by you. You are bound by your oaths as Klansmen to respect law and authority. If the Mayor decides that native-born American citizens cannot march through the streets of the city of Philadelphia, we shall obey the law." By early August, the Klan had decided to move its Klonvokation back to Washington, DC, the site of its great triumph in 1925.[39]

But the Invisible Empire would not allow W. Freeland Kendrick to escape unscathed. Rumors swirled that the Klan would exact its revenge by unearthing evidence of a deep, dark secret that it knew would destroy the mayor's personal life and professional career. It would prove, beyond the shadow of a doubt, that the Presbyterian, Scotch-Irish Kendrick had Jewish blood flowing in his veins.[40]

NOTES

1. Leuchtenburg, *The Perils of Prosperity 1914–32*, p. 149.

2. Austin and Hauser, *The Sesqui-Centennial International Exposition*, pp. 249–251, 256–257, 271, 276–277.

3. Selden, "Transforming Better Babies into Fitter Families," p. 217; "A Eugenics Catechism," American Eugenics Society, 1926; Kevles, *In the Name of Eugenics*, pp. 62–63.

4. Kevles, *In the Name of Eugenics*, pp. 47.

5. Ibid.

6. Ibid.

7. Austin and Hauser, *The Sesqui-Centennial International Exposition*, p. 287; Selden, "Transforming Better Babies into Fitter Families," p. 205; Kevles, *In the Name of Eugenics*, pp. 47, 59, 77.

8. Kevles, *In the Name of Eugenics*, pp. 46–47.

9. Luconi, *From Paesani to White Ethnics*, , pp. 44–45; Bruinius, *Better for All the World*, pp. 266; Dinnerstein, *Antisemitism in America*, p. 66; Braeman, Bremner, and Brody,

Change and Continuity, p. 226; Jenkins, *Hoods and Shirts*, p. 64; Kevles, *In the Name of Eugenics*, pp. 82–84.

10. Kevles, *In the Name of Eugenics*, pp. 82–84.

11. Kühl, *The Nazi Connection*, pp. 23–24; Bruinius, *Better for All the World*, pp. 9–10, 17, 72, 273, 290–291; Kevles, *In the Name of Eugenics*, pp. 111–118.

12. Greenberg, *Coolidge*, p. 81; Alexander, *Jazz Age Jews*, pp. 17, 31, 164; George Bornstein, *The Colors of Zion*, Cambridge, MA: Harvard University Press, 2011, pp. 149–150.

13. Braeman, Bremner, and Brody, *Change and Continuity*, p. 225.

14. Dinnerstein, *Antisemitism in America*, pp. 80–91; Bornstein, *The Colors of Zion*, p. 150; Feingold, *The Jewish People in America*, pp. 9–11; Watts, *The People's Tycoon*, pp. 376–397; Curcio, *Henry Ford*, pp. 131–158; Wallace, *The American Axis*, pp. 7–35.

15. "Inquirers Turn to Vare 'Machine," More Funds Found." *NYT*, June 16, 1926, p. 1.

16. "Seventy Volunteers as Drive Workers," *PI*, December 29, 1922; Greenfield, Albert M., speech to SCA, Bellevue-Stratford Hotel, October 12, 1925, HSP/AMG.

17. "17,000 Graduates Will Boost Sesqui," *PI*, July 14, 1922; "New Blood to Put Action into Fair," *PI*, July 13, 1922; "Committee Named to Manage Sesqui," *PI*, November 25, 1922; "New Sesqui Board 'Starts Something,'" *PI*, December 24, 1922.

18. M'Garry, "Philadelphia, Victim of Land Speculators, Sees Independence Fair Plans Fade Away," *DI*, March 10, 1923.

19. M'Garry, "Little Enthusiasm for Philadelphia Fair," *DI*, March 17, 1923.

20. "'Dearborn Independent' Objects to Jewish Participation in Sesqui-Centennial," JTA, April 26, 1926.

21. Evans, "The Klan's Fight for Americanism," *North American Review* 223 (March–May 1926): 60.

22. Ibid.

23. Ibid., pp. 44–52.

24. Ibid., pp. 40, 60–61.

25. Ibid., pp. 60–63.

26. Horowitz, *Beyond Left & Right*, p. 83; Braeman, Bremner, and Brody, *Change and Continuity*, pp. 247–248.

27. Jenkins, *Hoods and Shirts*, pp. 66, 70–72; Jackson, *The Ku Klux Klan in the City, 1915–1930*, pp. 172–173; Chalmers, *Hooded Americanism*, pp. 286–288.

28. Jenkins, *Hoods and Shirts*, pp. 68–69, 85; Jackson, *The Ku Klux Klan in the City, 1915–1930*, pp. 171, 173; *Who's Who in Philadelphia at the Time of the Sesqui-Centennial*, pp. 41, 274.

29. Jackson, *The Ku Klux Klan in the City, 1915–1930*, pp. 172–173; "Kendrick Denies Lu Lu Has Many Klansmen," *PB*, June 29, 1926; "Kendrick Frowns on Klan," *PB*, January 9, 1924; "Kendrick Scores Race Propaganda," *PB*, June 30, 1924; "Kendrick Assails Klan as Menace," *PPL*, June 30, 1924.

30. "Klan Day at S-C Celebration," Jewish Daily Bulletin, May 28, 1926.

31. "Klan Will Demonstrate at Sesqui-Centennial," *JDB*, May 12, 1926; "Klan Day at Sesqui-Centennial Celebration," *JDB*, May 28, 1926; "The Klan at the Sesqui-Centennial," JTA, May 30, 1926; "Sitting Pretty for the Sesqui-Centennial," *Baltimore Sun*, May 27, 1926.

32. "Klan Parade at Sesqui Is to Demonstrate Its Power, Organizer States," *JDB*, June 11, 1926.

33. "Sesqui Exhibit Shows Jewish Contribution to American Life," *JDB*, September 15, 1926; "Jews' Part in U.S. History Is Shown," *PB*, September 18, 1926.

34. "Rabbi Wolsey Protests to Phila Mayor against 'Klan Day' at Sesqui," *JDB*, June 18, 1926.

35. "Klan Day at S-C Celebration," *JDB*, May 28, 1926; "Wants Klan Barred at SC," *NYT*, June 22, 1926.

36. "Kendrick Forbids Klan at Sesqui," *PB*, June 23, 1926.

37. "Dispute on Klan Sesqui Program Threatens Rift," *Springfield Republican*, June 23, 1926; "Kendrick Bars Klan at SC," *NYT*, June 23, 1926; "Mayor's Klan Order Stands," *PB*, June 24, 1926; "Klan Barred from SC Celebration," *JDB*, June 24, 1926.

38. "America Is Ashamed of the Klan," JTA, June 26, 1926; "Baltimore 'Sun' on the Klan," JTA, June 27, 1926; "Mayor Hurls Defiance at Hooded Groups," *PB*, July 3, 1926.

39. "Kendrick Bars Klan at SC," *NYT*, June 23, 1926; "Klan Will Obey Mayor," *PB*, June 29, 1926.

40. "Klan Will Attempt to Prove Philadelphia Mayor Has Jewish Blood, Is Rumor," JTA, July 13, 1926.

10

★ ★ ★

The Ladies of the Street

HOW SHOULD WOMEN be represented at the Sesqui-Centennial, the first international exposition held in the United States since American women won the vote in 1920?

Long before suffrage, women had played a pivotal role in American expositions, starting with the Women's Centennial Executive Committee for Philadelphia's first world's fair. Appointed by the all-male United States Centennial Board of Finance in 1873, the thirteen-member women's committee saved the Centennial from financial extinction by persuading the Philadelphia City Councils and the U.S. Senate to appropriate millions of dollars for the fair. Once survival was assured, the committee spent more than $31,000 to build a Woman's Building, the first to appear at an international exposition. Filled with exhibits of feminine prowess in fields from embroidery to engineering, the Woman's Building proved to be one of the fair's most popular attractions. After 1876 a Woman's Building became a standard feature of international expositions both in America and abroad.[1]

By 1926, the role and self-image of American womanhood was in a state of flux. Most women still viewed themselves primarily as wives, mothers, homemakers, and consumers. Yet in the Sesqui-Centennial year, there were three female representatives in the Sixty-Ninth Congress, Wyoming had elected the first woman governor in America, and Seattle had a female mayor. By 1926, Margaret Sanger had founded the American Birth Control League , and Florence Sabin had been elected the first female member of the National Academy of Sciences.

Even women who maintained the traditional roles of wife and mother enjoyed greater freedom than their mothers: vivacious Grace Coolidge was considered the perfect helpmate to her taciturn, unsocial husband. Her official White House portrait shows her in a stylish gown of crimson, once the color of harlots. Cornelia Pinchot, wife of the Pennsylvania governor, also liked the color red. She dyed her hair bright red, wore flaming red dresses, and sped around the Commonwealth in a red car, winning the women's vote for her husband. The *North American* newspaper singled out Cornelia as the primary reason for Gifford Pinchot's victory over the Vare Organization in 1922.[2]

How could one exposition building contain such a polymorphous persona as the Woman of 1926?

It could not, announced Sarah Dickson Lowrie, the Philadelphia social reformer and writer who penned a popular column for the Philadelphia *Public Ledger*, "As One Woman Sees It." The women of 1926 "can't limit ourselves any longer to a Woman's Building . . . our great interest with women is in the community in which they live." No longer would a single building contain their interests and accomplishments. It would have to be an entire street of buildings, a colonial highway lined with the replicas of twenty-two historic structures that once stood on or near Philadelphia's central artery, High Street (renamed Market Street in 1853).[3]

Lowrie's coconspirator in the creation of the High Street of 1776 was Elizabeth Cornelius Price Martin, known to her friends as Lizzie and to the public as Mrs. J. Willis Martin. Martin was the most dynamic and influential woman involved with the Sesqui-Centennial Exhibition Association, serving as chairman of its Women's Committee. Both Elizabeth and her husband, Judge Jonathan Willis Martin Jr., ranked among the oldest of Old Philadelphians. Martin's Welsh ancestors had come to Pennsylvania in the 1680s, possibly with William Penn. Her grandfather was Eli Kirk Price, who had helped create modern Philadelphia through the Consolidation Act of 1854 and the establishment of the Fairmount Park Commission in 1867. Born in 1864, Lizzie spent her winters at a townhouse at 1709 Walnut Street and her summers at Edgecombe, a rambling mansion on Bethlehem Pike in Chestnut Hill. In 1884 she married attorney Martin, who would become one of Philadelphia's leading lawyers and judges.[4]

By the early 1920s, Elizabeth Martin occupied a position of unassailable authority in Philadelphia. As president of the Pennsylvania Council of Republican Women, she was a major participant in state and national politics, and a confidante of President Coolidge. With her husband and her brother, Eli Kirk Price II, she controlled an elite power bloc with ties to every Old

Elizabeth Price Martin (at left) and a friend rest outside the Russian Tea Pavilion during the Sesqui. (Courtesy of the Committee of 1926.)

Philadelphia institution in town, and wielded sufficient power to defy the Vare Organization. Given her impeccable credentials, powerful connections, and managerial talents, it was understandable that Mayor Kendrick would want her to play a major role in reviving the Sesqui-Centennial.

In April 1925 the SCEA executive committee unanimously appointed Martin as chairman of the Sesqui-Centennial Women's Committee. She accepted the position "temporarily" and reluctantly, since she considered the male management of the fair "a mass of putrid politics and graft." Martin insisted on having a free hand in running the Women's Committee, answering to no one at the SCEA or in City Hall. She refused to obey the Vare Organization's dictates on who to hire, what contractors to use, or what money to kick back.[5]

Despite Martin's insistence on the independence and integrity of the Women's Committee, its executive board reflected the *realpolitik* of Philadelphia. Mrs. W. Freeland Kendrick, the mayor's wife, was named honorary chairman. While Martin had little use for Eva Stotesbury personally, there was no question of excluding the wife of the city's wealthiest banker; Eva was named a vice chairman. Chicago-born Alma Viola Ennis Lorimer, wife of powerful *Saturday Evening Post* editor George Horace Lorimer, was named chairman of the States Committee. In this position, she would be responsible for welcoming national dignitaries on their frequent visits to the Sesqui. The committee's other officers were drawn from the city's oldest, wealthiest, and most aristocratic families: Biddle, Cassatt, Dixon, and Warburton. Besides the executive officers, more than two thousand women joined the Women's Committee, paying ten dollars apiece to support its activities.[6]

The original inspiration for the High Street of 1776 had come from Sarah Lowrie. She had been struck by the success of Addison Mizner's Alley (later the "Via Mizner"), a shop-lined walkway in Palm Beach. Since so much of Philadelphia's early life had centered on High Street between Second and Seventh Streets, Lowrie thought, why not build a "composite of the whole life of High Street and its environs comprised within one block"? Lowrie shared her concept for a High Street of 1776 with Martin, who immediately embraced it. The proposal received unanimous support from the Women's Committee, which voted to proceed with the project on November 27, 1925.[7]

By early 1926 the Women's Committee had forty-two active committees, reporting to Martin and the rest of the executive board. While the construction of High Street would be its primary objective, the Women's Committee identified other goals for 1926 that expanded its mission far beyond the Sesqui grounds. Hospitality was its overriding principle. "To receive and entertain our guests," stated the committee's Plan and Scope, "it will be the privilege of the women of this City to act as hostesses and guides and to conduct these visitors to the many shrines that are memorials of the beginning of this great nation." Specifically, the committee planned to establish a Center City information bureau, room registry, and travelers' aid office; provide access and guides to Independence Hall and other historic shrines; develop and distribute informational brochures; arrange walking tours of Center City and bus tours of outlying districts; and secure the loan of historic artifacts for public exhibition.[8]

During this period, Martin and Lowrie developed and refined their initial concept for the High Street of 1776. They consulted a panel of experts, including architect Clarence Clark Zantzinger, artist Frank Taylor, theater owner Jules Mastbaum, and Museum of Art Director Fiske Kimball. Thanks to the influence of Elizabeth Martin and Mrs. Barclay Warburton (daughter of John Wanamaker), Mayor Kendrick was able to convince the cash-strapped SCEA to appropriate $200,000 toward the project in mid-December. Soon after, the Women's Committee selected a location for High Street near the intersection of Pattison Avenue and Broad Street, in

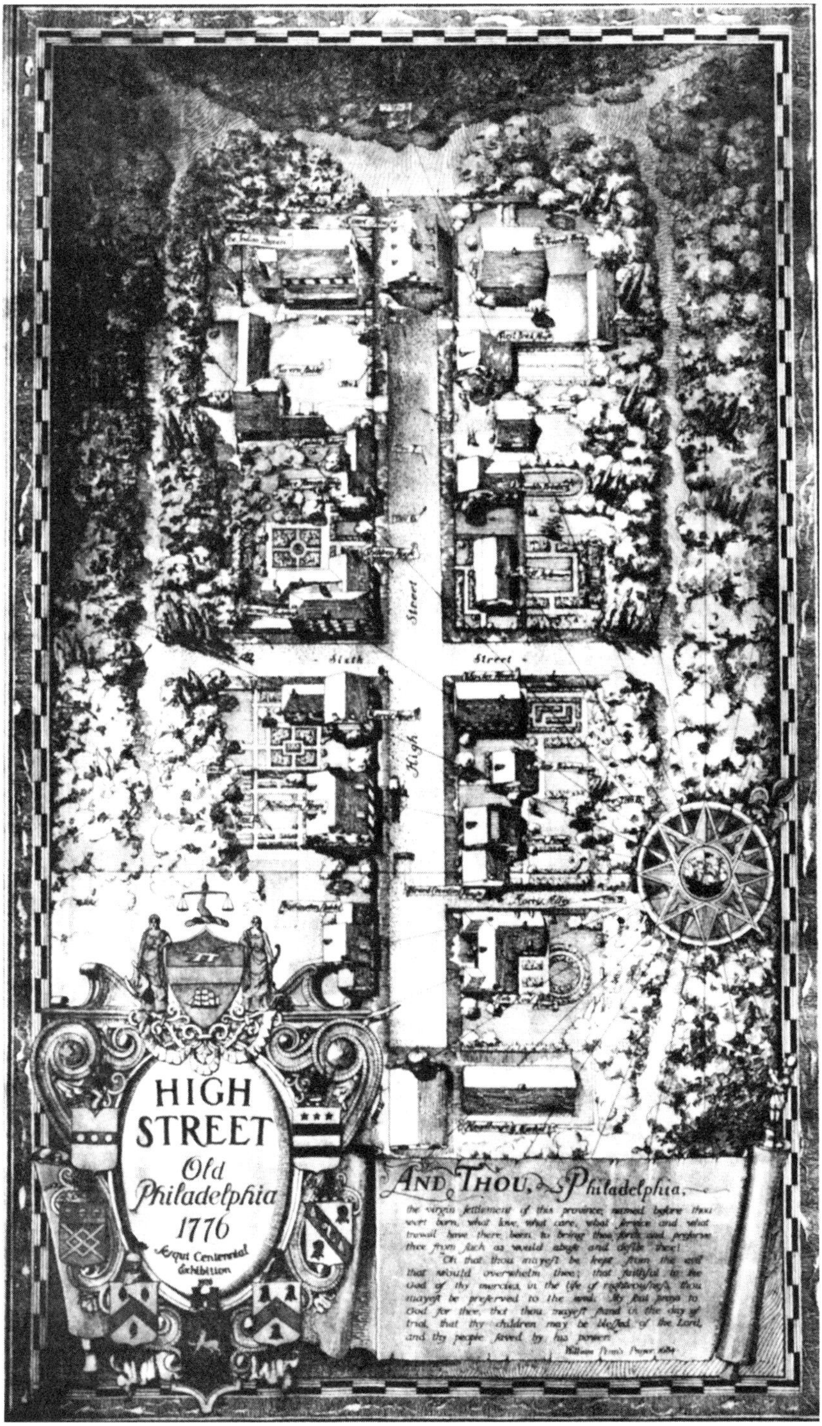

The idealized world of eighteenth-century Philadelphia, as depicted in a map of the High Street of 1776 by its architects.

the Sesqui's southwest quadrant. High Street would be approximately 800 feet long, and between 200 and 240 feet wide, with a cross street halfway along to allow passage between the India building to the north and Meadow Lake to the south.[9]

To design the street and its twenty-two buildings, the Women's Committee engaged three local architects who specialized in the Colonial Revival style: Richard Brognard Okie, E. Perot Bissell, and John P. B. Sinkler. Construction was handled by Frederick A. Havens, a reputable, non-Organization contractor recommended by the architects. Thanks to careful budgeting, the $200,000 allotted by the SCEA covered architectural design and engineering, site preparation, grading and paving roads, and construction of the main structures.[10]

To finish and furnish the buildings' interiors, and to landscape the site, the Women's Committee raised an additional $100,000 through leases to various groups, renting market stalls to vendors, arranging donations from corporate sponsors, and raising contributions from its members. The women convinced the SCEA to allocate an additional $52,500 to cover operational expenses, enabling them to open all houses to the public free of charge. In announcing the grant, Mayor Kendrick called it "a reward to the women of the Sesqui for their economical program carried out in the construction of High Street."[11]

High Street was anchored at its southeast end by the Jersey Market Head House, where farmers from New Jersey sold their produce, flanked on both sides by market stalls. At the northwest end stood the peak-roofed Town Hall and Court House, center of city and provincial politics until the State House (Independence Hall) was completed in 1753.

Along the south side of the street stood the low, rambling stables for the President's House, used as a theater. Next to the Washington Stables stood the President's House, a model of the mansion on Market between Fifth and Sixth where George Washington and John Adams lived until the capital moved to Washington in 1800. Next came the Robert Morris residence, home to the financier of the Revolution; the Graff House at Seventh and High Streets, where Thomas Jefferson wrote the Declaration of Independence; Dr. William Shippen's House, residence of the famous surgeon and director-general of military hospitals during the Revolution; the Office of Foreign Affairs, headquarters of America's first diplomatic corps; the Bake Shop of Christopher Ludwig, baker-general to Washington's army; and the Indian Queen Tavern, which served as an early meeting place for the First City Troop.

Beginning at Town Hall on the north side of the street stood replicas of the Friends' (Quaker) Meeting House at Second and High; the

First Brick House built in Philadelphia, in 1683; a Blacksmith shop; the Franklin Print Shop, where Benjamin Franklin printed the *Pennsylvania Gazette* and *Poor Richard's Almanack*; the Society Store House, repository of the records of the Society of Free Traders, founders of Society Hill; the Infirmary, Philadelphia's first official hospital, founded 1750; the Loxley House, reputed home of Revolutionary spy Lydia Darragh; the Little Wooden House, a generic example of early vernacular architecture; the Stephan Girard Mansion and Counting House, elegant home and office of the city's foremost merchant banker; and the Slate Roof House, where Proprietor William Penn lived and where he drafted the Charter of Privileges in 1700–1701.

Despite their sturdy appearance, all of the buildings were temporary wooden frames sheathed in staff or painted tin stamped to look like brick,

---

Workmen rush to finish the High Street of 1776 shortly before its June 5 dedication. The papier-mâché peaks of Treasure Island loom behind the Town Hall and Court House in the background.

their interior walls covered in plaster or paper board. Most of the structures had unfinished upper stories, while others had their dimensions carefully altered to reduce costs. White picket fences, hitching posts, and oil street lamps completed the illusion of a colonial thoroughfare.[12]

Each building was sponsored by a different society and staffed by volunteer hostesses provided by that organization. The Emergency Aid of Pennsylvania ran an "old-time restaurant" in the Indian Queen Tavern. The Philadelphia Teachers' Association sponsored a colonial "Dame School" in the First Brick House. The Pennsylvania Society of New England Women took over the Blacksmith Shop, renaming it the "Paul Revere Forge" in honor of their fellow Yankee. The Southern ladies who constituted the Jefferson Committee held sway at the Declaration House.

In the Society Store House, the National League of Women Voters set up displays "to arouse interest in voting and civic activity," noting that voting rates among adults had declined from 76 percent in 1876 to 51 percent in 1924. The Junior League sponsored the market stalls at the Jersey Market Head House, while the Daughters of the American Revolution held court in the Presidents' House. The Art Alliance of Philadelphia staged plays and puppet shows in the Washington Stables.

The Slate Roof House was the headquarters of the States Committee, and the personal fiefdom of committee chair Mrs. George Horace Lorimer. All receptions for governors and other American dignitaries would be held at the Slate Roof House, while ceremonies for foreign visitors would be held at the mansion of French-born merchant Stephen Girard. The most elegant building on High Street, the Girard House was the official "Hostess House" of the Foreign Relations Committee of the Women's Committee. Meanwhile, the Philadelphia Chapter of the War Mothers of America occupied the "Little Wooden House." This group's tenancy of the Street's most modest structure illustrated the receding presence of the Great War in an increasingly prosperous and frenetic America.[13]

Corporate sponsorship transformed some High Street houses into salesrooms for the updated Colonial Revival style enjoying a resurgence, thanks to the Sesqui-Centennial. The Shippen House resembled a suburban manse in Grosse Pointe or Winnetka. Decorated by Good Housekeeping Studios as "a house with Old-Time Charm and Modern Comforts," its mahogany furniture and chintz fabrics contrasted sharply with the gleaming porcelain of its Everhot Electric Cooker and Maytag Gyrafoam Electric Washer. Sarah D. Lowrie rationalized the anachronistic combination by explaining that the Shippen house demonstrated "how one may possess one's great-great-grandparent's house and still live comfortably in it."[14]

Philadelphia's major department stores played a leading role in the merchandising of High Street. Strawbridge and Clothier furnished the Declaration House, sending its decorators to Monticello and the homes of Jefferson descendants to research furniture belonging to the third president. Among their reproductions was the Tablet Arm Chair reputedly designed by Jefferson, a Windsor-style chair with a writing surface attached, where "rested the paper on which the original draft of the Declaration was made." All of the pieces on display were for sale in the Thomas Jefferson Room at the Strawbridge and Clothier store on Market Street. There, visitors could buy a "High Back Leather Chair," used when Jefferson was vice president, for $300, or $244 if muslin was substituted for leather.[15]

Snellenburg and Company outfitted the period school room at the First Brick House, while Gimbel Brothers provided the furnishings for the Loxley House. The Indian Queen Tavern was decorated by the John Wanamaker department store, with a sprinkling of genuine antiques lent by owner Rodman Wanamaker. The tavern was operated as an "old-time restaurant" where "dainty refreshments and all kinds of drinks within the law will be served throughout the day." The legal nature of the drinks had to be emphasized since many visitors, spying the tavern's antique bar festooned with ale mugs, immediately asked if there was anything on tap.

Since Elizabeth Martin was one of the founders of the Garden Clubs of America, it is not surprising that careful attention was devoted to landscaping High Street. The Committee of Associate Garden Clubs for the Planting of the Gardens of High Street solicited funds and donations from local nurseries. Volunteer gardeners from the Pennsylvania School of Horticulture for Women in nearby Ambler planted more than nine thousand flowers and four hundred shrubs. They had their hands full during the tumultuous summer of 1926. Elizabeth Martin later wrote of the "insurmountable obstacles that had to be overcome," including "soil which was a heavy muck, lack of proper drainage, thirty-seven days of rain and seven cloud-bursts." Despite these challenges, Martin felt that the gardens of High Street were a "constant delight" to tired visitors, happy to rest among the boxwood mazes and fragrant flowerbeds.[16]

Although unfinished, High Street was officially dedicated on a rainy June 5, 1926. While more than one thousand invited guests watched, three actors portraying the "Spirit of '76" escorted Mayor Kendrick and the officers of the Women's Committee along the length of the avenue, from the Market House to Town Hall. There, Elizabeth Martin presented Kendrick with the key to the Street. After formally accepting it, the mayor returned the key to Martin, a symbolic gesture that official Philadelphia was leaving High Street in the hands of the Women's Committee.[17]

A crowd of spectators and photographers watch the dedication ceremony for the High Street of 1776 on a rainy June 5, 1926. Like much of the Sesqui, the unfinished High Street was still swathed in scaffolding on its Opening Day.

For the rest of the Sesqui, High Street served as the setting for patriotic occasions and visits by national and foreign dignitaries. On Flag Day, June 14, after the ceremonies in the Stadium were routed by a torrential downpour, the executives' wives were treated to a soothing tea in the coolness of the Slate Roof House, headquarters of the States Committee. During the presidential visit on July 5, High Street was one of the few places at the Sesqui where the car bearing the Coolidges stopped, albeit briefly. At the Slate Roof House, Mrs. Lorimer reached through the window of the presidential motor to present Grace Coolidge with a diamond, ruby, and sapphire pin representing the first American flag. Mrs. Coolidge attached the pin to the lapel of her white suit, where it glittered during the rest of her brief visit to Philadelphia.[18]

Every Wednesday, the Philadelphia Art Alliance staged a historical pageant entitled "The Spirit of '76," climaxing with George Washington delivering his farewell address to the Continental Army. Even on ordinary days, the Street bustled with activity. A town crier in a tricorn hat and crimson greatcoat rang his bell, shouting news of upcoming events. Artisans hammered ornamental ironwork in the blacksmith's shop and operated the massive handpress at the print shop. A grand lady in a powdered wig fluttered her handkerchief from a sedan chair carried by liveried attendants. Hostesses in colonial dress greeted visitors and answered questions. At the theater, crowds laughed at puppets' antics, and listened to choruses sing eighteenth-century songs. Visitors were drawn by High Street's constant activity, its easily accessible attractions, and its irregular streetscape punctuated by shaded gardens and retreats. The street's human scale provided a welcome relief from the monumental plazas of the central fairgrounds, which even on the busiest days seemed strangely empty and lifeless. Roughly five thousand visitors walked the street each day, making it one of the most popular attractions at the Sesqui.[19]

The publicity committee of the Women's Committee kept High Street in the public eye with a stream of articles in newspapers and national magazines. The Women's Committee produced its own publications, starting with *The Sesqui-Centennial High Street (The Book of the Street)* by Sarah D. Lowrie and Martha Stewart Ludlum. More than ten thousand copies were sold of this ninety-six-page booklet, which described the historic significance of High Street's original buildings. Other books and pamphlets alerted visitors and natives alike to the city's heritage, including *Colonial Walks in Old Philadelphia, Historical Trails from Philadelphia,* and *Historic Germantown by Motor Bus.*[20]

The Women's Committee became involved in the campaign to preserve the string of colonial and federal mansions in Fairmount Park spearheaded by Fiske Kimball, new director of the Pennsylvania Museum of Art. Mount Pleasant, a 1761 mansion that Kimball called "the finest of the old houses of Philadelphia, and indeed of all the northern Colonies," had recently been restored by the museum. In a matter of weeks, the Women's Committee turned the empty house into a showcase. Assembling a rare collection of American furniture and art, the committee staged five period rooms dating from 1760 to 1776, open to the public between July 1 and November 1. Among the pieces on display was a pair of armchairs that once belonged to the Penn family; Benjamin Franklin's chess table; and a tall-case clock designed by David Rittenhouse. Seen by more than seven thousand visitors, the exhibition spurred public interest in restoring other neglected mansions in Fairmount Park.[21]

While the High Street of 1776 was the outstanding contribution made by Philadelphia women to the Sesqui, it was far from the only one. The Young Women's Christian Association erected a scaled-down replica of Mount Vernon, which served as a visitors' center throughout the Sesqui, with an information booth, rooms registry and employment bureau, and a cafeteria for Sesqui guests and employees. The National Society of the Colonial Dames of America erected a replica of Sulgrave Manor, sixteenth-century ancestral home of the Washington family in the Northamptonshire village of Sulgrave. The society's forty-two state societies raised $20,000 to construct the two-story Tudor house, which displayed relics from the original manor, portraits of Washington and his family, and antique Jacobean furniture. Neither Mount Vernon nor Sulgrave Manor came close to matching the popularity of the Street of 1776. Sarah Logan Wister Starr, chairman of Sulgrave Manor, recalled how visitors would stop there because it was the first thing they saw, "and then asked how to get to High Street."[22]

As autumn arrived and the Sesqui entered its final phase, the Women's Committee debated making their popular High Street a permanent attraction by rebuilding its temporary structures in steel and brick. Elizabeth Martin was a strong proponent of this movement, suggesting that various buildings could be used as the permanent headquarters of women's organizations. "Colonial architecture is fast fading from the country," she argued. "A permanent 'High Street' would be an incentive to the increase of Colonial buildings, so typically American." The Street's architects estimated that it would cost between $625,000 and $725,000 to reconstruct High Street buildings from sturdier materials, not counting the price of a new site. Given the tendency of League Island Park to flood at high tide, a move to higher ground in Fairmount Park would be advisable. Finally, even Martin and Lowrie were compelled to admit that a permanent High Street was financially unfeasible.[23]

When the initial postmortems were written on the Sesqui after its closing, it was universally acknowledged that the High Street of 1776 was one of the brightest spots in a gloomy landscape. It showed a healthy profit thanks to its popularity, its hefty subsidy, and the careful stewardship of the Women's Committee. Frances A. Wister called it "the outstanding Philadelphia exhibit during the past six months," providing greater benefits "than almost any other one separate feature of the Exposition." The executive committee of the SCEA awarded the Women's Committee a grand prize "as a symbol of the historic and artistic importance of High Street," issuing separate medals to Martin and Lowrie. The *Philadelphia Record* wrote that "if the men of Philadelphia had undertaken to serve their city with half of the zeal, enterprise and efficiency manifested by the women of this group during the Sesqui period, there would be a different story to tell of the celebration of the nation's birthday."[24]

Sulgrave Manor, the replica of the ancestral home of the Washington family, sponsored by the National Society of the Colonial Dames of America.

The Women's Committee gathers at High Street during its final days in late November 1926. (Courtesy of the Committee of 1926.)

In August 1927 the weather-beaten buildings of the High Street of 1776 were sold by Samuel Freeman's auction house for a total of $1,470, ranging from $30 for the Market Head House to $165 for the President's House. Most were in poor condition, damaged by the winter storms that had lashed League Island Park after the Sesqui closed. In noting the sale and demolition, several newspapers mourned the fact that the attraction could not have been preserved. A High Street "perpetuated indefinitely," editorialized the *Inquirer*, "would have become a permanent fixture for at League Island Park for the instruction of school children and shrines of interest to every intelligent visitor. A great opportunity has been lost."[25]

Not crying over spilled milk, the Sesqui-Centennial Women's Committee had moved on to its next project by then. It had reorganized as the Committee of 1926, dedicated to following "the same lines of hospitality and of historic and present-day interests that have been our record for that summer on High Street," in Martin's words. Buoyed by their success with Mount Pleasant, the committee decided to cooperate with the Museum of Art to restore another Fairmount Park villa. They settled on Strawberry Mansion, a federal country house in East Fairmount Park. The central house had been built around 1798 by the Lewis family; two large square wings had been added around 1835 by a later owner. After the Civil War, it had served as a beer garden, an Italian bistro, a "sailors' rendezvous," and finally as a police station that sold bootleg liquor out of the basement.[26]

Thanks to a generous gift from Joseph Horn, president of the Horn and Hardart Baking Company, a restored and refurbished Strawberry Mansion opened to the public in 1931. Its banquet room sparkled with star-sprinkled walls, a crystal-and-bronze chandelier, and imperial yellow silk draperies. In the Greek Revival ballroom, portraits by Thomas Sully looked down on a massive, circular ottoman covered in bright red silk. In the gardens behind the house, gravel paths led to benches offering breathtaking vistas of the Schuylkill River. Besides using Strawberry Mansion as a headquarters, the Committee of 1926 planned to operate the mansion as a reception center to welcome distinguished visitors to Philadelphia.[27]

After a series of heart attacks, Elizabeth Martin died on April 5, 1932, aged sixty-eight. Her friends created a garden walk that led from Strawberry Mansion to a point overlooking the Schuylkill River, contributing plants from their own gardens that Lizzie had admired. A bronze tablet honoring her contributions was mounted on the front door at Strawberry Mansion, noting that the house was "given to hospitality." Sarah Lowrie, who would live for another thirty-five years, wrote that her friend died "in the heyday of her usefulness."[28]

The impact of the Sesqui Women's Committee and the High Street of 1776 echoed long after the dismal summer of 1926. The success of Mount Pleasant and Strawberry Mansion helped advance Fiske Kimball's dreams of a network of notable mansions in Fairmount Park. By 1932 nine historic houses had been refurbished as part of Fairmount Park's "Colonial Chain," despite the deepening Depression. The reverberations from High Street might have been felt as far south as Williamsburg, Virginia. Dr. W. A. R. Goodwin of Bruton Parish Church had requested the assistance of the Rockefeller family with preserving some of the decaying Georgian structures in the former state capital as early as 1924. It was not until late 1926, after High Street had been featured in the *Saturday Evening Post* and other national publications, that John D. Rockefeller Jr. finally agreed to underwrite what became Colonial Williamsburg. Thirty years after the Sesqui, Ed Bacon and the other civic planners behind the rebirth of Society Hill would use High Street as a model for an eighteenth-century community adapted to the twentieth century. During the 1976 Bicentennial, women in colonial garb ushered hundreds of tourists through the colonial streets of Society Hill on candlelight tours, repeating the actions of their grandmothers at the 1926 Sesqui.[29]

The High Street of 1776 was the physical embodiment of an elitist fantasy about the creation of the United States: that it was accomplished solely by white Protestants of British ancestry, with sizable incomes and impeccable breeding, who had founded a homogenously patrician society as graceful and elegant as the highest ranks of the Old World. In the words of the *Saturday Evening Post*, High Street would show the American public, "thousands of whom never step foot inside a museum, exactly how our forefathers lived . . . [in] handsome aristocratic houses furnished in excellent taste with fine furniture, rare damasks, silver and paintings done by the foremost masters of the time."[30]

Fired by the enthusiasm and idealism of the Women's Committee, High Street transcended this narrow and erroneous vision. Through their activities, the Women of the Street educated thousands of Americans about the birth of their nation, and helped them understand precisely what they were celebrating in 1926. They gave visitors a glimpse of what their country had been in 1776, and how it had grown and evolved in 150 years. They enlightened Philadelphians about the beauty that existed within their city, and inspired them to preserve it. Finally, they showed women what they could achieve working together, while remaining within the traditional roles that were still comfortable for most of them.

Speaking to her associates at the final luncheon of the Women's Committee on December 6, 1926, Sarah Lowrie attempted to explain what the Street of 1776 had accomplished:

> If High Street has taught us nothing else, it has proved to us and to a very significant cloud of witnesses, that creed, race, social opportunities, education, personal bias, varying gifts, and much or little previous occupation cannot combine to separate women with a common purpose. . . . We can by our personal enthusiasm renew that clear vision of what are the essentials of life. Let us renew it as companions and united in our relation to our country and to one another to "show the world" the great treasure of Americanism that we hold in common as the joint inheritors of the pioneers who blazed a trail for us which is still the highway to life, liberty, and the pursuit of happiness.[31]

NOTES

1. Freedman, "The Women's Committee," p. 5; Scharf and Westcott, *History of Philadelphia 1609–1884*, 2:1699–1700; Hodos, "The 1876 Centennial in Philadelphia," pp. 30–31; Mary Frances Cordato, "Toward a New Century: Women and The Philadelphia Centennial Exhibition, 1876," *PMHB* 107, no. 1 (January 1983): 115–116.

2. Sklar, *The Plastic Age 1917–1930*, pp. 284–297; Leuchtenburg, *The Perils of Prosperity 1914–32*, pp. 158–167; Beers, *Pennsylvania Politics Today and Yesterday*, pp. 101–103.

3. *Report of the Sesqui-Centennial Women's Committee*, Independence Hall, February 8, 1926, Committee of 1926 Record Book Collection, pp. 5–6; Lowrie, "As One Woman Sees It," *PPL*, n.d., COM1926/SCA.

4. Rivinus, *Distaff Descent*, pp. 298–302; "Elizabeth Price Martin (Mrs. J. Willis Martin) 1864–1932," n.a., n.d., CHHS, 1997.23 CHHS.

5. Letter from David C. Collier to Elizabeth Martin, April 7, 1925, COM1926/SCA; letter from Elizabeth Martin to David C. Collier, April 25, 1925, COM1926/SCA; Freedman, "The Women's Committee," p. 14; Rivinus, *Distaff Descent*, pp. 200–203, 345–346, 359–360.

6. "Women of Sesqui Pick New Officers," *PPL*, December 15, 1925; Martin, Mrs. J. Willis, "Women's Patriotic Contribution," *The Sesqui-Centennial International Exposition*, p. 153.

7. Lowrie, "As One Woman Sees It," *PPL*, February 7, 1926.

8. "Plan and Scope for the Women's Division of the Sesqui-Centennial International Exposition," COM1926/SCA, p. 1.

9. Letter from R. J. Pearse, SCEA Director of Works, to Mrs. J. Willis Martin, December 21, 1925, COM1926/SCA; Sarah D. Lowrie, "Report of a Preliminary Survey of the Site for the Proposed Street of '76," December 27, 1925, COM1926/SCA; Freedman, "The Women's Committee," pp. 40–41; Rivinus, *Distaff Descent*, p. 364; Martin, "Women's Patriotic Contribution," *The Sesqui-Centennial International Exposition*, p. 151.

10. Sandra L. Tatman, "Okie, Richardson Brognard (1875–1945)," and "Bissell & Sinkler (fl. 1906–c. 1936)," *Philadelphia Architects and Buildings*, available at www.philadelphiabuildings.org; Freedman, "The Women's Committee," pp. 35–38; Elizabeth Frazier, "Our Sesqui-Centennial," *Saturday Evening Post* 198 (April 1926): 16.

11. Freedman, "The Women's Committee," pp. 38–40; "Women Get Sesqui Fund," *PB*, May 24, 1926; letter to Mrs. J. Willis Martin from W. Freeland Kendrick, May 18, 1926, COM1926/SCA; "Budget Estimate—June 10, 1926," COM1926/SCA.

12. "Sesqui to Have 'Street of '76,'" *PPL*, February 14, 1926; letter from Sarah D. Lowrie to Elizabeth Martin, January 23, 1926, COM1926/SCA; Lowrie and Ludlum, *The Sesqui-Centennial High Street*, pp. 1–54; Freedman, "The Women's Committee," pp. 42–44; "Describes Women's Part in the Sesqui-Centennial and the Patriotic Observance of Independence Week," *PPL*, July 4, 1926.

13. Freedman, "The Women's Committee," pp. 56–97; Lowrie and Ludlum, *The Sesqui-Centennial High Street*, pp. 57–87; Martin, Mrs. J. Willis, "High Street, the Memorable," *The Sesqui-Centennial International Exposition*, pp. 166–171; Lowrie, "As One Woman Sees It," *PPL*, n.d., COM1926/SCA; letter from Stuart G. Gibboney to Sarah D. Lowrie, February 18, 1926, COM1926/SCA; "Women Dedicate High Street House," *PB*, June 26, 1926; "Voter Indifferent to Duty at Polls," *PB*, July 26, 1926.

14. "Dr. Shippen's House"; Lowrie, "As One Woman Sees It," *PPL*, May 12, 1926; Dorothy Budd, "The Little Street of '76," *Woman Citizen*, August 1926, p. 36; Freedman, "The Women's Committee," p. 46.

15. Freedman, "The Women's Committee," pp. 47, 56–57, 92; "The Jefferson or Declaration House at the Sesqui-Centennial," *Strawbridge and Clothier Store Chat* 19, no. 9 (September 1926): 3–5.

16. Newhall, "Final Report of Committee for Planting the Gardens of High Street—November, 1926," COM1926/SCA; Newhall, "The Gardens of the High Street of 1776 at the Sesqui-Centennial, 1926," *Bulletin of the Garden Club of America* 12 (November 1926): 32–36; Freedman, "The Women's Committee," p. 49; Martin, "High Street, the Memorable," pp. 171–173.

17. "Old High Street Dedicated in Rain," *PB*, June 5, 1926; "Sesqui Peopled as in '76 Days on High Street," *PPL*, June 6, 1926.

18. Martin, "High Street, the Memorable," pp. 160, 164–166; "Wives of Governors Guests at Luncheon," *PPL*, June 15, 1926.

19. Freedman, "The Women's Committee," p. 81–82, 106; Martin, "High Street, the Memorable," pp. 160–161; "'In '76' Augments High Street Memories," *PPL*, July 22, 1926; "Washington Coach Rides on High Street," *PB*, July 27, 1926; "Sesqui Town Crier Finds Lost Child," *PPL*, July 21, 1926.

20. Martin, "Women's Patriotic Contribution," p. 156; "Colonial Walks in Heart of City," *PPL*, June 6, 1926; Lowrie, "As One Woman Sees It," *PPL*, n.d.; Mrs. Wilmer Krusen, "Story of the Women's Committee of the Sesqui-Centennial," COM1926/SCA, p. 5; "Historic Germantown Motor Bus Tours of 1926," COM1926/SCA.

21. Freedman, "The Women's Committee," pp. 111–112; Martin, "Women's Patriotic Contribution," p. 157; "Women Reopen Home of Arnold," *PPL*, n.d., COM1926/SCA; "Report of Committee on Mount Pleasant Mansion," November 8, 1926, COM1926/SCA; "Report of Mount Pleasant Loan Exhibition Committee, Louise H. Gillingham, Chairman," COM1926/SCA; "Furniture Styles of Colonial Period to Be Shown in Restoration of Mount Pleasant, Peggy Shippen's Bridal Home," *PPL*, July 4, 1926.

22. Freedman, "The Women's Committee," p. 102n160; Martin, "Other Activities of Women," pp. 179–180; Smith, *Sulgrave Manor*, p. 11; Hosmer, *Presence of the Past*, pp. 139–140.

23. Letter from R. Brognard Okie to Mrs. J. Willis Martin, October 7, 1926, COM1926/SCA; "Report of Sarah D. Lowrie on the Possibilities of a Permanent High Street at the Luncheon of the Woman's Committee of the Sesqui, December 6th, 1926," COM1926/SCA; Freedman, "The Women's Committee," p. 109; "Women Discuss Plans to Perpetuate 'High Street,'" *PB*, December 6, 1926.

24. "High Street 1776 Statistics of Gross Receipts, Nov. 29th and 30th, and Total to Nov. 30th," COM1926/SCA; "High Street 1926," COM1926/SCA; letter from Mrs. J. Willis Martin and Miss Sarah D. Lowrie to E. L. Austin, SCEA Comptroller, March 30, 1926, COM1926/SCA; "Preservation of High Street," *PR*, December 8, 1926; Wister, "High Street 'As One Woman Sees It,'" *PPL*, December 8, 1926.

25. "'Street of 1776' Brings Only $1,750," *PB*, August 9, 1927; "Passing of High Street," *PI*, August 12, 1927; "High Street Passes," *PPL*, August 12, 1927.

26. Letter from Sarah D. Lowrie to Elizabeth P. Martin, March 19, 1927, COM1926/SCA; Lowrie, *Strawberry Mansion*.

27. Letter from Joseph V. Horn to Mrs. J. Willis Martin, February 10, 1930, COM1926/SCA; letter from Mrs. J. Willis Martin to Joseph V. Horn, February 12, 1930, COM1926/SCA; letter from Elizabeth P. Martin to "High Street Members," March 29, 1930, COM1926/SCA; Lowrie, *Strawberry Mansion*, pp. 218–219; *The Chain of Colonial Houses*; Rivinus, *Distaff Descent*, p. 386.

28. Rivinus, *Distaff Descent*, pp. 392–393, 409; Lowrie, *Strawberry Mansion*, pp. 217–18.

29. Greenspan, *Creating Colonial Williamsburg*, pp. 18–20.

30. Freedman, "The Women's Committee," pp. 104–153.

31. "Report of Sarah D. Lowrie on the Possibilities of a Permanent High Street at the Luncheon of the Woman's Committee of the Sesqui, December 6th, 1926," COM1926/SCA.

11

★ ★ ★

The Philadelphia Negro at the Sesqui

WHILE THE OVERALL REACTION of Philadelphians toward their hometown fair might have been one of ennui, many African Americans greeted news of the Sesqui with excited optimism. "1926 is the year people from every nation, every clime . . . will assemble hard by the banks of the Delaware," enthused the *Philadelphia Tribune*, the city's leading black newspaper, in 1921. "Picture amid the throng of millions entering our fair domain, thousands of our own people!" For the next few years, the *Tribune* would exhort its readers to make the Sesqui a shining example of the accomplishments of the Philadelphia Negro:

> This is to be the one big chance for the Philadelphia Negro to prove to the world by deeds well done just how he stands in the outward march of events. . . . Splendid records have been made. Still greater records must be made. Since records are made to be broken, every thoughtful Negro must get into the record-breaking habit. He must use it in connection with producing something for the Sesqui-Centennial Celebration.[1]

The *Tribune* editorial acknowledged that while Philadelphia's black community (the second largest in America after New York) had achieved great things, it still had much to accomplish. Between 1910 and 1920, Philadelphia's African American population had jumped from 84,459 to 134,220. It boasted two hospitals, three banks, and more than a dozen building and loan associations. While the Philadelphia public school system was largely segregated, the city and its environs were home to four black colleges and industrial training schools. Although roughly one-quarter of Philadelphia blacks lived in poverty, income and home ownership levels were rising. African Americans were beginning to break out of the black ghettos of the Seventh and Thirtieth Wards in South Philadelphia, and were moving into previously all-white neighborhoods in North and West Philadelphia, Germantown, and Camden County, New Jersey.[2]

Thanks to their growing numbers, African Americans had become an attractive voting bloc for the Vare Organization, granting them greater leverage to demand favors for a select few. The Citizens' Republican Club delivered the black vote to the Vares in exchange for low-level municipal jobs for its members. Philadelphia blacks held 1,560 public service positions in 1920, the same number as in New York and significantly more than in Chicago. While most were menial positions, the city boasted 276 black teachers, 274 policemen, 145 mail carriers, eleven city and county officials, ten detectives, and four firemen. Thanks to the Vares, Amos M. Scott had been named Philadelphia's first black magistrate. In 1920, two African Americans from Philadelphia were elected to the Pennsylvania State Legislature with Vare backing: Major Andrew F. Stevens Jr. and John Cornelius Asbury.[3]

Despite these accomplishments, Philadelphia stood out from other major northern cities in its abusive treatment of its black citizens. African Americans in the City of Brotherly Love experienced a degree of racial separation as restrictive as in Birmingham or Atlanta. Racism prevented most blacks from earning a decent living. Albert M. Greenfield, owner of the Benjamin Franklin Hotel, ordered his manager to avoid using "colored service" because "in Philadelphia the highest class of hotels have only white service."[4] Dr. John P. Turner, chief surgeon at Frederick Douglass Memorial Hospital and the city's preeminent black doctor, was refused an appointment to a city hospital in 1924 because of his race. There were thirteen black lawyers in Philadelphia in 1910 and thirteen in 1920, showing no change during the decade when the city's black population had increased by more than 50 percent.

Philadelphia blacks were banned from Center City restaurants except for Horn and Hardart Automats, where they could serve themselves. They could not shop at any Market Street department store. At Jules Mastbaum's glittering movie palaces, they were banished to the upper balcony, no matter how empty the mezzanine and orchestra. When Mastbaum's luxurious Stanley Theatre opened in January 1921, Governor William Sproul and Mayor J. Hampton Moore headed a delegation of local legislators, who were led to choice seats in the parquet section. All except for State Representative John C. Asbury, who stormed out after being ordered to the rear balcony by an usher. When President Charles Dunbar King of Liberia visited Philadelphia in May 1921 at the invitation of Mayor Moore, the Bellevue-Stratford Hotel refused to give him a room. He stayed at the Hotel Dale, a black-owned hotel at Broad and Fitzwater Streets.[5]

Unlike New York and Chicago, where African Americans were mobilizing to challenge segregation, Philadelphia's black elite remained largely quiescent. When W. E. B. Du Bois had published *The Philadelphia Negro*, his groundbreaking sociological study of the Seventh Ward in 1899, he had commented on the lack of singularity among Philadelphia blacks aside from their vote, which was the undisputed "tool of the Republicans." He criticized their leaders for having "little social contact with the black masses." Instead, the primary impulse of "the best, the wisest and the richest is to segregate themselves from the mass." In the nearly three decades since *The Philadelphia Negro* had appeared, white authorities had used these internecine schisms to suppress African Americans even more ruthlessly than in 1899. When Representatives Asbury and Stevens agitated too strongly for civil rights legislation, Bill Vare forced both men to step down at the end of their terms in 1924. It was little wonder that the *Philadelphia Tribune* should consider the Sesqui-Centennial "the one big chance for the Philadelphia Negro."[6]

When Mayor Kendrick revived the Sesqui-Centennial in 1924, he approached the African American community for their support. On February 3, 1925, the first invitation to a foreign nation was issued to President King of Liberia. Soon after, Kendrick asked Magistrate Amos M. Scott to organize a national committee of "prominent colored citizens" to fund a $100,000 exhibit showing "the progress of the race." Encouraged, the *Tribune* painted a rosy picture of the riches that would accrue to the Philadelphia Negro from the Sesqui:

> Business will boom. Transportation will increase. Housing facilities will become more acute. There will be more jobs than men to fill them. Out of this vast wealth of opportunities, there will be particular benefits open to the members of our group in many lines of endeavor. We will receive increased commercial impetus and a fair share of the employment. Now is the time to prepare for the Sesqui-Centennial. We should begin to make plans at once. There will be a large influx of colored people and it is our duty to afford facilities for taking care of them.[7]

Enthusiasm for the Sesqui among African Americans reached a peak at a May 19 meeting of the Philadelphia Business League at the Royal, a black-owned theater at 1524 South Street. C. W. Crist, representing Director-General Collier, assured the audience of black merchants that there would be no segregation at the Sesqui, and that "all races will be treated the same."[8] Because there would be no segregation, Crist explained, it would be unnecessary to construct a separate building to showcase Negro accomplishments.

Not all African Americans were swept up in the Sesqui bubble. *Tribune* columnist Eustace Gay cautioned his race to stay aloof from the fair, given the rumors about graft and corruption. "It might be a good thing to let [the white establishment] have the Sesqui-Centennial Independence celebration 'independently' of our group, if there is going to be an aftermath of scandal." Other African Americans noted the irony of the Sesqui being relocated to Oregon Plaza, site of the 1913 Pennsylvania Emancipation Exposition. This celebration of the fiftieth anniversary of the Emancipation Proclamation, organized by the city's blacks as a showcase for their accomplishments, resulted in financial failure and political infighting.[9]

In the summer of 1925, blacks' euphoria burst when news spread that the Ku Klux Klan would hold its 1926 Klonvokation at the fair. Black leaders were further stunned when SCEA officials, led by Kendrick and Sutton, appeared to welcome the Klan with open arms. The black community joined forces with Jews and Catholics to protest sponsorship of the Klonvokation by both the city government and Sesqui management.[10]

It was time for spin control. Mayor Kendrick appeared to back away from the Klan presence at the Sesqui. He also followed the suggestion of Director-General Collier, who wrote the mayor, "I should very much like to suggest the advisability of the immediate organization of a Committee on Colored Participation. The situation is becoming acute, and I should like to get it settled." Kendrick announced the appointment of an executive committee of twenty-five "prominent Negro residents of Philadelphia" to "formulate a program showing the development of the Negro along educational lines," to be submitted to white Sesqui officials for approval. The executive committee would be augmented by a larger group of one hundred blacks.[11]

The executive committee leaders were handpicked by Kendrick and other SCEA officers. The vice chairman of what would become the Committee on Negro Activities was the Reverend Charles A. Tindley, pastor of the Bainbridge Street Methodist Episcopal Church. Leader of one of the largest black congregations in Philadelphia, Tindley was spearheading the construction of an impressive new sanctuary for his flock on South Broad

John C. Asbury, Philadelphia politician, lawyer, and banker. His appointment as chairman of the Sesqui Committee on Negro Activities was an example of the false promises made by white politicians and fair managers to Philadelphia's black community. (Courtesy of Howard University Library.)

Street, later known as the Tindley Temple. SCEA Executive Secretary George Hicks informed Ernest T. Trigg that the influential minister would do a great deal to help resolve the "race problem." "Dr. Tinsley," Hicks wrote, misspelling Tindley's name, "seems to have the larger endorsement [of black leaders] and appears to be the man who is able to control the situation."[12]

The SCEA selection for chairman was attorney and banker John Cornelius Asbury, one of the two black state representatives asked to step down by Vare in 1924 for his sponsorship of an equal rights bill. Despite this demotion, Asbury remained one of the most powerful African Americans in Philadelphia, politically and financially. He also remained a loyal Republican and Organization man. The office of Chairman of Negro Activities at the Sesqui was a concession to Asbury for his acquiescence in stepping down from the legislature. It was also a shrewd political move to ensure that the Negro program at the fair would be controlled by a dependable ally.[13]

While the Committee on Negro Activities included a few "New Negroes" like attorney Raymond Pace Alexander and *Tribune* editor E. Washington Rhodes, the majority of its one hundred members were older, more conservative blacks. Many of them depended on the Vare Organization for their livelihoods, like Assistant City Solicitor John A. Sparks; state representatives William H. Fuller and Samuel B. Hart; State Boxing Commissioner Charles Frederick White; and numerous police officers, municipal employees, and public school teachers and principals. The committee included several Asbury associates, like his business partner, the secretary of Asbury's Keystone Bank, and Asbury's wife, Ida. But there were also black leaders in business, finance, religion, and the professions. Among them was Dr. John P. Turner of the Frederick Douglass Memorial Hospital, who would be named the only black director of the SCEA.[14]

During this period, Colonel David Collier hired Albert L. Sutton as his executive assistant. Sutton, a Los Angeles resident born in the South, had worked with international expositions for over two decades. After Collier's departure, Sutton was named acting assistant director-general, helping E. L. Austin with the chaotic opening of the fair. He was also appointed director of domestic participation and special events. In these critical roles, Sutton was responsible for much of the event planning at the Sesqui. He managed a number of key departments, including Federal and State Participation, Municipal and Civic Participation, Congresses and Conventions, Fraternal Organizations, Special Events and Special Days, and the Committee on Negro Activities. Sutton's antipathy toward African Americans would grow more blatant over the following year, tainting the black experience at the Sesqui in a number of ways.[15]

After appointing the Committee on Negro Activities, the SCEA showed little interest in working with them to develop an agenda of black activities. Asbury's request for an African American speaker on opening day was ignored by Collier, while his application for a modest $25,000 for black exhibits was denied. Soon afterward, the white and socially prominent Elizabeth Martin and Mary Warburton easily secured $200,000 from the SCEA for their High Street project. A frustrated E. Washington Rhodes asked Collier why a colored committee had been named. Collier replied that it was in response to the numerous petitions received from local blacks, confirming Rhodes's fear that the committee was window dressing. African Americans also sensed that they were being shut out of all moneymaking aspects of the Sesqui, including the hiring of labor for construction projects. "I saw scores and scores of whites busily engaged in preparations," wrote Nahum Daniel Brascher, editor-in-chief of the Chicago-based Associated Negro Press (ANP) after visiting the Sesqui grounds in January 1926, "but not one black face."[16]

Despite his political experience, John Asbury appeared unable to persuade the SCEA to cooperate with his committee. Under his guidance, the Committee on Negro Activities had opened its offices in the Grand United Odd Fellows Building, headquarters of one of the largest black fraternal societies in America. Asbury, an officer in the society, had been instrumental in financing construction of its building at Twelfth and Spruce. The rest of the Sesqui organization was located in Congress Hall at Chestnut and Fifth Streets, preparing to relocate to the new Administration Building at Oregon Plaza on April 1. An Asbury spokesman dismissed talk of segregation, explaining that the separate facilities were "a means to facilitate the work of the various committees."[17]

Asbury's small but dedicated staff struggled to assemble exhibits and organize programs without SCEA support. His lieutenants were Assistant Director Ernest Ten Eyck Attwell and Manager of Exhibits Thomas J. Calloway. Attwell was field director of the Bureau of Colored Work with the Playground and Recreation Association of America, an agency dedicated to providing recreational spaces and activities for inner-city children. Calloway, a Maryland lawyer and educator, had organized the groundbreaking Negro Exhibit at the 1900 Paris Exposition with W. E. B. Du Bois. Calloway and Du Bois had assembled five hundred photographs depicting black life in one of the most highly praised displays at the fair.

Asbury's chief clerk was F. Grant Gilmore, a Philadelphia author and dramatist, who published a Sesqui guide for black visitors. W. Franklin Hoxter, church organist and music critic for the *Tribune*, served as director of music. A young woman named Harriette Wilson Parvis acted as investigator and researcher, while a Pennsylvania Academy of the Fine Arts graduate named Laura Wheeler supervised construction and decoration. Wheeler, who would later marry Walter Waring, would gain renown for her portraits of Marian Anderson, W. E. B. Du Bois, and other African American notables.[18]

The ANP noted acidly that "Mr. Asbury's plans have been advanced considerably farther than his cooperation from the general committee." The ANP, whose articles on the Sesqui appeared in the *Tribune*, attacked the

SCEA's treatment of blacks as "insulting" and "grossly unfair." It criticized the SCEA's "indifferent and sometimes insolent treatment" of the "patient and gentlemanly" Asbury. "The General Committee," wrote the ANP, "has pussy-footed and shunted Mr. Asbury until it really had placed him in an embarrassing position before his friends of Philadelphia and the country."[19]

The situation escalated when Nahum Brascher of the ANP protested to Federal officials that Sesqui managers were discriminating against Negroes and excluding them from all key aspects of the Sesqui. He cited the SCEA's refusal to allot funds to the Committee on Negro Activities for staff, programs, or exhibits, forcing Asbury to pay expenses out of his own pocket. Brascher's report came to the attention of President Coolidge, who asked Secretaries Hoover and Kellogg to investigate. Congressman Martin Madden of Chicago, the House Appropriations Committee chairman whose recommendations on federal funding would be crucial to the Sesqui's survival, also promised the Chicago-based ANP that he would explore the matter.

Sesqui management, which had ignored earlier inquiries from Brascher, sprang into action at this point. A. L. Sutton drafted a letter for Mayor Kendrick to sign, defending the Sesqui management as fair and unbiased. "I have gone very carefully into all matters relative to Negro activities," Sutton assured the mayor, "and have successfully straightened out the angles so that I believe we will now have hearty co-operation and full understanding on the part of Mr. Asbury and his Committee." During this period, the Organization offered to name Asbury as the city's first black assistant district attorney, possibly to ensure that he would toe the party line. The promise fell through later when District Attorney Charles Edwin Fox refused to appoint any blacks to his office.[20]

An official counteroffensive presented relations between the SCEA and the Committee on Negro Activities as harmonious. Asbury sent a public letter to Nahum Brascher, explaining that the SCEA had not denied his request for $25,000, but was simply "not appropriating any lump sums." Instead, "all monies allotted to all divisions of the work would be paid on orders from those divisions from one general fund." F. Grant Gilmore dismissed "disgruntled members of the race" who criticized the Committee on Negro Activities. "It's those of the race who put nothing into the project and want a lot out of it who are now crying," he insisted, "because they aren't getting anything out of the proposition." Not long after these statements appeared in the *Tribune*, the SCEA allocated $12,500 for black exhibits and programs. President Coolidge, who viewed racial conflict as "local problems which must be worked out by the mutual forbearance and human kindness of each community" rather than by "outside interference," did not press for any further investigation.[21]

For exhibit space, the SCEA allotted the Committee on Negro Activities twelve thousand square feet in the Palace of Agriculture near the booths for Japan and Los Angeles County. This assignment did not come until April 1926, giving the committee one month to organize its display. Telegrams and letters were sent to African American colleges and organizations around the country, asking them to contribute exhibit materials and photographs.

On April 27 Thomas J. Calloway contacted his former colleague W.E.B. Du Bois and asked for his assistance in assembling the Negro Exhibit. "The time is very short," he admitted, "but the possibilities seem so great that I believe it is worth the effort to attempt it." Calloway thought that the publication of a daily Negro newspaper at the Sesqui might attract national attention. Would Du Bois consider acting as editor in chief? "It would give you an opportunity to take up new causes to drive into the American public some of the things that you have been giving utterance to," Calloway urged, "and to take up new causes for which such an occasion would furnish the opportunity."[22]

Calloway was probably unaware that Du Bois had been corresponding for nearly a year with John Asbury and A. L. Sutton, vainly attempting to arrange a fourth Pan-African Conference at the Sesqui. Du Bois's frustration may have influenced the somewhat peevish tone of his two responses. The first rejected Calloway's plans for the Negro Exhibit, realistically based on what could be obtained from cooperative black organizations at minimal cost on short notice. Instead, Du Bois proposed fourteen original exhibits, quantifying the Negro population of America "from a scientific point of view" by key variables like geographic distribution, sex, age, education, occupation, and religion. In his second letter, Du Bois agreed to edit a daily paper, which he proposed calling *The Moon, Shining Daily for the Darker World*. Envisioning the paper as an eight-page tabloid, Du Bois anticipated that it would cost $50,000. Calloway, struggling to assemble an exhibit for less than $12,500, replied diplomatically that "the right business genius could put over the project," but that "neither you or I could put our hands on such a person."[23]

While Du Bois attempted to make his mark on the Sesqui from afar, a disturbing example of white resistance to black involvement on a local level was unfolding. In early 1926, Philadelphia's musical, social, and cultural institutions had joined forces to create a five-thousand-voice Sesqui-Centennial Festival Chorus. This massive ensemble would perform on special occasions like Opening Day, Flag Day, and the Fourth of July. Participants were drawn from a wide range of groups, including the National Society of the Colonial Dames of America, National Council of Jewish Women, Sons of St. George, German *Männenchor* Society, and Young Men and Young Women's Hebrew Associations. Not one black organization had been invited to sing in the Sesqui Chorus.

In late April a delegation from the Committee on Negro Activities, led by Chairman Asbury and Music Chairman Hoxter, met with Craig King, secretary of the SCEA music committee. King announced that while Negroes might participate in performances of the Sesqui chorus, their presence was not desired in rehearsals. "Colored only" rehearsals would be held in a separate location under the direction of Hoxter. How black singers would be treated during actual performances was not addressed. A furious Asbury reminded King of Mayor Kendrick's promise that there would be no segregation at the Sesqui. Hoxter noted that invitations had gone out to all Philadelphia public schools, including black and integrated ones, asking all good singers to audition. Were black children and teachers to be told that they could not rehearse or perform with their white counterparts? King informed the black delegation that the matter had already been decided and nothing could be done.

Asbury wrote an angry letter to Dr. Herbert J. Tily, chairman of the SCEA music committee, informing him that "under no circumstances" would he allow a "separate race group" of black singers. Tily assured Asbury that he was "personally quite in sympathy with your attitude," and that the Chorus "should be utterly and entirely democratic." But even though Tily was an SCEA director and chairman of the music committee, he announced that the matter of integration was beyond his control. The chorus was under the direction of the chairman of the festival chorus committee, while the school invitations had been handled by the Board of Public Education. Tily did offer to take Asbury's letter to the next meeting of the festival chorus committee to make sure that "your views are properly presented." Concluding, Tily admitted that he would "greatly like, for artistic reasons, to have some music given entirely by colored musicians," just as German singers were preparing a *Sängerfest* and Welsh musicians were organizing an *Eisteddfodd* at the Sesqui.[24]

In April several African Americans decided to attend Sesqui Chorus rehearsals and test the color line by applying for membership. Two of them, Rhoda Tilton and Bertha Harrison, were schoolteachers who had received invitations to audition from the board of public education. On April 13 the two women attempted to join the Central Unit of the chorus at the Girls' High School at Seventeenth and Spring Garden Streets. While waiting in the applicants' line, Harrison and Tilton were asked to take a seat and wait for a chorus official. Realizing that they had been the only two blacks in line, both women rejoined the queue. When they reached the desk where application cards were being distributed, the clerk ignored them and passed cards over their heads to white applicants behind them. Both women grabbed cards and filled them out.

At this point, the two determined teachers met the formidable Mrs. Frederick (Clara) Abbott, manager of the Sesqui Chorus and a leader in Philadelphia's most genteel musical circles. While white applicants entered the Auditorium, according to the *Tribune*, Abbott stopped the two black teachers and demanded that they surrender their application cards. She told both of them, "You cannot register here." When Tilton and Harrison asked why not, she responded, "We are going to form a unit for members of your group. When we know the time and place of meeting we will notify you. You will get your music then, and rehearse by yourselves."

When the teachers asked if they might enter the Auditorium and listen to the rehearsal, Abbott refused. The teachers sneaked in and listened to the music as well as to a speech on democracy from Tily. Tilton later wrote in the *Tribune* that as Tily spoke "[we] looked at each other and smiled, knowing from what had happened that it did not ring true." Both Tilton and Harrison soon received letters from the Philadelphia Music League, explaining that "we are making every effort to form a special unit for members of your race. We will be glad to notify you when and where the first rehearsal of the Unit takes place."[25] Although the correspondence parroted Abbott's language, both letters were unsigned.

Orrin C. Evans, a *Tribune* journalist whose efforts to join the Sesqui Chorus had also been rebuffed, interviewed Abbott afterward. He reported that Abbott confirmed the teachers' account, saying, "I most certainly did tell them that we would not take them at the Central Unit. I'll stand by my guns in that statement." Abbott explained that she was only doing as she had been instructed by "people at the headquarters." By this point, the Sesqui Chorus and black singers had reached an impasse that appeared to favor Abbott's camp. "Since the general committee refuses to permit colored singers to join the Central Unit," the *Tribune* editorialized, and "W. Franklin Hoxter, Chairman of the Colored Music Committee, refuses to train a special unit 'for colored,' it appears as if there will not be any colored voices in the Chorus."[26]

At a subsequent meeting of the SCEA Board of Directors, Dr. John P. Turner, the only African American director, demanded to know if a segregated choral unit was being formed. Mayor Kendrick insisted that "no lines would be, or have been drawn." W. O. Miller, assistant director of the Sesqui

Chorus, explained that a separate unit had been considered to provide Negro singers with special training, but had been abandoned since "very few members of the race had applied for membership." Miller suggested that if the two black teachers had been rejected, it was only because the sectional units had been filled. (Rhoda Tilton refuted Miller's argument, saying that she had been told that the Central Unit was only half filled.) He asked Dr. Turner to urge Miss Tilton and Miss Harrison to return to the Central Unit, where any confusion would be straightened out.[27]

Tribune coverage of the chorus segregation faded away soon afterward, overtaken by other concerns. Philadelphia's white press ignored the controversy completely, as it did most African American issues at the Sesqui. There is no way of knowing if Tilton, Harrison, or other blacks gained admittance to the five-thousand-member chorus. It is possible that a few lighter-skinned singers were allowed in to refute charges of complete segregation; even Abbott admitted to the *Tribune* that there were four or five "colored members" in the vast ensemble. African Americans formed a separate Sesqui-Centennial Chorus under the direction of W. Franklin Hoxter, deciding that it was better to sing by themselves than to remain silent.[28]

As Opening Day approached, African Americans in Philadelphia appeared increasingly alienated from both the Sesqui and their representatives to the fair. "There is something wrong with this whole Sesqui-Centennial business," complained the *Tribune*. "There has been much quibbling and 'crawfishing.' The colored participation has been side-tracked, switched off and discouraged. Apparently colored people didn't know what they wanted and the white folks were determined upon a policy of discrimination."[29]

Perhaps it was this alienation, and its possible impact on black voters in the fall elections, that persuaded Mayor Kendrick to include an African American orator in the Opening Day ceremonies at the last moment. According to one historian, a group of "representative colored citizens of Philadelphia" had petitioned the mayor to include a black speaker. On May 22 Kendrick wrote A. Philip Randolph, "I have the honor to invite you to be the Orator for the Negro Race of the World at the opening exercises of the Sesqui-Centennial Exposition on Monday, May 31, 1926."[30]

The thirty-four-year-old Randolph had become coeditor of the *Messenger* magazine in 1917, branding it "The Only Radical Negro Magazine in America." Randolph championed socialism, unionism, and racial equality, while dismissing Du Bois and other African American leaders as "conservative." In 1920, with the Red Scare in full throttle, he ran for New York State controller on the Socialist ticket, and lost. Randolph urged Philadelphia blacks, unsuccessfully, to boycott segregated schools in 1925. That

A. Philip Randolph as he appeared in 1964. Randolph's groundbreaking speech on Opening Day was one of the few bright moments for African Americans at the Sesqui-Centennial. (Prints and Photographs Division, Library of Congress.)

same year, he accepted an invitation to head a new black labor union, the Brotherhood of Sleeping Car Porters (BSCP), which battled the powerful Pullman Company for better wages and benefits. By the time of the Sesqui, Randolph had grown less radical, changing the *Messenger*'s masthead from "The Only Radical Negro Magazine in America" to "The World's Greatest Negro Monthly." He was still a surprisingly controversial addition to the Opening Day roster.

Kendrick offered his guest little in the way of hospitality. Randolph's name did not appear among the hundreds of dignitaries entertained at the mayor's reception on the morning of May 31. His name was also missing from the Opening Day program, so that few of his listeners at Sesqui Stadium had any idea who he was. Randolph's demands for complete racial equality and for recognition of the contributions made by Aframericans (his term for African Americans) were truly revolutionary for a nation where segregation was the everyday norm:

> If there are those, either because of ignorance or malice who would challenge the right of Aframericans to share in the glories and achievements of our country, my answer is that of all the Americans, the Negro is, doubtless, the most typically American. He is the incarnation of America. . . . The insistent cry for freedom on the part of the Negro has kept the American people face to face with the fact that a democracy has not fulfilled its highest mission so

> long as there are people in the country, black or white who cannot participate in the affairs of government, industry or society generally as free, intelligent human beings.[31]

Despite Randolph's challenge to the status quo, the *Tribune* reported that his speech was "surprisingly well received." The only objectors appeared to be a group of southern Shriners, who "evinced their impatience and displeasure by derogatory comments typical of their ilk," and A. L. Sutton, who passed notes to Kendrick begging him to cut off Randolph. Outside the Sesqui Stadium, Randolph's speech met with silence from the white community, vanishing into almost instant oblivion. Only African American newspapers covered his talk, while most white journals ignored it altogether. The Philadelphia *Bulletin*, which printed the speeches of Secretaries Hoover and Kellogg almost verbatim, did not quote one word of Randolph's speech. In an unusual slip for the accuracy-obsessed newspaper, it misspelled his name as "A. *Phillips* Randolph, colored, New York, who spoke for the American colored race."[32]

The *Tribune* estimated that between five thousand and six thousand African Americans, "largely of the laboring classes," attended Opening Day. Aside from Randolph, they were confined to the role of spectators. Only two blacks were among the hundreds of invited dignitaries: Dr. John P. Turner of the SCEA Board of Directors, and State Legislator Samuel D. Hart. Otherwise, the *Tribune* reported, "the only evidence of Negro representation . . . was a minstrel mimic laboring under the weight of a massive bass drum." African Americans were incensed that not one colored face appeared among the thousands of servicemen who led the Opening Day parade, since 350,000 African Americans had served overseas during the world war. *Tribune* editor Rhodes could not contain his anger at his race's exclusion from the procession:

> We wonder what was in the breasts of those black men who fought to make America safe for Democracy and on Monday stood on the sidelines, forgotten, as the Nordic strode by in all his vain pride. A few nights before some of them had heard the Mayor of the city—the recognized head of the Sesqui-Centennial, give several hundred Negroes the usual pap handed out by the white politicians to Negroes—"you people are as good as I am, etc."; and applauded to the echo by Negro hirelings and this duty done, he went safely on planning the great opening for the Sesqui, and ignoring them as usual. We hope the rest of the Negroes in America are as sorry for

Philadelphia Negroes as we are—the boast that we are Philadelphians doesn't mean very much—it has been proven.[33]

Black anger intensified when it became apparent that segregation would be the order of the day at the Sesqui. African Americans were not banned from the Alpine Haus or other Sesqui restaurants but were often made to feel unwelcome. Few African Americans would have enjoyed the ambience of the Indian Queen Tavern on High Street, where blacks costumed as field hands and Aunt Jemimas provided "Old Southern" entertainment. Instead, most African Americans ate at the cafeteria in the Colored Women's Hostess House, erected at a cost of $5,000 by the Federation of Colored Women's Clubs. The Hostess House also featured an emergency health station for black visitors, supervised by SCEA Director Dr. John P. Turner. Whites requiring medical treatment were taken to the fully staffed Sesqui

African American entertainers at the Indian Queen Tavern on High Street during the 1926 Sesqui. The tavern's white employees serve as a barrier between the blacks and the upper-class managers. The Indian Queen minstrels were the only black faces many Sesqui visitors would see. (Courtesy of the Committee of 1926.)

Hospitals. The location of the Hostess House, near High Street, was not indicated on any Sesqui maps.[34]

Ignoring these indignities, the Committee on Negro Activities focused on assembling an exhibit in the Palace of Agriculture that would illustrate the accomplishments of African Americans since 1876. Its showpiece was a plaque of Bishop Richard Allen, founder of the African Methodist Episcopal Church, executed by Henry Ossawa Tanner. Works of art by other African Americans, including several portraits by Laura Wheeler, alternated with photographs of student activities at Virginia's Hampton Institute, which counted Booker T. Washington among its alumni. Statistical charts tracked the growth in black college students, home owners, and business proprietors. A reproduction of the black-owned North Carolina Mutual Life Company represented the advances of African American entrepreneurs in the field of finance.

A booth featured current editions of the leading publications of the Negro Press in America, including Du Bois's *The Crisis*, the *Philadelphia Tribune*, the Baltimore *Afro American*, the Chicago *Broad Ax*, and the New York *Age*. Students from the Downingtown Industrial School, a vocational high school in Chester County, gave a daily demonstration of blacksmithing. African American musicians performed on a regular basis, and readings were given of works by Paul Laurence Dunbar and other contemporary black authors.[35]

On July 12 the Women's Committee on Negro Activities produced *Loyalty's Gift: A Historic Pageant in Song* in the Sesqui Auditorium. Written by Mrs. Dora Cole Norman, *Loyalty's Gift* presented a series of tableaux on black life. More than one thousand actors enacted scenes depicting the arrival of the first slaves in America in 1619; the horrors of slavery and the joys of emancipation; and the struggles and accomplishments of the American Negro in the modern era. The spectacle concluded with "Achievement," a pantheon of pioneers in race progress. Marian Anderson, Philadelphia's own "Negro contralto," represented achievement in song, bringing down the house with "O Mio Fernando" from Donizetti's *La Favorita*. Her rendition of this aria had won the National Music League competition at New York's Lewisohn Stadium in 1925.[36]

Loyalty's Gift was one of the few African American efforts at the Sesqui to attract favorable mention in the white press. The *Bulletin* reviewer praised it as "an entertainment quite unique and wholly interesting, produced on an elaborate and imposing scale." The reviewer noted that the audience was the largest that had ever gathered in the Auditorium, filling the ten-thousand-seat hall to capacity for the first time that summer. The only criticism was

"Loyalty's Gift"

(Mrs. Dora Cole Norman, Author and Director)

A HISTORIC PAGEANT IN SONG

Under Auspices of Women's Committee on Negro Activities

Sesquicentennial Grounds

IN THE AUDITORIUM

MONDAY EVE., JULY 12th

8.30 Daylight Saving

PORTRAYING THE STRUGGLES AND ACHIEVEMENTS OF THE NEGRO

FEATURING

A CHORUS OF 400 VOICES

SINGING SPIRITUALS IN THEIR ORIGINAL SETTINGS

THE CELEBRATED HAMPTON QUARTETTE

THE FAMOUS FISK QUINTETTE
With Its Splendid European Reputation

MISS MARIAN ANDERSON
Winner of the New York Stadium Contest
The Finished Product

GRINNELL'S CONCERT BAND
J. Lawrence Grinnell, Conductor

ADMISSION $1.00
PATRONS TICKETS (Reserved Seats) $2.50

NOTE: All tickets include admission to the Exposition Grounds. The afternoon or early evening may be devoted to other Sesqui Centennial attractions.

TICKETS ON SALE at Wanamaker's, Gimbels, Lit Brothers, Snellenburg's, Strawbridge & Clothier, Heppe's, Presser's, Philadelphia Tribune Office, 526 S. 16th St., Dabney's Pharmacy, 43rd & Fairmount Ave., Kessler & Kessler, 20th & Dickinson Sts., Glenn and Walker, 301 W. Queen Lane, Your Pharmacy, 18th & Christian Sts., Reading Advertising Service, 24 N. 59th St., or any member of the cast.

COMMITTEE ON NEGRO ACTIVITIES
1201 Spruce Street, Philadelphia, Pa.

Please mail me .... tickets for "Loyalty's Gift," to be held at the Auditorium, Sesqui Centennial Grounds, July 12th, 1926. I enclose check (or money order) for $..

Name .... Address ....

Make all checks or money orders payable to J. C. Asbury, Director.

Reading For Printing, 24 N. 59th Street

A program for *Loyalty's Gift*, the successful pageant presented by the Women's Committee on Negro Activities at the Sesqui Auditorium on July 12, 1926.

the length of the spectacle: it began after 9:00 P.M. and was still going strong at midnight, when the reporter had to leave to make deadline.[37]

On August 23 Committee on Negro Activities Chairman John Asbury and Music Director W. Franklin Hoxter staged a Spiritual Songfest in the Sesqui Stadium. In a challenge to the Festival Chorus, Asbury and Hoxter joined their singers with choirs from nearly a dozen southern cities, including Baltimore, Washington, and Richmond, to form a gospel chorus of one thousand voices. The concert attracted another sizable crowd.

Inspired by the success of the Songfest and *Loyalty's Gift*, the committee announced plans for an even larger spectacle to be staged at the Auditorium on Wednesday, September 22: *Ethiopia*, a "spectacular music drama" by Edward J. and Lillian White-McGoo. *Ethiopia* was an allegorical pageant that told the story of the Negro race from Egypt through modern-day America. Throughout the story, Ethiopia, a female character symbolic of the Negro race, battled Oppression and Leniency as she made her appeal before the mystical figure of Justice. "The general theme of the piece," according to publicity materials, "aims to advance world brotherhood by encouraging meekness with the Negro's demand for justice." Tickets for *Ethiopia* ($1.00 for general admission and $1.50 for reserved seats) were available at the *Tribune* offices, the Citizens Republican Club, and the black-owned Citizens and Southern Bank and Trust.[38]

Meanwhile, black conventioneers descended on the Sesqui as avidly as their white counterparts. The State Federation of Negro Women's Clubs held their convention in early July, followed by the National Association of Negro Musicians and the National Ushers' Association (for black church ushers and officers). August saw meetings of the National Negro Press Association, the Afro-American League of America, and the National Medical Association, the black counterpart to the then-segregated American Medical Association. Plans were under way for a Fraternal and Military Day in late October, which would convene the military companies associated with black fraternal organizations for a program of prize drills, athletic competitions, and a grand military ball.[39]

While the Committee on Negro Activities struggled to illustrate African American achievements, one retrogressive Sesqui policeman nearly triggered an international incident. Haiti, one of only fourteen foreign nations to acknowledge the Sesqui-Centennial officially, had mounted two exhibits at the fair. Despite being a virtual dictatorship under American military control, Haiti had much to celebrate in 1926 after decades of turmoil. Louis Borno, president since 1922, had stabilized Haitian finances, balanced the trade deficit, and modernized infrastructure. The bespectacled

Borno was a familiar figure to many Americans thanks to his appearances in movie newsreels and newspaper photos. In late June, Borno and his wife, Marie-Hélène, visited the White House, where President Coolidge welcomed the loyal ally of the United States.

The morning after the presidential visit, Borno and his party decided to motor from Washington to Philadelphia and visit the Sesqui-Centennial. After the limousine with Haitian flags flying from its fenders pulled up to the main gates, the policeman on duty snorted in disbelief when the driver told him that President Borno and the First Lady of Haiti were in the rear. "G'wan," he sneered. "I suppose you'll be telling me that it's General Grant and his wife next." When the driver protested, the policeman angrily told him, "I don't care who he is. If you ain't got a pass, you'll have to pay fifty cents each to get in this show."[40] After a brief discussion with the Bornos, the driver got out and paid two dollars for four tickets at an admission booth.

George Zimmer, an assistant to Director Austin, was driving through the Sesqui grounds later that day when he slammed on his brakes. He had just

Secretary of State Kellogg greets President Louis Borno of Haiti (center, wearing spectacles) upon his arrival in Washington, DC, to meet with President Calvin Coolidge. The following day, Borno would be publicly humiliated at the Sesqui-Centennial. (Prints and Photographs Division, Library of Congress.)

recognized the president of Haiti—a man who warranted a twenty-one-gun salute according to diplomatic protocol—munching a hot dog with his wife and two military aides at an outdoor table at the Alpine Haus. Zimmer introduced himself, and learned about the Bornos' humiliating welcome. Apologizing profusely, he whisked the Haitians to the Administration Building. Within an hour, an official escort gave the Borno party a blue-ribbon inspection of the Sesqui. The tour ended at Camp Anthony Wayne, where the Sixth Field Artillery treated the Haitians to a roaring twenty-one-gun salute. President Borno graciously excused the policeman's behavior, given that he had arrived without diplomatic notice. Both he and Sesqui officials overlooked the fact that a white policeman had refused to believe that four well-dressed blacks in a limousine could be anything other than a joke.[41]

The announcement on August 18 that the Sesqui would host the world heavyweight championship title bout between champion Jack Dempsey and challenger Gene Tunney in September thrilled white Philadelphia but left black Philadelphia cold. Civic leaders and boxing commissioners in New York and Chicago, promoter Tex Rickard's first two choices for the venue, had refused to sanction a Dempsey-Tunney match. They insisted that Dempsey fight the African American Harry Wills, lest their political machines lose the good will of their black voters. Philadelphia, with a black voting bloc in thrall to white Republicans, embraced the opportunity to host the fight. When Governor Pinchot asked the Pennsylvania State Boxing Commission to approve the fight, its two white members agreed without hesitation. Commissioner C. Fred White, an African American from Philadelphia, withheld his vote in protest and then resigned.[42]

Harry "Black Panther" Wills, a three-time World Colored Heavyweight Champion, had tried to secure a match against Dempsey since 1920. Dempsey had announced upon winning the heavyweight title in 1919 that he would "draw the color line" and refuse to fight black fighters. He later softened his stance, confessing in 1926 that "since I won the championship in 1919, I have wanted a bout with Wills." His sudden color blindness was greeted with derision by the black community. A *Tribune* sportswriter snickered that "Jack Dempsey would rather fight Harry Wills than anyone else. Now you tell one." Rickard offered to stage an elimination bout between Wills and Tunney, with Dempsey to fight the winner. Wills's manager refused the offer, leaving Dempsey free to fight his white challenger with a clear conscience. By then, Philadelphia blacks were referring to "the Fight of the Century" as "the Joke of the Century."[43]

The weeks following the announcement of the Dempsey-Tunney bout seemed to witness an escalation of calculated affronts to African Americans at the Sesqui. Most of these actions involved the office of Domestic Participation and Special Events, headed by A. L. Sutton. Given Sutton's sympathetic attitude toward the Ku Klux Klan, it is tempting to view these actions as part of a coordinated campaign on his part to exclude African Americans from the latter half of the Sesqui. They could also be interpreted as retaliation against blacks for their role in forcing Kendrick to cancel the September Klonvokation at the fair.[44]

In early September, Sutton fired Thomas J. Calloway, Asbury's director of exhibits, citing cost-cutting measures at the SCEA. The Committee on Negro Activities office in the Grand United Odd Fellows' Building was closed as well. Mincing no words, the *Tribune* disclosed that these actions were ordered by "Mr. Sutton, who it is understood, is a rabid Negro hater." The *Tribune* criticized the "dormant" Executive Committee of the Committee on Negro Activities for mounting no protest against Sutton's actions. Executive Committee members, "no more than figure heads," had not met in more than two months.[45]

The worst affront to the black community was saved until forty-eight hours before the pageant *Ethiopia* was to be staged. For weeks, *Ethiopia* had been slated for the Sesqui Auditorium on September 22, the night before the Dempsey-Tunney fight. Several prominent blacks, including ex-boxing commissioner C. Fred White, had invested thousands of dollars in the production. Anticipating another capacity crowd of ten thousand or more, *Ethiopia*'s backers expected to realize a substantial return on their investment.

On September 20 Sutton informed the producers that the Auditorium would not be available to them on September 22. They would have to stage *Ethiopia* there on September 23, the night of the championship fight. More than sixty thousand white Odd Fellows were holding their annual convention at the Sesqui, and had been booked for an evening program at the Sesqui Stadium on September 22. The normally efficient Sutton had evidently failed to realize that the Stadium, where the Dempsey-Tunney fight had been slated since August 18, would be crawling with workmen the night before the bout. The Odd Fellows were shunted to the Auditorium, and *Ethiopia* was pushed back twenty-four hours.

The producers of *Ethiopia* demanded that Sutton honor their contract. They had sold thousands of advance tickets for September 22, and there was insufficient time to alert everyone to the last-minute change in dates. Many African American households in Philadelphia did not have telephones or radios. Some ticketholders had other commitments on September 23, while others would be unwilling to brave the onslaught of fight fans. Sutton informed them that they could take the 23rd or cancel their production. As a feeble sop, he increased backers' take of receipts from 40 percent to 50 percent, and offered to distribute thirty thousand circulars throughout the city announcing the change. Their backs against the wall, the black producers consented.

When a *Tribune* reporter attempted to interview Sutton, he was told the director was unavailable. Sutton's secretary justified the last-minute change by explaining, "We couldn't afford to have the Odd Fellows, who were here 60,000 strong, go away from the Sesqui disgruntled, as did the Shriners, and spread word all over the country that the Sesqui officials had not given them due consideration." Hundreds of ticketholders for *Ethiopia* arrived at the Auditorium on September 22, mystified to find the great hall filled with thousands of white Odd Fellows rather than black performers. The thirty thousand circulars promised by Sutton had not been distributed until that morning.

The following night, September 23, approximately two hundred people braved the weather and traffic to see *Ethiopia* at the Auditorium, while almost 130,000 fight fans screamed for blood in the Stadium. The small audience clustered around the footlights, watching Ethiopia stand before Justice "and with a wistful face like the face of a blurred cameo plead for justice which was at that very moment being denied her." As could be expected, the production was a financial failure. The producers found cold comfort in the fact that they were receiving 50 percent of the roughly $200 gate, rather than 40 percent of the $10,000 to $15,000 they had anticipated. Plans for an October pageant were abruptly canceled.[46]

Ethiopia marked the swan song of African American efforts to participate in the Sesqui. Coverage of the fair by the *Tribune* dropped off substantially after the end of September. When the fair shut down at the end of November, the *Tribune* published an editorial, "The 'Big Show' Is Over." It offered a surprisingly restrained evaluation of what had become a bitter disappointment for African Americans in Philadelphia and elsewhere:

> In the beginning "sun-kissed" Americans were of the opinion that they would be able to present a clear picture of their progress in America to the civilized world. Hopes ran high. Expectations were great. It is seriously questioned that the colored people used the "Sesqui" to the best possible advantage. In some quarters it is believed that the hopes were blasted and the expectations were never realized. Then there are some who say that the colored people made a comparatively good record. . . . whether or not the colored people received their rightful proportion of the benefits will

> be discussed in barber shops long after the busy mechanics have wrecked the last building.[47]

Years after the white community conducted its relentless campaign to hinder black participation in the Sesqui, it continued to obliterate any record of black accomplishments at the fair. *The Sesqui-Centennial International Exposition*, the official history of the fair, was published in 1929. The 520-page tome painstakingly recorded nearly every aspect of the Sesqui, down to its parking lots and pigeon shows. But there was no room, evidently, for a chapter on African American participation at the Sesqui.

African Americans make a few, fleeting appearances throughout the book. In Chapter 14, "Other Activities of Women," Mrs. J. Willis Martin notes that "under the patronage of the Women's Committee was built a hostess house for negroes." Martin devotes a whole paragraph to the efforts of the Negro Women's Committee, who "exhibited rug making, uniforms, and negro dolls modeled from life." Mention is made elsewhere of *Loyalty's Gift*, the one Sesqui event to have filled the Auditorium to capacity. On page 469 of the appendix, the members of the Negro Activities Committee are listed, sandwiched in between the Naval Committee and the Polo Committee.

The most space devoted to African Americans in the book occurs in the first chapter, "The Exposition in Perspective." The authors try to list all of the "firsts" that made the Sesqui-Centennial a worthy successor to the 1876 Centennial. They end their list with a particularly noteworthy accomplishment:

> A unique exhibit at the Exposition was that showing the progress of the Negro race in industry, art and science. It was comprehensive in scope and offered a striking revelation of the remarkable advances that had been made by the race.[48]

Other than that self-congratulatory statement, African Americans are conspicuous in their absence from the official chronicles of the Sesqui-Centennial. Once again, they had been rendered invisible by the white men and women celebrating the 150th anniversary of life, liberty, and the pursuit of happiness.[49]

NOTES

1. "Fraternal Flashes: Sesqui-Centennial," *PT*, June 18, 1921; "Produce! We Must," Editorial, *PT*, March 21, 1925.

2. Countryman, *Up South*, pp. 17–20; Franklin, *The Education of Black Philadelphia*, pp. 25–27; Hardy, *Race and Opportunity*, pp. 75–76; "Real Estate for Rent and for Sale," *PT*, September 12, 1925.

3. Eric Ledell Smith, "'Asking for Justice and Fair Play': African American State Legislators and Civil Rights in Early Twentieth-Century Philadelphia," *Pennsylvania History* 63, no. 2 (April 1996): 184–185; Lane, *William Dorsey's Philadelphia and Ours*, p. 357; Hardy, *Race and Opportunity*, p. 558.

4. Franklin, *The Education of Black Philadelphia*, pp. 40.

5. "Notables Attend Stanley Opening," *PI*, January 29, 1921; "Stanley Thronged at Public Opening," *PI*, January 30, 1921; Franklin, *The Education of Black Philadelphia*, pp. 40, 50, 55–56, 69; Smith, "Asking for Justice and Fair Play," p. 185; Lane, *William Dorsey's Philadelphia and Ours*, pp. 357–361; Hardy, *Race and Opportunity*, pp. 514, 554.

6. Franklin, *The Education of Black Philadelphia*, pp. 84–85; Du Bois, *The Philadelphia Negro*, pp. 316–317. Untitled article, *PT*, July 19, 1928; cited by Francis Ryan, "The Quest for Local Power," p. 19; Hardy, *Race and Opportunity*, pp. 271–212, 282, 387, 540.

7. Hardy, *Race and Opportunity*, p. 527. "Sesqui-Centennial," editorial, *PT*, March 14, 1925.

8. "There'll be no Segregation at the S-C," *PT*, May 23, 1925.

9. Eustace Gay, "Facts and Fancies," *PT*, July 18, 1925; Charlene Mires, "Race, Place, and the Pennsylvania Emancipation Exposition of 1913," *PMHB* 128, no. 3 (July 2004): 258.

10. Rydell, *World of Fairs*, pp. 158–159.

11. SCEA Division of Publicity Press Release issued Sept. 4, 1925.

12. Memorandum from George W. B. Hicks to Ernest T. Trigg, PCA/SCEA, Folder 44.

13. Letter to W. Freeland Kendrick from David C. Collier, June 22, 1925, PCA/SCEA, Folder 44; memorandum from George W. B. Hicks to Ernest T. Trigg, PCA/SCEA, Folder 44; letter to W. Freeland Kendrick from Ernest T. Trigg, July 30, 1925, PCA/SCEA, Folder 44.

14. Press release, Division of Publicity, Sesqui-Centennial International Exposition, September 4, 1925; *Souvenir and Visitor's Guide,* 1926.

15. Memorandum from David C. Collier to all SCEA Department Heads, August 29, 1925, PCA/SCEA, Box A-1465, Folder 1; "Aide to Collier Named," *PB*, July 31, 1925.

16. Rydell, *World of Fairs*, p. 159.

17. "Sesqui Offices Opened with Asbury Head," *PT*, March 13, 1926.

18. Franklin, *The Education of Black Philadelphia*, p. 91; "Philadelphia," Baltimore *Afro American*, January 2, 1926; "The Negro Exhibit," *Report of the Commissioner-General for the United States to the International Universal Exposition, Paris, 1900, Vol. II*, pp. 463–466; *Souvenir and Visitor's Guide*, pp. 42–43; "Sesqui Offices Opened with Asbury Head," *PT*, March 13, 1926.

19. "Treatment of Colored Citizens by Sesqui Officials Branded as Insulting, Grossly Unfair," A.N.P. article published in *PT*, February 13, 1926.

20. "Visitor Sees Philadelphia as City that Clings to Past and Rich in Traditions," ANP article published in *PT*, January 9, 1926; "Fight on Real Representation at the Sesqui," *PT*, February 20, 1926; Letter from A. L. Sutton to W. Freeland Kendrick, February 25, 1926, PCA/SCEA, Folder 43; Hardy, *Race and Opportunity*, p. 534.

21. "Chairm'n Asbury Makes Statement on Exposition," *PT*, February 27, 1926; "Sesqui Offices Opened with Asbury Head," *PT*, March 13, 1926; Greenberg, *The American Presidents*, p. 87; Franklin, *The Education of Black Philadelphia*, p. 68; Hardy, *Race and Opportunity*, pp. 532–533.

22. Letter from Thomas J. Calloway to W. E. B. Du Bois, April 27, 1926, UMAL/WEBD (MS 312); Rydell, *World of Fairs*, p. 160.

23. Letter from W. E. B. Du Bois to Thomas J. Calloway, May 8, 1926; letter from W. E. B. Du Bois to Thomas J. Calloway, May 12, 1926; letter from Thomas J. Calloway to W. E. B. Du Bois, May 14, 1926, UMAL/WEBD (MS 312).

24. "Tily against Colored Unit in Sesqui Choir," *PT*, 1 May 1926.

25. Evans, "Sesqui Chorus Attempts to Raise Bars," *PT*, May 15, 1926.

26. Evans, "Sesqui Chorus Attempts to Raise Bars," *PT*, May 15, 1926; Tilton, "The Sesqui Chorus," *PT*, May 15, 1926; "The True Story of Segregation in Sesqui-Centennial Chorus," *PT*, June 19 and 26, 1926.

27. "Kendrick Denies Segregation in Sesqui Chorus," *PT*, May 22, 1926.

28. "Sesqui-Tribune Chorus Giving Big Musicale," *PT*, May 7, 1927.

29. "The Sesqui Chorus," *PT*, May 15, 1926.

30. Rydell, *World of Fairs*, p. 160.

31. A Philip Randolph, "The Negro Faces the Future," *African American Political Thought 1890–1930*, pp. 14–17, 253, 298, 309–331; Franklin, *The Education of Black People*, p. 80.

32. "Many Notables Accompany Mayor at Sesqui Opening," *PB*, May 31, 1926; "Kellogg, Hoover, and Mayor Speak at New Stadium," *PB*, May 31, 1926; "Sesqui-Centennial Opening Attended by Thousands of Visitors to the Quaker City," *PT*, June 5, 1926; Rydell, *World of Fairs*, p. 161.

33. *Souvenir and Visitor's Guide*, p. 17; Rhodes, "Remember!" *PT*, June 5, 1926.

34. "Large Number of Visitors See Sesqui Daily," *PT*, September 18, 1926; "Hostess House at Sesqui Is Dedicated," *PT*, October 23, 1926; Martin, *The Sesqui-Centennial International Exposition*, p. 177.

35. "Downingtown School Notes," May 15, 1926, *PT*; "Negro Exhibits at the Sesqui, *PT*, August 7, 1926; "Large Number of Visitors See Sesqui Daily," *PT*, September 18, 1926.

36. "20,000 See Loyalty's Gift Philly's Sesqui Pageant," Baltimore *Afro American*, July 24, 1926, p. 9; "'Loyalty's Gift' Will Draw Big Crowd at Sesqui," *PT*, July 10, 1926.

37. "A Negro Pageant," *PB*, July 13, 1926.

38. "Famous Tenor Will Sing at Sesqui Songfest," *PT*, August 14, 1926; "Ethiopia," *PT*, September 11, 1926; "20K Expected to See Ethiopia Musical Drama," *PT*, September 18, 1926; "Negro Pageant Staged at Sesqui," *PPL*, September 24, 1926.

39. "Negro Exhibits in Palace of Agriculture at Sesqui Grounds," *PT*, June 19, 1926; "Methodists to Hold Immense Chautauqua," *PT*, September 25, 1926.

40. "Sesqui Guard Halts Haitian President," *PI*, June 27, 1926.

41. Ibid.

42. "Dempsey Title Bout Suddenly Shifted to Philadelphia," *NYT*, August 19, 1926.

43. "Jack Dempsey, New Heavyweight Champion, Announces He Will Draw the Color Line," *NYT*, July 6, 1919; J. M. Howe, Sports Sidelight, *PT*, May 15, 1926; Cavanaugh, *Tunney*, pp. 251–253; Rydell, *World of Fairs*, pp. 159, 164.

44. "Klan Konklave to Meet in Washington Because of Philadelphia Ban," *JDB*, August 3, 1926.

45. "Sesqui Exhibit Head Released by E. L. [*sic*] Sutton," *PT*, September 11, 1926.

46. "Negro Pageant Staged at Sesqui," *PPL*, September 24, 1926; "Ethiopia Pleads for Justice but Gets Deaf Ear," *PT*, October 2, 1926.

47. "The 'Big Show' Is Over," editorial, *PT*, December 4, 1926.

48. Austin and Hauser, *The Sesqui-Centennial International Exposition*, p. 24.

49. Austin and Hauser, *The Sesqui-Centennial International Exposition*, pp. 24, 177, 469.

12

★ ★ ★

The Fight of the Century and a Half

ON SEPTEMBER 23, 1926, W. Freeland Kendrick's fairy godmother grudgingly granted his wish and transformed his woebegone Sesqui-Centennial into Cinderella for one magical night. Tens of thousands of people thronged Philadelphia, dropped money like crumpled cigarette packs, and stormed the fairgrounds en masse. For the first and only time in 1926 it was impossible to find an empty hotel room in town. The Sesqui took in more money in one night than it normally earned in six weeks. All that it took were two phenomenal boxers, the country's savviest sports promoter, a fistic-fanatic America, and enough ballyhoo to float the giant dirigible *Shenandoah* for a year.

On August 18, after weeks of secret negotiations between Sesqui officials, city and state politicians, and fight promoter Tex Rickard, a stunned *New York Times* announced that the world heavyweight boxing championship bout had been "suddenly shifted to Philadelphia." On September 23 reigning champ Jack "Manassa Mauler" Dempsey would defend his title against ex-Marine sergeant Gene "Fighting Marine" Tunney in the Sesqui Stadium. Sports writers were already calling the match the "fight of a century and a half." While the *Times* implied that Philadelphia had scored a tremendous coup, the Quaker City was the third choice of an increasingly desperate Rickard. Only the willingness of Philadelphia politicians to trample the aspirations of their black electorate diverted the Dempsey-Tunney bout from Jersey City.[1]

In early 1926, Tex Rickard, America's biggest sports promoter, had announced a championship bout between Jack Dempsey and Gene Tunney to

George Lewis "Tex" Rickard, who rose from running a Klondike saloon to become the most powerful sports mogul in America. For Rickard, the Dempsey-Tunney fight was the biggest and most profitable fight he had ever engineered. (Prints and Photographs Division, Library of Congress.)

be held in either August or September. Its site would be the three-year-old Yankee Stadium in the South Bronx. Rickard's plans went awry when Tammany Hall refused to play ball. Fearful of alienating black voters, Tammany politicos insisted that Dempsey fight Harry "Black Panther" Wills rather than Tunney. Many in the boxing world considered Wills, the reigning World Colored Heavyweight Champion, to be the rightful challenger to Dempsey. Rickard refused, unwilling to break the "color line" drawn after African-American Jack Johnson surrendered the heavyweight title to Jess Willard in 1915.

By July Rickard was telling Chicago reporters how delighted he was to be staging "the most anticipated fight" of the decade in the Windy City. Despite Rickard's offer to donate part of the gate to the families of slain Chicago policemen, he encountered the same political opposition in the Second City as in the First. Blocked by a coalition of Chicago's black leaders, reform politicians, and newspapers, Rickard decided to try his luck once more in the Big Apple. Again, Tammany's will prevailed. Citing a technicality that a reigning champion must defend his title every six months, the New York State Athletic Commission forbade the bout on the grounds that Dempsey had not engaged in a fight for three years. At this point, a frustrated Rickard considered moving the fight to Jersey City.[2]

Keeping his options open, the promoter had entered into secret negotiations in July to move the fight to Sesqui Stadium in Philadelphia. Frank L. Wiener, chairman of the Pennsylvania Boxing Commission, had contacted Rickard after being tipped off about the New York deadlock. Wiener's overtures were seconded by E. L. Austin of the Sesqui-Centennial Exhibition Association and Assistant City Solicitor James F. Ryan. Mayor Kendrick, who had fiercely opposed a Dempsey-Wills fight at the Stadium earlier in the year, played dumb until the Dempsey-Tunney deal was finalized, asserting in early August that it was "all news to me." Governor Gifford Pinchot, a boxing fan, made sure that both the Pennsylvania Athletic Commission and Boxing Commission sanctioned the fight in record time. Everyone played ball, except for C. Fred White, the one black member of the three-man State Boxing Commission, who resigned in protest after being overruled by his two white colleagues. As a promise that he would not switch venues again, Rickard posted a bond for $50,000 to the SCEA and a check for an equal amount to the state boxing commission.[3]

Conforming to a new Pennsylvania boxing law, the Dempsey-Tunney bout would last a maximum of ten rounds, with a decision by two officials and the referee at the end of the tenth round. Ticket prices would range from $3 for general admission to $27.50 for ringside seats. Attendance was expected to reach an unprecedented 150,000. The SCEA would receive 10 percent of an anticipated $2 million gate, plus $30,000 to $50,000 in program and concession rights. The Commonwealth of Pennsylvania would receive 5 percent of the gate in taxes. Both the Sesqui and the city of Philadelphia expected to reap millions in secondary spending by the throngs of spectators. Two days after Rickard announced the fight's move to Philadelphia, a group of 118 Sesqui creditors agreed to delay legal action against the SCEA. The announcement of the September 23 fight—the first good news for the luckless Sesqui in weeks—played a critical role in the creditors' decision to grant the SCEA more time to get its financial house in order.

Champion Jack Dempsey agreed to accept a $700,000 fee while challenger Gene Tunney would receive $200,000, regardless of who won or lost. The two fighters were required to relocate their training camps from upstate New York to what was loosely defined as the Philadelphia region. Dempsey moved from Saratoga Lake to Atlantic City, sixty miles from City Hall. Tunney relocated from Speculator, New York to Stroudsburg in the Pocono Mountains, ninety miles north of Philadelphia.[4]

On August 19 Tex Rickard visited Philadelphia to inspect the fight's new venue and to organize his local office, detraining at Broad Street Station with a full retinue of clerks, ticket sellers, and publicists. He told reporters, "Chicago had a chance at this fight. New York had a chance at it. Philadelphia took it away from both of them because the Philadelphia Sesqui-Centennial management was far-seeing." While half of Rickard's entourage set up shop at the Bellevue-Stratford, the other half accompanied him while he toured the Sesqui Stadium with Mayor Kendrick and Director Austin. "This is wonderful!" the promoter exclaimed. "It beats anything I had expected. It has always been the dream of my life to build an arena like this one."[5]

The fifty-six-year-old Rickard, whose curriculum vitae included stints as a Texas cowboy, Klondike casino owner, and South African diamond prospector, was the biggest fight promoter of all times, having arranged more than two hundred bouts since 1906. He had made a fortune from Dempsey, arranging lucrative bouts between the Manassa Mauler and Jess Willard, Georges Carpentier, and Luis Angel Firpo. The one-man sports empire was also the owner/operator of the Madison Square Garden arena in Manhattan, and the creator of a new National Hockey League franchise known as "Tex's Rangers" (later renamed the New York Rangers). Tanned and lean, Rickard favored conservative three-piece suits that made him look more like a stockbroker than a sports promoter.[6]

On Sunday, August 23, fifty thousand onlookers cheered William Harrison "Jack" Dempsey when he arrived at Philadelphia's Broad Street Station with his wife, Hollywood starlet Estelle Taylor, and his new manager, Gene Normile. After a visit to City Hall, Mayor Kendrick treated the Dempseys to a tour of the Sesqui fairgrounds and Stadium. Dempsey appeared distracted as Kendrick tried to persuade him to train at the Sesqui rather than in Atlantic City. He had recently dumped his longtime manager "Doc" Kearns, who had masterminded his rise to champion while appropriating one-half of his earnings. Kearns immediately filed three lawsuits against Dempsey totaling $750,000. Dempsey later wrote, "I was afraid to shake hands with anybody, for process servers usually used a handshake to serve a 'plaster' on me." Besides Kearns' harassment, Dempsey was plagued by marital problems with Taylor, criticism over his three-year absence from the ring, and lingering rumors that he had dodged the draft during the World War. Suffering from dermatitis and chronic indigestion, he had started to drink olive oil every morning as a tonic.[7]

Warm as Dempsey's welcome to Philadelphia was, it paled in comparison to Gene Tunney's reception a week later. His train was met at Broad Street Station by thousands of admiring fans, including hundreds of Marines stationed at Camp Samuel Nicholas on the Sesqui grounds. When the tall young man stepped onto the platform, the cheering crowd surged

Mayor Kendrick shows Jack Dempsey and his wife, movie actress Estelle Taylor, the wonders of the Sesqui Stadium during their August 23 visit.

forward and the U.S. Marine Band crashed into a Sousa march. Tunney was encircled by a protective ring of Marines, while Rickard and manager Billy Gibson were engulfed by the surging mob. Acting as a flying wedge, the Marines escorted their former comrade through the crowded station and across the street to City Hall, where police escorted him to the mayor's office. After a formal welcome by Mayor Kendrick, the party headed out to Penn Square and a waiting row of limousines for the trek to the Sesqui.

Tunney was escorted to Tun Tavern and then to Camp Samuel Nicholas, where hundreds of ecstatic Devil Dogs lifted him high in the air and cheered him for fifteen minutes. The Marines finally relinquished Tunney to officials, who escorted him to the Sesqui Stadium. Tunney exuded confidence throughout his visit, dismissing Dempsey as "a gymnasium fighter" who "punches hard, but he does little boxing." After lunch at the Alpine Haus, Tunney spent a quiet hour reminiscing with an old friend, Major Anthony J. Drexel Biddle. "I never thought that one of my students would ever fight for the championship of the world," an ecstatic Biddle told reporters as he gazed proudly at Tunney. The scion of two of Philadelphia's most blue-blooded families, Biddle was the martial arts expert who had

Gene Tunney poses with members of Colonel Cummings's Wild West Stockade at the Stadium. (Prints and Photographs Division, Library of Congress.)

instructed the young Marine in boxing at Quantico. Tunney, who had learned how to box as a youngster on the mean streets of Greenwich Village, credited Drexel with instilling a "killer instinct" in him.[8]

On the afternoon of September 11, a cigar-chomping Tex Rickard left his offices at the Bellevue-Stratford and boarded a train for New York. In his wallet were bank receipts for more than $1,370,000 in advance ticket sales. By this time, the odds favoring Dempsey ranged between three to one and four to one. New York bookies had placed more than $1 million on the fight, with much of the "smart money" backing the champion. "Most of the intelligentsia of the pugilistic world," noted the *New York Times*, "believes that Dempsey has retained at least 90 per cent of his punching power and that he will knock Tunney out." Other sports stars, including Babe Ruth, favored their fellow champion. "Dempsey will murder him," opined the Sultan of Swat. Most of the major sportswriters also favored Dempsey, including Damon Runyon, Ring Lardner, and Paul Gallico. Even Doc Kearns paused in his legal harassment of Dempsey to predict that the champion would win; he was rumored to have bet between $50,000 and $150,000 on his former client.

Twelve days before the bout, the demand for ringside seats had reached fever pitch. Samuel Vauclain, president of the Baldwin Locomotive Works, spent $27,000 on fight tickets; E. T. Stotesbury also purchased a large ringside consignment. William K. Vanderbilt, Percy Rockefeller, and Vincent Astor would lead a society contingent from Gotham, while the New York Racquet Club reserved seven hundred tickets. So many requests had been received from J. P. Morgan and Co. and other Wall Street firms that Rickard declared ringside would look like a bankers' convention. Samuel T. Bodine, chairman of Philadelphia's United Gas Improvement Company, who had never seen a prize fight, requested when he ordered his tickets: "Be sure to get me near the ring, as my eyes are not so good and I don't want to miss anything." Less distinguished fight fans were forced to wait in long lines at the two ticket offices opened by Rickard, on Walnut Street near the Bellevue-Stratford and at Jules Mastbaum's Arena at 4530 Market Street. They paid between $3.30 and $11 for tickets in the wooden bleachers beyond ringside, or in the concrete rows of the Stadium.[9]

The market for hotel rooms was as bullish as that for ringside seats. Besides the fight, the city was hosting nearly sixty thousand guests attending four major conventions during the week of September 23. Philadelphia's luxury hotels—the Bellevue-Stratford, Ritz-Carlton, and Benjamin Franklin—were completely booked, as were the less glamorous Adelphia, St. James, Stenton, Sylvania, Spruce, and Walton. Every day, manager Richard O'Neil of the Bellevue-Stratford sent out hundreds of telegrams refusing requests for rooms. He was already juggling assignments for the governors of Pennsylvania, New Jersey, New York, Delaware, Illinois, Maryland, and Nebraska, and the governor-elect of Texas, as well as their entourages. Jules Mastbaum, who had spent $27,500 on fight tickets, needed twenty of the Bellevue's best rooms for his party of Broadway and Hollywood luminaries. William Randolph Hearst was hosting fifty guests. Already, bellboys were squeezing extra cots into many rooms, and setting up five hundred more on the parquet floor of the Grand Ballroom.[10]

Municipal authorities prepared to handle crowds on a scale not seen since the Great War. Besides its regular hourly service between New York and Philadelphia, the Pennsylvania Railroad made plans for thirty additional trains known as "Rickard Specials," and as many relief trains as might be needed to handle the fifty thousand New Yorkers expected to attend. The New Jersey Central Railroad also added numerous "Tunney Rooter" specials to its hourly service. Dozens of private railroad cars belonging to

Gifford Pinchot, governor of Pennsylvania and fistics fanatic, consults with Richard Dunn, superintendent of construction, on the site for his ringside private box for the Dempsey-Tunney fight.

wealthy individuals or organizations had to be hitched onto trains leaving New York and then assigned to railroad sidings throughout Philadelphia, further complicating logistics. For those venturing south by car, the *New York Times* published detailed maps and directions to the faraway land of Philadelphia. Director of Public Safety Elliott had already assigned four thousand of Philadelphia's finest to direct traffic the day of the fight, with five hundred policemen assigned to the fairgrounds.[11]

At the Sesqui, an army of laborers struggled to finish transforming the Stadium into a giant boxing arena. Tiers of wooden bleachers across the open northern end added an additional twenty-two thousand seats. The twenty-three-square-foot canvas ring in the middle of the Stadium was surrounded by a ringside section consisting of forty rows of nearly fifteen thousand chairs, although the number kept growing as scalpers sold more premium tickets. Despite Rickard's earlier vow that there would be no boxes, several enclosures had been erected near the ring section to accommodate select parties like Governor Pinchot's.

Carpenters begin construction on the hundreds of ringside seats for the Dempsey-Tunney fights. Some disappointed ticket holders found that their expensive ringside seats were hundreds of feet away from the action.

While all ringside tickets were priced at $27.50, only the seats in the first twelve rows were commanding top prices from scalpers. Tickets in the outer rows were being discounted at $15 or less. Fans realized that they would have trouble viewing the fight from those seats, located on the flat ground several hundred yards from the canvas. Instead, they were snapping up seats in the first rows of the tiered concrete sections of the Stadium, priced at $11.50. While these seats would require field glasses because of their distance from the ring, their elevation would offer an unobstructed view. Days before the fight, more than five thousand tickets were still unsold, most of them for $3 and $5.50 seats in the Stadium's stratosphere. Rickard, after viewing the ring from a $5.50 seat, ordered the canvas to be jacked up an additional four inches to increase visibility and ticket sales.

As workmen struggled to raise the ring, electricians labored underneath it to lay and connect more than one hundred telegraph lines that would convey more than two million words from more than three hundred journalists around the world as the fight progressed. Plans were in place to broadcast the match live via radio throughout the world, including to more than one hundred ocean liners at sea.[12]

While technicians were wiring the Stadium for sound, the question of radio broadcast rights almost torpedoed the entire enterprise. Tex Rickard, seeking to recoup the fortune he had spent on the bout, demanded the exorbitant sum of $50,000 for broadcast rights. In doing so, he underestimated the growing corporate power of radio, as represented by the newly created National Broadcasting Company, the first countrywide radio network. Although the network would begin operation on November 15, newspaper ads trumpeting its formation appeared in mid-September. Refusing to pay Rickard's ransom, NBC announced that its New York flagship stations, WEAF and WJZ, would broadcast round-by-round descriptions provided by newswire service reporters at ringside. In retaliation, Rickard decreed that the fight was a "private show" and that he would ban all press coverage.

At this point, the SCEA stood up to the promoter, threatening to revoke his license if he banned the press. On September 21 the conflict was resolved when the Royal Typewriter Company, a major Sesqui exhibitor, purchased the radio rights for $15,000. Royal Typewriter would broadcast the fight via a network of thirty-one stations that would cover two-thirds of the country. Graham McNamee and Major J. Andrew White of WEAF, who had announced the Dempsey-Carpentier fight of 1921, would call the bout. Although Rickard's compensation was far less than what he had originally sought, it allowed him to back away gracefully from a potentially disastrous standoff.[13]

The day before the bout saw both fighters indulging in light exercise, followed by relaxation for Dempsey and further preparation for Tunney. In Atlantic City, Dempsey started September 22 with a four-mile hike and then spent the rest of the day reading the sports page and playing checkers with his bodyguard Mike Trant. He assured reporters that he was "in excellent condition and ready for the battle of my life." That evening, Dempsey received a message from his wife, Estelle Taylor, in Hollywood, relayed by Hearst sob sister Louella "Lolly" Parsons in her daily column. "Win or lose," read Estelle's tender note, transmitted in a manner that guaranteed maximum nationwide publicity, "hurry back, dear."[14]

At Stroudsburg, Gene Tunney played eighteen holes of golf, carding a ninety-two, his best round of the year. A *Bulletin* reporter asked him about rumors that he planned to travel to Philadelphia via airplane the next day. "No, I certainly am not going to fly to Philadelphia," Tunney laughed. "If Tex Rickard believes this crazy rumor, he will be up here after me with

A crowd of neatly dressed, respectable admirers accompany challenger Gene Tunney as he plays a round of golf at the Glen Brook Country Club, prior to the big fight.

a machine gun, and I wouldn't blame him." Assured that Tunney would motor to Philadelphia in the morning, most reporters left Stroudsburg that afternoon.[15]

One sportswriter, Jackie Farrell of the New York *Daily News*, remained behind to watch Tunney engage in a sparring session, one round apiece with three partners. Farrell later said that it was the best boxing exhibition he had ever seen. Tunney never threw a punch, but he either blocked or dodged his opponents' punches, emerging untouched after nine minutes of sparring. Despite this bravura performance of defensive skills, Farrell still favored Dempsey.[16]

As darkness fell on Philadelphia, a full moon rose above a carnival city. "To say that not only Philadelphia but the country at large has gone completely fight-mad about this encounter is no exaggeration," wrote one reporter. An advance guard of thirty thousand out-of-town fight fans had already joined tens of thousands of conventioneers invading the city. "One out of every three persons one passed on Broad Street tonight," wrote the *New York Times*, "wore a badge or a fez or an Admiral's uniform complete with gold sword, and the other two were hunting for a place to sleep." Hotel lobbies were jammed with men besieging the front desks, begging in vain for a spot to rest their heads. All of the city's twenty-eight thousand hotel rooms were booked, as were one hundred thousand beds in boardinghouses and private residences. Scalpers demanded fifty dollars or more for fleabag hotel rooms that usually rented for eight dollars. Visitors swarmed around the Women's Committee information booths at railroad stations, desperate to find a spare bed or sofa anywhere in Philadelphia. Many would spend the night in Camden or Trenton.[17]

September 23 dawned bright and dry, continuing an unusual stretch of fine weather in the Sesqui City. Some forecasters were predicting a light drizzle later, as the remains of the deadly hurricane that had devastated Miami earlier in the week reached the northeast. The first of nearly fifty thousand visitors expected from New York that day began to flood the city's railroad stations. Many were young men who looked distinctly collegiate in their sports jackets and summer suits, snap-brimmed felt hats, and brightly colored neckties, carrying umbrellas, raincoats, and field glasses. Meanwhile, bookies were reporting a sudden surge of betting on Tunney, cutting the odds in Dempsey's favor nearly in half, from four to one to twelve to five.[18]

Latecomers scrambled to secure choice fight seats. One scalper boasted of selling two sixth-row ringside seats to a Cleveland millionaire for $1,295. Ticket broker Mike Jacobs later told Jack Dempsey about a September 23 visit from Max "Boo Boo" Hoff, notorious King of Philadelphia Bootleggers. Hoff told Jacobs that he needed twenty-five ringside seats for his politico friends. When Jacobs protested that ringside had been sold out for weeks, Hoff pulled out a roll of bills "that would choke an elephant" and peeled off twenty-five $1,000 bills. Jacobs consulted his seating chart, squeezing in chairs and moving people he knew wouldn't gripe too much. He handed over the tickets to Hoff and pocketed the $25,000. When Hoff started to walk away, Jacobs stopped him. "You forgot to pay me for the tickets," he told the King of the Bootleggers. "They're fifty bucks each." Hoff, well versed in Philadelphia's "pay-to-play" etiquette, obligingly handed over $1,250 for the tickets.[19]

Shortly before 10:00 A.M., Gene Tunney stepped outside the Glen Brook Country Club and climbed into the Duesenberg of Wade Morton, a Philadelphia racecar enthusiast. The two men drove six miles to the Shawnee Country Club, where World War ace Charles "Casey" Jones was waiting to fly them to Philadelphia in his red Curtiss Oriole biplane. Tunney had kept the flight a secret until the last minute. "It's really the sensible thing to do," he told a reporter. "First, I'll have a little diversion which will keep my mind off the fight. And second it will be much quicker than by train or motor car, and there won't be that continuous bumpy motion that is very hard on the nerves." Tunney concluded his press statement with these fatalistic words: "If I crash, it won't matter. After all, the longest life is very short." The plane lifted off at 11:49 A.M., circled twice, and headed toward Philadelphia.

In Philadelphia, Tex Rickard stood in front of the Bellevue-Stratford with a group of reporters when someone rushed up and broke the news about Tunney's flight. "God damn that son of a bitch!" Rickard exploded. "What's he trying to do to me?"

"To you?" retorted W. O. McGeehan of the *Herald-Tribune*. "What about himself?"

At that moment, Tunney was probably asking himself the same question. Jones had gotten lost in fog over the Pocono Mountains, and the "little diversion" had turned into a stomach-churning flight that caused Tunney to vomit twice. After half an hour, Jones got his bearings and proceeded south. The plane made a smooth landing at the Philadelphia Navy Yard aviation field at 1:07 P.M. before a crowd of one hundred reporters, photographers, and marines. Tunney's teeth were clenched in a broad grin for the cameras, although his face looked sallow and sweaty.

"How did you like it, Gene?" Jones asked his passenger.

"Oh, it was grand, Casey," Tunney responded gamely as he struggled to extricate himself from the cockpit. "I enjoyed it a lot."[20]

Tunney climbed into a car that raced to the offices of the Pennsylvania State Athletic Commission at Fifth and Chestnut Streets for his weigh-in. Stripped down to his boxer shorts, the challenger weighed in at 185.5 pounds. Dr. Abraham Baron, commission staff physician, pronounced Tunney in perfect condition, "with an air of optimism that speaks well of his frame of mind for the fight tonight. He apparently has that 'winning mood.'" After weighing in, Tunney went to the Spruce Hotel, a men's residential hotel at 261 South Thirteenth Street. By 4:00 P.M., he had recovered sufficiently to eat a steak and take a nap.[21]

At this point, one of the most intriguing mysteries of the Dempsey-Tunney fight occurred, although the specifics vary depending on the storyteller. Years later, Tunney would write that he was awakened from his nap by his manager, Billy Gibson, accompanied by Max "Boo-Boo" Hoff and Hoff's lawyer, U.S. Congressman Ben Golder. Gibson explained that he needed money to cover their expenses for the fight, and that Tunney needed to witness a document related to a $20,000 loan Hoff had offered to extend. If Tunney lost the bout, Hoff would forgive the loan. But when Tunney read the document carefully, he realized it was a long-term contract giving Hoff

20 percent of all Tunney's purses for future fights. A furious Tunney threw the contract at Gibson and ordered everyone out of his room.

Tunney would later write that Hoff and his lawyer were "trying to assure themselves of something in case I lost by a knockout. They had undoubtedly bet that way." If Tunney had signed the contract and then lost, he could have been accused of taking a $20,000 dive while Hoff would have raked in $3 for every $1 he bet. If Tunney had won, Hoff would have lost in the short term but would have stood to gain a fortune over the course of Tunney's boxing career. Trying to explain why he offered the soul of his fighter to the King of Philadelphia Bootleggers, Gibson would later claim that he had enlisted Hoff's help only to ensure that the fight wouldn't be stolen from Tunney by other gangsters.[22]

When Hoff brought suit against Tunney in January 1927, he told a different story. In his version, the meeting took place in Tunney's changing room at Sesqui Stadium before the fight. Tunney signed the contract willingly, entitling Hoff to twenty percent of Tunney's earnings during his reign as champion. Congressman Golder showed the press a copy of the last page of the supposed contract, with four signatures: Max Hoff, William Gibson, Philadelphia attorney Michael Serody, and Eugene Joseph Tunney. Unfortunately for Hoff, Tunney's legal name was James Joseph Tunney. "Gene" was a childhood nickname. Either the contract was a fake, or Tunney had signed a name that wouldn't stand up in court. All the judges who heard the case thought the first scenario was more plausible. Hoff would pursue his case all the way up to the New York Supreme Court before admitting defeat in January 1931, long after Tunney had retired as undefeated champion.[23]

While Gene Tunney was defying Boo-Boo Hoff, Jack Dempsey was suffering his own gastrointestinal issues. He had awakened that morning with a nasty rash, an indication that his chronic dermatitis had returned. Dempsey began to feel queasy after his bodyguard, Mike Trant, gave him his usual dose of olive oil. His nausea worsened on the private railroad car that carried Dempsey and his entourage across New Jersey, arriving at North Philadelphia Station around 6:40 P.M. During the car ride to the Adelphia Hotel at 1229 Chestnut Street, the driver had to stop several times so that Dempsey could vomit in the street. While Dempsey thought he had a mild case of ptomaine, his illness gave rise to rumors of real poisoning.[24]

As the two fighters made their way toward Philadelphia under increasingly cloudy skies, they seemed to be joined by the rest of the known universe. Dozens of special trains—the Rickard and Tunney Expresses—were shunted directly to the Pennsylvania Railroad Sesqui Station on Packer Avenue, half a mile north of the Stadium. But most arriving trains waited to pull into Broad Street Station, creating the greatest locomotive gridlock the city had ever seen. The Chinese Wall, the elevated viaduct between Broad Street Station and the main northeast corridor line in West Philadelphia, was lined with railroad cars. The last fight-bound train to arrive in Philadelphia, at almost 8:00 P.M., was the "Mastbaum Special," chartered by Jules Mastbaum and carrying three hundred New York politicians, officials, and theatrical luminaries.[25]

At 5:00 P.M., Broad Street was closed to all but fight traffic from Walnut Street south to the Sesqui. Neighboring streets were jammed with commuters struggling to get home in a nightmarish rush hour. Nearly thirty-five hundred policemen directed traffic while another five hundred struggled to handle the growing crowds at the Sesqui. As fight time grew near, South Broad Street became a snarling mass of taxis, private cars, buses and trolleys, defying all traffic regulations. Among them were limousines carrying Jules Mastbaum's glittering guests, including Hollywood stars Constance Talmadge, Tom Mix, and William S. Hart. "All caution was thrown to the wind," wrote Louella Parsons, covering the fight for the Hearst newspapers, "and that the casualty list did not assume huge proportions was due more to fate than caution."

Before the police opened the Sesqui Stadium at 3:00 P.M., they had to evict more than two hundred squatters who had hidden in the labyrinthine complex. Ticket holders had to run a gauntlet of sixteen policemen, two firemen, and one official bouncer, who scrutinized their pasteboards, making sure that no freeloaders or fraudsters crashed the fight. Once inside the Stadium, fight-goers were directed to their seats by an army of thirteen hundred red-capped ushers, who managed the flow with almost military precision. As darkness fell, a dozen batteries of huge searchlights mounted at the top of the Stadium flickered into life, illuminating the field below. Over the ring itself, thirty-seven cone-shaped lights glared down on the white canvas square. Dance music filled the air, broadcast over a radio hooked up to the Stadium's amplification system. Airplanes unnerved the crowds in the upper reaches of the Stadium as they zoomed past, advertising slogans spelled out on their sides in electric lights.[26]

Around 8:00 P.M., the first of five preliminary fights began. Few spectators paid any attention to it or to the other prelims. They were too busy ogling the stream of celebrities flowing down the aisles to their ringside seats. Picked out by a blazing spotlight, their names were announced over loudspeakers. The Dempsey-Tunney bout had truly attracted "the most cosmopolitan crowd that ever attended an outdoor event in the United States," according to the *Bulletin*, with an estimated two thousand millionaires surrounding the canvas. Screen sirens Constance Talmadge and Gloria Swanson, in furs and evening gowns, took seats at ringside. They were among an estimated ten thousand female spectators, the "largest number of the fair sex ever to attend a fight."

Official America was represented by Secretary of War Dwight F. Davis and Secretary of the Navy Curtis P. Wilbur. Archie, Kermit, and Theodore Jr., the three sons of former president Theodore Roosevelt, were on hand, as was their sister Alice and her husband, Speaker of the House Nicholas Longworth. The governors of seven states and the governor-elect of Texas were among the crowd, as were the mayors of New York City, Atlantic City, Jersey City, Pittsburgh, and Baltimore. A number of infamous characters were sprinkled among all the famous ones. Besides Philadelphia's own Max "Boo Boo" Hoff, the crowd included Arnold Rothstein, the New York racketeer who fixed the 1919 World Series. Many local politicians enjoyed ringside seats, possibly as a result of Hoff's last-minute largesse. Mayor Kendrick was there, along with most of City Council and the mayoral cabinet.

A touch of Chestnut Hill class was provided by Judge J. Willis Martin and his wife, Elizabeth, who hosted a party of twenty in their private box. Major Anthony J. Drexel Biddle, Tunney's former trainer, also entertained twenty guests in his enclosure. In the adjoining box, the Stotesburys hosted a large party that included Eva's daughter Louise, her son James H. R. Cromwell, and James's wife, Delphine, heiress to the Dodge Motor Company fortune. Louise's husband, General Douglas MacArthur, was absent, fueling the growing rumors of marital discord between the couple. During the preliminaries, an exhausted yet elated Tex Rickard worked his way through the ringside crowds, greeting friends and acquaintances.[27]

Separated from the celebrities in their ringside seats by a five-foot aisle were more than three hundred journalists and telegraph operators, each one allotted sixteen inches in four rows of tightly packed benches hugging the ring. While the reporters opened their portable typewriters, the telegraph men tapped their keys to open a circuit, preparing to relay the first leads on the big fight to newspaper offices around the country. Doc Kearns, Dempsey's litigious ex-manager, squeezed between Gene Fowler of the *Mirror* and a Los Angeles sportswriter named Mark Kelly.

Graham McNamee and Major J. Andrew White took their places before the radio microphones. Their narration of tonight's fight would be heard not only throughout most of the continental United States, but in Central and South America, Europe, the Philippines, and South Africa. Passengers on the luxury ocean liners *Berengaria* and *Belgenland* would hear the fight in the middle of the Atlantic Ocean; so would riders on all Pennsylvania Railroad trains; so would patients at veterans' hospitals, thanks to the secretary of war and the secretary of the navy. Forty feet north of the canvas, two elevated platforms rose from the ringside seats, reserved for still photographers and motion picture crews. Each platform was supported by a single pole, and the men crowded on top were asked to move as little as possible.[28]

After the fourth preliminary between Dempsey sparring partner Tommy Loughran and Tunney sparring partner Jimmy Delaney, announcer Joe Griffo informed the crowd that Tommy Reilly of Philadelphia would referee the championship bout. Frank Brown of Pittsburgh and Mike Bernstein of Wilkes-Barre would serve as judges, while Jim Hendon and Byron Hayes would supervise the taping of the fighters' hands. As he made these announcements, the first drops of rain fell on the sea of spectators, who donned raincoats, raised umbrellas, and covered their heads with newspapers.

At exactly 9:30 P.M., challenger Gene Tunney climbed through the ropes, receiving a huge ovation as he took the southwest corner of the ring. The "Fighting Marine" was resplendent in purple trunks and a scarlet-trimmed blue silk dressing gown with the Marine Corps emblem emblazoned in gold on the back. The magnificent robe had been given to Tunney by Marine Corps Major General John A. Lejeune on behalf of eighteen thousand Marines "at home and abroad, ashore and afloat." Regardless of the odds, Elmer Davis of the *Times* later estimated that "about 90 percent of the 130,000 people who saw the encounter were for Tunney." Among them were a mob of Marines, who crowded around the press benches and acted as a cheering section for the challenger throughout the match.

A few minutes later, a double row of twelve policemen escorted Jack Dempsey to the ring, making sure that Kearns and his process servers did not spoil the moment with a subpoena. Dempsey wore navy blue silk trunks piped in gold and a white, V-neck tennis sweater. His entrance was greeted with a smattering of applause, followed by a murmur of surprise. Fistic fanatics had expected to see Dempsey's ratty old red "good luck" sweater, which he had worn to all of his major fights since winning the heavyweight title. His gleaming new sweater was a gift from his wife, Estelle. When announcer Joe Griffo introduced Dempsey as "the heavyweight champion who has defended his title for the past six years," a chorus of boos and hisses rippled through the Stadium, led by the Marines lining the ring.[29]

When the opening bell rang, a scowling Dempsey charged forth, driving Tunney back to his own corner. Tunney, displaying the same agility he had shown during the previous day's sparring practice, evaded Dempsey's onslaught. Deftly retreating from Dempsey's powerful left hooks, Tunney jarred Dempsey with surprisingly strong right crosses to his cheekbone. By the end of round one, Tunney appeared to be in control. As the Fighting Marine continued to deliver sharp jabs to Dempsey's face, the Manassa Mauler began to stagger. Dempsey bobbed and ducked, trying to evade the curving right hand that kept appearing out of the darkness and crashing into his head.

By the end of round two, it was pouring rain. Curses rose from the press benches as telegraph wires shorted out, paper turned to pulp, and waterlogged typewriters jammed. Ring Lardner, covering the fight for the *World* after Heywood Broun bowed out, was able to file only half of his story because of electrical problems. "It broke off in such a manner," he later wrote F. Scott and Zelda Fitzgerald, "that people must have said to themselves that I was very drunk."[30] Some reporters took shelter in the space under the raised ring, bobbing out to observe the action and then diving back under to type their stories in relative dryness. At the end of the third round, announcer Graham McNamee told radio listeners that Tunney "is outboxing the champion from start to finish. Dempsey is absolutely unable to get going. He seems to have nothing."[31]

During round four, James Dawson of the *Times* noted that Tunney had opened a bad cut under Dempsey's right eye, "from which a crimson stream flowed and flecked the beautiful bronzed body which had been so liberally praised in song, story, and picture." Tunney staggered Dempsey with a

The big fight, held in the pouring rain before a crowd of nearly 130,000 spectators.

right to the jaw, followed by a rapid succession of left jabs and hooks, and right crosses and swings. By the fifth round, Dempsey was on the defensive, causing the Marines around the ring to jeer, "Are you too proud to fight?" Dempsey stunned Tunney once in the sixth round, landing a left hook to the Adam's apple that caused the challenger to cough up a little blood. But Tunney had recovered by the seventh round. Dempsey's power and accuracy diminished steadily as Tunney attacked him with a string of "rapier-like lefts and lightning-like rights." Fight analysts would later determine that Dempsey landed only fifty blows during all ten rounds, while Tunney hit Dempsey three blows for each one he received.

By the eighth round, according to one reporter, Dempsey "was a sorry looking spectacle, with his left eye blackened and swollen and a cut under his right eye, from which blood continued to flow." Many of Dempsey's blows began to miss wildly, while he left himself open to sharp jabs from Tunney. The champ began to use the illegal rabbit punch during his clinches with Tunney, striking his neck repeatedly despite being warned by the referee. In the one-minute break between rounds, trainer Jack O'Brien struggled to staunch the flow of blood from Dempsey's wounds with court plaster, chloride, and liquid skin.

By round ten—the final round as decreed by the Pennsylvania Boxing Commission—the ring was so wet from the downpour that both boxers begin to slip, despite the resin sprinkled on the canvas. Deflecting Dempsey's final charge, Tunney drove home a right that opened a cut from the inside of Dempsey's left eyebrow to the top of his temple, followed by another right that sent him back on the ropes. As the half-blind champion lunged at his opponent, Tunney pummeled the champ's face, now "a matrix of blood and battered flesh." Ready for the kill, the rain-soaked crowd howled for Tunney to "finish him off!" By this time, Dempsey was "a human hurricane petered out. . . . weary of body and mind, wobbling and staggering around."[32] Glancing at his neighbor, sportswriter Mark Kelly noticed that Doc Kearns was crying over the fate of the man he was suing for hundreds of thousands of dollars.

When the Round Ten bell rang at 10:25 P.M., Dempsey staggered to his corner and slumped in his chair. As the judges passed the soggy slips of paper containing their decision to the referee, a phalanx of Philadelphia policemen stormed into the ring to surround the winner, a standard procedure at prize fights. Even before hearing the decision, they gathered around Tunney. While the entire Stadium waited for the final verdict, announcer Major J. Andrew White informed millions of radio listeners around the country, "There is no question but that Tunney won the fight." A few seconds later,

Griffo announced, "The judges are agreed on giving the decision to Gene Tunney, the new heavyweight champion."[33] It was the first time in history that the world heavyweight championship had changed hands on points; Tunney had won each of the ten rounds.

Griffo's voice was inaudible beyond the first few rows, but as the ringside spectators rose to cheer Tunney, a chain reaction spread throughout the entire Stadium. Within a few seconds, all spectators were on their feet, saluting the new champion. A dazed Dempsey staggered across the ring and shook hands with the man who had just beaten him, embracing him briefly. Within moments, Andrew White was holding a radio microphone under Tunney's nose, broadcasting his first words as champion: "I have realized my ambition," Tunney said, "and I will try to defend the title that I have worked so hard for six years, and I am going to try to defend it as becomes a Marine."[34]

The phalanx of policemen cleared a path to a waiting car for the Fighting Marine, who appeared untouched except for a split lip and a small cut over one eye. Tunney returned to his dressing room to shower and change. His ablutions were interrupted by former sparring partner Bernard Gimbel, who burst fully clothed into the shower with the naked victor, unable to contain his enthusiasm. The new champion rushed back to the Spruce Hotel to call his worried mother in the Bronx and assure her that he was fine. Over a cup of tea, he told reporters, "I am through with planes." He also assured them, "Jack Dempsey is one of the cleanest boxers I have ever met in the ring." Before bidding the army of journalists good night, he promised, "I am going to give my best to be a popular champion and will leave it all to the public."[35]

Dempsey's handlers maneuvered the fallen champion back to his changing room, a towel thrown over his head to keep photographers from immortalizing his ravaged face. Two doctors examined his injuries, concerned that he might need to go to a hospital. The gaping cut over his left eye was stitched up and bandaged, as was the gash on his right cheek. Luckily, Dempsey's nose, reconstructed at a cost of $10,000 for his brief career before the Hollywood cameras, was intact. A patched-up Dempsey was driven back to his suite on the sixth floor of the Adelphia Hotel, looking like "a man who had been in a railroad wreck," according to the *Bulletin*. Yet his attitude was oddly euphoric, as if he was relieved to be done with the great ordeal. "Well, kid," Dempsey laughed to a member of his entourage, "you can't fight always, can you?" Dempsey's handlers undressed the ex-champ and eased him into a warm bath infused with Epsom salts. As they put Dempsey to bed, the ex-champ remembered that he had been invited to a dinner party at the Locust Club. It took most of his handlers to keep him in bed until his exhilaration subsided, and the Manassa Mauler finally drifted off to sleep.[36]

While Dempsey slid into oblivion, an army of soaked and exhausted fight fans struggled to leave the Sesqui. The lucky notables who had watched the fight from ringside were ushered into their limousines, or walked the short distance to the railroad sidings where their private cars waited. But the Pennsylvania Railroad terminal north of the fairgrounds stood empty. While the Pennsy ran special trains directly to the Sesqui grounds before the fight, it had stopped service before the fight ended. The bulk of the 125,732 spectators fought for the handful of available taxis, or waited for trolleys at the PRT station above the Stadium in a crowd that soon reached monstrous proportions.

Packed with humanity, the few streetcars heading north on Broad Street resembled "a working model of the steam room of a Turkish bath,"[37] and took more than an hour to traverse the three miles to Center City. At Broad Street Station, thousands of travelers were forced to wait outside in the rain until well past midnight, while thousands of riders inside with tickets for the Tunney and Rickard specials could be dispatched. The first regular local train didn't leave the station until 1:30 A.M., arriving in Trenton around 3:00 A.M. By this point, reported the Trenton *Times*, "If there is one thing the bulk of dripping customers never want to see again, it is a world's heavyweight fight in Philadelphia."

Thousands of drenched men and women trudged up South Broad Street in the rain, having lost hope of finding any other way to reach their hotels or train stations. Some of them made the trek in stocking feet, their shoes swallowed by the thick mud of the waterlogged fairgrounds. Delivery wagons on South Broad Street were besieged by pedestrians desperate for a ride uptown, their drivers making a tidy profit in the bidding wars on fares.

While movie stars, governors, and business tycoons settled into their luxurious suites at the Bellevue-Stratford, the cot-filled grand ballroom resembled an army barracks as several hundred men stripped off their soaked clothing. The hotel's exhausted bellboys were nearly smothered under a mountain of soiled, sodden garments. The Bellevue-Stratford laundry would clean and press nearly seven hundred suits over the next day, setting a new record. Despite this efficiency, some fight-goers would not get their suits back until the weekend. In the following days, stories would abound of an army of men in their pajamas or BVD's haunting hotels throughout the city, waiting for their missing clothes. One suite occupied by eight New York businessmen would be able to reclaim only one suit and three shoes by Saturday.[38]

While half of the hotel guests were trying to get their clothes back, the other half were writing newspaper features on the bout, or trying to find someone sober enough to do it for them. *Chicago Tribune* sportswriter Ring Lardner, sharing a hotel room with friend and New York *Herald-Tribune* writer Grantland Rice, ended up writing Rice's story as well as his own when his colleague passed out on his bed, under the weather and under the influence. While Rice had planned to glorify both boxers, Lardner as Rice blasted them both for staging a lousy fight, then phoned the story in to the *Herald-Tribune*. Neither Dempsey nor Tunney would speak to Rice for months.[39]

The morning after the fight dawned sunny and dry but broiling hot, ushering in yet another heat wave. The Sesqui Stadium looked as if the Florida hurricane had touched down in Philadelphia. Workmen had begun to dismantle the bleachers across the northern end, piling the lumber in jumbled heaps. The central field was a wasteland of churned mud, a foot deep in some places. The arena was littered with thousands of muddy newspapers used as headgear during the previous night's deluge, along with dozens of derelict umbrellas, discarded hats, and mud-mired shoes abandoned during the post-fight exodus.

In Tex Rickard's suite at the Bellevue-Stratford, government bureaucrats, SCEA managers, and fight officials divvied up the loot from the championship bout. In the final analysis, the fight attracted 125,732 attendees and generated $1,893,733 in revenues. While less than the $2 million Rickard had expected, this gate made Dempsey-Tunney the richest prize fight to date, earning $267,353 more than the 1921 Dempsey-Carpentier bout. Tunney received $200,000 and Dempsey $700,000, per their contracts. Rickard walked away with $500,000, barely enough to cover the hefty sums he had laid out for Stadium renovations, staff, office rental, sportswriter bribes, and other expenses. Of the remaining half million in revenues, $172,339 was surrendered for federal taxes, $86,150 for state taxes, and $170,000 went to the SCEA. No explanation was given for why the association received 9 percent of the purse and the state 4.5 percent, rather than the full 10 percent and 5 percent originally stipulated. Their shares may have been adjusted to reflect the lower-than-anticipated gate.[40]

An elated Rickard told reporters that he intended to rematch Dempsey and Tunney in 1927, location to be determined. Already cities across America were clamoring to host the sequel. The owners of Wembley Stadium outside London, site of the 1924–1925 British Empire Exhibition, proposed that the two Americans meet there on Derby Day, June 1, 1927. Rickard dismissed talk of a Tunney-Wills bout, insisting that Dempsey was now the leading challenger. "Dempsey was handicapped by many legal proceedings and his mind was not working as actively as it should," Rickard noted. "Dempsey was only a shell of his former self and his timing of punches was very bad." But by 1927, Rickard expected the Manassa Mauler to be back up to snuff.[41]

That afternoon, Estelle Taylor arrived from Hollywood, alighting from the Pennsylvania Limited at Broad Street Station in a chic suit and red toque. She had learned of her husband's defeat on the train the previous night. By the time she reached Philadelphia, the Hollywood starlet was prepared for her biggest role to date: Loyal and Loving Wife of the Defeated Champ. While her "finely moulded lips trembled," Taylor told waiting reporters, "I am still his wife, no matter what he is to the fighting world. I am glad also that he is alive and that means more than everything in the world to me." She then rushed to the Hotel Adelphia, where a now-subdued Dempsey waited in seclusion with his retinue. "Ginsberg," Estelle gasped when she saw her battered husband, "what happened?"

"Honey," came Jack's immortal reply, "I forgot to duck."[42]

Soon after Estelle's arrival, Gene Tunney stopped by the Adelphia to pay a courtesy call on the man he had vanquished. Aside from slightly swollen lips and a plaster over his left eye, the new champ looked untouched by his ten rounds with the Manassa Mauler. "I always thought you were a great champion," Tunney told Dempsey. "And I want to say now that you are a fine, clean opponent and fought as clean and game a fight as any man who has been in a ring. Any man can be proud to have met you in the fight you made." After Tunney left, the Dempseys departed the Adelphia via the rear entrance, where taxis were waiting to speed them to an Atlantic City train. At least six process servers were waiting in the hotel lobby to serve Dempsey with papers, hoping to secure a share of his purse for Kearns and other claimants.[43]

Tunney left Philadelphia on the morning of the 25th. A few hours later, Gotham's first heavyweight champion was given a hero's welcome by his hometown, with a reception at New York City Hall and a gala luncheon at the Biltmore Hotel. By Saturday morning, Tunney had been commissioned as a first lieutenant in the Marine Reserve Corps. Fans lined up outside movie theaters across America to see films of the bout, shown on a double bill with Gene Tunney's sole Hollywood effort, *The Fighting Marine*, shot in 1925. The weekend papers were filled with photographs of the fight, most showing Dempsey retreating from Tunney's barrage of jabs.[44]

Despite its soggy climax, the Dempsey-Tunney bout was hailed as a boon to the struggling Sesqui-Centennial and its host city. "Not only did

Gene Tunney win in the rain-soaked affair," noted the *New York Times*, "but Philadelphia and the Sesquicentennial won also, in money and prestige alike." Local businessmen pronounced the fight to be "the greatest thing that ever happened to Philadelphia." Officials estimated that between $3 million and $5 million were added to the city coffers by eighty-five thousand out-of-town fight fans. The *Times* noted that while "Philadelphia has become sensitive in recent years about its reputation for somnolence," the recent past had seen "an awakening so brisk that it could almost be called a boom." The successful handling of the Dempsey-Tunney fight, the *Times* augured, "will send tidings of this new Philadelphia spirit all over the country." A radiant Mayor Kendrick immediately announced plans to bring another mammoth sporting event to Sesqui Stadium. The giant arena appeared poised to emerge as one of the city's greatest assets.

With the world clamoring for a rematch, Rickard arranged for Dempsey to meet Tunney at Soldier Field in Chicago on September 22, 1927. The A-list attendees, including Charlie Chaplin, Irving Berlin, Al Jolson, and Princess Xenia of Greece, made the ringside crowd at Philadelphia look like a suburban bridge party. Although the rematch attracted fewer paying customers than the Sesqui bout, its $2.7 million gate set a new record. Much had changed in the year since the Fight of a Century and a Half. In Chicago, Tunney received the larger check, $990,445.54 vs. a mere $450,000 for Dempsey. Tunney gave Rickard a check for $9,554.46 so that the promoter could present him with a check for a cool million.

The goodwill between Dempsey and Tunney had evaporated by the time they reached Chicago. "Tell Truth about 1926 Fight, Dempsey Challenge to Tunney," screamed a Chicago headline a week before the Soldier Field fight. Underneath was an open letter from Dempsey that accused Tunney of fixing the Philadelphia fight with the help of Max "Boo Boo" Hoff. During the fight itself, the straight arrow Tunney became the center of controversy over what became known as the Long Count. A referee appeared to stall his count when Tunney was knocked down in round seven, giving him several seconds to recover, while beginning the ten-count immediately when Tunney floored Dempsey in round eight.[45]

Rumors about the 1926 fight would circulate for decades afterward. Someone had slipped a Mickey Finn into Dempsey's coffee on the morning of the 23rd. Tunney and Gibson had enlisted Max Hoff's help to intimidate Dempsey into throwing the fight in exchange for a share of Tunney's future purses, and then reneged on the deal. Dempsey had taken a dive in exchange for $1 million from Hoff, Al Capone, and other gangsters who made a fortune betting on underdog Tunney. Sportswriter Ring Lardner was a strong proponent of the latter theory, having lost $500 on Dempsey. A month after the fight, Lardner wrote Scott and Zelda Fitzgerald that "the thing was a very well-done fake."[46]

All the conspiracy theories couldn't prevent Cinderella from enjoying her magical night at the ball. September 23 was the one time during the Sesqui that Philadelphia got it right. Despite the rain and the mud, the lost suits and Turkish-bath trolleys, many guests carried away glowing memories of the city. They praised the efficient management of the championship bout, the technological wonders of the vast new Stadium, Center City's lively atmosphere and decked-out streets, the elegant hotels and restaurants, the ease of access provided by the Delaware River Bridge and Roosevelt Boulevard, and even the courteous and capable police. For one night during the sorry, soggy Sesqui season, the City of Brotherly Love was downright sexy. Jazzed by the Fighting Marine and the Manassa Mauler, the Gray Quaker Lady kicked up her heels, revealing rolled silk stockings on a pair of shapely legs.[47]

NOTES

1. "Dempsey Bout Suddenly Shifted to Philadelphia," *NYT*, August 19, 1926.

2. "Tex Picks Tunney, Drops Harry Wills," *PI*, January 22, 1926; "Rickard Selects Tunney as Rival," *PPL*, n.d.; "Dempsey-Tunney Fight in Chicago," *PT*, July 21, 1926; Evensen, *When Dempsey Fought Tunney*, pp. 54–63.

3. Evensen, *When Dempsey Fought Tunney*, pp. 70–73; "Seek Again to Bring Big Fight to Sesqui," *PB*, August 5, 1926; "Dempsey Bout Suddenly Shifted to Philadelphia," *NYT*, August 19, 1926; Cavanaugh, *Tunney*, p. 254.

4. "Facts about the Fight," *PB*, September 23, 1926.

5. "Dempsey Bout Suddenly Shifted to Philadelphia," *NYT*, August 19, 1926; "Dempsey to Fight Tunney in Stadium," *PB*, August 19, 1926; "Creditors to Wait," *PB*, August 20, 1926; "Rickard Inspects Philadelphia Bowl," *NYT*, August 20, 1926; Cavanaugh, *Tunney*, p. 266.

6. "Pinchot Appeals for Ideals of '76," *PB*, August 30, 1926; Cavanaugh, *Tunney*, pp. 160–166.

7. Cavanaugh, *Tunney*, pp. 269–270; Dempsey, Consodine, and Slocum, *Dempsey*, p. 197; Roberts, *Jack Dempsey*, pp. 223–224.

8. Vidmer, "Tunney Welcomed by Philadelphia," *NYT*, September 2, 1926; "Gene Tunney Gets Big Ovation Here," *PB*, September 1, 1926; Biddle, *My Philadelphia Father*, pp. 24–25, 185–188; Cavanaugh, *Tunney*, p. 76.

9. "$1,370,000 Advance for Dempsey Bout," *NYT*, September 12, 1926.

10. "Big Bout Thursday Will Surpass All," *NYT*, September 19, 1926.

11. "Five Auto Routes from Here to Bout," *NYT*, September 19, 1926; "Railroads Prepare to Transport 50K," *NYT*, September 19, 1926; "Sidelights on the Fight," *TT*, September 23, 1926, p. 13.

12. "Title Bout Site Will Be Enlarged," *NYT*, September 5, 1926; "Carpenters Start on Seats in Field," *NYT*, September 14, 1926; "Dempsey to Defend His Title Tonight;

130,000 to See Bout," *NYT*, September 1926; "Fight Fans Told to Start Early," *TT*, September 23, 1926, p. 12.

13. Rudel, *Hello, Everybody!* pp. 92–95, 137–138.

14. "Dempsey Arrives at 7.49 Tonight," *PB*, September 23, 1926.

15. Thayer, "Only One Thing Can Scare Gene—a Girl!" *PB*, September 22, 1926; Cavanaugh, *Tunney*, pp. 275–276.

16. Cavanaugh, *Tunney*, pp. 278–279.

17. "Avalanche of Fans Hits Philadelphia," *NYT*, September 23, 1926; "Increasing Thousands Fast Filling Stadium," *PB*, September 23, 1926.

18. Elmer Davis, "Dempsey to Defend His Title Tonight; 130,000 to See Bout," *NYT*, September 23, 1926; "75,000 Fight Fans Leave City by Rail," *NYT*, September 24, 1926.

19. Dempsey, Consodine, and Slocum, *Dempsey*, p. 192; "Fight Fans Told to Leave Early," *TT*, September 23, 1926, p. 12.

20. Cavanaugh, *Tunney*, p. 287.

21. Cavanaugh, *Tunney*, pp. 283–287; "Tunney Flies Here by Air to Battle Dempsey Tonight," *PB*, September 23, 1926; "Airplane Carries Tunney to Scene," *NYT*, September 24, 1926.

22. Cavanaugh, *Tunney*, p. 288.

23. "Max Hoff Claims He Has Contract with Tunney," *PB*, January 18, 1927; "Hoff Agreement Calls for Fifth of Tunney Pursues," *PPL*, January 19, 1927; "Max Hoff May Sue Champion Tunney," *PB*, January 26, 1927; "'Boo Boo' Sues Tunney," *PB*, November 30, 1927; "To Hear Hoff Suit against Tunney," *PB*, July 7, 1928; "Against Tunney," *PB*, November 12, 1930; "Hoff Drops Suit against Tunney," *PB*, January 13, 1931; "Hoff Drops Suit to Have Tunney Share Earnings," *Herald Tribune*, January 14, 1931.

24. "Dempsey Arrives at 7.49 Tonight," *PB*, September 23, 1926; Cavanaugh, *Tunney*, p. 287.

25. "75,000 Fight Fans Leave City by Rail," *NYT*, September 24, 1926.

26. Parsons, "Cosmopolitan Crowd Sees Battle for Championship," *CPD*, September 24, 1926; "Fight Fans Get the 'Once Over,'" *CPD*, September 24, 1926; "Sidelights on the Fight," *TT*, September 24, 1926, p. 4.

27. "10,000 Women See Tunney Win Crown," *PB*, September 24, 1926; "Sidelights on the Fight," *TT*, September 24, 1926, p. 4.

28. Evensen, *When Dempsey Fought Tunney*, pp. 91–92.

29. "10,000 Women See Tunney Win Crown," *PB*, September 24, 1926; Rudel, *Hello, Everybody!* p. 139.

30. Letter to F. Scott and Zelda Fitzgerald dated October 13, 1926, Lardner, *Letters of Ring Lardner*, p. 206.

31. Kahn, *A Flame of Pure Fire*, p. 398

32. Dawson, James F., "Tunney Always Master," *NYT*, Sept. 24, 1926.

33. Elmer Davis, "Victory is Popular One," *NYT*, Sept. 24, 1926.

34. Kahn, *A Flame of Pure Fire*, p. 399.

35. Elmer Davis, "Victory Is Popular One," *NYT*, September 24, 1926; James Dawson, "Tunney Always Master," *NYT*, September 24, 1926; Robert Edgren, "Dempsey Never Gave Way a Step As Gene Battered Him to Defeat," *PB*, September 24, 1926; "Dempsey Landed Only 50 Blows In Entire Fight, Says Leonard," *PB*, September 24, 1926; "Tunney Hit Jack 3 Blows for One," *PB*, September 24, 1926; "Sidelights on the Fight," *TT*, September 24, 1926; "Realization Greater than Anticipation, Gene Says,

As He Begs to be Alone," *PPL*, September 24, 1926; Kahn, *A Flame of Pure Fire*, pp. 397–400; letter to F. Scott and Zelda Fitzgerald dated October 13, 1926, Lardner, *Letters of Ring Lardner*, p. 206.

36. Raymond Hill, "'I Have No Alibi,' Asserts Dempsey," *PB*, September 24, 1926; Raymond Hill, "Dempsey's Downcast Friends Shocked by Smiles after Fight," *PB*, October 1, 1926.

37. "Sidelights on the Fight," *TT*, September 24, 1926.

38. "Hotel Tailors Establish World Mark in Pressing Drenched Fight Fan Suits," *Boston Herald*, September 25, 1926; "Where Are My Pants? That's Philly's New Yell," Consolidated Press feature, Seattle *Daily Times*, September 26, 1926, p. 21; McCullough, *World's Fair Midways*, p. 90.

39. McCullough, *World's Fair Midways*, p. 85.

40. "Tunney Wins Dempsey's Title as 125,732 Cheer," *PPL*, September 24, 1926; "$1,895,733.40 Paid to Witness Title Fight," *CPD*, September 25, 1926, p. 25.

41. "Rain Saved Jack from a Knockout, Says Gene's Aide," *PPL*, September 24, 1926; "Tunney Is Offered Derby Day Fight," *World*, September 26, 1926.

42. "Ginsberg" was Estelle's nickname for Dempsey, adopted after he told her that he might have Jewish relatives. "'He's My Champion,' Estelle, Here, Says," *PPL*, September 24, 1926; "Dempsey Jests with Estelle; Ex-Champ Tells Wife He 'Forgot to Duck,'" *CPD*, September 25, 1926, p. 25.

43. "Gene Pays Visit to Jack's Room," Greensboro *Record*, September 26, 1926, p.23.

44. "Champion Seeks Rest in Gotham," *CPD*, September 25, 1926, p. 25; "New York Acclaims Tunney as Champion," *TT*, September 25, 1926, p.1.

45. "Dempsey Accuses Gene of 'Frame-Up,'" *PB*, September 19, 1927; Hauser, *The Boxing Scene*, pp. 125–128; Dempsey, Consodine, and Slocum, *Dempsey*, p. 124; Roberts and Roberts, *Triumph on Fairmount*, p. 253; Kahn, *A Flame of Pure Fire*, p. 414.

46. "Dempsey Poisoned with Punches Only, Tunney Declares," *PB*, October 2, 1926; letter to F. Scott and Zelda Fitzgerald dated October 13, 1926, Lardner, *Letters of Ring Lardner*, p. 206.

47. "Philadelphia Sees Bout a Great Boon," *NYT*, September 25, 1926.

13

★ ★ ★

A Royal Visit

LESS THAN A week after her triumphant night at the Dempsey-Tunney bout, Kendrick's Cinderella was back in rags and crouched among the ashes. While Center City restaurateurs, hoteliers, and dry cleaners had reaped a handsome windfall on September 23, the Sesqui-Centennial Exhibition Association soon realized that the fight offered few substantive benefits. The $170,000 cut of the gate received by the SCEA was a drop in the bucket of the fair's multimillion-dollar debt, and was nearly offset by the money spent preparing for the fight. Similarly, any profit that the city of Philadelphia might have accrued from the fight had been offset by its expenditures, especially overtime for police and other municipal employees.

By the end of September, the Sesqui's leading creditors had also realized that the Dempsey-Tunney bout was not going to resolve the fair's financial woes. Some of these large contractors had bills for work on the fairgrounds and structures dating back to 1925. The lawyer retained by the Sesqui-Centennial Creditors' Committee, George C. Klauder, informed the press that his clients "are becoming restive and will not wait much longer for their money." Klauder, one of the city's most powerful attorneys, was also politically well-connected. His law partner was City Treasurer Harry A. Mackey, former campaign manager for the Vare Senate race.[1]

Creditors' anger reached new heights when Mayor Kendrick signed an ordinance authorizing a thirty-year extension of the city-owned Frankford Elevated Line to the Philadelphia Rapid Transit Company on October 14, after City Council approved the deal eighteen to two. In exchange for being given control of the profitable Frankford El for another three decades, the

PRT assumed full interest and sinking fund charges on the $14 million bond issue on the elevated transit line. Since this ordinance immediately increased the city's borrowing capacity, Sesqui creditors felt they should be paid at once. But City Council President Charles B. Hall announced that the additional borrowing capacity would have to be diverted to more pressing municipal expenses. Instead, a referendum would be placed on the November ballot that, if approved by voters, would transfer $7.5 million from the city's long-term plans for extending rapid transit to its northern districts to pay down Sesqui debt.

Sesqui creditors were not the only parties outraged by the new PRT contract. The United Business Men's Association, a powerful lobby of Philadelphia merchants, and the Northeast Philadelphia Chamber of Commerce threatened taxpayers' suits to block what they saw as yet another sweetheart deal for the transit monopoly. Dissension erupted within the Kendrick administration when City Controller WillB Hadley charged that the PRT had published misleading documents which understated the profitability of the Frankford El, enabling it to underpay the city by millions of dollars. A furious Kendrick swore that he stood solidly behind City Solicitor Gaffney, who had championed the PRT deal. When PRT President W. K. Myers acknowledged that Hadley was correct, and that the new lease would allow his firm to reduce its payments to the city by $4 million, Kendrick declined comment and referred all questions to Gaffney.[2]

During the same period, the lawyer representing the Sesqui concessionaires announced plans to file yet another taxpayers' suit to block any payments to contractors and other creditors. The SCEA had extracted hefty fees from hundreds of commercial exhibitors, amusement ride operators, and hot dog and lemonade vendors, their lawyers argued, by promising that between twenty-five million and forty million customers would visit the Sesqui. Fewer than four million had actually materialized to date. That spelled financial ruin for many of these concessionaires, whose lawyers demanded priority compensation for their losses.[3]

With the Sesqui's financial status shaky and legal threats looming from both contractors and concessionaires, SCEA managers instituted another round of cost-cutting. Earlier in September, Director of Domestic Participation and Special Events A. L. Sutton had used budget shortfalls as an excuse to cut the staff and close the offices of the Committee on Negro Activities. Now all musical events scheduled for the Sesqui Auditorium during October and November were canceled, including concerts by the New York and Cleveland Symphony Orchestras. Otherwise, the SCEA would have been forced to pay $25,000 to install a heating system in the

Auditorium. With the Sesqui losing roughly that amount every week, the SCEA debated whether or not to close the fair on October 31 rather than on November 30. Even as Sesqui officials struggled to control costs, exposition debt mushroomed to $6 million by the end of October.[4]

As the Sesqui's problems mounted, so did allegations of incompetence and corruption at the highest levels of management. In early October, Director of Exhibits Axel Malm resigned abruptly, telling the press that the Sesqui "will become the greatest scandal ever witnessed" without radical changes. The only way to save the Sesqui, Malm insisted, was to have concessionaires, exhibitors and creditors elect new management and craft an operational agreement, like a large corporation undergoing bankruptcy proceedings. Malm fingered Director-General Austin as the major reason for the fair's failure. The Sesqui "czar," Malm charged, was an ineffective bureaucrat "without any human touch or soul. . . . who locks himself in his private office and tries to run an exposition." Due to Austin's bad management and poor salesmanship, Malm charged, the Sesqui had never been properly boomed, resulting in its inadequate attendance. Kendrick defended his Sesqui director, asserting that "the exposition has been very fortunate in having a man at its head with the courage, vision and capability that characterize Mr. Austin."[5]

By this time, the whiff of scandal had begun to waft to the upper levels of City Hall. In early October, a *Bulletin* reporter named Davis submitted a confidential memo to Managing Editor William B. Craig. It included a list of rumors the reporter had compiled concerning the illegal involvement of Mayor Kendrick's colleagues or relatives with Sesqui concessions. Walter R. Rodgers, assistant director of public works at City Hall, was said to hold the concession on lavatories at the Sesqui. Edward Loeb, Kendrick's confidential secretary, supposedly owned the main parking concession under a false name. Loeb's business partner allegedly held the Sesqui program concession. Finally, the Quaker City Laundry Company, owned by the mayor's brother Charles H. ("Chick") Kendrick, was "the fair-haired baby in getting all laundry work at Sesqui, competitors being banned."[6] While none of these rumors could be substantiated, the earlier scandals involving Director of Concessions William Abrahams lent them some credence.

The biggest bombshell came from an anonymous source that appeared to connect the mayor's elegant wife directly with the sordid corruption of the Sesqui. Davis's contact passed along a story told him by a friend, Charles H. Evans. When Evans had made a deposit at the Aldine Trust Company at 2020 Chestnut Street in May 1926, his teller pointed out a woman customer and identified her as Mrs. Kendrick, the mayor's wife. The teller held up a check and told Evans: "This check was deposited for Mrs. Kendrick. It is for $50,000. It was made to her order by a builder or contractor who is doing Sesqui work."[7] For corroboration, Davis sought out Charles H. Evans, a partner in the construction firm of Evans-Steele. Davis's notes for the off-the-record interview were forwarded the next day to *Bulletin* City Editor Charles Israel. Evans explained that he himself had not witnessed the transaction; he had been told the story by a friend. Despite this remove, Evans was able to specify that the amount of Mrs. Kendrick's check had been $25,000 rather than $50,000. He also identified the check's signer as Philip H. Johnson, one of Philadelphia's most politically connected architects. Johnson, a brother-in-law of the late boss Israel W. Durham, had been granted a lifetime contract with the City Health Department which would net him roughly $2 million in fees before his death in 1933. During the Kendrick administration, Johnson was the architect on major projects like the Philadelphia General Hospital, the Hospital for Contagious Diseases, and the Hospital for Mental Diseases at Byberry.

Evans had worked with Philip Johnson on the Byberry Hospital project, but he told Davis that he had lost $8,000 on the deal. Johnson's office had ordered Evans to use cement from the Nazareth Cement Company, a favored supplier. Evans had done so, but when he refused to provide kickbacks for his participation in the project, Johnson had arranged for his allies in the Bureau of Building Inspection to condemn the Evans-Steele work. Evans described the "round table" at the Manufacturers Club where Johnson held court, dividing up deals on municipal projects with key figures. These men included C. Albert Kuehnle of the Kuehnle Paint Company; a representative of the Nazareth Cement Company; and F. W. Mark, whose construction company handled most of the work on the Museum of Art, the Free Library, and the Pennsylvania State Building at the Sesqui. "It is suicide for anyone else to bid" against Mark, Evans told Davis. "He has been heard to openly boast around the Penn Athletic Club and the Manufacturers Club that the city lost $100,000 on [the Byberry] job."[8]

Given the lack of substantive proof and Evans' refusal to go on record, Davis's notes never took the form of an article in the *Bulletin*. "All this gossip is just between ourselves," the contractor had told Davis. "I want to continue in business, you see, and if I can get any city work on the level, of course I want it." Instead, the *Bulletin* demanded that the city release a detailed accounting of Sesqui finances to city taxpayers, warning that:

> Rumor has been continually accumulating since the first of the contracts for the filling of the Sesqui grounds was awarded. And

> persistence and multiplication of these rumors have been possible largely because the affairs of the Sesqui-Centennial have been kept under cover and the public has been denied an open showing of the expenditure of its money. Millions have been spent. The management has not had sufficient faith in the people to show them from time to time how and where these large appropriations have been expended, and the public, in the dark, and without enlightenment from official authority, naturally have listened to whispered rumor.[9]

At the October meeting of the SCEA Board of Directors, an emotional Mayor Kendrick defended himself against the growing talk of malfeasance. Beating his hand against his breast, he declared, "There can't be any scandal because we have taken nothing; have given all we had. I have done nothing since becoming Mayor except to conduct my office for the best interests of all the citizens."[10] The assembled crowd, which included numerous City Hall officials in addition to the SCEA Board of Directors, gave the mayor a standing ovation that lasted several minutes. The board unanimously approved the issuance of $5 million in short-term notes, to be turned over to Sesqui creditors starting the following week. They agreed that the Sesqui would still end on November 30, but tabled a proposal to extend it into 1927. At the conclusion of the meeting, the SCEA Board passed a resolution expressing their "100 per cent support of the Mayor and his policy to carry on the exposition and to meet the obligations incurred."[11]

"Philadelphia Expo a Failure; Unpaid Bills Total More Than $3M," shouted the headline on the front page of the *New York Times* the next morning. "Mayor Kendrick said today the Sesquicentennial is a financial failure," the article began. "Fewer than five million people have passed through the gates, leaving the city to shoulder a big deficit." The following day, the *Times* headline announced "Philadelphia Fair Never Had Chance." The front-page article enumerated the reasons for the Sesqui's failure: lack of preparation and rushed construction; the Shriners' negative word-of-mouth; the growing evidence of mismanagement, graft, and favoritism; and the incessant rain. It had become painfully clear that "the exposition which Philadelphians hoped at one time would make their city the centre of the United States for several months has become a white elephant." An accompanying editorial noted that "no great international exposition of recent years has met with such public apathy as the Sesquicentennial."[12]

Defying its negative press and the specter of its financial collapse, the Sesqui-Centennial had become a fully functional world's fair by October, with nearly every attraction operating at 100 percent capacity. Kicked off by a record crowd of 125,968 on October 3, when Cardinal Dougherty of Philadelphia celebrated Catholic High Mass at the Stadium, turnout remained high throughout the month. The total October attendance of 1,048,987 would represent the second-highest month for the Sesqui, after September with 1,210,756 visitors. Wet weather would continue to be a problem: it rained on fifteen days during October, including all five Sundays. But after a heat wave at the start of the month, the cooler temperatures of early fall attracted many Americans who realized that the Sesqui's wonders would soon vanish.[13]

Large national conventions and special theme days kept the fairgrounds crowded throughout October. With less than two months before Closing Day, the same date had to serve double and sometimes triple duty for the many organizations that wished to make their presence felt. October 1 had to be shared between the blue-blooded descendants of those who had sailed on the *Mayflower* in 1620, and the rugged pioneers of South Dakota, a state for less than forty years. October 5 marked Maine Day and Japan Day, as well as Civil Engineers' Day and Pennsylvania Firefighters' Day, honoring two associations celebrating their annual conventions at the Sesqui that week. October 9 was Cuba Day, Chicago Day, and Public School Children Day. October 12 honored Christopher Columbus, Italy, and Spain, as well as the residents of Cape May, New Jersey, and Danbury, Connecticut. The next day, British Consul General Frederick Watson shared British Day with the residents of Lehighton in Carbon County, Pennsylvania, and members of the Ohio American Legion.[14]

Hardly had the thousands of firemen and civil engineers departed Philadelphia when 150,000 members of the American Legion began to arrive for their national convention from October 11 to 15. Founded in 1919, the American Legion was the biggest veterans' organization in the country, with 673,229 active members in 1926. Another 247,000 wives, widows, sisters, mothers and daughters constituted the Legion Auxiliary. A mutual aid and lobbying organization for the country's surviving 4.5 million World War veterans, the Legion was dedicated to "Keeping the Spirit of the Great War Alive" in a nation that seemed determined to forget about the conflict. Its first commander in 1919–1920 had been Franklin D'Olier, the former SCEA president.[15]

The 150,000 American Legionnaires descending on Philadelphia, accompanied by ten thousand members of the Women's Auxiliary, represented the largest contingent of a single organization to invade the city since the Shriners had landed at the end of May. On Monday, October 11, the city's train stations were thronged with multitudes of men in military uniforms, or in colorful hybrids created by their individual posts. Several delegations brought along samples of their states' flora and fauna. The Montana delegation arrived with a menagerie of burros, jackrabbits, and snakes, while Colorado's entourage featured mules and coyotes.[16]

At the fairgrounds, three thousand Legionnaires gathered in the cavernous Sesqui Auditorium for the opening session of their five-day convention. A message from President Coolidge was read in which he praised the Legion for its work to build up America's shrinking voter base, admonishing that "shirkers in peacetime are to be condemned as severely as slackers during a war." Governor Pinchot lectured the assembled Legionnaires on the need for clean government, only to have his speech disrupted when the Colorado chapter led a tame bear down the aisle and presented it to Mayor Kendrick. As dusk descended, the Legionnaires headed north. Soon, the streets of Center City had become an outdoor dance hall, "filled with marching bands, groups of men wearing some of the weirdest uniforms ever seen outside a circus, laughing and yelling and singing." A spotlight on City Hall picked out Legionnaire Harry Gardiner as he scaled the gigantic statue of William Penn atop the central tower, executing a handstand on the broad brim of the proprietor's hat while the crowds below cheered.[17]

On October 12 a crowded Auditorium hailed General John Joseph "Black Jack" Pershing, commander of the American Expeditionary Forces in Europe during the World War. Although the sixty-six-year-old Pershing had retired from active service in 1924, he retained his title of "General of the Armies of the United States" and five-gold-star status, reflecting his supreme command of all armed forces. Because of ill health, he had not been expected to attend the convention; his presence was cause for jubilant celebration among the Legionnaires. Pershing was followed by the principal speaker, Vice President Charles G. Dawes, who warned the Legion that the men who had played such a great role in the Great War were in danger of becoming the Lost Generation, "living heedlessly, almost recklessly, and with little thought of the future."[18]

After Dawes's talk, a vintage Renault AG1 taxicab puttered up the aisle. It was a Taxi of the Marne, one of six hundred that had ferried three thousand French infantry troops from Paris to the front during the First Battle of the Marne in September 1914. In what became known as the Miracle of the Marne, the city's fleet of Renault taxis prevented the German Army from capturing Paris in the opening weeks of the Great War. The taxi carried messages from French generals and politicians, inviting the Legionnaires to celebrate their 1927 convention in Paris.

The vote on the site for the 1927 convention was tabled until the next day so that the Legionnaires could rush back to Center City for "the Parade

A Taxi of the Marne, one of the six hundred Parisian cabs that ferried French troops to the front and averted a German capture of Paris in September 1914, made an appearance at the American Legion Convention in September.

of a Century and a Half." Beginning at 1:00 P.M., more than forty-five thousand men and women marched down the Parkway and South Broad Street to the Sesqui Stadium, with General Pershing, Vice President Dawes, Governor Pinchot, and Mayor Kendrick leading them in open limousines. The massive parade featured one hundred bands, a vintage tank with its Gatling gun firing blanks, and the Taxi of the Marne. In the sky above the Stadium, tiny Martin bombers and scout planes buzzed around two dirigibles, the U.S. Army's TC-5 and the U.S. Navy's *Los Angeles*. By the time the last of the forty-five thousand marchers passed the reviewing stand, it was

Led by Florida veterans wearing bright orange uniforms, the "Parade of a Century and a Half" makes its way under the Liberty Bell into the Sesqui fairgrounds.

7:30 P.M. and the Stadium was nearly empty of spectators aside from the weary dignitaries in the stand.[19]

Unlike the Shriners, Legionnaires were able to enjoy one of the most festive and eventful weeks at the Sesqui, with lavish parades and ceremonies marking Columbus Day, Spanish Day, and British Day. When the nearly two hundred thousand men and women of the American Legion left Philadelphia in mid-October, their feelings toward the fair were significantly warmer than those of the disgruntled Shriners in June. Unfortunately, the Legionnaires' goodwill came three months too late to save the Sesqui.[20]

As the Legionnaires departed, fair planners turned their attention to the next major event on their agenda: the arrival on October 21 of Queen Marie of Romania, one of the most romantic and controversial figures of the era. She had been born Princess Marie of Edinburgh in England in 1875 to the second-oldest son of Queen Victoria and the only surviving daughter of Czar Alexander II of Russia. Although the Prince of Wales (the future King George V) had proposed to the beautiful young princess, Marie's mother forced her into a loveless marriage with Crown Prince Ferdinand of Romania, ten years her senior. At least three of Marie's six children were rumored to have been fathered by men other than Ferdinand, for whom Marie felt an initial "distaste, which grew to revulsion."[21]

During the Great War, Queen Marie earned the loyalty of her subjects and the admiration of foreigners by serving as a Red Cross nurse, using her own wealth to feed starving refugees, and arranging much-needed foreign loans. The British-born Marie made sure that Romania backed the Allies, resisting the country's pro-German faction even when two-thirds of her country was occupied by the Central Powers. Her loyalty to the Allies paid off at the Paris Peace Conference in 1919 where, as an unofficial delegate, she helped to obtain the neighboring provinces of Bessarabia, Bukovina, and Transylvania. These acquisitions more than doubled the country's area, creating a new entity known as *România Mare* or Greater Romania.

By the mid-1920s, Marie's halo had taken on more than a touch of tarnish. Her eldest son, Crown Prince Carol, had abandoned his wife, renounced the throne, and was living a dissolute life in Paris with his mistress, Magda Lupescu. Seven years after the Armistice, Romania remained mired in poverty. Three-quarters of a million Romanians had died during the war, while its occupiers had stripped the country of its resources. Despite being the second-largest oil producer in Europe, Romania was saddled with $342 million in debt. Its Byzantine government was condemned for both its corruption and its persecution of Jews and other minorities. Although many Americans were still fascinated by the haggardly beautiful queen with soulful eyes and exquisite jewels, they were increasingly disenchanted with her realm.

In 1926 American dancer Loie Fuller, a friend of Marie, suggested a United States tour as a way for the queen to raise funds for her impoverished country. At stops along the way, Marie would solicit donations for Romania and preside over performances of Fuller's ballets. The fifty-year-old queen traveled across Europe, stopping briefly in Paris to beg Carol not to attempt a coup d'état in her absence. She set sail in early October on the luxury liner SS *Leviathan* with her younger children, Prince Nicholas and Princess Ileana, fifteen attendants, and 168 pieces of luggage.

Americans had mixed feelings about Marie's visit. Although her trip was unofficial, the queen made it known that she expected to be received by President Coolidge and honored by dignitaries along her route. "Is the object of Marie's visit pleasure, or is it business?" queried the New York *World*. "If it is pleasure, why the elaborate political discussions in Roumania, and the elaborate diplomatic preparations throughout the better part of the civilized world?" William H. Fineshriber, rabbi of Philadelphia's Congregation Keneseth Israel, was appalled by the popular enthusiasm that attended Marie's American tour. While acknowledging that the queen was "a woman of undoubted charm" who had performed "excellent war work," Fineshriber

Queen Marie of Romania arrives in the United States on October 18, accompanied by her younger children, Prince Nicholas and Princess Ileana. (Prints and Photographs Division, Library of Congress.)

reminded Americans that her nation's record on human rights remained abysmal. "What has she done for humanity?" Fineshriber asked of Marie. "What has she done for her own country?"[22]

Ignoring this skepticism, Philadelphia begged to be squeezed into Marie's schedule. To establish its credibility as an international exposition, the

Sesqui needed a visit from at least one crowned head of state, its counterpart to Emperor Dom Pedro II of Brazil at the 1876 Centennial. While Gustaf Adolf had been perfectly charming in June, he was merely the heir apparent to the Swedish crown. Conversely, the autocratic ruler of a reactionary country could only benefit from using the Liberty Bell and other symbols of democracy as a backdrop. After much negotiation, October 21 was fixed as the date when the Romanian Queen would grace the Quaker City. As with Calvin Coolidge, planners put a brave face on Marie's abbreviated visit. The Romanian royal party would arrive at 4:00 P.M. and depart by midnight, giving Philadelphia eight hours to rub shoulders with royalty.

By the time the *Leviathan* arrived in New York harbor on October 18, 1926, a wicked *lele*, or Romanian sprite, seemed to have cursed Marie's American visit, transforming it into a high-class vaudeville routine. Marie, dressed for the role in a sable-trimmed burgundy coat and gold turban, played Margaret Dumont to Mayor Jimmy Walker's Groucho Marx at her reception. While the nervous mayor struggled to pin a medal on Marie's ample bosom, he admitted sheepishly, "Your Majesty, I've never stuck a queen, and I hesitate to do so now."

"Proceed, Your Honor," Marie assured him. "The risk is mine."

"And such a beautiful risk it is, Your Majesty," murmured Beau James.

Later, as the mayor and the majesty shared an open limousine up Broadway in the brisk October air, the chivalrous Walker reached over to cover Marie's legs with a lap robe. A construction worker, viewing the gesture from a girder high overhead, yelled, "Hey, Jimmy! Have you made her yet?"

The queen observed diplomatically that everyone in New York seemed to know Walker.

"Yes, Madam," the mayor responded. "And some of them know me very well indeed."[23]

The following day, Marie called upon the Coolidges at the White House, spending four minutes with a visibly uncomfortable president who had heard that Marie sought a $100 million loan from his tight-fisted administration. The formal dinner at the White House that evening lasted 105 minutes, the blink of an eye by the standards of Washington diplomacy. During that brief period, the queen shocked her fellow guests by wearing a knee-length Patou gown (White House protocol dictated floor-length dresses for official dinners) and smoking a cigarette with Alice Roosevelt Longworth.[24]

By the time Marie's act reached Philadelphia on October 21, it had degenerated into slapstick. Event planners had packed her brief visit with blue-ribbon events. After her arrival at the Baltimore and Ohio station at

4:00 P.M., Marie was to be honored with a parade to City Hall, where she would be the guest of Mayor Kendrick at a gala reception. The customary tour of the Sesqui-Centennial would follow. After that, Marie would be escorted to the Bellevue-Stratford Hotel, to meet a delegation of women war workers headed by Mrs. J. Willis Martin. The queen and her party would be guests of honor at a banquet in the hotel's Grand Ballroom. A "Soirée de Gala" at the Sesqui Auditorium would follow, with the Philadelphia Orchestra accompanying Loie Fuller's ballet troupe. The Auditorium had been remodeled to accommodate a royal box to the right of the proscenium. Two rows of elevated boxes had also been constructed on either side of the stage, capable of holding fifteen hundred people. An entire box for eight was available for $440, a single box seat could be had for $50, and orchestra seats ranged from $1.10 to $7.50. After the soirée was over, a reception would be held at the Palace of Fine Arts for box holders. Gala proceeds would be split between the SCEA and Queen Marie's charities.

The SCEA had charged the Women's Committee with selling forty-eight boxes for the "Soirée de Gala" at the recommended price of $440. Committee chairman Elizabeth Martin denounced the SCEA demand as "outrageous," and refused to ask more than $300 a box. Even that, she told the Women's Committee, was "too much—we only ask you if you know anybody who wants to buy them." The tepid response of the Women's Committee to the SCEA amounted to an upper-class boycott of the gala, and box sales languished. Perhaps the wicked *lele* carried word of Martin's lack of fealty back to Queen Marie. The day before her arrival in Philadelphia, Marie informed her hosts that she would like to begin her visit by attending an afternoon service at the Church of the Descent of the Holy Ghost, a Romanian Orthodox church in Northern Liberties. The church had sent Marie an invitation several months earlier, which she had just acknowledged. The queen's last-minute request played havoc with the meticulously planned agenda for her visit.[25]

As dusk descended on October 21, the queen's train rolled up to its scarlet-carpeted platform at the Baltimore and Ohio Station at Twenty-Fourth and Chestnut Streets. Queen Marie, in a heavy fur coat and feathered hat, and her two children were received by Alexander P. Moore, former ambassador to Romania, and Edward T. Stotesbury, chairman of the Sesqui Welcoming Committee. Escorted by the First City Troop on horseback, the Romanian royal party proceeded down streets lined with cheering crowds to City Hall. There, they were received by Mayor Kendrick, who presented Queen Marie with a golden key to the city, an oversize bouquet, and a block of wood from Independence Hall.

After this hasty reception, the royal party drove to Northern Liberties, a grim working-class neighborhood near the Delaware River. There, at American and Brown Streets, stood the Church of the Descent of the Holy Ghost, a neoclassical brick structure designed by William Strickland in 1815 as St. John's Episcopal Church. In 1926 the *New York Times* described it as a "dingy little church" where whitewash peeled off the walls in huge flakes, and electric lights glowed dimly through dusty globes. Despite the humble surroundings, the passionate devotion of Philadelphia's Romanian community to their queen was manifest. Thousands of admirers struggled to touch their monarch as they cried, *"Traisoia, Regina!"* (Long live the Queen!) After the service, Marie addressed her admirers in their native language. "I came here to see you all, my people, and I am very happy that I have had the opportunity to be among my own. *Teraiti!*" (Long life to you!)[26]

The royal party sped back to the Bellevue-Stratford, where the queen and her children spent a few moments with Elizabeth Martin and four hundred uniformed women war workers. The royals hurried upstairs to change for dinner, only to discover that their luggage had gone astray between the railway station and the hotel. The *lele*, who obviously had seen a few Mack Sennett comedies, had struck again. Constance Lily Morris, one of Marie's ladies-in-waiting, arrived late to find a scene of chaos at the hotel, where "a confused mob of people, policemen and men in extraordinary Revolutionary costumes" surged through the lobby and corridors. "Anybody that wanted to could get in. If I had been bent on some nefarious mission, I might have had a good opportunity that day to do my worst."[27]

While emissaries hunted down the missing trunks, six hundred of Philadelphia's most distinguished citizens waited patiently in the Grand Ballroom for their guests of honor. Finally, Queen Marie appeared, serene and regal in a scarlet gown, an ermine robe, and a diamond-and-pearl tiara. Prince Nicholas arrived a little later, in evening clothes, only to discover that the ballroom doors had been locked, with no one able to locate the key. The laughing prince was rushed through the adjacent kitchen by a general, an admiral, and a distracted hotel manager, while tray-laden waiters jumped out of the way.

The hasty dinner was followed by another frenzied drive, this time to the Sesqui Auditorium. Marie and her party took their places on thronelike chairs in their royal box, hung with gold brocade curtains and adorned with a large electric *M* on the front panel. They looked out on a half-full Auditorium, and on scores of empty boxes lining both sides of the stage. After Martin's pronouncement, only 150 people had paid for box seats. Most of the audience

Queen Marie of Romania and entourage in her royal box at the Sesqui Auditorium, which allowed her to be seen to great advantage while blocking her view of the stage.

had been waiting for ninety minutes, listening to recordings of the Philadelphia Orchestra punctuated by radio announcements updating the queen's progress downtown. Both Queen Marie and Princess Ileana kept their fur coats on. The unheated Auditorium was chilly, despite hundreds of oil stoves scattered around that permeated the air with an acrid smell.

The performance began around 9:00 P.M. with Tchaikovsky's *Capriccio Italien*, followed by *Nell Gwyn*, a ballet performed by the Loie Fuller dance troupe. As the ballet progressed, it became apparent that while the royal box was angled to allow Marie and her party to be viewed to their best advantage by the sparse audience, it prevented them from watching the action onstage. Hoping to accommodate the queen, two of Mayor Kendrick's aides startled the monarch by lifting up her throne and moving it to one side of the box. It did not help. The performance was halted while the royal party moved to a humble fifty-dollar box, from which they watched the rest of the performance.

The select reception for box holders at the Palace of Fine Arts had been canceled because so few boxes had been purchased. Once Marie had returned to her throne, the announcement was made that "Her Majesty has graciously consented to receive the audience before her box. We ask you to pass before the royal box with as little confusion as possible."[28] Hundreds of spectators rushed forward, ignoring the pleas of ushers as they pushed and shoved their way in front of the royal box. More than one commentator noted the irony of well-heeled Americans celebrating the 150th anniversary of their independence by groveling before a third-tier monarch like Balkan peasants.

At 11:20, the queen and her party returned to their limousine for a whirlwind tour of the Sesqui. At the queen's request, they stopped for fifteen minutes at the Palace of Fine Arts. Marie pronounced the Rodin sculptures "beautiful" and wished she had time to see all of the wonderful paintings. After the royal family climbed back into their limousine, the procession of motorcars tore around Edgewater Lake at breakneck speed, and then raced up Broad Street at fifty miles per hour. The only element needed to complete the farcical scene was a paddy wagon filled with Keystone Kops pursuing the procession. Shortly before 1:00 A.M., the royal train departed Philadelphia, returning to New York prior to setting out on a four-week, coast-to-coast tour of the United States and Canada. As Marie boarded the *Leviathan* for her return voyage in November, she assured reporters that "the official functions were strenuous, of course, but I've met some lovely mayors."[29]

Philadelphia had less than twelve hours to kick itself over its numerous faux pas with the Romanian royal family. The following morning, Mayor Kendrick was back in his silk hat and morning dress and standing on a red carpet at the Broad Street Station, waiting for the representatives of twenty-one Latin American nations to arrive and celebrate Pan-American Day at the Sesqui. A week after Philadelphia had entertained its Romanian and Latin American guests, Mayor Kendrick asked City Council to appropriate an additional $12,500 for entertaining Sesqui visitors, bringing the total for the year to $30,500. Kendrick assured Philadelphia taxpayers that "the money has been well spent and the city has been advertised in a way that is bound to rebound not only to the credit but to the advantage of the municipality in years to come."[30]

While Mayor Kendrick was ready to drop from exhaustion, Congressman William S. Vare had never felt better in his life. Vare had enjoyed a lengthy European vacation over the summer, sailing in mid-July on the SS *Majestic*. He had been accompanied by his beloved daughter Beatrice, and by his friend and backer Jules E. Mastbaum. Among Vare's shipmates was Secretary of the Treasury Andrew W. Mellon, patron of Vare's main opponent in the May primary, incumbent U.S. Senator George Wharton Pepper. Mellon had been the soul of graciousness, shaking the congressman's hand warmly and greeting him with the words, "Hello, Senator." Vare returned home, tanned and relaxed, in mid-August on the SS *Leviathan*.

He spent the rest of August at his summer cottage in Atlantic City, fishing from his yacht and holding informal political conferences with other power brokers on the front porch. Vare did not return to Philadelphia until the end of August to begin his senatorial campaign in earnest. His first step was to resign his long-held post as Republican City Committee member from the Twenty-Sixth Ward, turning it over to Recorder of Deeds James M. Hazlett. City Hall watchers understood that the transfer of power meant nothing, and that Vare was still the guiding spirit of the Organization. Vare's campaign kicked off on September 25 with a speech in Hazleton in northeastern Pennsylvania, and continued with a statewide tour throughout October.[31]

As the Republican candidate in an overwhelmingly Republican state, with the financial resources of the Organization behind him, there should have been no reason for Vare to hurry back from the beach before Election Day on Tuesday, November 2. But the U.S. Senate Committee investigating expenditures in the Pennsylvania Republican primary had reconvened after its summer break, uncovering financial and voting irregularities among all three candidates' campaigns. At least 395 voting districts in the state had counted more votes than there were registered voters. The total amount of primary spending tabulated by the Senate committee had risen from $1.1 million to nearly $3 million. The recorded expenditures of the Pepper camp amounted to roughly $1,800,000, more than twice the $786,000 identified as being spent by the Vare team. (By contrast, the penny-pinching Pinchot spent a measly $187,000.) Yet the Senate committee focused most of its attention on potential fraud in the Vare campaign. Determined that "there will be no millions spent for the election of the next U.S. Senator from Pennsylvania," the Senate tacked a rider on a Postal Salary Increase Bill which limited the amount spent by an individual on a Senate race to three cents per vote, not to exceed $25,000.[32]

Vare was also the target of vituperative opposition, led by Pennsylvania Governor and former senatorial candidate Gifford Pinchot. After toying with the idea of accepting the Labor Party nomination for U.S. Senator, Pinchot withdrew from the race. The Republican governor then did the unthinkable: he announced his support of the Democratic candidate, William B. Wilson. "I am a Republican," he told astounded reporters, "but I cannot stand for Vare. He is not fit to represent Pennsylvania in the Senate of the United States. . . . Vare cannot possibly be elected even if he receives the nomination. Vare must go. . . . The whole country knows that Vare's nomination was partly bought, partly stolen." Pinchot called on President Coolidge to publicly repudiate Vare's candidacy. The congressman, hoping that Pinchot's jeremiads would be forgotten by November 2, smilingly assured the press that he was "not alarmed."[33]

Most of Philadelphia's daily newspapers dutifully endorsed William S. Vare for U.S. Senator once he became the official nominee of the Republican Party. The city's one Democratic paper, the reform-minded *Record*, gleefully reprinted the attacks that these newfound friends had aimed at Vare during the spring primary, when they had backed either Pepper or Pinchot. The *Record*'s favorite target was the *Inquirer*, which had performed the most adroit about-face from its earlier support of Pepper. In October the *Record* reprinted a May 3 editorial from the *Inquirer* that had asked Republican voters: "Are you going to support a man for whom you would continually be called upon to apologize to every State in the Union? Do you dare humiliate your State by sending Vare to the Senate?" Since the *Record* knew that most of its readers were Democrats, it urged them, "Cut this out and hand it to a Republican friend."[34]

In the same issue, the *Record* addressed an open letter to Congressman Vare, accusing the politician "of the rankest and most disgusting hypocrisy" for using "Give an American His Rights" as a campaign slogan:

> While you are undermining the very foundation of those rights with the aid of the crew of crooked registrars and conscienceless election

> officers who manufacture the majorities you predict in advance. . . . The only votes you will get, besides those of your river-wards' Foreign Legion and of persons actuated by self-interest and willing to drag the honor of the State in the mud for the fancied advantage to be derived through maintaining the ascendancy of the Republican party, are those that will be counted for you without having been cast.[35]

While the *Record* led the charge against Vare on his home territory, a group of national figures broadcast his flaws to a wider audience. The Senate investigation into the Pennsylvania primary had electrified many Progressive politicians from outside the state into taking action against the man who represented the worst abuses of the boss system in their minds. Supporters of Prohibition feared the election of the "wet" Vare as the first step in modifying the Volstead Act to permit the sale of light wines and beer. Senator George W. Norris of Nebraska fell into both categories, being a Progressive Republican and a staunch Prohibitionist. Acting as a "patriotic citizen," Norris barnstormed across Pennsylvania during October, warning voters of the dangers of Vareism. Shortly before Election Day, Norris chaired a rally at the Academy of Music in Philadelphia. He promised that if Vare was elected on November 2, the Senate would not allow him to be seated.[36]

Wayne B. Wheeler, general counsel for the Anti-Saloon League (ASL), also campaigned against Vare. The November 2 election, announced the influential spokesman for the nation's foremost Prohibition organization, would determine who had the upper hand in Pennsylvania. Would it be "Vare's foreign legion in the first twenty wards of machine-ridden Philadelphia, backed by brewers' contributions," or "the respectable true Americans [who] will forget partisan lines and send to Washington the clean and able opponent of the Quaker City boss"? Influenced by ASL lobbying, many religious groups opposed Vare. The Pennsylvania General Baptist Convention adopted a resolution condemning the congressman for his "unstatesmanlike principles in upholding the liquor traffic."[37]

Defying his local and national foes, William S. Vare won the election for United States Senator on November 2. He polled 822,178 votes statewide, compared with 648,680 for Democratic candidate William B. Wilson. As usual, the Philadelphia Organization assured his victory: Vare carried each of the city's forty-eight wards, polling 306,000 votes to Wilson's 73,000. While Vare crowed about his "handsome majority," the election results indicated that the campaign against him had made an impact. In the state excluding Philadelphia, the Democratic Wilson was the victor, with nearly 576,000 votes to Vare's 516,000. Vare's edge of 173,507 votes constituted the narrowest margin of victory to date for a Pennsylvania Republican senatorial candidate.

Within days of the election, Vare's detractors descended on the senator-elect like vultures on fresh roadkill. Senator George W. Norris insisted that the election had been brought about by "fraudulent manipulation." While Vare was technically the winner, he had been repudiated by the "honest, patriotic people of Pennsylvania." Norris announced plans to investigate both the primary and the general election. On Capitol Hill, rumors abounded that the Senate Committee on Elections planned to impound all Philadelphia ballot boxes for a complete recount of votes in the city. The same election that had won Vare his Senate seat had reduced his potential allies in that body: the number of Republicans in the U.S. Senate shrank from fifty-four to forty-eight, while Democratic senators increased from forty-one to forty-seven. Since the sole Farmer-Labor senator, Henrik Shipstead, usually voted with the Democrats, Senate Republicans would enjoy no majority except for Senate President Charles G. Dawes in the event of tied votes.[38]

Unwilling to wait for the Senate, Philadelphia's Committee of Seventy had already begun to investigate Vare. By Thanksgiving counsel for the reform organization had accused nine election officials of the Fourth Ward in West Philadelphia of fraud and vote manipulation. The Committee focused on the Sixteenth Division in the Fourth Ward, one of about thirty "zero divisions." Out of a total registration of 404 voters, election officers turned in a tally sheet showing 401 votes for Vare and zero votes for William Wilson. Twenty-eight residents of the Sixteenth Division testified under oath that they had not voted on November 2, even though election records showed them as having cast their ballots for Vare—twice, in several cases. The Committee of Seventy promised to conduct further investigations of Vare precincts where Wilson "was accorded zero treatment by Vare gangsters." If fraud could be proved in more than one division, it would open the way for a comprehensive investigation of the senatorial election, including a federal seizure of all ballot boxes and a complete recount of all votes. It would provide anti-Vare forces in the U.S. Senate with concrete reasons to block the senator-elect from taking his seat.[39]

Vare tried to proceed as though everything was above board and beyond reproach. Immediately after the election, he escaped to his winter retreat in St. Lucie, Florida, pursued by reporters who wanted his reaction to the latest developments in Washington and Philadelphia. "There is no ground for the charges," Vare insisted. "Norris and some of his men could not see how one man could get such a large vote honestly, so they brought these charges, which have no basis." He dismissed Senator Norris as a turncoat, who was working with Western Democrats in the Senate rather than loyally supporting his own party. After giving his statement, Vare asked to "be left alone," so that he could recuperate from his strenuous campaign.[40]

His refuge was a sprawling Victorian manse with a two-story wrap-around veranda that caught the breezes from the Indian River. Originally, the building had been the St. Lucie Club, built by "Sunny Jim" McNichol and other Philadelphia Republican bigwigs in 1902. Over the years, the St. Lucie Club had served as the winter getaway for the Organization. Bill Vare had spent many years there with his late brothers and political allies, alternating strategy sessions with hooking tarpon and playing baseball. As the last living member of the corporation that built the club, Vare had inherited it as his own private property under a tontine agreement. Now, the senator-elect and sole survivor could use St. Lucie as a haven where he could remember the past and plan for the future.

Ten days later Vare was in Washington, where he personally delivered his campaign expense report to the Secretary of the Senate and took an oath before a notary public as to its veracity. The report showed that his entire senatorial campaign against William Wilson had incurred expenses of only $7,668.28. This worked out to roughly $0.009 per vote, well below the three-cent-per-voter limit established by the Senate. It remained to be seen whether this parsimony would end what Vare later termed "the most merciless investigation ever conducted by any committee of the United States Senate." His conscience was clear. As he later wrote, there had been no testimony offered before the Reed Committee that demonstrated "the slightest improper act on my part or any one act illegally committed on my behalf." William S. Vare saw nothing that would prevent his admittance to the world's greatest deliberative body in 1927.[41]

NOTES

1. "Hadley Fires Four Aids, Protégés of Mackey and Hall," *PB*, January 3, 1927.

2. Hadley was given the name WillB by his mother, who wanted to commemorate her late husband, William, but did not want to name her son "William Hadley Jr." "Sesqui Proposes Raising $5M upon Note Issue," *PB*, August 9, 1926; "Sesqui Creditors Grow Impatient," *PB*, September 28, 1926; "Kendrick Extends Elevated Rail Lease," *NYT*, October 14, 1926; "Sesqui Creditors Can Get Notes Now," *PB*, October 21, 1926; "Sesqui Deficit Growing," *PB*, October 22, 1926; "Serious Tangles to Be Cleared in Sesqui-Centennial Financing," *PB*, October 23, 1926; "Claims Philadelphia Loss $4,000,000 in 'L' Lease Terms," *Electric Railway Journal*, November 6, 1926; "City Officials at Odds over 'L' Lease Renewal," *Electric Railway Journal*, November 20, 1926.

3. "Showmen Demand Sesqui Next Year," *PB*, September 30, 1926.

4. "Sesqui Exhibit Head Released by E. L. [*sic*] Sutton," *PT*, September 11, 1926; "Sesqui Cancels Concerts," *PB*, September 29, 1926; "Mayor Praises Austin; Sesqui to End Nov. 30," *PB*, October 7, 1926; "Sesqui Deficit Growing," *PB*, October 22, 1926.

5. "Sesqui Officials Resign after Row," *PB*, April 27, 1926; "Sesqui Official Resigns," *PB*, October 5, 1926; "Sesqui's Failure Due to Managers, Says Axel Malm," *PB*, October 6, 1926.

6. Letter and notes from "Davis" to William B. Craig, dated October 5, 1926, TUUA/SCA.

7. Ibid.

8. Letter and notes from "Davis" to William B. Craig, dated October 5, 1926, TUUA/SCA; "Memo for Mr. Israel Concerning Attached Memo of Davis," dated October 6, 1926, TUUA/SCA.

9. "Sesqui Accounting Wanted," *PB*, October 28, 1926.

10. "Mayor Praises Austin; Sesqui to End Nov. 30," *PB*, October 7, 1926.

11. Ibid..

12. "Philadelphia Expo a Failure; Unpaid Bills Total More than $3M," *NYT*, October 8, 1926; "Philadelphia Fair Never Had Chance," *NYT*, October 9, 1926; "An Unlucky World's Fair," editorial, *NYT*, October 9, 1926.

13. "'Sesqui Weather' Is Wet According to the Official Records," *PB*, November 3, 1926; "4,622,211 Persons Paid to See Fair," *NYT*, December 2, 1926.

14. Austin and Hauser, *The Sesqui-Centennial International Exposition*, pp. 376–379, 400–405.

15. Pencak, *For God & Country,* pp. 171–207, 300.

16. "Pouring into Philadelphia," *NYT*, October 10, 1926; "Legion Gathers in Ph," *NYT*, October 11, 1926.

17. "Coolidge Applauds Legion's Vote Drive," *NYT*, October 12, 1926; "National Legion Convention Awakens Slumbering Philadelphia," Brewster (NY) *Standard*, October 15, 1926, p. 1; Pencak, *For God & Country*, p. 95.

18. "Host of Legionnaires in Picturesque Parade," *Reading Eagle*, October 12, 1926, pp. 1, 3; "Dawes Sees Danger in Voting Apathy," *NYT*, October 13, 1926.

19. "Host of Legionnaires in Picturesque Parade," *Reading Eagle*, October 12, 1926, pp. 1, 3; "Pershing May Lead Legion to France," *NYT*, October 13, 1926; "National Legion Convention Awakens Slumbering Philadelphia," Brewster (NY) *Standard*, October 15, 1926, p. 1.

20. "British Marchers Thrill at Sesqui," *NYT*, October 13, 1926; Austin and Hauser, *The Sesqui-Centennial International Exposition*, 434–435.

21. Pakula, *For God & Country*, pp. 341–345.

22. Pakula, *For God & Country*, pp. 341–345; "News Brief," *JTA*, November 24, 1926.

23. Fowler, *Beau James*, p. 187.

24. Pakula, *For God & Country*, pp. 346–349; Fowler, *Beau James*, p. 187; Walsh, *Gentleman Jimmy Walker*, pp. 94–95.

25. "Mrs. Martin Scores High Cost of Seats," *PB*, October 18, 1926.

26. "Queen Marie Hailed in Rumanian Church by Her Own People," *NYT*, October 22, 1926.

27. Morris, *On Tour with Queen Marie*, pp. 50–54.

28. "Carry Queen in Chair So She Can See Dancers," *PB*, October 22, 1926.

29. "Await Arrival of Queen Marie in Philadelphia," *Reading Eagle*, October 21, 1926; "Counting 'Soiree' Receipts," *PB*, October 22, 1926; "Keys to Quaker City

Presented to Queen Marie," *Herald-Tribune*, October 22, 1926; "Queen Marie Hailed in Rumanian Church by Her Own People," *NYT*, October 22, 1926; "Carry Queen in Chair So She Can See Dancers," *PB*, October 22, 1926; "Whirlwind Tour Made at Sesqui by Royal Party," *PB*, October 22, 1926; "Thousands Hailed Queen Marie Here," *PB*, July 18, 1938; Austin and Hauser, *The Sesqui-Centennial International Exposition*, pp. 201–202; Morris, *On Tour with Queen Marie*, pp. 50–54.

30. "Mayor Asks $12,500 More for Entertaining Visitors," *PB*, October 28, 1926.

31. "Vare Starts for Europe," *PB*, July 16, 1926; "Mellon and Vare Meet aboard Ship," *PB*, July 17, 1926; "Congressman Vare Home from Europe," *PB*, August 16, 1926; "Vare Resigns Post on City Committee; Hazlett Is Elected," *PI*, August 31, 1926.

32. "Pepper-Fisher Ticket Outlay Put at $841,795," *PB*, July 11, 1926; "Penna. Probe over with Primary Cost Set at $3,000,000," *PB*, July 7, 1926; "Cunningham Ready for Senate Inquiry about $50,000 Gift," *PB*, July 9, 1926; "$25,000 Limit Placed on Expenses for Next Vare Campaign," *PB*, August 18, 1926; Beers, *Pennsylvania Politics Today and Yesterday*, p. 65.

33. "Pinchot Bolting, Aids Fight on Vare," *PB*, September 14, 1926; "Pinchot Not Aiding Vare, Will Keep Out of Fight," *PB*, September 14, 1926; "Vare Not Alarmed," *PB*, September 14, 1926.

34. "Information Wanted," *PR*, October 8, 1926; "A Republican View of Vare," *PR*, October 14, 1926; "An Open Letter to Congressman Vare," *PR*, October 14, 1926.

35. "An Open Letter to Congressman Vare," *PR*, October 14, 1926.

36. Speech by Norris, July 26, 1930, cited by Folsom, *No More Free Markets or Free Beer*, p. 72; "Norris Continues Tour," *PB*, October 20, 1926; "Calls Vare Plea Insult," *PB*, November 1, 1926.

37. "Dry League Head Denounces Vare," *PB*, October 18, 1926; "Baptists Condemn Vare," *PB*, October 22, 1926.

38. "Vare Denies Fraud Won Seat for Him," *NYT*, November 6, 1926; "Charges of Fraud Enter into the Senatorial Complications," *PB*, November 6, 1926.

39. Barton, "Vare's Hopes Dim as Zeroes Pile Up," *PR*, November 7, 1926; "Charges of Fraud Enter Into the Senatorial Complications," *PB*, November 6, 1926; Barton, "Frauds Exposed as Zero Division Men Are Given Hearing," *PR*, November 23, 1926.

40. "Vare Denies Fraud Won Seat for Him," *NYT*, November 6, 1926.

41. "Vare Denies Fraud Won Seat for Him," *NYT*, November 6, 1926; "General Election Campaign Cost Vare $7,668.28, He Says," *PB*, November 16, 1926; "Election Expenses Cost Vare $7668.28," *PI*, November 17, 1926; Vare, *My Forty Years in Politics*, pp. 169–183.

14

★ ★ ★

Follies of 1926

ON NOVEMBER 1, 1926, the Ziegfeld *Follies* opened at the Forrest Theater, located on South Broad Street between Sansom and Walnut. The Forrest possessed one of the largest stages in Philadelphia, making it the theater of choice for road companies of large revues like the *Follies*. The 1926 *Follies* would be one of the last shows to grace the twenty-year-old theater, scheduled to be demolished in early 1927. In its place would rise a twenty-nine-story office building, designed by Sesqui Stadium architects Simon and Simon, which would house the newly formed Fidelity-Philadelphia Trust Company.[1]

The 1926 *Follies* was not one of Flo Ziegfeld's stronger efforts, which may explain why it toured the provinces rather than opening at his legendary New Amsterdam Theater on Forty-Second Street. The score by Rudolf Friml and James Hanley contained no songs that became instant hits, like Irving Berlin's "A Pretty Girl Is Like a Melody." The show starred none of the famous Ziegfeld headliners like Fanny Brice or Will Rogers, but featured second-string players like James Barton and Edna Leedom. Still, the 1926 *Follies* had its share of attractions. Among them was a nubile sixteen-year-old named Paulette Goddard, her blond curls and baby fat making her unrecognizable as the brunette gamine who would gambol through Charlie Chaplin's *Modern Times* a decade later. In the *Follies*, her primary function was to look luscious while the leading men crooned songs like "Florida, the Moon, and You" into her baby-blue eyes.

Goddard did not appear in the opening number, "The Passing of the Champions," which featured actors impersonating fallen sports idols littering the Great White Way. Among them was Jack Dempsey, who had lost his title to Gene Tunney in the Sesqui Stadium in September. He was joined by other sports figures who had suffered setbacks in 1926, including tennis players Helen Wills and Bill Tilden and golfer Bobby Jones. A group of chorus boys ushered the has-beens offstage while singing "We're Cleaning Up Broadway." The writers did not include the 1926 Sesqui-Centennial in their number, perhaps to spare Philadelphians' feelings, or perhaps because the fair had never been a champion in the first place.[2]

The day after the Ziegfeld *Follies* opened at the Forrest, Philadelphia voters went to the polls to approve the transfer of $5 million from the $7.5 million Roxborough rapid transit appropriation of 1919, to be used for payment of Sesqui-Centennial debts. This vote to spend yet more money on the Sesqui was not a sign of public support for the fading world's fair. It represented the ongoing obedience of Philadelphia voters to the whims of the all-powerful Organization, along with an intense desire to bury the Sesqui once and for all. On November 22 a silent City Council passed the ordinance making the $5 million available to Mayor Kendrick to pay Sesqui bills, sixteen to zero, with four councilmen absent.[3]

With funds authorized to pay the fair's biggest bills, City Hall released an itemized register detailing the thousands of Sesqui creditors and their associated debts. This public disclosure was done at the insistence of City Controller WillB Hadley, whose signature was required along with Mayor Kendrick's on any bill approved for payment. The voluminous document, issued in four segments, was a revelation to even the most jaundiced of Philadelphia voters. The creditors' list illustrated the complete lack of organized planning behind the fair, along with the explosion of frenetic activity expended to cobble together an approximation of an international exposition at the eleventh hour. It also hinted at secret deals made in the dining room of the Manufacturers Club between city and SCEA officials and favored contractors, deals which ensured that millions of taxpayer dollars were diverted from the Sesqui infrastructure to insiders' wallets.

The total amount owed to Sesqui creditors was $5,098,172. Of this amount, $4,421,060 was in the form of development or construction expenses, while $657,120 fell in the category of operating expenses. The rush to complete the Sesqui in the months of May and June alone had generated $189,664 in extra labor and material costs. It had also resulted in the hiring of multiple companies to handle a single area like sewers, or in the primary construction company subcontracting work to smaller firms to complete a major assignment on schedule. Hundreds of contractors and suppliers were listed, many with overlapping claims: seventeen companies submitted invoices relating to the Tower of Light and the thirteen state pylons in the Forum of the Founders. Conversely, many large contractors submitted one invoice covering work on a dozen different jobs without itemizing fees. It was nearly impossible to determine the cost of a single project or building.

The most striking item was the enormous cost of preparing the swamplands of South Philadelphia in 1925 and early 1926, before a single building was erected. Prior to the Sesqui, the city's Department of Public Works had allocated $2,750,000 to grade the Sesqui site and adjacent streets, plus $1,910,000 to pave these streets, for a total of $4,660,000 dedicated to "South Philadelphia Improvements." The November creditors' lists revealed that the city had spent an additional $660,000 to grade and drain the marshlands on either side of Broad Street where the Sesqui buildings stood. Even with all of this advance work, the invoices from private contractors contained hefty tabs for site preparation. Building No. 1, the Palace of Liberal Arts and Manufactures, cost $763,865. This was in line with the original estimate of $758,000 made by its contractor, Austin & Company, in August 1925. One-fifth of Austin's total construction cost, $150,300, had gone to fill and grade the site of the Sesqui's major palace. The Turner Construction Company, which submitted invoices for construction on the Sesqui Stadium, the Auditorium, and the Palace of Fine Arts, also billed the SCEA $384,855 for "drainage, grading and improvement of grounds."

The cost of fill dirt emerged as one of the biggest controversies surrounding Sesqui expenditures. Millions of cubic yards of soil had been transported to the Sesqui site in 1925 and early 1926. The prices charged for this fill ranged from forty cents to $1.15 per cubic yard, depending on the supplier and project. The 400,000 cubic yards needed for the Sesqui Stadium site had been provided by the Keystone State Construction Company, once headed by the late "Sunny Jim" McNichol. Now run by rising contractor king Jerome Louchheim, Keystone provided dirt at a relatively reasonable sixty-two cents a yard. This price appeared less competitive when Philadelphians realized that City Hall was paying Keystone more than $6 million to excavate and construct two stretches of the Broad Street Subway. Louchheim had sold the city its own dirt, and charged sixty-two cents to truck each cubic yard from one end of Broad Street to the other. Defending Louchheim, a former city official insisted that sixty-two cents was cheap for a cubic yard of dirt. "I don't know where the city could have obtained the amount of dirt used cheaper," the anonymous bureaucrat protested. "The Keystone Company had the right to sell the dirt to anyone at any price it could get."[4]

City Hall had allocated $2 million in municipal funds to build the Sesqui Stadium, the one permanent showpiece of the fair. Besides this amount, the Stadium had required another $25,847 for reinforcement of its foundations, after concerns arose that sections of the massive arena were settling into the swampy soil at different rates. The repair work was handled by the Underpinning and Foundation Company of Philadelphia, which filed a separate invoice of $15,746 for labor. At a time when the average hourly factory wage hovered around forty cents, the carpenters and pitmen shoring up the Sesqui Stadium had earned between $1.35 and $2.10 an hour. The pay scale had been approved by George H. Biles, director of the Department of Public Works, after U&FCP engineers had told him that "a high type of workmen must be employed to strengthen the foundations."[5]

Separate invoices relating to Stadium construction covered issues like "replacing heads over entrances and trimming where they had settled," "fixing granite bases that settled around the Stadium," and "painting up cracks," all per instructions of the architects, Simon and Simon. Besides the more than $100,000 that the firm received in architectural fees, Simon and Simon also submitted an invoice for $23,952 for its supervision of the construction work, and another one for $5,272 for designing the stage and dressing rooms used for the ill-fated *Freedom*. It cost the city another $123,836 for the Turner Construction Company to transform the Simon and Simon designs for *Freedom* into reality.

Compared with the Stadium, the $99,220 charged by Frank G. English and Son to construct the giant Liberty Bell at Oregon Plaza seemed like a relative bargain, until two additional bills surfaced for $75,662. The thirteen ornamental pylons representing the original colonies in the Forum of the Founders had cost $19,200 for the Conneen Construction Company to erect, or $1,477 per column. All of these figures paled when compared with the $365,093 charged by the Michael J. Melody Company, Inc., for the Tower of Light, construction of which never progressed past a naked steel skeleton with a cramped reception room at its base. The total invoice for the Melody Company, which included miscellaneous work on the Liberal Arts and Transportation palaces, amounted to $566,891.

Another large bill, for $528,676, was presented by Ford and Kendig, a construction company located at 1428 Callowhill Street. The invoice covered work done by the company on the Gladway and the Palace of Education, the Sesqui firehouses, and water pumping stations. The "Ford" of Ford and Koenig was Albert E. Ford, an uncle of Mrs. W. Freeland Kendrick. When reporters attempted to question Mr. Ford about his work, they were informed that the elderly man had left for California on November 11, accompanied by a nurse. Rumors circulated that Ford, in his eighties and in ill health, was a straw man who had not been active in the management of his company for more than a year.

Before the Sesqui, the Vare Construction Company had earned $73,600 grading Pattison Avenue from Seventh to Tenth Streets, and Seventh Street from Bigler Street to Pattison Avenue. After the fair, the firm submitted three relatively small invoices totaling $12,461, all for providing fill dirt for various sites. This was chump change. Insiders understood that the senator-elect had made his real money on his take on the more than four hundred contracts for construction, land preparation, and supplies that had been vetted by his Organization in the fair's planning period.[6]

Public anger mounted when the exorbitant salaries of Sesqui employees and officers were made public. Between November 1925 and November 1926, Sesqui salaries aggregated more than $2.7 million, exclusive of construction wages. At the fair's midsummer peak, its payroll of more than four thousand employees amounted to more than $150,000 a week. Many senior officials received salaries of $10,000 or more, at a time when $5,000 was a comfortable middle-class income. There was grudging acceptance of the $10,000 annual salary received by Director-General Erastus L. Austin. Even the harshest critics acknowledged that Austin had devoted countless hours to making the fair function on a daily basis. His salary was considerably less than the $25,000 paid to Colonel David G. Collier, or the $15,000 paid to his immediate predecessor, Captain Archer C. Baker. Satisfaction with Austin would wane when it was later revealed that he had been awarded a $19,000 "honorarium" to compensate for the difference between his salary and those of his predecessors.

Incredulity greeted the news that William W. Matos, chairman of pageantry at the Sesqui, was the highest-paid SCEA official, earning $5,000 more a year than the man who actually ran the fair. Matos, described by the *Bulletin* as an "advertising man and personal friend of Mayor Kendrick," received $15,000 a year for his work staging the numerous pageants and spectacles that had enlivened the Sesqui during its six months. Among his accomplishments was coauthoring the cumbersome script for the ill-fated extravaganza *Freedom*. R. H. Burnside, the New York impresario who acted as director of pageantry, received $1,000 a week during the six months that he spent staging *Freedom*, which saw eighteen of its twenty-eight scheduled performances get washed out.

Besides Austin, three other Sesqui employees received yearly salaries of $10,000: R. J. Pearse, director of works; W. E. Cash, director of concessions; and Odell Hauser, director of publicity. Most of the other officials were paid on a monthly basis, including A. L. Sutton, the director of domestic participation and special events, who received $650 a month. The only senior Sesqui official not to receive a salary was Mrs. J. Willis Martin, who served as chairman of the Women's Committee on a volunteer basis. Dozens of minor functionaries received monthly wages ranging between $250 and $500. Asked to defend the exorbitant salaries, a defensive Kendrick replied that the short-term nature of the positions made them a necessity. "We were very fortunate," the mayor concluded, "in being able to obtain some men who left big jobs to come here and help make the Sesqui a success." Kendrick would later admit that money originally designated for construction work had been diverted to pay salaries instead.[7]

Soon after the public learned of the Sesqui's salaries and expenses, a Sesqui-Centennial Exhibition Association participating certificate for $1,000 came up at public auction. This was one of the nearly $3 million in certificates sold to the public in September and October 1925 by Albert M. Greenfield and his army of canvassers, which allowed Kendrick to make the Sesqui a reality. The $1,000 certificate fetched $40, or 4 percent of its face value. Based on that sale, the entire issue of $2.6 million in Sesqui bonds was worth $104,000. In addition to the recent spate of negative financial news, the forty-dollar auction price was blamed on City Council President Charles B. Hall, who had recently announced that certificate holders "would never receive a cent" on their investment.[8]

Mayor Kendrick called for the demolition of the fair's main structures immediately after closing day on November 30, 1926. He hoped that speedy salvaging of the building materials might yield as much as $1.2 million, which could be used to pay down the fair debt. A bid of $75,000 had already been received for the magnificent organ in the Sesqui Auditorium, which had cost $150,000. The *Record* protested against this hasty destruction, since "there has yet been no accounting to the public of the millions of dollars that have been expended on the construction contracts." The paper insisted that the buildings stand "until after the contracts and books of the sesqui-centennial enterprise shall have been opened before the public, if for no other reason, than to avoid the slightest appearance of anything like destroying evidence."[9]

While Kendrick sought to destroy his fair at the first opportunity, SCEA Finance Chairman Albert M. Greenfield searched for ways to reopen it in 1927. A second season might redeem the Sesqui from complete financial ruin, and would offer some hope to its concessionaires. Greenfield organized the Committee of the Sesqui-Centennial Exhibition Association to Consider the Advisability of Continuing the Exposition Throughout 1927, which included SCEA Directors Mrs. J. Willis Martin, Herbert J. Tily, and William C. Sproul. As the Sesqui entered its final month, Greenfield estimated that it would cost at least $6 million to revive the fair another year. Of this amount, $3 million would come from the federal government, $1 million from the state of Pennsylvania, and $2 million from subscriptions by the "financial, industrial, and commercial interests of Philadelphia." Greenfield and other committee members conducted confidential interviews with political leaders, corporate executives, and newspaper editors to assess the feasibility of raising this amount.[10]

An embittered Mayor Kendrick placed the blame for the Sesqui's failure on changing cultural tastes. "I guess the day of expositions is over," he rationalized. "The big department stores of today are an exposition in themselves and things move so fast now that people see everything new before it can be placed in an exposition." City Council President Charles B. Hall agreed: "The truth is that people are tired of expositions." Despite this fair fatigue, Hall still felt that once the history of the exposition was written, "it will be a splendid tribute to the city." Northeast Councilman Clarence K. Crossan, who had criticized runaway spending on the Sesqui in the past, now praised it as having "heightened the ideals of our young people." According to Crossan, "America itself is to blame if the Sesqui was not a complete financial success."[11]

Others were willing to place the blame much closer to home. Rumors that the Kendricks and members of their circle had enriched themselves by looting the Sesqui's coffers were now rampant. Kendrick was forced to hold several press conferences and tell reporters that "everyone who knows me probably realizes as I do that I will retire from office a poorer man than when I entered it." He enumerated and denied all of the "poison gas rumors" currently in circulation: that he and his wife had seven-figure bank accounts; that Mrs. Kendrick was the president of the company that provided all of the lumber to the Sesqui; that the mayor was buying Grey Towers, the baronial Glenside mansion of late sugar king William Welsh Harrison. Kendrick challenged his detractors to locate the large cash deposits he was supposed to have made at numerous banks, promising to donate "every cent" of these "alleged huge sums" to charity. "I don't know of any single piece of graft in connection with the Sesqui-Centennial or with any city contract since I have been Mayor," Kendrick insisted. "I have nothing to worry me."[12]

Kendrick announced that he would retire from public life at the end of his term, a fact many reporters considered a foregone conclusion. Gone were the days when the governor's mansion in Harrisburg seemed like the next step for "Freel," with the White House visible on the far horizon. William S. Vare had already distanced himself from his fellow Shriner and former protégé. City Treasurer Harry A. Mackey announced that Vare would not assume responsibility for any decisions made at City Hall during Kendrick's increasingly troubled tenure. The senator-elect, Mackey insisted, "had little influence with this administration, and is not entitled to share in either credit or censure."[13]

During the fair's final month, Kendrick and other officials went through the motions of hosting a great international exposition. November began with back-to-back celebrations of Austrian Day, Irish Day, and Czechoslovak Day, each one with its contingent of parades, receptions, and colorful native costumes. Czechoslovak Day on November 6 had special significance for Philadelphians. In October 1918, the city had hosted a celebration of a Czechoslovakian "Declaration of Independence" at Independence Hall. Now the prosperous, multicultural democracy, carved from the corpse of the Austro-Hungarian Empire, was prized as one of the few solid pieces of proof that the War to End All Wars had not been fought in vain. On Czechoslovak Day, a capacity crowd watched dozens of *sokols* (athletic societies) perform in a *slet* or mass gymnastic demonstration in a Sesqui Auditorium festively decorated with the red, white, and blue flags of Czechoslovakia and the United States.[14]

Thursday, November 11, marked the eighth commemoration of Armistice Day in the United States, in remembrance of the estimated 117,465 Americans who had died during the World War. On June 4, 1926, Congress had passed a resolution directing the president to issue an annual proclamation calling for the national observance of Armistice Day. The day would be marked with the display of the American flag on all government buildings, and by "inviting the people of the United States to observe the day in schools and churches, or other suitable places."[15] As the site of the Sesqui-Centennial, the Liberty Bell, and Independence Hall, Philadelphia would become a giant shrine to honor those who died in the nation's service.

Shortly before 11:00 A.M. on November 11, 1926—the hour and day when the Armistice was signed in 1918—a military guard escorted a squad of National Guard buglers to City Hall, symbolic crossroads of Philadelphia. While one bugler stood in the center of the courtyard, surrounded by the guard, the others took their positions at the four entrances of the building. As the four clocks in City Hall tower struck eleven, the five men raised their trumpets to their lips and sounded the "Roll Call," summoning Philadelphia to honor the dead. A pall of silence spread over the entire city. Automobiles and trolley cars ground to a halt. Pedestrians stood silently with heads bowed. Two minutes later, the five buglers sounded "Taps," bringing the city back to life.

With another flourish of trumpets, a military parade kicked off at Twentieth Street and the Fairmount Parkway. Major-General William G. Price Jr. led the fifty-five hundred men of the National Guard of Pennsylvania down the Parkway to City Hall and then down South Broad Street to the Sesqui. Directly behind Price marched a detail of U.S. Marines carrying forty-eight national service flags, one for each state, provided by the War Mothers of America. Each silk banner bore two stars: a blue star showing the number of men from that state who served in the Great War, and a gold star showing the number who had died. The parade reached the Sesqui Stadium at 12:20 P.M., passing before a reviewing stand containing Mayor Kendrick and representatives of the armed forces. Directly behind the stand sat seven hundred War Mothers, each one carrying an individual service flag that illustrated her sacrifice.

After the parade had ended, the War Mothers were escorted to the Little Wooden House on the High Street of 1776, the Sesqui headquarters for their organization. There, Mrs. J. Willis Martin raised a national service flag, showing the total number of men and women in the American forces during the war, and the total number who made the supreme sacrifice. Officers who had participated in the parade were treated to lunch in the Indian Queen Tavern and in the nearby "Taj Mahal," while enlisted men mustered in the cavernous Alpine Haus for their meal. The day that began

The Little Wooden House, headquarters of the National War Mothers of America.

with silence and mourning ended with music and dancing: three thousand distinguished guests were invited to a Military Concert and Victory Ball in the Auditorium, with the 108th Field Artillery Band providing the music. For other ranks, the Sesqui grounds were open free to any service man in uniform, active duty or veteran, along with a lady guest of his choice.[16]

As the Sesqui stumbled through its final days, nature once again seemed determined to destroy it. On November 16, a nor'easter slammed eastern Pennsylvania. Heavy rains and forty-five-mile-per-hour winds caused widespread damage throughout Philadelphia, battering the already badly weathered buildings at the Sesqui. After the storm, an early cold spell settled in, reducing attendance even further. Indian performers at Colonel Cummins' Wild West show, their tepees and wigwams ruined by the storm, huddled around open campfires.[17]

SCEA officials attempted to dispel the gloom by announcing the grand prize awards, the medals denoting excellence that had been a part of world's fairs since London's Great Exhibition of 1851. For each of 145 classes of exhibits, "from false teeth and locomotives to embroidery and international peace exhibits," there were five classes of awards: the medal of honor, gold, silver, bronze, and honorable mention. Philadelphia, still touting itself as the "workshop of the world," won the lion's share of grand prizes, especially in the manufacturing categories. Among the winners were the Baldwin Locomotive Works, the Pennsylvania Railroad, the Sun Oil Company, and John B. Stetson Company. Bethlehem Steel alone received twenty-five gold medals for its vast array of products. Among educational institutions, gold medals were awarded to the University of Pennsylvania, Temple University, Haverford College, Girard College, and the Philadelphia School of Design for Women. The students of Holy Cross College were honored for performing Euripides's *Hecuba* in the original Greek in the Stadium.

Not every award went to local groups: honors were bestowed on such diverse entities as the Republic of Haiti (perhaps to atone for the shabby welcome accorded President Borno), the American Birth Control League, the Division of Negro Education of the State Department of Public Instruction, the National Council of Jewish Women, the Pennsylvania League of Women Voters, and the United States Marine Corps. The actual medals would not be delivered until the spring of 1927. When they were distributed, some recipients were surprised to discover that the "gold," "silver," and "bronze" medals were all bronze, with those in the first two categories covered with a thin plating of gold or silver. With Sesqui finances in such fragile condition, buying enough gold to mint the 388 gold medals was unthinkable.[18]

On Tuesday, November 30, guns boomed and bugles sounded for the last time at the Sesqui grounds, as the ill-fated fair drew to a close under gray skies "which seemed symbolic of the end," according to the *Public Ledger*. The final guest of honor was Governor John H. Trumbull of Connecticut, who toured the fairgrounds with Mayor Kendrick. After a visit to the Connecticut Building, the party walked the short distance to the Slate Roof House on the neighboring Street of 1776. There, Turnbull presented the Connecticut state flag to Mrs. George Horace Lorimer. As States Committee chairman, Lorimer had been collecting the flags of the various states from governors and other official envoys all summer long. A proxy gave her the flag of New Mexico, the only one of the forty-eight states not to have sent a representative to the Sesqui. To top off her now-complete collection, Mayor Kendrick presented Lorimer with a silk United States flag. After a military review at the Court of Honor, the party repaired to the Alpine Haus for one last dinner in honor of Director-General Austin.

That evening, a special concert was held at the Auditorium to mark the closing of the Sesqui, featuring the Twelfth Infantry Band, the Sesqui Festival Chorus (reduced from five thousand to twenty-five hundred voices), the Matinee Musical Club Chorus, and Kendrick's beloved all-boy Harmonica Band. There were speeches by Governor Turnbull and Mayor Kendrick, the presentation of medals, and dancing to music by the Sesqui-Centennial Band, led by Lieutenant Joseph J. Frankel. Kendrick presented Frankel, who had serenaded the Coolidges, Queen Marie, and other Sesqui guests, with "the oldest and most historical baton in the country." The eighteen-inch baton, mounted in silver, was fashioned from one of the original joists from Independence Hall, removed during a 1917 renovation. With the playing of "The Star-Spangled Banner" on the stroke of midnight, the Sesqui-Centennial International Exposition came to an end.[19]

Except it didn't. Like the owners of a terminally ill pet who could not bear to put their darling out of its misery, the SCEA postponed the official closing of the exposition until December 31, 1926. The one-month extension had been advanced by Samuel M. Vauclain, the man who had once warned that the Sesqui would be as welcome as "jazz music at a funeral." SCEA Finance Chairman Albert M. Greenfield had soundly backed Vauclain's proposal, having realized that a 1927 Sesqui was an impossible dream. Interviews with local leaders indicated that interest in prolonging the fair was minimal, especially with SCEA participating certificates selling at four percent of face value. City Council President Charles B. Hall had already announced that the council would "not vote a cent" toward a second season for the Sesqui.

Greenfield favored the one-month extension because it gave the city another month to avoid paying its creditors. A recently passed law specified that Sesqui debts could not be paid until after the fair had ended. The SCEA hoped that an extra month of operations might add a few extra dollars to its depleted coffers. "People will pay to see the Sesqui while the work of salvaging it is progressing," Director Austin insisted, "just as they did before it was completed."[20]

The December closing was also touted as a concession to the Sesqui's unhappy concessionaires, most of whom were already packing up their wares. For foreign exhibitors, the U.S. Customs bond permitting the display of their items expired on November 30. If they exhibited after that date, they would be forced to pay duty on all merchandise on display, whether it sold or not. Calling the decision to run the Sesqui another month a "deathblow," one official reported that "the public should be informed that as far as the foreign exhibitors are concerned they are officially through on December 1."[21] Those few concessionaires who chose to remain were allowed to set up their wares in the Auditorium for a nominal fee of twenty-five cents per square foot, in a giant "going out of business" sale.

Plans were made to keep the Sesqui open from 9:00 A.M. through 9:00 P.M. during December, with admission slashed from fifty to twenty-five cents. The Sesqui payroll, which had run as high as five thousand employees in mid-August, was slashed to a skeleton crew of 870 on November 30. Desperate to spend as little as possible, the SCEA instituted a program of rigid economy. Of the major buildings, only the Auditorium, the Palace of Liberal Arts and Manufactures, and the Palace of Fine Arts remained officially open after November 30. Many of the most popular exhibits, including the High Street of 1776, were shuttered that day. By early December the Liberty Bell at Oregon Plaza no longer blazed forth at night. Darkening the gigantic bell saved the SCEA $4,000, and so many of its twenty-seven thousand bulbs had already burned out that it was beginning to look pockmarked.[22]

Although "technically open" for business, the Sesqui was a "deserted village" by December 2, according to the *Bulletin*, and the entire fairgrounds "seemed bleak and dreary." Cold winds and an early snowfall conspired with the lack of attractions to keep visitors to a minimum. Visitors to the Palace of Liberal Arts and Manufactures had to dodge dozens of workmen dismantling exhibitors' elaborate displays. Laborers were also busy stripping the walls of paintings at the Palace of Fine Arts. At the Palace of Agriculture and Foreign Exhibits, the booths for Austria, China, Czechoslovakia, and Denmark offered carpets, tapestries, ceramics, and glassware to visitors at greatly reduced prices before the building closed for good. At the U.S. Government Palace, workers were disassembling turbines and other oversize machinery, while engineers backed huge diesel and steam locomotives out of the great hall onto the adjacent railroad tracks.

All the secondary structures south of Pattison Avenue were closed, with the exception of the Argentine Pavilion. The Argentineans had not completed their exhibits until early November; now they were determined to show their wonders to the world until the last possible moment. A few curious visitors peeked in the windows of the locked houses on High Street, while across the way workmen removed antique furniture from Sulgrave Manor. At Camp Anthony Wayne, the doughboys of the Sesqui Expeditionary Force were pulling down their tents, mess halls, and public buildings. The Gladway was devoid of life except for the occasional small boy, climbing the fence to stow away on the pirate ship at Treasure Island.[23]

Ralph Bencker's Pennsylvania State Building had been praised as one of the most handsome and sophisticated buildings at the Sesqui, and a number of architects had recommended that it be made a permanent fixture. Governor Pinchot decreed that the pavilion be stripped of its exhibits and artwork beginning on December 1, and that it be sold and demolished as soon as possible. The murals by Joseph T. Pearson, Jr., Daniel Garber, and other artists were dismantled and either placed in storage, or dispersed to various schools and institutions around the Commonwealth.

On December 3 Pinchot journeyed to Philadelphia to take charge of the six historic Liberty Bells that had been on display at the Pennsylvania pavilion. These bells, lent by the cities of Allentown, Chester, Easton, Lancaster, Reading, and York, had all rung on July 8, 1776, to announce the public reading of the Declaration of Independence. Prior to their being returned to their home towns, the six bells were moved to Independence Hall. They were grouped around the main Liberty Bell in the central vestibule, while Pinchot posed for photographs with the mayors of the six towns that had lent them. Mayor Kendrick was not present.

Pinchot used the occasion to harangue the citizens of Philadelphia over their blind acceptance of the political machine run by Senator-Elect William S. Vare. Standing in front of the seven Liberty Bells, Pinchot referred to them as "the stilled voices of America's fathers—stilled in tone but speaking eloquently in their silent appeal." Recalling the Revolutionary era battle cry of "Taxation without representation is tyranny," Pinchot mourned because "that same call today leaves Philadelphia coldly indifferent":

The six Liberty Bells of Pennsylvania on display at Independence Hall, surrounding the original Liberty Bell. Governor Pinchot used their removal in December to rail against the tyrannical rule of the Philadelphia Organization.

> Taxation without representation is exactly what is happening to you, yet you do nothing. Large numbers do not vote at all and when they do vote, their votes are either not counted or, what is worse, they are counted falsely. The citizens of Philadelphia or of any community that suffers thieves to steal votes are victims of tyranny—gang tyranny. They are dominated, their politics is controlled by a mere handful of politicians who have the presumption and the cunning to override the will of the masses. Does the blood of Philadelphians today run less warm than that of their ancestors? Has their pulse become sluggish? Is there no fight left in them?[24]

Pinchot's scolding was only one of a number of public outbursts against Vare and his Organization as 1926 drew to a close. With the Sixty-Ninth Congress preparing to leave Washington for Christmas recess, Vare's senatorial bid was safe from any official action until the New Year. But public discontent with the Organization seemed to be spreading, fueled by revelations over the cost of transferring the Sesqui from the Parkway to Vare's home base. On December 21 the *Bulletin* published an article entitled "Two Dictatorships" by local reformer Imogen B. Oakley. A leader of the Civic Club of Philadelphia, Oakley compared the Philadelphia of Vare with the Rome of Mussolini, with the Fascist getting the better end of the bargain:

> Rome is a dictatorship. Philadelphia is a dictatorship.
>
> In the Italian city Mussolini has gathered all the functions of government into his own hands and rules frankly and openly as an autocrat. In the city where the Declaration of Independence was signed the constitutional authorities are under the control of an invisible dictatorship. The actual members of this invisible dictatorship are unknown to the community at large, but it is conceded that not the least of them is Mr. William S. Vare, who claims nomination and election as U.S. Senator from Pennsylvania.
>
> Under the Italian dictator, Rome has become an orderly and healthful city. . . . Under the invisible dictatorship of Philadelphia the city is unbelievably dirty. . . . In South Philadelphia, known locally as Vare's bailiwick, the inquiring visitor will find incredible slums and smell indescribable odors. Hundreds of cesspools pollute the soil and air. Many miles of streets are without sewers.
>
> Laws are disregarded. The Police Department is honeycombed with politics. . . . The invisible dictatorship of Philadelphia proclaims through its agents its obedience to the will of the people as expressed at the polls, but it controls the polls by stuffing ballot-boxes and counting phantom voters.[25]

As midnight approached on December 31, 1926, the revelry that engulfed Center City was barely audible in the ghost town at the southern tip of Philadelphia, where the Sesqui-Centennial was breathing its last, artificially sustained breaths. The Sesqui's skeleton crew had left the grounds hours before, leaving all one thousand acres of the abandoned exposition in the care of a single guard. Was he the unlucky fellow who pulled the short straw?

By now an army of statisticians had compiled and released their findings on the fair. To no one's surprise, they confirmed that the Sesqui-Centennial was the least successful international exposition of modern times. Only 4,622,211 visitors had paid to see the Sesqui, compared with 8,004,325 visitors who had paid to visit the Centennial fifty years before. In 1876, the

The Liberty Bell in the snow during the Sesqui's final days.

population of the United States was thirty-eight million, roughly one-third of the more than 117 million who filled the country in 1926. There were no moving pictures or radio to broadcast the wonders of the Centennial to a global audience, and no automobiles, airplanes, or luxury liners to transport them over vast distances in speed and comfort.

Yet the Centennial, held in an America that seemed unbelievably primitive to modern Americans, had attracted millions more visitors than its awkwardly named bastard child. So had the 1893 Columbian Exposition in Chicago, the 1904 St. Louis fair, and even the Panama Pacific International Exposition held in remote San Francisco during the wartime year of 1915. The Sesqui did surpass the Centennial in one aspect: more than 1,230,000 complimentary passes had been distributed in 1926, versus fewer than 200,000 in 1876. More than 20 percent of all Sesqui visitors had seen the fair for free, thanks primarily to the largesse of City Hall officials.

Meanwhile, meteorologists had determined scientifically what the most casual observer had known all summer: that the Sesqui had taken place during one of the rainiest periods ever recorded in Philadelphia. It had rained on 107 of the 184 days between May 31 and November 30, or roughly 60 percent of the days that the Sesqui had been open. Only one out of four days during the Sesqui's run had been completely clear and dry. The amount of precipitation had broken records for four of the six months of the Sesqui's run. It had rained when the fair opened, on Flag Day, on Independence Day, during the presidential visit on July 5, during the greatest prize fight of modern times on September 23, and when Queen Marie of Romania visited on October 21. It was raining on December 31, the fair's final day.[26]

As the church bells of South Philadelphia struck twelve, the solitary guard took his last walk along the rain-streaked Forum of the Founders, avoiding the puddles in the pockmarked pavement. To his right, the huge masses of the once-colorful palaces stood tall and stark and silent. The formerly festive gardens and lagoons of the Gladway, stripped of their tawdry amusements, now resembled the swamps from which they had risen a few months before. As the guard reached the Court of Honor, the pylons representing the thirteen colonies loomed overhead, while the mocking skeleton of the Tower of Light was mercifully hidden by the night. The gigantic horses and massed marchers of the *Philadelphia Progressive* statue were already stained and crumbling. A few blocks north, the huge bulk of the Liberty Bell stood shrouded in darkness, its twenty-seven thousand lightbulbs extinguished for all time. The guard passed by the storm-battered entrance pavilions that had once gleamed with bright red and gold paint. He closed and locked the gates at the main entrance at Packer Avenue, and walked home in the frigid rain.[27]

The Sesqui-Centennial year had ended.

NOTES

1. Glazer, *Philadelphia Theaters*, pp. 11, 46.

2. *Plays and Players*, Forrest Theater, Week of November 1, 1926.

3. "$5 Million Voted to Pay for Sesqui," *PB*, November 22, 1926.

4. "Sesqui Grading Cost Up to $1.15 Yd.," *PB*, n.d.

5. "Draining Marshes and Sesqui Grading Cost over $600k," PB, Nov. 13, 1926.

6. "Draining Marshes and Sesqui Grading Cost over $660,000," *PB*, November 13, 1926; "Sesqui Grading Cost Up to $1.15 YD," *PB*, n.d.; Evensen, "Saving the City's Reputation," pp. 10–11; "Council Gets Sesqui Bills for $2,701,584; Total is $4,800,000," *PB*, November 24, 1926; "Page Full List of Debtors and Categories into Which Their Debts Fall," *PB*, November 30, 1926; "Unfinished Towers of Light at Sesqui Cost $365,092.94," *PB*, December 1, 1926; "Sesqui 'Light' Cost Fortune; Never Lit," *PPL*, December 1, 1926.

7. "Sesqui Salaries Run into Millions," *PB*, December 16, 1926; "Approves $4,859,773 Sesqui Measure," *PB*, December 17, 1926; "Reveal Salaries Paid by Sesquicentennial," *NYT*, December 17, 1926; "Sesqui's Payroll Peak Was $152,499," *PB*, December 18, 1926; "Paid Salaries out of Sesqui Building Fund, Says Mayor," *PB*, January 5, 1927.

8. "Unfinished Towers of Light at Sesqui Cost $365,092.94," *PB*, December 1, 1926; "4,622,211 Persons Paid to See Fair," *NYT*, December 2, 1926.

9. "Sesqui-Centennial Buildings," editorial, *PR*, November 8, 1926; "Demand Inquiry into Sesqui Costs," *PB*, November 17, 1926; "Mayor Expects $1,200,000 on Sesqui Salvage," *PPL*, November 21, 1926; "$1,000 Sesqui Certificate Brings $40 at Public Auction," *PB*, December 1, 1926.

10. Minutes from the meeting of the Committee of the Sesqui-Centennial Exhibition Association to Consider the Advisability of Continuing the Exposition Throughout 1927, October 27, 1926, HSP/AGMP, Correspondence 1926–1927, Box 78, Folder 1; letter from Jno. T. Dickinson to W. Freeland Kendrick, November 5, 1926, HSP/AGMP, Correspondence 1926–1927, Box 90, Folder 8; letter from B. H. Patrick to Albert M. Greenfield, November 8, 1926, HSP/AGMP, Correspondence 1926–1927, Box 90, Folder 8; letter from E. L. Austin to Albert M. Greenfield, November 9, 1926, HSP/AGMP, Correspondence 1926–1927, Box 90, Folder 8; "Greenfield Favors Running 1927 Sesqui," *PI*, October 16, 1926; "Sesqui Heads Plan Exposition in 1927," *PB*, October 21, 1926; "Consider Sesqui Plans for 1927," *PB*, November 15, 1926; "1927 Sesqui Plans in 3 Men's Hands," *PB*, November 15, 1926.

11. "Advance Sesqui Closing to Jan. 1," *PB*, November 20, 1926; "Mayor Expects $1,200,000 on Sesqui Salvage," *PPL*, November 21, 1926; "Council Gets Sesqui Bills for $2,701,584; Total Is $4,800,000," *PB*, November 24, 1926.

12. "'I Leave Office a Poorer Man,' Declares Mayor," *PB*, November 26, 1926; "Kendrick Demands Gossipers Prove Charges of Graft," *PB*, November 27, 1926.

13. "'I Leave Office a Poorer Man,' Declares Mayor," *PB*, November 26, 1926; "Kendrick Demands Gossipers Prove Charges of Graft," *PB*, November 27, 1926; "Kendrick Invites Bank-Book Proof," *PPL*, November 27, 1926.

14. Austrians Have Sesqui Day," *PB*, November 5, 1926; "Irish Day at Sesqui," *PB*, November 6, 1926; "Sesqui to Have 'Sokol,'" *PB*, November 8, 1926; Austin and Hauser,

The Sesqui-Centennial International Exposition, p. 411; Mires, *Independence Hall in American Memory*, p. 175.

15. "History of Veterans Day," U.S. Department of Veterans Affairs Office of Public Affairs web site, http://www.va.gov/opa/vetsday/vetdayhistory.asp.

16. "Parade and Ball to Mark Armistice," *PPL*, November 10, 1926; "Martial Parade Leads Observance of Armistice Day," *PPL*, November 11, 1926; Austin and Hauser, *The Sesqui-Centennial International Exposition*, pp. 205–207.

17. "Pennsylvania Hard Hit," *NYT*, November 17, 1926; "Expo Nears End," *NYT*, November 29, 1926; "Sesqui Made Rain Record; About Half of Days Wet," *PB*, November 30, 1926; "'Heap Cold,' So Sesqui Indians Resort to Traditional Campfires," *PPL*, November 26, 1926.

18. "Sesqui Grand Prize Awards Announced," *PB*, December 2, 1926; "Award Sesqui Medal of Honor," *PB*, December 3, 1926; "Award 388 Medals to Sesqui Exhibits," *PB*, December 7, 1926; "87 Sesqui Medals Awarded," *PB*, December 10, 1926; "Three Medals Shown by Chestnut Street Perfume Dealer," *PPL*, April 7, 1927; "Winners of Sesqui Gold Medals Find They Are Made Only of Bronze," *PPL*, August 5, 1927.

19. "Connecticut Day Finishes Program of Sesqui Fetes," *PPL*, November 30, 1926; "Sesqui Conductor Honored," *PB*, December 1, 1926; "Sesquicentennial Fair Comes to an End, Leaving a $5M Deficit to Be Paid," *NYT*, December 1, 1926; Austin and Hauser, *The Sesqui-Centennial International Exposition*, pp. 207–209.

20. "Will Extend the Sesquicentennial to Jan. 1; Reopening Next Year Held in Abeyance," *NYT*, November 20, 1926.

21. Ibid.

22. "Will Extend the Sesquicentennial to Jan. 1; Reopening Next Year Held in Abeyance," *NYT*, November 20, 1926; "Advance Sesqui Closing to Jan. 1," *PB*, November 20, 1926; "1,000 on Sesqui Staff Dismissed," *PB*, November 20, 1926; "Mayor Expects $1,200,000 on Sesqui Salvage," *PPL*, November 21, 1926; "Will Not Continue Sesqui Next Year," *PB*, November 21, 1926; "1,000 on Sesqui Staff Dismissed," *PB*, November 20, 1926; "Ask 25-Cent Sesqui Fee for December," *PB*, November 22, 1926; "High Street Closes Nov. 30," *PPL*, November 22, 1926; "Sesqui Admission Cut to a Quarter," *PPL*, November 25, 1926; "Alien Exhibitors Quit Sesqui Mart," *PPL*, November 25, 1926; "Only 870 Employees Still Have Work at the Sesqui," *PB*, December 1, 1926.

23. "25-Cent Sesqui Charge Draws Few Visitors," *PR*, December 2, 1926; "Sesqui Grounds Gloomy Spot Now," *PB*, December 6, 1926.

24. "Pinchot Scores Vote Laxity Here," *PB*, December 3, 1926; "Pinchot in Speech Scolds Philadelphians," *NYT*, December 4, 1926; *Report of the Pennsylvania Sesqui-Centennial Commission*, pp. 35–41.

25. Imogen B. Oakley, "Two Dictatorships," *PB*, December 21, 1926.

26. "Paid Attendance at Sesqui 4,622,211," *PB*, December 1, 1926; "4,622,211 Persons Paid to See Fair," *NYT*, December 2, 1926; "1,230,572 Saw Sesqui Free," *PB*, December 7, 1926.

27. "Philadelphia Fair Ends," *NYT*, January 2, 1927.

15

★ ★ ★

For Sale: One Sesqui

ON JANUARY 3, 1927, the Sesqui-Centennial returned to life when the first auction of fair property took place on the Gladway. The twenty-nine animals of the Sesqui Zoo, one of many concessions bankrupted by poor attendance, went under the sheriff's hammer at the orders of a Common Pleas Court judge. Among those bidding were several fur dealers, ready to transform the cuddly zoo denizens into a silver fox stole or mink-trimmed wrap for fur-crazed flappers. Bernadine Thorne, daughter of the insolvent zoo owner, paid the hefty sum of $227 to save her pet silver fox, "Sister," from being skinned. "Only about one in every 5,000 foxes can be tamed," Thorne explained as she cradled the rescued creature in her arms. "I handled 'Sister' since she was a pup and I couldn't think of letting anybody else have her if it took all the money I have."[1]

For $111, "a hot-tempered, high-spirited cinnamon bear" named Sonny was sold to Benjamin Satler, who lived on Ninth Street near Buttonwood in the Spring Garden district. Satler felt sure that his neighborhood of narrow row houses with small backyards would be the perfect habitat for a half-grown bear. When Satler asked the auctioneer to deliver the bear to his home, he was informed that all purchases were cash and carry. With the assistance of two volunteers, Satler tried to wrestle Sonny out of its cage and into his car. A fierce tug-of-war developed between the bear and the three men, with bystanders betting three-to-one on Sonny. After a protracted struggle, the aggravated animal was finally manhandled into Satler's car, where it proceeded to shred the interior. When Satler opened the car door, Sonny tumbled out and sought refuge in a nearby taxi, to the dismay of its driver. "Get him out of there!" the cabbie yelled. "I just started on my afternoon work, and I work on commission!"[2]

The resourceful Bernadine Thorne enticed Sonny out of the cab and back into his cage with a tray of coffee cake. Having lost any desire to keep his new pet, Satler telephoned the Philadelphia Zoo and offered them "a nice cinnamon bear" for free. Soon, two zookeepers arrived with an offering of apples. After eating a couple, a sated Sonny clambered into the zoo van and departed for his new home. The taxi driver took Satler's helpers to Methodist Hospital to have their scratches patched, a sadder but wiser Satler departed in his battered car, and a joyful Thorne took her pet fox Sister safely home.[3]

While Sister the fox and Sonny the bear were making headlines, a political circus raged elsewhere in Philadelphia, with the mayor's office, city controller's office, and Sesqui Administration Building as its three rings. In late December, City Controller WillB Hadley had requested "a full and detailed statement of the receipts and disbursements of the Sesqui-Centennial Exhibition Association" from Mayor W. Freeland Kendrick and SCEA officials. The ambitious Hadley was using the chaotic finances of the city and Sesqui to position himself as Philadelphia's financial guardian, in hopes of becoming its next mayor.

After three weeks without a response, Hadley issued a subpoena on January 10, demanding that Mayor Kendrick appear at the controller's office at 2:00 P.M. the following day, accompanied by "all relevant financial information." For two days, Hadley peppered Kendrick and City Solicitor Gaffney with questions on SCEA organization and procedures, asking who had hired employees, contracted construction, ordered supplies, and solicited bids. At the end of it, a browbeaten Kendrick sighed that "this baby [the Sesqui] was laying on my doorstep when I walked into office. I have done everything I could from patriotic motives, and this is a sample of the reward I'm getting. . . . It's over, and I'm glad it's over." Kendrick and Gaffney got their revenge by sending Hadley not only "all relevant financial information" for the Sesqui, but the entire physical contents of the SCEA offices, including its staff. Controller Hadley returned from lunch on January 13 to find his offices crammed with desks, chairs, typewriters, adding machines, safes, and seventy laughing, chattering young female stenographers.[4]

The subpoena from a civil servant who was technically the mayor's employee was only one of many attacks on an embattled Kendrick as 1927 got under way. The man who had once inspired parades, roses, and romantic ballads now seemed to be under siege from all sides. In mid-January, Kendrick was summoned to Washington, DC, along with other officials of the Philadelphia Registration Committee, to testify before Senator James Reed's committee investigating the Vare election. Kendrick had refused Reed's initial request to turn over more than two thousand ballot boxes from the November election, forcing the senator to serve him with a court order. Now the boxes resided at City Hall behind doors sealed by the Sergeant at Arms of the U.S. Senate, who had also impounded all voter registration lists from November. Arrangements were being made to transport the boxes to Washington in a guarded freight train for an official recount. Kendrick's earlier reluctance to cooperate with Reed guaranteed that he would be treated as a hostile witness by the Senate committee.

The erstwhile darling of Philadelphia politics had become the whipping boy for the city's growing list of problems. At a meeting of the Pennsylvania League of Women Voters, one female Republican leader blamed the Kendrick administration for "a subway that doesn't run, an incomplete art museum where a great deal of money and material was wasted, a never-to-be forgotten Sesqui, a sinkable Stadium, a Delaware River bridge overrun with

Sealed boxes of ballots in the Vare-Wilson election case arrive at the United States Capitol on January 18, 1927. (Prints and Photographs Division, Library of Congress.)

P.R.T. buses, and we gained and lost Smedley D. Butler." One journalist noted, "The Sesqui was Freel's funeral."[5]

If the Sesqui was Kendrick's funeral, then City Controller Hadley was the uninvited guest in the back pew, cracking jokes. In his most serious assault on City Hall, Hadley refused to sign off on $5 million in bills submitted by Sesqui creditors and approved by the SCEA. "The management of the Sesqui-Centennial was so irregular," he claimed, "as to justify me in declining to countersign these warrants." Hadley questioned the legality of an earlier $5 million bond issue underwritten by Albert M. Greenfield and Company and the Franklin Trust Bank to cover Sesqui debt, accusing Kendrick of strong-arming his cronies into paying for "Freel's Folly." He even wrote the new governor of Pennsylvania, John S. Fisher, detailing the legal ambiguities in both the Sesqui bond issue and the voter-sanctioned transfer of $5 million in transit funds in November. With less than $200,000 in the bank, the SCEA discharged most of its remaining employees without issuing their last paychecks. Only a $15,000 loan from Albert M. Greenfield enabled the SCEA to pay the laid-off workers, mostly guards, mechanics, and laborers who had earned between twenty-five and forty dollars a week.[6]

On a broader scale, Philadelphia was paralyzed financially by the ongoing war between Hadley and Kendrick. Hadley issued increasingly dire warnings about the state of municipal finances, charging that 1927 city loans would be "greatly in excess" of $25 million, that the 1927 budget was more than $1 million over actual revenue, and that the city had a borrowing capacity of only $16 million to cover $30 million due on outstanding contracts. He cast doubts on the city's ability to float a meager $4 million councilmanic loan to cover its most pressing obligations. With Philadelphia facing a liquidity crisis, Kendrick instructed his cabinet and department heads "to cut every item of expense to a minimum during the remainder of my administration." Having told his underlings to practice a "rigid economy," Kendrick left in a private railroad car for a two-week vacation in Florida and Cuba.[7]

To raise desperately needed capital, the SCEA announced plans to sell its remaining assets in a massive auction at the fairgrounds in early March. Samuel T. Freeman and Co., the city's oldest auctioneer, would run the sale. Their 150-page catalog included everything from the giant Liberty Bell to items like mechanically operated lions and tigers from the *Freedom* pageant, rolls of unused tickets from the Dempsey-Tunney fight, and a "nicely carved wooden leg." Mayor Kendrick and Director-General Austin were confident that this gigantic sale would generate more than $1 million in salvage revenue, allowing the SCEA to pay off its operating deficit and remain solvent.

An offer of $50,000 had already been made for the magnificent Austin organ in the Auditorium. SCEA officials had declined the offer. They were confident of realizing at least $75,000 on the organ, even though rats had devoured the leather and felt of its pallets and gussets, and sparrows roosted in its pipes. The SCEA needed to make as much as possible, since they still owed $37,000 on the $150,000 bill to the manufacturer.[8]

A few items had already been sold besides the denizens of the Sesqui Zoo. State Senator George Woodward had paid the National Society of the Colonial Dames of America $3,500 for their replica of Sulgrave Manor. By early spring, he had arranged for the structure to be dismantled and its key elements moved to West Willow Grove Avenue in Chestnut Hill. Architect H. Louis Duhring redesigned the structure, maintaining its general layout while enlarging it and adding modern conveniences. Reconstructed with an exterior of Wissahickon schist, Sulgrave Manor became an elegant private residence in the city's toniest district.[9]

Ralph Bencker's Pennsylvania State Building, one of the architectural gems of the Sesqui, met a sadder fate. The structure, which belonged to the Commonwealth and not the SCEA, had been offered at auction in early January. Governor Gifford Pinchot insisted that the building be sold before he left office on January 18, 1927. He might have been nervous that his successor, John S. Fisher, would let the building remain as a permanent fixture. On January 5 the pavilion, which cost roughly $500,000, was sold to the Stanley Iron and Steel Company of Philadelphia for $9,274. Demolition began almost at once, but did not go smoothly. Stanley Iron and Steel filed a suit against the State Treasurer to prevent him from cashing the company's check. The firm charged that the building contained only 475 tons of structural steel, not the 800 tons advertised.[10]

The destruction of the Pennsylvania State Building was only one of Pinchot's parting shots before he left office. He took further steps to prevent his formal rival, William S. Vare, from gaining admittance to the United States Senate. After a senatorial election, the governor of Pennsylvania was obliged to send a letter to the U.S. Senate certifying the returns and declaring the victor the legitimate representative of the Commonwealth. On January 8 Pinchot sent a letter to the president of the Senate, stating that "on the face of the returns filed in the Office of the Secretary of the Commonwealth . . . William S. Vare appears to have been chosen by the qualified electors of the State of Pennsylvania a Senator."[11] Pinchot's tentatively worded missive became known as the "Certificate of Doubt."

Pinchot was less ambivalent in private, charging that Vare's election was "partly bought and partly stolen," and that fraud had "tainted both the primary and the general election." Under heavy pressure from the Organization, Pinchot's successor, Governor John S. Fisher, issued an amended certificate in early March stating that Vare was "duly chosen" as senator by Pennsylvania's voters. By the time Fisher's revised certificate was issued, the Sixty-Ninth Congress had adjourned. Vare would not present his credentials until the First Session of the Seventieth Congress convened on December 5, 1927. Forced to wait another eight months for his prize, the normally temperate Vare started to smoke and drink heavily. Pinchot's "Certificate of Doubt," combined with a petition charging election fraud filed by Democratic loser William B. Wilson, would provide the two Senate committees investigating Vare's expenditures and other campaign irregularities with plenty of ammunition.[12]

Like nearly everything else about the Sesqui, the March auction of its assets was a bitter disappointment. The buildings and fixtures that had cost so much more than expected in 1926 fetched far less than expected in 1927, in some cases realizing pennies on the hundreds of dollars. The Palace of Agriculture and Foreign Exhibits had been erected at an official cost of $850,000, although the actual outlay probably exceeded $1 million. It received one bid of $19,501. The cavernous Alpine Haus restaurant, which had cost $50,000 to build and which had bankrupted its original proprietors, was knocked down for $2,125. Most of the other large structures did not receive any bids. Albert M. Greenfield tried to convince the Chamber of Commerce to buy the U.S. Government Palace and convert it into a convention center, since the city had no money to build Victory Hall on Logan Circle.

Thousands of shrubs and trees used to landscape the grounds, valued at $300,000, sold for $3,005. More than thirteen hundred pieces of office furniture, for which the SCEA had paid $109,000, fetched $7,402. One bidder paid $1,452 for all of the equipment used to outfit the Sesqui police, including hundreds of billy clubs, pistols, and uniforms. One of the most popular lots, a fleet of forty-one motor vehicles, received more than four hundred bids and was finally knocked down for a blanket bid of $4,000. The biggest shock came when the $150,000 Organists' Organ, for which the SCEA had spurned an earlier offer of $50,000, received a single bid of $1,260 from a curio dealer. Chastened SCEA officials decided to cancel the rest of the auction and reschedule it for the summer. A stunned Mayor Kendrick learned that the total proceeds amounted to less than $250,000, only a quarter of what he had expected to earn.[13]

The failure of the March auction was the last gasp for the Sesqui-Centennial Exhibition Association. Drowning in debt, SCEA officials asked that their organization be placed in receivership in U.S. District Court on April 23. Director-General Austin stated that the SCEA had liquid assets of about $150,000 against debts of $5,501,349, of which $500,000 was the responsibility of the association while the balance would be paid by the city. The valuation of the SCEA's remaining buildings and physical assets was not stated, since the recent auction had proven that they were essentially worthless. The federal judge appointed Austin to serve as coreceiver for the SCEA, along with former Pennsylvania Attorney General Francis Shunk Brown. One of the city's leading lawyers, the blue-blooded Brown was chancellor of the Philadelphia Bar Association. Brown was familiar with the SCEA, having represented Tex Rickard's legal interests in Philadelphia during the Dempsey-Tunney bout. He was also a loyal Organization man who had tutored the young Bill Vare on rhetoric and civic affairs. As Vare's chief counsel, Brown handled the former congressman's prickly legal dealings with the Senate committees investigating his election.[14]

Austin and Brown announced that the remaining Sesqui property would be sold at a series of five auctions run by Freeman and Co. at the fairgrounds between July 18 and August 10. Unfortunately, the returns for the second round of auctions were as disappointing as the spring sale. Most of the shabbily built Sesqui structures, in wretched condition after a year without maintenance, sold for less than the wholesale cost of their structural components. Prices remained low because there was confusion over who would be responsible for removing the buildings' concrete floors and foundations. Austin assured bidders that they would not have to remove them. He was contradicted by the Fairmount Park Commission, which insisted that League Island Park be restored to its original condition. Individual landowners who had leased their property to the SCEA also threatened to sue if the floors and foundations of Sesqui structures were not demolished. Unsure of their potential liability, salvage companies lowballed their bids, paying $38,000 for buildings with a cumulative price tag of nearly $2.5 million.

The Palace of Education and Social Economy, which cost $346,000, was knocked down for $10,750 to the Newman House Wrecking Company. Newman also acquired the Palace of Liberal Arts and Manufactures for $11,000 and the smaller Palace of Fine Arts for $950. They had originally cost $758,000 and $241,000, respectively. Philip Wright, a Philadelphia iron dealer, bought the Auditorium (original cost: $399,000) for $4,800 and the U.S. Government Palace (original cost: $714,500) for $10,500. Wright flipped the Auditorium, selling it for $11,000 to the Starlight Amusement Park in the Bronx. The $45,000 Electrical Fountain on the Gladway, which had delighted fairgoers with its dancing plumes of multicolored water, sold for $500. It too began a new life at an amusement park in Birmingham, Alabama.[15]

The Sesqui's two landmarks, the Tower of Light and the giant Liberty Bell, suffered especially ignominious fates. The Tower of Light—the naked metal framework known as the "Sesqui Folly" or "The Light that Failed," which cost the SCEA $365,093 before they gave up on it—fetched $1,050. Two dimmers for the "Light of Independence," the largest searchlight in the world that was never installed atop the tower, sold for $440. Unused and still in their original packing crates, they had cost $5,000. A sixteen-foot chandelier of leaded glass sold for $3,405. Purchased for $23,000, it was to have graced the grand entrance hall to the Tower of Light, but was far too large for the cramped rotunda erected at the base of the steel skeleton.[16]

The Liberty Bell was sold for sixty dollars to Arthur C. Baumann, a South Philadelphia contractor, who tore it apart for its valuable components. The bell's twenty-seven thousand light sockets had a resale value of a penny apiece, its thirty-five thousand feet of lumber might have fetched $700, and the ninety-seven tons of structural steel were worth roughly eight dollars a ton. Then there were the thousands of light bulbs, the sheet-iron sheathing, and the miles of copper wiring. Even after paying for dismantling and removal, Baumann stood to clear several thousand dollars on his sixty-dollar investment. Local residents were glad to see the bell disappear. Once the Sesqui had closed, its hollow interior and stanchions had become a thriving "hobo hotel," filled with dozens of vagrants.[17]

The white-domed "Taj Mahal" sold for $600; the Japanese teahouse for $165. The elegant Spanish palace, the Modernist Cuban cube, and the Beaux-Arts Argentine pavilion had all been deeded to the city of Philadelphia by their respective governments in gestures of goodwill. Each one was sold for less than $100. Andrew Rebori's Illinois pavilion was a bargain at only thirty dollars, produce included. One wing of the Modernist structure had housed a display of Prairie State corn, including murals composed of countless red, white, and blue kernels. After eight months of rain pouring through its leaky roof, the wing had been transformed into a miniature cornfield, with a fine crop of two-foot-high stalks.

Even those with only a few bucks in their pocket could take home a piece of the Sesqui, provided they could move it. The thirteen ornate state columns that lined the Forum of the Founders sold for $4.50 apiece, while the badly weathered statue of "Philadelphia Progressive" fetched a single dollar. The two thrones that had serviced Queen Marie and Princess Ileana of Romania went for twenty dollars apiece, while the 871 portable oil stoves that had failed to warm them sold for eighty cents each. The 7,781 beer steins from the Alpine Haus, advertised as "unfilled," brought a penny apiece.[18]

In the one bright note of the auction, the great organ from the Auditorium was rescued from oblivion in a curio shop when an anonymous bidder paid $25,000 for it. While only half of the $50,000 refused by SCEA officials earlier in the year, the offer was still significantly more than the $1,260 bid in March. The benefactor was later revealed to be Cyrus H. K. Curtis, the music-loving publisher of the *Saturday Evening Post* and *Ladies' Home Journal* magazines and the *Public Ledger* newspaper. In 1928, the renamed Curtis Organ became a permanent fixture of the new William B. Irvine Auditorium at the University of Pennsylvania. The addition of the organ forced architect Horace Trumbauer to redesign the structure to include a soaring central tower as a sounding chamber for the mammoth instrument.[19]

Auctioneer George Freeman rang down his last hammer on August 10, selling the remaining Sesqui shrubbery, valued at nearly $98,000, for a total of $3,488. The six summer auctions run by Freeman's generated a total of $238,000. Added to the proceeds of the March auction, the Sesqui-Centennial salvage process had yielded less than $500,000. E. L. Austin proudly announced that this would be more than enough to cover the operating deficit for the SCEA, which he calculated to be a mere $206,987. But it would not begin to pay for the $5 million the city still owed to major creditors, still in limbo thanks to taxpayers' suits and other legal challenges. And there remained the matter of the roughly $20 million spent by the city on Kendrick's Karnival, which included more than $4 million to develop its South Philadelphia site, and $3 million to build the Sesqui Stadium, the one major structure that would survive the fair.

Some critics protested that these figures were far too low, and did not reflect millions in sparsely documented general appropriation bills and councilmanic loans pushed through City Council since 1924. As an example, they pointed to the recent loan for $1,250,000 for the stated purpose of repaving and resurfacing city streets. Nearly $200,000 was used instead to pay the outstanding Sesqui bills of "favored" firms. The Turner Construction Company received almost $90,000 for its work on the Stadium, the Vare Construction Company was paid $20,365, and the Keystone State Construction Company was paid $15,084. By branding this work as part of the South Philadelphia Improvements, City Council could bypass the legal bottleneck blocking other Sesqui claims. Through methods like these, critics charged, the Kendrick administration had diverted millions of dollars in municipal funds to its business allies since 1924, meaning that no one would ever know the true cost of the Sesqui.[20]

Ruminating on the paltry legacy of the Sesqui, a *Bulletin* columnist imagined what the exposition might have been like if it had been staged on the Fairmount Parkway, as originally planned. "Most of the millions which would have been spent in such a program," the writer mused, "would have been of permanent value." In this alternative universe, the Parkway would be lined with a completed Art Museum and Free Library, a new Municipal Court, a Victory Hall capable of attracting the 1928 Republican National Convention (which in the real world would be held in Kansas City, Missouri), and the elegant homes of the city's leading cultural institutions. In West Philadelphia, a revitalized Commercial Museum would be "permanently endowed with buildings suitable for its important service to the industry and commerce of Philadelphia."

These missed opportunities, the writer concluded stoically, were "only vain regrets. There is no use in crying over spilt milk." The only comfort that the writer could find was in the reclamation and development of the South Philadelphia swamps. The real estate slump gripping the city meant that the only beneficiaries of this work at present were the few inhabitants of the region and their political representatives. But the writer was sure that at some future point, "attention will be turned to South Philadelphia ultimately," and growth in that district would "bring about the completion of the work started under the Sesqui-Centennial scheme."[21]

Unlike the *Bulletin*, an optimistic Mayor Kendrick announced, "I have no regrets over the Sesqui or anything connected with it." On August 2, Kendrick was awarded a gold medal for his "faithful, disinterested and continued services as Mayor of Philadelphia to the Sesqui-Centennial celebration of American independence." The award was presented by former directors and officers of the SCEA in a quiet ceremony in the Mayor's Reception Room. Acknowledging that "the Sesqui was a very difficult proposition to handle," Kendrick insisted that "it was not money that we were after. It was to impress upon this and the growing generation the great sacrifices of our forefathers, and we were highly successful along that line."[22]

While Kendrick basked in his fading glory, the Organization was selecting his successor. In mid-August, Vare and his forty-eight ward lieutenants settled on the Republican mayoral nominee: City Treasurer Harry Arista Mackey, who had managed Vare's senatorial campaign in 1926. "Thus benevolently," sighed the *New York Times*, "does [Vare] instruct the voters in their duty." As leader of the Forty-Sixth Ward in West Philadelphia, Mackey had been a loyal Organization man since 1906. The stocky ex-football

The Lame Duck: Mayor Kendrick offers the key to the city to Baby Snookums, "the youngest movie star in America," in May 1927.

player was an exemplary practitioner of Philadelphia *Realpolitik*, as illustrated by his blunt description of Vare's hold over the city's "first twenty" wards before the Reed Committee in May 1926. In 1927, he delivered the same message to the North Philadelphia Chamber of Commerce, instructing them on how to obtain the benefits that Vare had bestowed upon the Neck:

> If you want to get anything for your community you've got to play politics and cater to politicians. Line up with those who have power and influence. Don't think you can go down to City Hall and make demands upon some director. He may listen to you, but it won't get you anything. Be friendly to the men who can get things done for you and they will take care of your needs.[23]

Mackey launched his mayoral campaign by assailing the extravagance and corruption of the Kendrick regime. While vowing to implement long-delayed improvements in the city's water supply and transportation systems, the City Treasurer promised voters an economical administration, "with no more art galleries, no more Sesquicentennial Expositions, no instrumentalities of public justice as vehicles to public graft." Mackey demanded an investigation of the Philadelphia police department, which he called a graft-ridden organization that accepted hundreds of thousands of dollars every month to protect criminals. Despite fierce opposition from three independent Republican candidates (including City Controller WillB Hadley and former mayor J. Hampton Moore), Mackey was the winner of the Republican primary with 235,000 votes.[24]

The 1927 Philadelphia mayoral campaign attracted national attention as a portent of Senator-Elect Vare's fortunes. The Mackey candidacy, noted the *New York Times*, "is almost the same as if Vare himself were running for that office. If [Mackey] should lose, or be elected by only a scant majority, it would seriously affect Vare's prestige in Washington and might be the turning point that would cause his rejection by the Senate." On November 8, Election Day, Philadelphia awarded Mackey the mayoralty by nearly 169,000 votes. In a further sign of Vare's continuing power, all twenty of the Organization-backed City Council candidates won handily. Turnout was heavy, with more than four hundred thousand votes cast. James M. Beck, the former chairman of the National Sesqui-Centennial Advisory Commission who had succeeded Vare as congressman from the First Congressional District, viewed the election as proof that Philadelphians had no sympathy with the "attempt to deprive William S. Vare of the seat in the Senate to which he was unquestionably elected."[25]

A month after Mackey was elected mayor, the Organization learned that its local machinations did not represent the voice of the people as embodied on Capitol Hill. On December 5, 1927, Senator-Elect William S. Vare presented his credentials to the Seventieth Congress, including the amended certificate granted by Governor John S. Fisher. The documents were refused and he was prevented from entering the U.S. Senate. A humiliated Vare later described his "roughshod" treatment by saying, "I was stopped at the threshold of the chamber as though I were some common thief awaiting an opportunity to rob the so-called statesmen of their personal belongings."[26]

Vare's opponents in the Senate labored to bar him permanently from its hallowed halls. Senator George W. Norris of Nebraska sponsored a resolution that renewed Senator James A. Reed's now-defunct Special Committee on Expenditures, delaying Vare's installment until the committee had produced a final report on his election. The Norris Resolution passed the Senate by a vote of fifty-six to thirty. Norris claimed that Vare's tabulated expenditures, exceeding $785,000, were "harmful to the dignity and honor of the Senate and dangerous to the perpetuity of a free government."

The resolution continued to overlook the fact that former Senator George Wharton Pepper had spent over $1.8 million on his campaign. Vare's overspending, along with charges of irregularities made by Pinchot and Wilson, served to "taint with fraud and corruption the credentials of the said William S. Vare."[27]

Progressive and Prohibitionist elements of the Senate united across party lines to block Vare. The thirty-eight Democrats voting to deny Vare his seat were joined by seventeen Republicans, along with Senator Shipstead of the Farmer-Labor Party. The anti-Vare Republicans were primarily from the agricultural states of the Midwest and Great Plains. Like Vare, many were self-made men who had come from humble origins. Charles McNary of Oregon was a shopkeeper's son; Frank B. Willis of Ohio was a farmer's boy; Peter Norbeck of South Dakota was born in a mud hut on the Dakota Territory to Scandinavian immigrants. To these small-town Progressives and Prohibitionists, the Duke of South Philadelphia was as anathematic as he was to their Democratic counterparts. Both camps viewed Vare as a corrupt machine boss from the urban Northeast who favored looser immigration laws, heavy industry, high tariffs, and most damning of all, the Modification of Prohibition to permit the sale of beer and light wine.[28]

A dejected Vare announced that the loss was not his, but that of "the Great State of Pennsylvania, comprising approximately one-tenth of the population." For the first time in history, the Keystone State stood "without the representation in the national Government to which she is legally and morally entitled."[29] Vare retreated to his South Broad Street brownstone, disappearing from the public view with what was described as a bad case of flu. Francis Shunk Brown, who had witnessed Vare's disgrace, reported that his client was on the verge of a nervous breakdown. Poor health, including an inflammation of the lungs known as pleurisy, would plague Vare well into 1928.

David A. Reed, now the sole senator from Pennsylvania, staunchly defended Vare's right to be seated. He argued that a failure to admit Vare would deprive his state illegally of full representation, violating the constitutional rights of its citizens. He recommended that the Senate admit Vare and then expel him if the final report of the Special Committee indicated that such a course was justified. This was the usual protocol in cases where elected representatives with valid credentials were under investigation. Reed noted that a bloc of Progressive and Prohibitionist senators had used similar tactics recently to prevent the admission of Frank L. Smith, Republican senator-elect from Illinois. The disqualification of both Vare and Smith gave Democrats effective control of the ninety-six-seat Senate, since it left the body with forty-six active Republicans, forty-seven Democrats, and one Farmer-Labor senator who usually voted Democratic. "I do not charge that the Democrats are trying to steal the Senate," Reed announced on the Senate floor, "but will not the country think so?"[30]

"We can't help that," snapped Senator Duncan Fletcher (D-Florida). "We didn't bring the situation here."[31]

Vare's former protégé, W. Freeland Kendrick, adopted a valedictory pose during his final days on the public stage. On December 30 Kendrick signed six ordinances in the same reception room where nineteen months earlier he had welcomed the civilized world to celebrate his Sesqui-Centennial. They dealt with such matters as the establishment of cab stands throughout Center City to discourage taxi cruising and the relocation of PRT tracks in the northern suburbs. To Kendrick, these ordinances were "of very great importance," because "they will do much to make our city more attractive, more beautiful." By signing them, Kendrick would leave office without having vetoed a single piece of councilmanic legislation during his four years as mayor. He took pride in being the first Philadelphia mayor to achieve this record of compliance, part of his original campaign promise of "Cooperation and Action." The following day, Kendrick left City Hall for the last time, ending his sixteen years as a public servant.[32]

Kendrick's withdrawal from public service was far more dignified than that of his onetime mentor. In May 1928 William S. Vare was scheduled to appear before the reconvened Reed Special Committee to defend himself against charges that his election was the result of "wholesale fraud and corruption." At the last moment, he called in sick. His counsel, Francis Shunk Brown, explained that Vare was prostrate with "acute indigestion" at his Atlantic City cottage. The indignant senators insisted that Brown contact Vare by telephone from the committee room. When Brown reached the cottage, Vare's physician, Dr. Ellwood Kirby, refused to let his patient speak on the phone. A few days later, Dr. Kirby reported that Vare had suffered another attack of pleurisy, and had to be kept under observation. Vare remained too ill to appear before the Reed Committee when the Senate adjourned for the summer.

By preventing the Reed Committee from filing its final report until Congress reconvened, Vare postponed the increasingly inevitable option that the Senate would reject him permanently. He had recovered sufficiently to attend the Republican National Convention in Kansas City as a delegate-at-large in mid-June. There, he attempted to play kingmaker for the final time, convincing the Pennsylvania delegation to back Vice President Herbert Hoover. While Hoover's nomination was never in serious doubt, Vare's avid support might have been an attempt to garner support for his Senate bid from the man certain to be the next president. "I am feeling fine now," an ebullient Vare assured reporters. "After a thorough physical examination, my physicians informed me there is no organic disorder anywhere."[33]

On the evening of August 1, Vare motored back to Atlantic City after spending the day at his office in the Lincoln Building. He had left his office early, complaining of feeling ill. Soon after he had gone upstairs to bed, his family heard a thud. They ran to Vare's bedroom to find him on the floor, unconscious. He had suffered a severe cerebral hemorrhage that left him paralyzed on his left side. Dr. Kirby informed Vare's family that their patriarch would probably die within a day or two. Immediately, speculation focused on who would be the new head of the Philadelphia Organization, and who would be appointed to fill the Senate seat. Instead, the tough kid from the Neck clung to life. By early September, he was able to move his left hand and foot and speak in brief sentences. "I want to get out of here," he told his daughters, Beatrice and Mildred. "I want to get out and help Hoover's campaign."[34]

By midmonth, Vare was holding political powwows at his Atlantic City home with Mayor Mackey and other Organization leaders. Soon the city's forty-eight ward leaders were shuttling between Philadelphia and Atlantic City to get their marching orders. They were told to tone down the Organization's illegal activities lest they attract the attention of the Reed Special Committee. In early October, Governor Fisher paid a call on Vare, telling reporters that he was astonished to find the senator-elect in such splendid condition. Unable to campaign for Hoover, Vare listened with pride as his daughter Beatrice gave a radio address promoting the candidate. He was delighted when Hoover won the presidency by a wide margin on November 6, carrying forty of the forty-eight states.

In early 1929, Vare's day of reckoning with the Senate finally arrived. His chief counsel and physician, Francis Shunk Brown and Ellwood Kirby, appeared before the Reed Special Committee in January, declaring that to compel Vare to testify at that time would "kill him." If their testimony was meant to muster compassion for the senator-elect, it failed. The Reed Committee submitted its final report a few weeks later, declaring that Vare was not entitled to his seat because of excessive campaign expenditures. By this time, the Senate Committee on Privileges and Elections had also presented its findings, alleging widespread voter fraud and coercion on the part of the Organization, including thousands of fake registrations. A Philadelphia voter, the latter committee concluded, had a one-in-eight chance of having his or her ballot counted correctly.

Senator James A. Reed agreed to postpone his committee's final verdict until Vare was well enough to testify before the U.S. Senate. For the rest of 1929, Vare struggled to regain his health and vigor. On December 4, thirty-seven months after winning the election as Junior Senator from Pennsylvania, William S. Vare appeared on the Senate floor to plead his case. Clutching a cane in his right hand and supported on his left side by his son-in-law, the sixty-two-year-old senator-elect hobbled onto the floor and took a seat at a vacant desk. His face was flushed a dark red, and the left side of his mouth still drooped noticeably. Pennsylvania Senator David Reed interrupted Senator George Norris of Nebraska, who was delivering a bitter denunciation of the Vare machine. "Mr. Vare is here," Reed informed the Senate, "and has something to say."[35]

Vare rose to his feet slowly, leaning the right side of his body against the desk for support. In the packed galleries, his wife and two daughters watched him anxiously. Talking slowly to minimize the slurred speech caused by his paralysis, Vare spent twenty minutes trying to convince the silent senators to let him sit among them:

> During all of my political career I have never been accused of any crime. I have tried to lead an upright life both socially and politically. I have never participated in any political juggling. I never stole an election, nor have I ever asked anyone to make a false return or to change any election records to decide a close contest in my favor. In fact, I would never countenance any such action, and I have always used all of my influence against such practices.[36]

Responding to charges of excessive expenditures, Vare noted that "there are senators sitting on this floor today whose election cost more per vote, more per capita, and more per voting district" than his campaign. He spoke of how the charges against him "so preyed upon my mind and body that in that terrible month of August, 1928, I trembled on the verge of eternity."[37]

He cited his fifteen years as a member of the House of Representatives, and the service he rendered to his constituents and to his country. Finally, he asked that the Senators respect not only his right to be seated, but the constitutional rights of Pennsylvanians to full representation.

Vare was present two days later when the Senate voted to oust him, fifty-eight to twenty-two. His face flushed and set, Vare hobbled down the center aisle and out of the Senate Chamber for the final time. He returned to Philadelphia the following day, to tell a throng of cheering supporters at Broad Street Station that he was in a "fight to the finish" for his Senate

William S. Vare arrives at the U.S. Capitol on December 4, 1929, to plead for his admission as a senator, accompanied by his wife, Ida, and his daughter Mildred. The effects of the stroke he suffered in 1928 are apparent in his drooping mouth and his palsied left arm.

seat. On December 11 Governor Fisher of Pennsylvania appointed his own political mentor, Joseph R. Grundy, to fill Vare's empty seat. For the first time in nearly three years, Pennsylvania was represented by two senators. Vare considered a campaign for the next Senate primary in 1930, but he gave up when Dr. Kirby warned him that he would not survive its demands. His most bitter disappointment was that Herbert Hoover, whom he had supported so vocally in Kansas City, had never lifted a finger to help him throughout the Senate ordeal.[38]

While Vare was fighting for his political life, the city of Philadelphia was fighting to regain its reputation after the disgraces of the Sesqui-Centennial, the Vare debacle, and a 1928 Grand Jury investigation that had disclosed rampant corruption in the Philadelphia Police Department. In April 1929, a consortium of civic leaders launched a multimillion-dollar advertising and public relations campaign to promote Philadelphia's strengths to the outside world. Campaign leaders admitted that they were responding to negative publicity generated by recent scandals, specifically the Sesqui. "That undertaking," noted the *New York Times*, "cost upward of ten times the sum now sought, but most Philadelphians are content to drop the subject of the Sesquicentennial Exposition with an exclamation or two."

Among the achievements touted by the campaign was the explosive development of Center City. As the decade ended, the Philadelphia skyline was being transformed by over a dozen new skyscrapers, including the Aldine Trust Company, Fidelity-Philadelphia Trust Company, and Rittenhouse Plaza. Logan Circle was now graced by the beautiful Swann Fountain, and by the Free Library of Philadelphia. The Museum of Art, opened in early 1928, had attracted more than a million visitors during its first year. Greater things were in the works. The Pennsylvania Railroad had begun work on its Suburban Station and would soon break ground for its new Thirtieth Street Station. At Twelfth and Market Streets, construction had started on the new headquarters of the Philadelphia Savings Fund Society, a futuristic skyscraper designed by local architect George Howe and Swiss-born William Lescaze. Looking confidently into the future, the Philadelphia Planning Commission was preparing a Fifty-Year Plan that would guide the city's progress into the 1980s, when its population would top three million.

The cheerful campaign masked a more desperate agenda. It was designed to counter a noticeable slowdown in business growth and industrial expansion in the "Workshop of the World." Philadelphia's economy was fraying, even as America reached new heights of prosperity under the Hoover Administration. Despite millions spent on docks and harbor facilities, the Port of Philadelphia kept losing trade. Of the $5 billion in foreign commerce received by all East Coast ports in 1928, Philadelphia attracted only $304 million, compared with New York's $3.75 billion. Before the World War, twenty-two transatlantic passenger steamships docked at Philadelphia; in 1928, not one ship left its harbor for Europe.

Heavy industry, the lifeblood of Philadelphia's prosperity, was deserting the city. Manufacturing jobs in Philadelphia were at the same level in 1929 as they were in 1925. Textile firms were relocating to other cities where labor and materials were cheaper. Samuel Vauclain ended his reign as president of the Baldwin Locomotive Works by moving all production from North Broad Street to its industrial campus in Delaware County. He hoped that this relocation to a modern facility would reverse his company's decline. Baldwin's gross revenues had dropped from over $100 million in 1923 to only $22.5 million five years later. William Cramp and Sons Shipbuilding, which had employed more than ten thousand workers at its Kensington shipyard during the war, closed its doors in 1927, devastating the local community. Even the mighty Pennsylvania Railroad had reduced its workforce from 280,000 to 186,000 between 1920 and 1928.

A U.S. Bureau of Labor Statistics study found that in April 1929 more than 10 percent of Philadelphia workers were unemployed. This was more than double the national level and on a par with unemployment figures for 1915, "a period of severe depression and desperate idleness." Of those without jobs, 30 percent had been unemployed for at least six months. The Philadelphia Family Society was caring for 750 families a month in 1929, and could handle no new applicants. More than four thousand local families had lost their homes to foreclosure in the Sesqui-Centennial year of 1926. Three years later, that figure had jumped to nine thousand. Well before the term *Hooverville* entered the English language, shantytowns populated by the homeless had begun to sprout up on the east bank of the Schuylkill below the new art museum and near the former Sesqui grounds.[39]

By early 1929, the municipal government was struggling to meet expenses, hobbled by its massive expenditures on the high-profile projects of the Kendrick Administration: the Delaware River Bridge, Free Library, Broad Street Subway, Byberry Hospital, Museum of Art, and the Sesqui-Centennial. A report released in April calculated the city's gross outlay for the Sesqui at $23,320,000, excluding the $10 million appropriated separately for the Stadium and the South Philadelphia Improvements.[40]

Not long after the report detailing Sesqui expenditures was released, the official history of the ill-fated fair was finally published: *The Sesqui-Centennial International Exposition: 150 Years of American Independence*. Edited by former Sesqui Director-General E. L. Austin and Publicity Director Odell Hauser, the 520-page tome featured an introduction by W. Freeland Kendrick and articles written by key figures in the SCEA. After exhausting every possibility for private or official sponsorship, Austin and Hauser had published the book at their own expense, selling it by popular subscription. It found few takers.

The Sesqui-Centennial International Exposition cast the disappointing celebration in the best possible light, beginning with its first paragraph:

> Three years ago a city was reared as if by the wave of a magic wand and all the world was invited to come and view its wonders. Treasures of many lands were assembled there. The streets of the city were traversed by millions of people, including royalty and rulers, statesmen and diplomats, leaders in every walk of life. The facades and towers and domes and minarets of its many buildings formed a skyline of rare beauty. It was the daily scene of colorful events, pageantry, spectacles, and festivals. Because of its many-hued structures it was called "The Rainbow City."[41]

After this fairy-tale opening, Austin and Hauser presented a list of the Sesqui's "biggest" and "first" accomplishments. "No other exposition on so large a scale," they proclaimed, "was ever built in so short a time," an assertion that might have been disputed by the disappointed Shriners who attended its opening. The illuminated Liberty Bell was "the largest electrical structure ever erected." The Sesqui featured the largest collection of airplanes and flying machines in one location to date, as well as the largest assemblage of Diesel engines. Thanks to Jules Mastbaum, the Palace of Fine Arts contained the largest and finest collection of works by Rodin outside of Paris. The Auditorium was home to one of the biggest and greatest organs ever constructed. The on-site mint struck coins depicting a living president for the first and only time. The Sesqui was the only world's fair where an outdoor Catholic mass was celebrated, and where a world's heavyweight boxing championship was fought, both on the same ground. The fair featured the "greatest livestock show the East has ever seen." And of course, there was that "unique exhibit . . . showing the progress of the Negro race in industry, art and science. . . . a striking revelation of the remarkable advances that had been made by the race."[42]

After setting forth the many achievements of the Sesqui, the authors acknowledged that its birth had been premature. If the Sesqui had opened on July 15, 1926, it would have been "an unqualified success." If it had been postponed until 1927, it would have been "a triumphant success." Unfortunately, the fair's initial stumbles provided grist for "a certain portion of the population of the city which William Penn founded" that was "firmly addicted to the habit of destructive criticism." These naysayers failed to realize that "it was the duty of all good citizens to drop their personal inclinations and pull together for the city's greatest glory."[43] Because of these hometown haters, the authors asserted, the rest of the United States decided to snub the Sesqui.

Despite this negativity, Austin and Hauser believed, the Sesqui succeeded in its original purpose of "the appropriate and adequate celebration of 150 years of American independence." Thus, the authors concluded, "an event of such deep import and far-reaching influence, with a total attendance of 6,408,289, is worthy not only of a historical record such as this but also of an honorable page in the history of the nation."[44]

There is something pathetic in Austin and Hauser's apologia for the Sesqui, including their overinflating its attendance by more than half a million visitors. The idea that Philadelphia could spend more than $33 million in 1926 dollars for a world's fair that turned out to be nothing more than "appropriate and adequate" makes one want to weep. For all of its faults, the Sesqui-Centennial International Exposition deserved a nobler obituary. It had been more than a waste of time, materials, and money. It had done more than expose the greed, dishonesty, and hypocrisy of the Philadelphia political establishment to the entire country.

It had taken a barren expanse of swamps and marshes and transformed it into a fully functioning neighborhood, ready to be inhabited by the next wave of Philadelphia's ever-increasing population.

It had given the people of Philadelphia a magnificent new Stadium that would become one of the great sports centers of the twentieth century, attracting the Army-Navy Game and other major events.

It had assembled the nations of the world in peaceful harmony a decade after the holocaust of the World War, just as the Centennial had united Northerners and Southerners a decade after the Civil War.

It had shaken the smug, self-satisfied nature of Americans in the 1920s, and exposed them to new nations, new technologies, new artists, and new ideas.

It had taught visitors about the history and the heritage of their country, and made them proud to be citizens of the United States.

It had attracted the movers and shakers of the world to Philadelphia for one incredible night in September to witness the crowning of a new heavyweight boxing champion.

It had given Philadelphians a glimpse into the history of their city, and made them realize that it was worthy of preservation and restoration.

It had shown Philadelphians a vision of what their city could accomplish, if its ruling classes lifted their eyes beyond their own selfish needs.

It had created a dazzling Rainbow City of romantic towers and pastel palaces, of illuminated fountains and exotic citadels, a carefree Cockaigne where Philadelphians danced the Charleston in the streets while bathed in a kaleidoscopic flood of colored lights.

The Sesqui-Centennial International Exposition, like the Great War to End All Wars, had not been in vain.

It had possessed purpose, meaning, and value.

It was a world's fair that people would always remember.

NOTES

1. "Will Sell Sesquicentennial Zoo," *NYT*, December 30, 1926; "Bear-Taxi-Wow! Biff-Bang-Zow!," *PB*, January 3, 1927.

2. Ibid.

3. "Ibid.

4. "Paid Salaries out of Sesqui Building Fund, Says Mayor," *PB*, January 5, 1927; "Answers Hadley's Subpoena Threat," *PB*, January 8, 1927; "Hadley Subpoenas Kendrick to Bring Sesqui Accounts," *PB*, January 10, 1927; "Hadley, Quizzing Mayor, Raps Site Picked for Sesqui," *PB*, January 11, 1927; "Gaffney Clashes with Hadley at Quiz of Kendrick," *PB*, January 12, 1927; "Sesqui 'Exhibits' by Truckloads Swarm Hadley," *PB*, January 13, 1927; "Austin Again Sends 'Office' to Hadley," *PB*, January 14, 1927.

5. "Senate Committee Summons Kendrick," *NYT*, January 15, 1927; "Republican Woman Hits Kendrick Rule," *PB*, March 15, 1927; Ferris, "Freel Kendrick of Philadelphia," pp. 91–92.

6. Letter to W. Freeland Kendrick from WillB Hadley, January 21, 1927, HSP/AMG, Box 1.131; "Hadley Refuses to Sign $5 Million in Sesqui Bills," *PB*, January 21, 1927; "Hadley Again Hits Sesqui Debt Act," *PB*, February 28, 1927; "Asserts He Bought Bonds to Aid Claim," *PB*, April 22, 1927; "200 Sesqui Workers Fired without Two Weeks Salary," *PB*, January 22, 1927; letter to Albert M. Greenfield from Chas. A. Bonyun, SCEA Chief Accountant, January 26, 1927, HSP/AMG, Box 1.131.

7. "Warns City Faces $25,000,000 Loans," *PB*, January 6, 1927; "Hadley's Report Blow to Council," *PB*, February 18, 1927; "Mayor Goes South, Asks City Economy," *PB*, February 10, 1927.

8. Letter from Samuel T. Freeman & Co. to SCEA, February 10, 1927, HSP/AMG, Box 1.131; "Entire Sesqui Debt Now Near $5,250,000," *PB*, November 18, 1926; "Mayor Expects $1,200,000 on Sesqui Salvage," *PPL*, November 21, 1926; "Like Ichthyosauri? Sesqui to Sell 'Em," *PB*, February 14, 1927; "For Sale—One Sesqui," *PB*, February 15, 1927; "Would Keep Sesqui Organ in Phila.," *PB*, January 26, 1927.

9. Pennsylvania Society of the Colonial Dames of America Archives, Notebook No. 6: Meeting Minutes 4/15/25–1/28/28, February 16, 1927, p. 128; "Sulgrave Manor 'Moved,'" *PPL*, April 6, 1927; CHHS, *Chestnut Hill Historic District Inventory: Prospect Avenue to Wyndmoor Street*, pp. 365–366.

10. "State Sesqui Building Sold," *PB*, January 5, 1927; "Sesqui Gem Goes to Scrap Heap," *PB*, January 8, 1927; "Sesqui Building Sale Causes Suit," *PB*, February 26, 1927.

11. Vare, *My Forty Years in Politics* pp. 176–178.

12. Vare, *My Forty Years in Politics*, pp. 176–178; Weigley, *Philadelphia*, p. 584; "Vare Supported by Certificate," *Pittsburgh Press*, March 2, 1927, p. 11.

13. "$1,250 Only Offer for Sesqui Organ," *PB*, March 2, 1927; "Commerce Board Seeks Sesqui Hall," *PB*, March 18, 1927; "$3,005 Is Best Bid for $300,000 Sesqui Shrubs," *PB*, March 3, 1927; "$1,250 For $150,000 Organ," *NYT*, March 3, 1927; "Bids $7,402.12 for Sesqui Furniture Costing $100,000," *PB*, March 4, 1927; "Bids $2,125 on Alpine Haus," *PB*, March 8, 1927; "Bid for Sesqui Police Gear," *PB*, March 15, 1927; "Open Bids on Sesqui Cars," *PB*, March 11, 1927; "Will Consider

Sesqui Buildings," *PB*, March 14, 1927; "Low Bids on Sesqui Astonish Kendrick," *PPL*, April 19, 1927.

14. Salter, *The People's Choice*, p. 16; Beers, *Pennsylvania Politics Today and Yesterday*, p. 92.

15. "Will Sell Sesqui at Auction," *PB*, 30 June 30, 1927; "Sesqui Auditorium Sold for $4,800," *PB*, 8 August 8, 1927; "Sesqui Auditorium Resold for $10,000," *PB*, 9 August 9, 1927; Gray, "Streetscapes: The New York Coliseum: From Auditorium to Bus Garage to . . ." *NYT*, March 22, 1992; "Sesqui Fountain Sold," *PB*, August 19, 1927.

16. "Tower of Light Cheap at Auction," *PB*, July 28, 1927.

17. "Sesqui Bell is Hobo Hotel," *PB*, March 9, 1927; "Demolishing Sesqui Bell," *PB*, August 17, 1927; "Liberty Bell Soon Memory at Sesqui," *PPL*, August 22, 1927; Arkell and Saunders-Watson, *The Vendue Masters*, pp. 89–91.

18. "Sesqui Remnants Bring Fair Prices," *PB*, July 18, 1927; "Sesqui's 'Royal' Chairs Bring Only $20 Each," *PB*, July 22, 1927; "Sesqui Auditorium Sold for $4,800," *PB*, August 8, 1927; "Sesqui Auditorium Resold for $10,000," *PB*, August 9, 1927; "Sesqui Flora Worth $98,000 Brings but One $500 Offer," *PB*, August 10, 1927; "Sesqui Offices Moving," *PB*, August 11, 1927; "Sesqui Fountain Sold," *PB*, August 19, 1927.

19. "Great Sesqui Organ Sold for $25,000," *PI*, August 27, 1927; "Buys Big Organ for U. of P.," *NYT*, November 22, 1927; "Curtis Organ Rededication: Breathing New Life into Those Old Pipes," *University of Pennsylvania Almanac* 49, no. 7 (October 2002): available at http://www.upenn.edu/almanac/v49/n07/organ.html.

20. "Approve $200,000 Bills for Sesqui," *PB*, May 14, 1927; "Philadelphia Loss on Fair Is $206,987," *NYT*, June 19, 1927.

21. "Salvage Sales at the Sesqui-Centennial Suggest Retrospect and Prospect," *PB*, August 10, 1927.

22. "Kendrick Receives Sesqui Gold Medal," *PB*, August 3, 1927.

23. In Mr. Vare's City," *NYT*, August 17, 1927.

24. "In Mr. Vare's City," *NYT*, August 17, 1927; "Seething Politics Grip Philadelphia," *NYT*, August 21, 1927.

25. "Philadelphia Stirred By Mayoralty Fight," *NYT*, October 9, 1927; "Vare Ticket Wins in Philadelphia," *NYT*, November 9, 1927; "Philadelphia Vote Stirs Talk on Vare," *NYT*, November 9, 1927.

26. Vare, *My Forty Years in Politics*, pp. 179–180.

27. Salter, *The People's Choice*, p. 17.

28. Ibid.

29. Vare, *My Forty Years in Politics*, pp. 179–181.

30. Beers, *Pennsylvania Politics Today and Yesterday*, p. 65.

31. "Senate, By 56 to 30, Refuses Vare Seat," *NYT*, December 10, 1927; "Vare Reported Improved," December 17, 1927; Beers, *Pennsylvania Politics Today and Yesterday*, p. 65; Vare, *My Forty Years in Politics*, pp. 179–181.

32. "Kendrick Publicly Signs Six Ordinances," *PB*, December 30, 1927; "Says City Needs $7,847,743," *PB*, June 25, 1927; Weigley, *Philadelphia*, pp. 597, 623–624.

33. "Vare Ill, Senate Probe Is Delayed," *PB*, May 19, 1928; "Vare Has Pleurisy, Phila. Physician Finds," *PI*, May 22, 1928; "Vare Too Ill for Quiz," *PB*, May 26, 1928; "Vare Leaves Sick Bed," *PB*, May 31, 1928; "Vare Back from Shore," *PB*, June 4, 1928; Vare, *My Forty Years in* Politics, pp. 184–186.

34. Salter, *The People's Choice*, pp. 71–75.

35. "The Election Case of *William B. Wilson v. William S. Vare of Pennsylvania* (1929)," *United States Senate*, Senate Historical Office, available at www.senate.gov/artandhistory/history/common/contested_elections/109Wilson_Vare.htm.

36. Ibid.

37. "The Vare Waterloo," *Literary Digest*, December 21, 1929, pp. 9–15; Vare, *My Forty Years in Politics*, pp. 189–205; "The Election Case of William B. Wilson v. William S. Vare of Pennsylvania (1929)," *United States Senate*, Senate Historical Office, available at www.senate.gov/artandhistory/history/common/contested_elections/109Wilson_Vare.htm.

38. "Vare in Politics Over Forty Years," *PB*, n.d.; "William S. Vare Dies of Heart Attack at Shore Home," *PB*, August 7, 1934; "Wielded Great Power," *NYT*, August 8, 1934; "The Vare Waterloo," *Literary Digest*, December 21, 1929, pp. 9–15; Vare, *My Forty Years in Politics*, pp. 189–205; Salter, *The People's Choice*, pp. 71–75; "The Election Case of William B. Wilson v. William S. Vare of Pennsylvania (1929)," *United States Senate*, Senate Historical Office, available at www.senate.gov/artandhistory/history/common/contested_elections/109Wilson_Vare.htm.

39. "Quaker City Nerves Worn Raw by Gibes," *NYT*, April 21, 1929; Brown, *The Baldwin Locomotive Works 1831–1915*, p. 241; Westing, *The Locomotives That Baldwin Built*, p. 125; Burgess and Kennedy, *Centennial History of the Pennsylvania Railroad Company 1846–1946*, pp. 807–808; Roger D. Simon, "Great Depression," *The Encyclopedia of Greater Philadelphia*, available at http://philadelphiaencyclopedia.org/archive/great-depression/; Weigley, *Philadelphia*, pp. 601–605; Miller et al., *Still Philadelphia*, p. 110; Bill Ecenbarger, "A Fraying City Torn Asunder," *PI*, May 31, 2009; Bonnie R. Fox, "Unemployment Relief in Philadelphia, 1930–1932: A Study of the Depression's Impact on Volunteerism," *PMHB*, *93* no. 1 (January 1969): 86–108.

40. "How Much Did the Sesqui Cost?" *PB*, April 21, 1929.

41. p. 19.

42. pp. 21–24.

43. pp. 24–25.

44. The authors never explained how they arrived at their attendance figure of 6.4 million, which was 556,000 higher than the official attendance of 5.8 million. "Sesqui History to Appear in May," *PB*, April 16, 1929; Austin and Hauser, *The Sesqui-Centennial International Exposition*, pp. 19–26, 54.

Epilogue

★ ★ ★

IN SEPTEMBER 1934 a Philadelphia *Bulletin* reporter named Laura Lee journeyed to League Island Park to discover what remained of the Sesqui-Centennial nearly eight years after its closing. Before the Sesqui had opened in 1926, one journalist had described it as a "city of dreams done in rose and turquoise."[1] In 1934, Lee found that this "gorgeous and glittering reality" had given way to a desolate landscape of automobile graveyards and tar-paper shacks. Despite the millions of dollars spent to improve the local infrastructure, only a few houses stood between Packer Avenue, where the giant Liberty Bell had once towered, and Pattison Avenue, site of the main entrance. Most of the former fairgrounds were open fields that served as truck gardens or as makeshift parking lots on the rare occasion that the nearby Stadium was in use. By the time the Sesqui site had been cleared, the real estate slump and the Depression had deterred any development south of Packer Avenue.

At the southwest corner of Broad and Packer, all that remained of the Auditorium was its cracked concrete floor, covered with wrecked automobiles and a second-hand car shop. Across Broad Street, the Palace of Liberal Arts and Manufactures had given way to a poster-covered fence surrounding the South Philadelphia Base Ball Park. The lagoons and gardens of the Gladway had been supplanted by the steel skeleton of the new United States Naval Hospital. The framework of the structure's large central block had begun to take shape at one of the few active construction sites in the Depression-stricken city.

Across Pattison Avenue from the Naval Hospital stood an elegant rectangular building topped by a delicate spire. This was the American Swedish

Historical Museum, a monument to the contributions of Swedish immigrants to the United States like Declaration of Independence signer John Morton, inventor John Ericsson, and botanist Peter Kalm. The museum had been funded by Swedish Americans around the country, led by Dr. Amandus Johnson of the Philadelphia-based Swedish Colonial Society. Shortly after the Sesqui opened, Crown Prince Gustaf Adolf of Sweden had laid the cornerstone for what was then called the John Morton Memorial Building. But the shell had not been completed until November 1928, and the museum would not be dedicated until 1938. Although the facility was open to the public in 1934, Laura Lee noted that this "building of beauty and dignity" was "not frequently visited." It was able to remain in operation only because curator Amandus Johnson maintained it out of his own pocket. Johnson slept in his office many nights, acting as a watchman to protect the isolated structure from intruders.[2]

On the east side of Broad Street loomed the Sesqui-Centennial Stadium, now called the Municipal Stadium. Despite Mayor Kendrick's hopes after the Dempsey-Tunney bout, the rarely used arena had turned out to be a white elephant for the city, earning less than $100 during all of 1933. The coveted Army-Navy football game, one of the major rationales for building the Stadium, had returned to Philadelphia in 1932. But the two service academies had avoided the remote arena. Instead, they had played at

The American Swedish Historical Museum as seen from League Island Park in 1934.

Franklin Field on the University of Pennsylvania campus in 1932 and 1933, and were scheduled to meet there in 1934 as well.[3]

While all of the other major buildings erected for the Sesqui had been torn down by 1934, a few smaller structures survived. The Sesqui police station and emergency hospitals were used as maintenance buildings for League Island Park. The Russian Tea House and Outlook gazebo, holdovers from the park's first incarnation, still stood on the northern shore of Edgewater Lake. Stripped of its decorations and furnishings, the brick-and-concrete shell of the tea pavilion served as a boathouse. Another survivor was the Model Playground and Recreation Center. Painted a dignified white during the fair, the center was covered in bright orange in 1934. Large black letters spelled out its current attractions: "Spaghetti—Hot Dogs—Beer—Sandwiches—Dine-and-Dance." Detritus from the Sesqui could be found on the trash dumps dotting the area, including the rusted remains of some of the oil stoves that had failed to warm Marie of Romania during her visit to the Auditorium. This was all that remained of the "endless chain of fantastic palaces equaled in grandeur only by those of legendary Spain" that had once constituted Philadelphia's "Rainbow City."[4]

Philadelphians couldn't even take solace in the oft-repeated refrain that the Sesqui had failed because world's fairs were anachronistic in the age of the airplane and department store. In September 1934, the Century of Progress international exposition was nearing the end of its second triumphant season in Chicago's Grant Park. The Century of Progress had accomplished everything that the Sesqui had not. In the depths of the Depression, it had attracted nearly thirty-nine million visitors; captured their imagination through innovative and futuristic displays; launched new trends in architecture, design and technology; enhanced the reputation of its host city; and even turned a profit. Philadelphians could sniff that Chicago succeeded because its fair had legal beer and burlesque queen Sally Rand, but other critics realized that the Second City had crafted a fair brimming with modernity and vitality, qualities that the Sesqui sadly lacked.[5]

The woebegone condition of the Sesqui fairgrounds reflected the decrepitude of the City of Brotherly Love in 1934. Despite the optimism generated by the election of Franklin D. Roosevelt in 1932 and the enactment of New Deal legislation, Philadelphia seemed mired in despair. Its economy, sputtering before October 1929, had crashed along with the stock market. New construction, valued at $150 million in 1925, had plunged to less than $4 million by 1933. Average wages in 1934—for those lucky enough to have a job—had dropped 38 percent from their all-time high in 1926. Although business conditions had begun to improve slightly by 1934, 37 percent of Philadelphia workers remained unemployed at the start of the year, compared with a national average of 22 percent.[6]

With unemployment came hunger and homelessness. Nearly fifty thousand Philadelphia families went to bed hungry in 1934, while another seventy-one thousand struggled to survive with inadequate food, heat, or clothing. Delaware Avenue by the docks was haunted by dozens of idle men, women, and children, waiting to pounce on any vegetables that fell off passing produce wagons. When warm weather came, the fields of Fairmount Park were quickly denuded of dandelions. Their edible greens were a desperately needed source of nourishment for the hungry.[7]

In 1934 Philadelphia's municipal government was effectively bankrupt. The city had entered the fifth year of the Great Depression with a deficit of $10 million and more than $33 million in delinquent taxes. While Philadelphia had been able to pay the interest and sinking fund charges on its bonds at the end of 1933, it still owed $6 million on a loan taken out to meet municipal payrolls. The city's borrowing capacity was nonexistent. By

Homeless and unemployed veterans set up a Hooverville below Philadelphia's new Museum of Art during the summer of 1932. By October, Fairmount Park guards would burn down the shantytown.

the end of 1934, the city was $42 million over its legal debt limit, and debt service consumed one-half of all revenue.

Despite the city's desperate financial condition and high unemployment, Mayor J. Hampton Moore (elected to a second term in 1931) refused to seek or accept federal funds that would generate much-needed jobs. A disgusted Governor Gifford Pinchot (also reelected in 1930) did an end run around the intractable Moore, appointing a state-run Philadelphia County Relief Board that supplied some destitute Philadelphians with the necessities of life.[8]

Between 1930 and 1933, fifty Philadelphia banks had closed their doors because of insolvency. By 1934, they had been joined by sixteen hundred of the city's thirty-four hundred building and loan associations. The collapse of these institutions cost local investors and depositors a grand total of $5 billion. The largest failures were the two banks most closely associated with the Sesqui-Centennial and its finance chairman, Albert M. Greenfield: the Franklin Trust Company, with $37 million in deposits, and Bankers Trust Company, with $35 million in deposits. After watching his financial empire crumble, Greenfield would declare bankruptcy by the end of the decade. It would be another decade before he began his phoenixlike resurrection, ending his career as the universally respected "Mr. Philadelphia."[9]

Center City was filled with new buildings in 1934, the legacy of the last, heady days of the Roaring Twenties. Yet signs of the economic collapse were everywhere. Philadelphia had a new Pennsylvania Railroad terminal at Thirtieth Street, its crisp Modernist design a welcome change from the Victorian pile of Broad Street Station. Yet on the maze of tracks leading into the station, children searched for stray lumps of coal to heat their homes. At Twelfth and Market Streets, the streamlined skyscraper of the Philadelphia Savings Fund Society soared above its neighbors like an Art Moderne emissary from another galaxy. Soon after it opened in 1932, city residents joked grimly that the twenty-seven-foot-tall, red neon letters atop the building that spelled out "PSFS" represented "Philadelphia Slowly Faces Starvation."[10]

Amid the gleaming facades of its new structures, Philadelphia crumbled. All work on its subway system had been suspended when Moore took office, except for completion of the Ridge Avenue spur to Eighth and Market Streets. The South Broad Street subway to Snyder Avenue would remain without tracks or stations until 1937. The $6 million tunnel built for the Locust Street subway between Eighth and Eighteenth Streets was sealed off, to be left unused until 1952. Meanwhile, the once-mighty Philadelphia Rapid Transit Company declared bankruptcy. Philadelphians began to wonder if they would even have a transit system by the end of 1934.

Much of the city was dark at night: burned-out streetlights were rarely replaced, while working ones were switched off in low-traffic areas. Drivers proceeded with caution along unlit streets, afraid of damaging their cars on the numerous potholes that remained unfilled. Horse-drawn wagons still collected much of the city's garbage. With no funds available to upgrade the city's inadequate water system, many Philadelphians collected their drinking water from streams in Fairmount Park. Bad storms in the coal regions of Northeast Pennsylvania would cause "a bluish-black liquid stinking of chlorine, puckery with alum" to gush from kitchen taps. Before long, the fiscal crisis would leave Philadelphia with 248 policemen to patrol its 143 square miles, and a brigade of pre-Depression fire engines that often broke down before they reached the fire.[11]

As the Depression stretched on, the reassuring rituals that softened the harshness of life gradually disappeared. For the first time since 1918, when America was at war, the Mummers did not parade on Broad Street on January 1, 1934. There was no city money available for prizes. Unwilling to let the tradition die completely, about twenty string bands donned old costumes and paraded around their neighborhoods. One of the few groups to buy new outfits was the Quaker City String Band, who wore helmets topped by a large blue eagle with red feathers. Their costumes celebrated the National Recovery Administration or NRA, established the previous summer as the keystone in President Roosevelt's New Deal. Although Philadelphia would not elect a Democratic mayor until 1951, the Mummers' outfits were a portent that the great monolith of the Republican Organization was beginning to crumble.[12]

On August 7, 1934, William S. Vare suffered a heart attack at his Atlantic City home and died within half an hour. The sixty-six-year-old Vare, who still walked with a cane and spoke with a slur as a result of his 1928 stroke, had been in ill health for some time. His physical condition had deteriorated after the May 1934 Republican primary, when an anti-Vare bloc had wrested power away from his ward leaders throughout the city. In early June, the "Duke of South Philadelphia" was stripped of his title of honorary chairman of the Republican City Committee. The *New York Times* crowed that Philadelphia had experienced a "real coup" that included "the downfall of National Committeeman William S. Vare as dictator of the Philadelphia Republican Machine."[13]

Like his brothers Edwin and George, Bill Vare left behind much less money than people expected. When Vare's will was probated, his estate was calculated to be $1,459,917, a fortune in 1934 but roughly one-tenth of his estimated worth. Once his debts were discharged, the estate was reduced to $1,035,923. That was enough for his family to live comfortably, but not enough to underwrite a dynasty after his death. Much of Vare's wealth, including the estimated $15 to $20 million in contracts his construction company had been awarded during the Kendrick administration, had gone into the maintenance of the massive Organization and the preservation of his power base.

Every Christmas Vare had personally distributed thousands of dollars when he made the rounds at City Hall, handing out ten- or twenty-dollar gold pieces to as many functionaries as possible. Tens of thousands more were distributed to the army of policemen, committeemen, and poll watchers who enforced Vare's will throughout the city. Then there were the untold millions spent over the decades on his constituents in the name of "Service"—the baskets of food and firewood given to destitute households; the candy and toys handed out to South Philly kids at Christmas parties; and the cash box filled with five and ten dollar bills, doled out to any loyal voter who needed a few bucks. Even as his power waned, Vare spent $10,000 for a dinner at the Bellevue-Stratford for five hundred influential guests. For the Duke of South Philadelphia, nothing could stand in the way of his complete control of the Organization and local politics.[14]

W. Freeland Kendrick lasted nearly two decades longer than his erstwhile political patron. His political career truncated by the Sesqui, Kendrick went to work for Albert M. Greenfield's Commonwealth Casualty Company after leaving City Hall. He remained active in the Shriners, helping to engineer the construction of seventeen hospitals for crippled and chronically ill children around the country. In the 1940s Kendrick was named president of Greenfield's Benjamin Franklin Hotel Company, occupying a suite at the hotel with his wife. In March 1953 the seventy-eight-year-old Kendrick died of a cerebral hemorrhage. The ex-mayor who was once rumored to have millions of dollars stashed in secret accounts left his wife a modest estate valued at $58,427. His assets included one of the largest collections of fraternal jewelry in Philadelphia, valued at $1,265. It was a memento of the long-gone days when thousands of Shriners had paraded around City Hall, celebrating the election of "Brother Freel" as the imperial potentate of the Ancient Arabic Order of the Nobles of the Mystic Shrine.[15]

THE TRAUMATIC EXPERIENCE of the Sesqui-Centennial may have transformed Philadelphia into a city wary of undertaking any major celebrations for decades afterward. Planning for a Bicentennial International Exposition began in the 1950s, when Philadelphia was riding high as a model of enlightened urban renewal. City Planning Commissioner Ed Bacon had transformed the decrepit burg by restoring the eighteenth-century splendor of Society Hill, replacing Broad Street Station and the Chinese Wall with a modern office complex called Penn Center, and initiating an entertainment/retail development on the Delaware riverfront called Penn's Landing. Bacon envisioned a magnificent world's fair as completing Philadelphia's transformation into a modern Utopia, with no slums, plenty of green space, and an integrated transportation system. But after years of political squabbling, social unrest, economic retreat, and millions of wasted dollars, Philadelphia abandoned the idea of hosting a third world's fair. Instead, it celebrated the Bicentennial on a modest scale, assisted by $50 million in federal funds. It restored its historic shrines, built replicas of others like the Declaration House and City Tavern, constructed a Liberty Bell Pavilion and Visitors' Center, and fitted out a few new museums.[16]

Philadelphia's Bicentennial turned out to be a pleasant affair, even after Mayor Frank Rizzo scared away tourists by calling for federal troops to combat the hordes of hippie protestors he felt sure would descend on the city. Between fourteen and twenty million visitors came to Philadelphia in 1976, far short of the fifty to one hundred million originally expected. Among them was President Gerald Ford, who addressed the nation from Independence Hall on July 4. Two days later, Queen Elizabeth II of Great Britain visited the city and gave the people of America a new Bicentennial Bell. Despite these high points, the Bicentennial became one of Philadelphia's most bitter disappointments. "The new Atlantis described in 1965," wrote one reporter, "has become the Big Block Party of 1975."[17] The inability to produce a viable world's fair after two decades of planning and millions of wasted dollars wounded the city's collective self-confidence and tarnished its national image for years.

Unfortunately, the 1976 festivities shone in comparison with Philadelphia's attempt to mark the bicentennial of the signing of the U. S. Constitution in Independence Hall in 1787. By April 1987, the celebration had been derided as a "fiasco" by the Philadelphia *Daily News*. What planners had envisioned as a six-month celebration of the Constitution had dwindled to a fifteen-hour spectacle on September 17, culminating in the "Great American Picnic" at Penn's Landing. The only lasting benefit of the event to Philadelphia was that the statue of William Penn atop City Hall, which had grown corroded and green over the years, was finally cleaned. *Newsweek* sighed that "if the people planning Philadelphia's tribute to the Constitution had been in charge in 1786, we'd probably be driving on the left side of the street today."[18]

THE PHILADELPHIA OF 2016 is a very different city than the Philadelphia of 1926, in both positive and negative ways. It is smaller today than it was in the Sesqui-Centennial year, when it boasted roughly 1.9 million inhabitants. After reaching an all-time peak of 2.07 million in 1950, Philadelphia's population shrank 26 percent to 1.53 million in 2010. Reversing this long-term trend, it has begun to regain inhabitants in recent years, as immigrants, empty-nesters, and college graduates have flocked to a revitalized Center City.[19]

Philadelphia is poorer today than it was in 1926, when the Workshop of the World could offer a decent factory job to any reasonably intelligent person. Its median household income of $36,836 puts it near the bottom of the ten largest cities in the United States, outranking only Cleveland and Detroit. Twenty-six percent of Philadelphia households live in poverty. In some tracts of North Philadelphia, home to the abandoned factories that once employed tens of thousands, poverty is nearly universal. The city's rate of deep poverty—households with incomes of less than $12,000 for a family of four—is 12.3 percent, the highest among the ten largest American cities. Yet Philadelphia is safer than it has been in recent years: the number of homicides dropped from 406 in 2006 to 247 in 2014.[20]

Philadelphia in 2016 is a more honest city than it was in 1926. Much of the credit for this goes to Michael A. Nutter, who served as the city's ninety-eighth mayor between 2008 and 2015. Nutter labored to eliminate the "pay-to-play" ethos and culture of corruption that were endemic features of Philadelphia government for decades. Between 2008 and 2015, his legal team instigated seventy arrests and the firing or resignation of 209 city workers, saving Philadelphia taxpayers an estimated $46 million. Nutter's administration also worked to improve access to city services, reform planning and zoning policies, overhaul its archaic property tax system, and create a land bank to make the city's thirty-two thousand vacant or abandoned properties available for redevelopment. His willingness to increase taxes and cut services gave the city an A+ bond rating, its highest in decades.

Like Blankenburg, Moore, and other reform mayors, Nutter was criticized for his inability to play the political game and strike deals with power brokers. His administration was marked by ongoing stalemates with City Council and public-sector unions. One City Hall staffer called Nutter "a failed politician" who "never learned to play with the other children in the sandbox." As 2016 begins, Philadelphians are waiting to see how Nutter's successor, former Democratic City Councilman James F. Kenney, will maintain his legacy.[21]

Despite the city's serious social ills—including a struggling educational system described by one educator as "the most under-resourced urban school district in the nation"—Philadelphia is enjoying an enhanced public profile in 2016. The visit of Pope Francis to the city in September 2015 was a major coup, although business leaders blamed overly stringent security measures for disappointing attendance and revenues. Planning is well underway for the National Democratic Convention, to be held in the Wells Fargo Center in South Philadelphia (site of the former Sesqui-Centennial Stadium) in July 2016. More and more, Philadelphia is growing accustomed to shining on the national and international stage.[22]

Center City, Penn's original Green Country Town, has blossomed into a dazzling civic center. This twelve-hundred-acre rectangle is still home to Philadelphia's municipal government, largest businesses, and major civic organizations. It is the heart of the recent renaissance, filled with multimillion-dollar properties; four-star restaurants; chic nightspots; and dozens of theaters, concert halls, and museums. Real estate is booming: in 2014, the city issued building permits for nearly four thousand units with an estimated value of $879 million. Comcast Corporation, one of the city's largest employers, has begun construction on its second downtown office tower, a 1,121-foot-tall Innovation and Technology Center that will replace its original tower as the city's tallest skyscraper. The revitalization of Center City has extended into once-marginal neighborhoods on its fringes, like Northern Liberties, East Kensington, Brewerytown, and Point Breeze.

On the west side of City Hall, the concrete wasteland known as Dilworth Plaza has been transformed into Dilworth Park, a green public space that hosts concerts, holiday markets, and winter ice skating. Initiatives to create more parkland within Center City have resulted in the extension of the Schuylkill River Trail via the Schuylkill Banks Boardwalk, the development of the Race Street Pier, and the refurbishment of Sister Cities Park on Logan Circle. On the Benjamin Franklin Parkway, the world-famous Barnes Collection has joined the Museum of Art, Rodin Museum, and Franklin Institute to create a civic "cultural campus." Outdoor cafés, refurbished parks, and improved pedestrian amenities are helping to bring the Parkway closer to its original conception as Philadelphia's Champs-Élysées.

Philadelphia, once the epitome of self-doubt and self-criticism, is growing accustomed to receiving accolades like being named one of *Travel + Leisure*'s top restaurant cities, and being rated number three (behind Milan and Cuba) on the *New York Times*'s list of "52 Places to Go In

2015." UNESCO named Philadelphia as the first World Heritage City in the United States in 2015, putting it in the same league as Jerusalem, Prague, and Paris. For the first time in decades, the Quaker City is becoming positively chic.[23]

CAPITALIZING ON THIS rebound, a group of civic leaders has banded together to mark the nation's 250th birthday in Philadelphia in 2026. USA250, the organization dedicated to planning a major celebration of America's quarter millennial, is betting that this event will enhance and extend the city's current upswing, and cement its status as a world-class metropolis. By bringing together citizens and leaders from all fifty states, it hopes "to renew the American project through a year-long celebration and exploration of Equality, Life, Liberty and the Pursuit of Happiness in the modern era."[24] Headed by Board Chairman Andrew Hohns and Director Jon Grabelle Herrmann, the organization had raised more than $200,000 as of early January 2016. In a potentially ominous echo of 1926, donors are being thanked with red, white, and blue buttons marked "Semiquin," shorthand for Semiquincentennial.

Specific information on how USA250 will manifest itself is rudimentary at present. Hohns has thrown out such possibilities as Philadelphia hosting blockbuster events like Major League Baseball's All-Star Game, or even Super Bowl LX. He envisions urban improvements like a new subway line along the Delaware River, or covering over the Vine Street Expressway, the sunken interstate that slices through some of the city's most historic neighborhoods. Physical improvements, however, would play a secondary role to the development of shared goals that would advance the quality of American life. These might include major drug companies committing to curing or eradicating a disease; individual states vowing to increase childhood literacy; or environmental agencies pledging to improve water quality within a specific region.

Echoing John Wanamaker, both Hohns and Herrmann insist that while USA250 should be a national celebration, it should be centered in the City of Brotherly Love. "Philadelphia's DNA," Hohns states, "is a reflection of that of the United States." The city's multicultural and multiethnic makeup, its legacies of personal and religious freedom, and its traditions of tolerance and innovation make it the perfect place for America to set a course for its future. "Philadelphia is America and America is Philadelphia," Hohns explains. "Our hopes, challenges, dreams, accomplishments can be reflected in every neighborhood in this city."[25]

The surest sign that USA250 was a success, Hohns augurs, "would be that on July 5, 2026, the celebrations would begin rather than end." Concurring, Herrmann would like the final legacy of USA250 to be that "in its 250th year, we reinvigorated the American project with Philadelphia as the center." With what may be a nervous glance over his shoulder at past celebrations, Herrmann insists that hopes for the outcome of the event must be kept within reason. "We are starting with zero public expectations beyond 'Don't screw it up' and 'Be careful about any use of public resources.'"[26]

A WORLD'S FAIR is a concrete illusion—or perhaps, more accurately, a plaster illusion. It is a chimerical city of dreams, a magical mirage of a metropolis that rises overnight from a swamp, dazzles onlookers for a few months, and sinks back into the earth as quickly as it appeared, usually taking taxpayers' money along with it. In a few lucky instances—Philadelphia in 1876, Chicago in 1893, New York in 1939—the magic persists long after the buildings and budget have evaporated. This afterglow can enchant an entire city into accepting an image of itself as a noble entity, a place that freely gives its residents and visitors its gifts and its heart's affections, to paraphrase Roman Payne.

In other instances, a world's fair can suck the soul of a city into its demolition pit, along with the cracked concrete of its fairy palaces and pulverized plaster of its heroic statuary. A failed world's fair is like a disastrous love affair, leaving behind anger, disillusionment, and self-recrimination among the surrounding community in its wake. Nine decades after the Sesqui-Centennial raised and then dashed the aspirations of the Quaker City, it remains to be seen whether the Semiquincentennial (dear God, do people learn nothing from the past?) will transform Philadelphia into a City of Dreams in 2026.

NOTES

1. "Sunset Ideal Time for Visiting Sesqui," *PB*, May 20, 1926.

2. "Dr. Amandus Johnson and the Museum Founding," *PR*, June 28, 1938; Johnson, *The American Swedish Historical Museum*, pp. 7–32, ASHM Archives.

3. Keels, *Forgotten Philadelphia*, pp. 200–202.

4. Laura Lee, "Weeds and Junk Adorn Sesqui Site," *PB*, September 8, 1934; "From Sesqui Site to Ghost Village in 12 Years," *PB*, July 19, 1939.

5. Findling and Pelle, *Encyclopedia of World's Fairs and Expositions*, pp. 268–277; Ganz, *The 1933 Chicago World's Fair*, pp. 59–62, 68–70.

6. Hamilton, *Mr. Philadelphia*, p. 121; Miller et al., *Philadelphia Stories*, pp. 45–46; "Philadelphia Idle 37%," *NYT*, March 21, 1934.

7. Miller et al., *Philadelphia Stories*, pp. 47–48.

8. "Philadelphia," *NYT*, January 8, 1934; "Ph. Rolls Up 2.22 Per Cent in Year," *NYT*, August 29, 1934; "Uncertainty in Philadelphia," *NYT*, September 23, 1934.

9. Weigley, *Philadelphia*, pp. 609, 611–612.

10. Tatum, *Penn's Great Town*, pp. 131–132.

11. "Philadelphia Utility Faces Receivership," *NYT*, June 13, 1934; Weigley, *Philadelphia*, pp. 610–611; "Philadelphia's Hole," *Time* Magazine, January 8, 1940.

12. "No Mummers' Parade," *NYT*, January 2, 1934.

13. "Wm. S. Vare Dies of Heart Attack at Shore Home," *PB*, August 7, 1934; "G.O.P. Leader Succumbs at Shore Home," *PR*, August 8, 1934; "W.S. Vare Dies at 66 of a Heart Attack," *NYT*, August 8, 1934; "Vare No Longer Philadelphia Boss," *NYT*, June 17, 1934; Lawrence E. Davies, "Philadelphia G.O.P. Seeks after Votes," *NYT*, August 19 1934; J. T. Salter, "The End of Vare," *Political Science Quarterly* 50, no. 2 (June 1935): 214–235.

14. Salter, *The People's Choice*, pp. 84–85.

15. "Masons Name Kendrick," *PB*, January 10, 1948; "15,000 Hail Shriners' Potentate," *PI*, December 7, 1948; "Former Mayor Kendrick Dies Suddenly at 78," *PB*, March 20, 1953; "W. F. Kendrick, 78, of Shrine Is Dead," *NYT*, March 21, 1953; "W.F. Kendrick Dies; Ex-Mayor of Philadelphia," *Herald-Tribune*, March 21, 1953; "Kendrick Estate Set at $58,427," *PI*, May 15, 1953.

16. Knowles, "Staying Too Long at the Fair," pp. 104–108; Wolf, "The Bicentennial City 1968–1982"; Weigley, *Philadelphia*, pp. 726–728; "Scattered Anniversary," *Time*, June 12, 1972; Keels, *Forgotten Philadelphia*, pp. 248–249.

17. "The Big 200th Bash," *Time*, July 5, 1976.

18. Philip Lentz, "Philadelphia's Festival for Constitution Bicentennial Flounders," *Chicago Tribune*, April 12, 1987; William K. Stevens, "Constitution Event Off to Rocky Start; Philadelphia's Reputation at Stake in Bicentennial Observance," *NYT*, March 23, 1987; William K. Stevens, "After 2 Centuries, Great Day for Constitution," *NYT*, September 18, 1987.

19. Pew Charitable Trusts, *Philadelphia 2015: The State of the City*, pp. 6–8; "State & County QuickFacts: Philadelphia County, Pennsylvania," United States Census Bureau, available at http://quickfacts.census.gov/qfd/states/42/42101.html.

20. Pew Charitable Trusts, *Philadelphia 2015: The State of the City*, pp. 2–5; Alfred Lubrano, "Among the 10 Largest Cities, Philly Has Highest Deep-Poverty Rate," *PI*, October 1, 2015; Zuylen-Wood, "What's Your Problem with Michael Nutter, Philadelphia?" *Philadelphia*, January 4, 2015.

21. Patrick Kerkstra, "The Power Crowd: Incorruptible," *Philadelphia*, July 2014, pp. 32–38; "Accomplishments," *City of Philadelphia*, available at http:///www.phila.gov/InformationCenters/Accomplishments/Pages/default.aspx.

22. Denisa R. Superville, "School Budget Problems Have Deep Roots in Philadelphia," *Education Week*, May 6, 2014, available at http:///www.edweek.org/ew/articles/2014/05/07/30philly.h33.html; "Papal Visit Was Disappointing to Many Businesses, Nutter Blames Media," 6ABC Action News, available at http://6abc.com/business/papal-visit-was-disappointing-to-many-businesses-nutter-blames-media/1006794; "2016 Democratic National Convention," Visit Philadelphia, http:///available at www.visitphilly.com/events/philadelphia/2016–democratic-national-convention-in-philadelphia. .

23. Hurdle, "5 Big Projects: Status Update," Philadelphia *City Paper*, pp. 10–14; "52 Places to Go in 2015," *NYT*, December 21, 2015, available at www.nytimes.com/interactive/2015/01/11/travel/52–places-to-go-in-2015.html; Anya von Bremzen, "T+L's Best

New Restaurants: 2015," Travel + Leisure, January 14, 2016, available at http:///www.travelandleisure.com/slideshows/tls-best-new-restaurants-2015–edition.

24. USA250, available at www.usa250inc.org.

25. Telephone interview with Andrew Hohns, August 20, 2014.

26. USA250, available at www.usa250inc.org; telephone interview with Jon Grabelle Herrmann, July 17, 2014; telephone interview with Andrew Hohns, August 20, 2014; "USA250: By the People, for the People," Presentation prepared by USA250; Michael Callahan, "Can USA250 Make Philly the Star of America's 250th Birthday?" *Philadelphia*, September 26, 2013; Matt Gelb, "Planning the Nation's Birthday Party . . . for 2026," *PI*, January 17, 2016, p. 1.

Bibliography

★ ★ ★

PERIODICAL KEY

CPD: Cleveland *Plain Dealer*
DI: Dearborn Independent
JDB: Jewish Daily Bulletin
JTA: Jewish Telegraphic Agency
NYT: New York Times
PMHB: Pennsylvania Magazine of History and Biography
PB: Philadelphia *Bulletin*
PI: Philadelphia *Inquirer*
PNA: Philadelphia *North American*
PP: Philadelphia *Press*
PPL: Philadelphia *Public Ledger*
PR: Philadelphia Record
PT: Philadelphia Tribune
TT: Trenton *Times*

REPOSITORY/COLLECTION KEY

APS: American Philosophical Society
ASHM: American Swedish Historical Museum
CHHS: Chestnut Hill Historical Society
COM1926/SCA: Committee of 1926 Sesqui-Centennial Archives
HSP/AMGP: Historical Society of Pennsylvania/Albert M. Greenfield Papers (Collection 1959)
PCA/SCEA: Philadelphia City Archives/Sesqui-Centennial Exhibition Association Records.
TUUA/SCA: Temple University Urban Archives/Sesqui-Centennial Archives.
UMAL/WEBD: University of Massachusetts Amherst Libraries, W. E. B. Du Bois Papers, Special Collections and University Archives.
VR/AJA: Victor Rosewater Papers/American Jewish Archives

BOOKS

Albrecht, Harry A. *Broad Street Station, Pennsylvania Railroad, Philadelphia, 1881–1952.* Clifton Heights, PA: Steam Locomotives of Yesteryear, 1972.

Alexander, Michael. *Jazz Age Jews.* Princeton, NJ: Princeton University Press, 2001.

Allen, Frederick Lewis. *Only Yesterday and Since Yesterday.* New York: Bonanza Books, 1986.

Arkell, Roland, and Catherine Saunders-Watson. *The Vendue Masters.* Philadelphia: Samuel T. Freeman, 2005.

Arrigale, Lawrence M., and Thomas H. Keels. *Philadelphia's Golden Age of Retail.* Charleston, SC: Arcadia Publishing, 2012.

Asbury, Herbert. *The Great Illusion: An Informal History of Prohibition.* Garden City, NY: Doubleday, 1950.

Austin, E. L., and Odell Hauser. *The Sesqui-Centennial International Exposition: A Record Based on Official Data and Departmental Records.* Philadelphia: Current Publications, 1929.

Bach, Penny Balkin. *Public Art in Philadelphia.* Philadelphia: Temple University Press, 1992.

Baldwin, Lou, Monsignor Michael J. Carroll, Joseph J. Casino, Father John P. Collins, Shawn Weldon. *Our Faith-Filled Heritage: The Church of Philadelphia Bicentennial as a Diocese 1808–2008.* Philadelphia: Archdiocese of Philadelphia, 2007.

Baldwin, Neil. *Henry Ford and the Jews: The Mass Production of Hate.* New York: Public Affairs/Perseus Books Group, 2001.

Baltzell, E. Digby. *Philadelphia Gentlemen: The Making of a National Upper Class.* Chicago: Quadrangle Books, 1971.

Barry, John M. *The Great Influenza: The Epic Story of the Deadliest Plague in History.* New York: Viking Press, 2004.

Beers, Paul B. *Pennsylvania Politics Today and Yesterday: The Tolerable Accommodation.* University Park: Pennsylvania State University Press, 1980.

Bencker, Ralph. "The Pennsylvania State Building at the Sesqui-Centennial International Exposition," *The American Architect*, Volume 130, CXXX, 1926, p. 384.

Biddle, Cordelia Drexel. *My Philadelphia Father.* New York: Doubleday, 1955.

Biddle, Francis. *The Llanfear Pattern.* New York: Charles Scribner's Sons, 1927.

Biddle, Gertrude B., and Sarah D. Lowrie, eds. *Notable Women of Philadelphia.* Philadelphia: University of Pennsylvania Press, 1942.

Binzen, Peter, ed. *Nearly Everybody Read It: Snapshots of the Philadelphia* Bulletin. Philadelphia: Camino Books, 1998.

Birmingham, Stephen. *The Grandes Dames.* New York: Simon and Schuster, 1982.

Biswanger, Ray. *Music in the Marketplace: The Story of Philadelphia's Historic Wanamaker Organ from John Wanamaker to Lord & Taylor.* Bryn Mawr, PA: Friends of the Wanamaker Organ Press, 1999.

Blankenburg, Lucretia L. *The Blankenburgs of Philadelphia.* Philadelphia: John C. Winston, 1929.

Blaszczyk, Regina Lee. *The Color Revolution*, Cambridge, MA: M.I.T. Press, 2012.

Blodget, Lorin. *The Industries of Philadelphia as Shown by the Manufacturing Census of 1870, Compared with 1860 and Estimates for 1875 and 1876.* Philadelphia: Collins, 1877.

Boisseau, T. J., and Abigail M. Markwyn, eds. *Gendering the Fair: Histories of Women and Gender at World's Fairs.* Urbana: University of Illinois Press, 2010.

Bok, Edward W. *The Americanization of Edward Bok: The Autobiography of a Dutch Boy Fifty Years After*. New York: Charles Scribner's Sons, 1922.

———. *Twice Thirty: Some Short and Simple Annals of the Road*. New York: Charles Scribner's Sons, 1925.

Bond, Birgitta H. "PA Impressionists at the SC Intl Expo, 1926." In *PA Impressionism*, edited by Brian H. Peterson, pp. 330–331. Doylestown, PA: James A. Michener Art Museum, 2002.

Bornstein, George. *The Colors of Zion*. Cambridge, MA: Harvard University Press, 2011.

Braeman, John, Robert H. Bremner, and David Brody, eds. *Change and Continuity in Twentieth-Century America: The 1920s*. Columbus: Ohio State University Press, 1968.

Breslin, Jimmy. *Damon Runyon*. New York: Ticknor and Fields, 1991.

Brown, John K. *The Baldwin Locomotive Works 1831–1915: A Study in American Industrial Practice*. Baltimore, MD: Johns Hopkins University Press, 1995.

Brownlee, David. *Building the City Beautiful: The Benjamin Franklin Parkway and the Philadelphia Museum of Art*. Philadelphia, PA: Philadelphia Museum of Art, 1989.

———. *Making a Modern Classic: The Architecture of the Philadelphia Museum of Art*, Philadelphia, PA: Philadelphia Museum of Art, 1997.

Bruinius, Harry. *Better for All the World: The Secret History of Forced Sterilization and America's Quest for Racial Purity*. New York: Alfred A. Knopf, 2006.

Burgess, George H., and Miles C. Kennedy. *Centennial History of the Pennsylvania Railroad Company 1846–1946*. Philadelphia: Pennsylvania Railroad, 1949.

Burt, Nathaniel. *The Perennial Philadelphians: The Anatomy of an American Aristocracy*. Boston: Little, Brown, 1963.

Cardinell, John. A Pictorial Record of the Sesqui-Centennial International Exposition. Philadelphia: Author, 1926.

Cavanaugh, Jack. *Tunney: Boxing's Brainiest Champ and His Upset of the Great Jack Dempsey*. New York: Random House, 2006.

Chalmers, David M. *Hooded Americanism: The History of the Ku Klux Klan*. Durham, NC: Duke University Press, 1987.

Chasins, Abram. *Leopold Stokowski: A Profile*. New York: Hawthorn Books, 1979.

Chernow, Ron. *The House of Morgan: An American Banking Dynasty and the Rise of Modern Finance*. New York: Atlantic Monthly Press, 1990.

Clark, Dennis. *The Irish in Philadelphia: Ten Generations of Urban Experience*. Philadelphia: Temple University Press, 1973.

Conn, Steven. *Museums and American Intellectual Life, 1876–1926*. Chicago: University of Chicago Press, 1998.

Contosta, David R. *A Philadelphia Family: The Houstons and Woodwards of Chestnut Hill*. Philadelphia: University of Pennsylvania Press, 1988.

———. *Suburb in the City: Chestnut Hill, Philadelphia, 1850–1990*. Columbus: Ohio State University Press, 1992.

Coolidge, Calvin. *The Autobiography of Calvin Coolidge*. New York: Cosmopolitan Book, 1931.

Cooper, John Milton. *Woodrow Wilson: A Biography*. New York: Random House, 2009, pp. 286–287.

Countryman, Matthew J. *Up South: Civil Rights and Black Power in Philadelphia*. Philadelphia: University of Pennsylvania Press, 2006.

Curcio, Vincent. *Henry Ford*. New York: Oxford University Press, 2013.

Davenport, Walter. *Power and Glory: The Life of Boies Penrose*. New York: G. P. Putnam's Sons, 1931.

Davis, Marni. *Jews and Booze: Becoming American in the Age of Prohibition*. New York: New York University Press, 2012.

Dempsey, Jack, Bob Consodine, and Bill Slocum. *Dempsey by the Man Himself*. New York: Simon and Schuster, 1960.

Di Giacomo, Donna J. *Italians of Philadelphia*. Charleston, SC: Arcadia Publishing, 2007.

Dinnerstein, Leonard. *Antisemitism in America*. New York: Oxford University Press, 1994.

Donaghy, Thomas J., FSC. *Philadelphia's Finest: A History of Education in the Catholic Archdiocese, 1692–1970*. Philadelphia: American Catholic Historical Society, 1972.

Dorwart, Jeffrey M., with Jean K. Wolf. *The Philadelphia Navy Yard from the Birth of the U.S. Navy to the Nuclear Age*. Philadelphia: University of Pennsylvania Press/Barra Foundation, 2001.

Dubin, Murray. *South Philadelphia: Mummers, Memories, and the Melrose Diner*. Philadelphia: Temple University Press, 1996.

Du Bois, W. E. B. *The Autobiography of W. E. B. Du Bois*. New York: International Publishers, 1997.

———. *The Philadelphia Negro: A Social Study*. New York: Schocken Books, 1967.

Evensen, Bruce J. *When Dempsey Fought Tunney: Heroes, Hokum and Storytelling in the Jazz Age*. Knoxville: University of Tennessee Press, 1996.

Fairmount Park Art Association. *Sculpture of a City: Philadelphia's Treasures in Bronze and Stone*. New York: Walker Publishing, 1974.

Fausold, Martin L. *Gifford Pinchot: Bull Moose Progressive*. Syracuse, NY: Syracuse University Press, 1961.

Feingold, Henry L. *The Jewish People in America: A Time for Searching: Entering the Mainstream 1920–1945*. Baltimore, MD: Johns Hopkins University Press/American Jewish Historical Society, 1992.

Findling, John E., and Kimberly D. Pelle, eds. *Encyclopedia of World's Fairs and Expositions*. Jefferson, NC: McFarland, 2008.

Ford, Henry, with Samuel Crowther. *My Life and Work*. Garden City, NY: Garden City Publishing, 1922.

Fowler, Gene. *Beau James: The Life and Times of Jimmy Walker*. New York: Viking Press, 1949.

Franklin, Vincent P. *The Education of Black Philadelphia: The Social and Educational History of a Minority Community, 1900–1950*. Philadelphia: University of Pennsylvania Press, 1979.

Freedman, Ellen. "The Women's Committee and Their High Street Exhibit at the Philadelphia Sesquicentennial Exposition of 1926." Master's thesis, University of Pennsylvania, 1988.

Friedman, Murray, ed. *Jewish Life in Philadelphia 1830–1940*. Philadelphia: ISHI Publications, 1983.

Ganz, Cheryl R. *The 1933 Chicago World's Fair: A Century of Progress*. Urbana: University of Illinois Press, 2008.

Gatewood, Willard B. *Aristocrats of Color: The Black Elite, 1880–1920*. Bloomington: Indiana University Press, 1990.

Gibbons, Herbert Adams. *John Wanamaker*. New York: Harper, 1926.

Giberti, Bruno. *Designing the Centennial: A History of the 1876 International Exhibition in Philadelphia*. Lexington: University Press of Kentucky, 2002.

Glassberg, David. *American Historical Pageantry: The Uses of Tradition in Early Twentieth-Century America*. Chapel Hill: University of North Carolina Press, 1990.

Glazer, Irvin R. *Philadelphia Theaters: A Pictorial Architectural History*. New York: Athenaeum of Philadelphia and Dover Publications, 1994.

Gray, William F. *Philadelphia's Architecture*. Philadelphia: City History Society, 1915.

Greenberg, David. *The American Presidents: Calvin Coolidge*. New York: Times Books/Henry Holt, 2006.

Greenspan, Anders. *Creating Colonial Williamsburg*. Washington, DC: Smithsonian Institution Press, 2002.

Grossman, Elizabeth Greenwell. *The Civic Architecture of Paul Cret*. Cambridge: Cambridge University Press, 1996.

Hauser, Thomas. *The Boxing Scene*. Philadelphia: Temple University Press, 2009.

Hershberg, Theodore, ed. *Philadelphia: Work, Space, Family and Group Experience in the 19th Century*. New York: Oxford University Press, 1981.

Hodos, Jerome. "The 1876 Centennial in Philadelphia: Elite Networks and Political Culture." In *Social Capital in the City: Community and Civic Life in Philadelphia*, edited by Richardson Dilworth, 19–39. Philadelphia: Temple University Press, 2006.

Hosmer, Charles B., Jr. *Presence of the Past: A History of the Preservation Movement in the United States before Williamsburg*. New York: G. P. Putnam's Sons, 1965.

Hunter, Ruth H. *The Trade and Convention Center of Philadelphia: Its Birth and Renascence*. Philadelphia: City of Philadelphia, 1962.

Jackson, Anna. *Expo: International Expositions 1851–2010*. London: V&A Publishing, 2008.

Jackson, Joseph. *Prints, Documents and Maps illustrative of Philadelphia Real Estate in the Office of Mastbaum Brothers & Fleisher*. Philadelphia: Mastbaum Brothers and Fleisher, 1926.

Jackson, Kenneth T. *The Ku Klux Klan in the City, 1915–1930*. New York: Oxford University Press, 1967.

Jacobs, Timothy. *The History of the Pennsylvania Railroad*. New York: Smithmark Publishers, 1994.

Jarvis, Elizabeth Farmer. *Mount Airy*. Charleston, SC: Arcadia Publishing, 2008.

Jenkins, Philip. *Hoods and Shirts: The Extreme Right in Pennsylvania, 1925–1950*. Chapel Hill: University of North Carolina Press, 1997.

Johnson, Amandus. *The American Swedish Historical Museum. Its Origin; Its Functions; Its Activities; Its Aims and the Plan of Its Sixteen Rooms*. Philadelphia: American Swedish Historical Museum, 1966.

Kahn, Roger. *A Flame of Pure Fire: Jack Dempsey and the Roaring '20s*. New York: Harcourt Brace, 1999.

Kathrens, Michael C. *American Splendor: The Residential Architecture of Horace Trumbauer*. New York: Acanthus Press, 2002.

Katz, Michael B., and Thomas J. Sugrue, eds. *W. E. B. Du Bois, Race, and the City: The Philadelphia Negro and Its Legacy*. Philadelphia: University of Pennsylvania Press, 1998.

Keels, Thomas H. *Forgotten Philadelphia: Lost Architecture of the Quaker City*. Philadelphia: Temple University Press, 2007.

———. *Philadelphia Graveyards and Cemeteries*. Charleston, SC: Arcadia Publishing, 2003.

———. *Wicked Philadelphia: Sin in the City of Brotherly Love*. Charleston, SC: History Press, 2010.

Kevles, Daniel J. *In the Name of Eugenics: Genetics and the Use of Human Heredity*. Cambridge, MA: Harvard University Press, 1995.

Kühl, Stefan. *The Nazi Connection: Eugenics, American Racism, and German National Socialism*. New York: Oxford University Press, 1994.

Kuklick, Bruce. *To Every Thing a Season: Shibe Park and Urban Philadelphia 1909–1976*. Princeton, NJ: Princeton University Press, 1991.

Lane, Roger. *William Dorsey's Philadelphia and Ours: On the Past and Future of the Black City in America*. New York: Oxford University Press, 1991.

Lardner, Ring. *Letters of Ring Lardner*. Edited by Clifford M. Caruthers. Alexandria, VA: Orchises Press, 1995.

Larson, Erik. *The Devil in the White City: Murder, Magic, and Madness at the Fair That Changed America*. New York: Vintage Books, 2003.

Leach, William. *Land of Desire: Merchants, Power, and the Rise of a New American Culture*. New York: Vintage Books, 1994.

Leighton, Isabel, ed. *The Aspirin Age, 1919–1941*. New York: Simon and Schuster, 1967.

Leuchtenburg, William E. *The Perils of Prosperity 1914–32*. Chicago: University of Chicago Press, 1969.

Lewis, David Levering. *W. E. B. DuBois: Biography of a Race, 1868–1919*. New York: Henry Holt, 1993.

———. *W. E. B. DuBois: The Fight for Equality and the American Century, 1919–1963*. New York: Henry Holt, 2000.

Lewis, Michael. "Kahn's Graphic Modernism." In *Drawn from the Source: The Travel Sketches of Louis I. Kahn*, edited by Eugene J. Johnson and Ralph Lieberman. Cambridge, MA: MIT Press, 1996.

———. *Frank Furness: Architecture and the Violent Mind*. New York: W. W. Norton, 2001.

Lewis, Sinclair. *Main Street & Babbitt*. New York: Library of America, 1992.

Lief, Alfred. *Family Business: A Century in the Life and Times of Strawbridge & Clothier*. New York: McGraw-Hill, 1968.

Luconi, Stefano. *From Paesani to White Ethnics*, Albany, NY: SUNY Press, 2001.

Lukacs, John. *Philadelphia: Patricians and Philistines, 1900–1950*. New York: Farrar, Straus, Giroux, 1981.

Lutz, Jack. *The Poor Richard Club: Its Birth, Growth and Activities; and Its Influence on Advertising, the City, State and Nation*. Philadelphia: Poor Richard Club, 1953.

Maass, John. *The Glorious Enterprise: The Centennial Exhibition of 1876 and H. J. Schwarzmann, Architect-in-Chief*. Watkins Glen, NY: American Life Foundation, 1973.

Maher, James T. *The Twilight of Splendor: Chronicles of the Age of American Palaces*. Boston: Little, Brown, 1975.

Marion, John Francis. *Within These Walls: A History of the Academy of Music in Philadelphia*. Philadelphia: Academy of Music, 1984.

McCabe, James D. *The Illustrated History of the Centennial Exhibition*. Philadelphia: National, 1975.

McCaffery, Peter. *When Bosses Ruled Philadelphia: The Emergence of the Republican Machine, 1867–1933*. University Park: Pennsylvania State University Press, 1993.

McCullough, Edo. *World's Fair Midways*. New York: Exposition Press, 1966.

McGeary, M. Nelson. *Gifford Pinchot: Forester-Politician*. Princeton, NJ: Princeton University Press, 1960.

Mendte, J. Robert. *The Union League of Philadelphia Celebrates 125 Years, 1862–1987*. Devon, PA: William T. Cooke Publishing, 1987.

Meyers, Allen. *The Jewish Community around North Broad Street.* Charleston, SC: Arcadia Publishing, 2002.

Miller, Frederic M., Morris J. Vogel, and Allen F. Davis. *Philadelphia Stories: A Photographic History, 1920–1960.* Philadelphia: Temple University Press, 1988.

———. *Still Philadelphia: A Photographic History, 1890–1940.* Philadelphia: Temple University Press, 1983.

Morley, Christopher. *Travels in Philadelphia.* Philadelphia: J. B. Lippincott, 1937.

Morris, Charles R. *American Catholic: The Saints and Sinners Who Built America's Most Powerful Church.* New York: Random House/Times Books, 1997.

Morris, Constance Lily. *On Tour with Queen Marie.* New York: Robert M. McBride, 1927.

Mosby, Dewey F., Darrell Sewell, and Rae Alexander Minter. *Henry Ossawa Turner.* Philadelphia: Philadelphia Museum of Art, 1991.

Moss, Roger W. *Historic Houses of Philadelphia: A Tour of the Region's Museum Homes.* Philadelphia: University of Pennsylvania Press, 1998.

———. *Historic Landmarks of Philadelphia.* Philadelphia: University of Pennsylvania Press, 2008.

———. *Historic Sacred Places of Philadelphia.* Philadelphia: University of Pennsylvania Press, 2005.

Nicolai, Richard R. *Centennial Philadelphia.* Bryn Mawr, PA: Bryn Mawr Press, 1976.

Norton, Frank H., ed. *Frank Leslie's Historical Register of the United States Centennial Exposition 1876.* New York: Frank Leslie's Publishing House, 1877.

O'Donnell, George E. *St. Charles Seminary Philadelphia: A History of the Theological Seminary of Saint Charles Borromeo, Overbrook, Philadelphia, Pennsylvania, 1832–1964, with a Chronological Record of Ordinations and Pictures of the Living Alumni.* Philadelphia: St. Charles Seminary, 1964.

O'Gorman, James F., Jeffrey A. Cohen, George E. Thomas, and G. Holmes Perkins. *Drawing toward Building: Philadelphia Architectural Graphics, 1732–1986.* Philadelphia: Pennsylvania Academy of the Fine Arts/University of Pennsylvania Press, 1986.

Okrent, Daniel. *Last Call: The Rise and Fall of Prohibition.* New York: Scribner, 2010.

Opperby, Preben. *Leopold Stokowski.* New York: Hippocrene Books, 1982.

Pakula, Hannah. *The Last Romantic: A Biography of Queen Marie of Roumania.* New York: Simon and Schuster, 1984.

Parker, Dorothy. *The Portable Dorothy Parker.* Edited by Brendan Gill. New York: Penguin Books, 1982.

Pegram, Thomas R. *One Hundred Percent American: The Rebirth and Decline of the Ku Klux Klan in the 1920s.* Chicago: Ivan R. Dee, 2011.

Pencak, William. *For God & Country: The American Legion, 1919–1941.* Boston: Northeastern University Press, 1989.

Pennell, Elizabeth Robins, and Joseph Pennell. *Our Philadelphia.* Philadelphia: J. B. Lippincott, 1914.

Pepper, George Wharton. *Philadelphia Lawyer: An Autobiography.* Philadelphia: J. B. Lippincott, 1944.

Philadelphia War History Committee. *Philadelphia in the World War, 1914–1919.* New York: Wynkoop Hallenbeck Crawford, 1922.

Post, Robert C., ed. *1876: A Centennial Exhibition.* Washington, DC: National Museum of History and Technology, Smithsonian Institution, 1976.

Radtke, Terry. *The History of the Pennsylvania American Legion*. Mechanicsburg, PA: Stackpole Books, 1993.

Randel, William Peirce. *Centennial: American Life in 1876*. Philadelphia: Chilton Book, 1969.

Ray, Jim. *The Story of American Aviation*. Philadelphia: John C. Winston, 1946.

Report of the Sesqui-Centennial Committee of the Engineers' Club of Philadelphia on Sites, Philadelphia, PA: Engineer's Club, 1927.

Ristine, James D. *Philadelphia's 1926 Sesqui-Centennial International Exposition*. Charleston, SC: Arcadia Press, 2009.

Rivinus, Marion Willis. *Distaff Descent*. Philadelphia: Privately published, 1943.

———. *The Story of Rittenhouse Square, 1682–1951*. Philadelphia: Privately published, 1951.

Roberts, George, and Mary Roberts. *Triumph on Fairmount: Fiske Kimball and the Philadelphia Museum of Art*. Philadelphia: J. B. Lippincott, 1959.

Rudel, Anthony. *Hello, Everybody! The Dawn of American Radio*. New York: Harcourt, 2008.

Rumer, Thomas A. *The American Legion: An Official History 1919–1989*. New York: M. Evans, 1990.

Robert W. Rydell, *World of Fairs: The Century-of-Progress Expositions*, Chicago: University of Chicago Press, 1993.

Rydell, Robert W., John E. Findling, and Kimberly D. Pelle. *Fair America: World's Fairs in the United States*. Washington, DC: Smithsonian Institution Press, 2000.

Salter, J. T. *The People's Choice: Philadelphia's William S. Vare*. New York: Exposition Press, 1971.

Samuel, Lawrence R. *The End of the Innocence: The 1964–1965 New York World's Fair*. Syracuse, NY: Syracuse University Press, 2007.

Sann, Paul. *The 20s: The Lawless Decade*. New York: Da Capo Press, 1984.

Saunders, George M. *A Short History of the Shrine*. Chicago: A.A.O.N.M.S., 1971.

Scharf, Thomas J., and Westcott, Thompson. *History of Philadelphia, 1609–1884*. Philadelphia: L.H. Everts & Co., 1884

Schmidt, Hans. *Maverick Marine: General Smedley D. Butler and the Contradictions of American Military History*. Lexington: University Press of Kentucky, 1987.

Schotter, H. W. *The Growth and Development of the Pennsylvania Railroad Company: A Review of the Charter and Annual Reports of the Pennsylvania Railroad Company 1846 to 1926, Inclusive*. Philadelphia: Allen, Lane, and Scott, 1927.

Segal, Geraldine R. *Blacks in the Law: Philadelphia and the Nation*. Philadelphia: University of Pennsylvania Press, 1983.

Shinn, Earl. *A Century After: Picturesque Glimpses of Philadelphia and Pennsylvania*. Philadelphia, PA: Allen, Lane & Scott, 1875.

Shlaes, Amity. *Coolidge*. New York: HarperCollins, 2013.

Skaler, Robert Morris. *Philadelphia's Broad Street South and North*. Charleston, SC: Arcadia Publishing, 2003.

Skaler, Robert Morris, and Thomas H. Keels. *Philadelphia's Rittenhouse Square*. Charleston, SC: Arcadia Publishing, 2009.

Sklar, Robert, ed. *The Plastic Age 1917–1930*. New York: George Braziller, 1970.

Sky, Alison, and Michelle Stone. *Unbuilt America: Forgotten Architecture in the United States from Thomas Jefferson to the Space Age*. New York: Abbeville Press, 1976.

Smith, H. Clifford. *Sulgrave Manor and the Washingtons: A History and Guide to the Tudor Home of George Washington's Ancestors*. London: Jonathan Cape, 1933.

Speth, Henry. "The History of the Shrine and Lu Lu." Unpublished manuscript. Plymouth Meeting, PA: Lu Lu Shrine Archives.

Sports Complex Special Services District. *Looking Back & Moving Forward*. Philadelphia: Sports Complex Special Services District, 2010.

Stafford, Hartwell, ed. *Who's Who in Philadelphia at the Time of the Sesqui-Centennial*. Philadelphia: Stafford's National News Service, 1927.

Steffens, Lincoln. *The Shame of the Cities*. New York: Hill and Wang, 1995.

Talbot, Francis X., SJ. *Jesuit Education in Philadelphia: St. Joseph's College, 1851–1926*. Philadelphia: St. Joseph's College, 1927.

Thomas, George E., Jeffrey C. Cohen, and Michael J. Lewis. *Frank Furness: The Complete Works*. Rev. ed. New York: Princeton Architectural Press, 1996.

Threston, Christopher. *The Integration of Baseball in Philadelphia*. Jefferson, NC: McFarland, 2003.

Tirella, Joseph. *Tomorrow-Land: The 1964–65 World's Fair and the Transformation of America*. Guilford, CT: Lyons Press, 2014.

Trotter, Joe William, Jr., and Eric Ledell Smith, eds. *African Americans in Pennsylvania: Shifting Historical Perspectives*. University Park: Pennsylvania State University Press, 1997.

Vare, William S. *My Forty Years in Politics*. Philadelphia, PA: Roland Swain Company, 1933.

Venzon, Anne Cipriano, ed. *General Smedley Darlington Butler: The Letters of a Leatherneck, 1898–1931*. New York: Praeger, 1992.

Wallace, Max. *The American Axis: Henry Ford, Charles Lindbergh, and the Rise of the Third Reich*. New York: St. Martin's Press, 2003.

Walsh, George. *Gentleman Jimmy Walker: Mayor of the Jazz Age*. New York: Praeger, 1974.

Warner, Sam Bass. *The Private City: Philadelphia in Three Periods of Its Growth*. Philadelphia: University of Pennsylvania Press, 1991.

Watts, Steven. *The People's Tycoon: Henry Ford and the American Century*. New York: Alfred A. Knopf, 2005.

Weigley, Russell F., ed. *Philadelphia: A 300-Year History*. New York: W. W. Norton, 1982.

Westing, Fred. *The Locomotives That Baldwin Built. Containing a Complete Facsimile of the History of the Baldwin Locomotive Works, 1831–1923*. New York: Bonanza Books, 1966.

Weymouth, Lally. *America in 1876: The Way We Were*. New York: Vintage Books, 1976.

White, Theo B. *Paul Philippe Cret: Architect and Teacher*. Philadelphia: Art Alliance Press, 1973.

———. *The Philadelphia Art Alliance: Fifty Years 1915–1965*. Philadelphia: University of Pennsylvania Press, 1965.

Wilson, Martin W. "From the Sesquicentennial to the Bicentennial: Changing Attitudes toward Tourism in Philadelphia, 1926–1976." PhD. diss., Temple University, 2000.

Winkelman, Barnie F. *John G. Johnson: Lawyer and Art Collector, 1841–1917*. Philadelphia: University of Pennsylvania Press, 1942.

Wintz, Cary D., ed. *African American Political Thought 1890–1930: Washington, Du Bois, Garvey and Randolph*. Armonk, NY: M. E. Sharpe, 1996.

Wister, Frances Anne. *Twenty-Five Years of the Philadelphia Orchestra 1900–1925*. Philadelphia: Edward Stern, 1925.

Wister, Owen, and James A. Butler, eds. *Romney & Other New Works about Philadelphia*. University Park: Pennsylvania State University Press, 2001.

Wister, Owen. *The Philadelphia Club 1834–1934, Being a Brief History of the Club for the First Hundred Years of Its Existence, Together with Its Roll of Officers and Members to 1934*. Philadelphia: Privately printed, 1934.

Yount, Sylvia. "Rocking the Cradle of Liberty: Philadelphia's Adventures in Modernism." In *To Be Modern: American Encounters with Cezanne and Company*, edited by Sylvia Yount and Elizabeth Johns, 9–25. Philadelphia: Pennsylvania Academy of the Fine Arts/University of Pennsylvania Press, 1996.

Zulker, William Allen. *John Wanamaker: King of Merchants*. Wayne, PA: Eaglecrest Press, 1993.

Zwicker, Charles G. and Edward C. Zwicker. *Annual Report of the Department of Wharves, Docks and Ferries of the City of Philadelphia for the Year Ending December 31, 1916*. Philadelphia: City of Philadelphia, 1917.

———. *Fairmount Park Art Association: An Account of Its Origin and Activities from Its Foundation in 1871. Issued on the Occasion of Its Fiftieth Anniversary, 1921*. Philadelphia: Fairmount Park Art Association, 1922.

———. *The Garden Club of America: History, 1913–1938*. Philadelphia: Privately printed, 1938.

———. *John Wanamaker: The Record of a Citizens' Celebration to Mark His Sixty Years as a Merchant April 1861–April 1921*. Philadelphia, PA: Printed for the Committee, 1921.

———. *Paintings, Sculpture and Prints in the Department of Fine Arts, Sesqui-Centennial International Exposition*. Philadelphia: Department of Fine Arts, Sesqui-Centennial International Exposition, 1926.

———. *Philadelphia: Three Centuries of American Art. Bicentennial Exhibition April 11–October 10, 1976*. Philadelphia: Philadelphia Museum of Art, 1976.

———. *Phila-Nipponica: An Historic Guide to Philadelphia & Japan*. Philadelphia: Japan America Society of Greater Philadelphia, 1999.

———. *Report of the Sesqui-Centennial Commission of the Commonwealth of Pennsylvania*. Harrisburg, PA: Privately printed, 1927.

———. *Whitemarsh Hall: The Estate of Edward T. Stotesbury*. Charleston, SC: Arcadia Publishing, 2004.

MAGAZINES/PAMPHLETS

American Society of Civil Engineers. Fifty-Sixth Annual Convention, Phila., PA, October 4–9, 1926. In connection with the Sesqui-Centennial Exposition.

Flags of America: From the Time of Columbus to the Present Day. Sesqui-Centennial ed. Philadelphia: John Wanamaker, 1926.

A Friendly Guide-Book to Philadelphia. Philadelphia: John Wanamaker, 1918.

A Friendly Guide-Book to the Wanamaker Store. Philadelphia: John Wanamaker, 1922.

A Greater Philadelphia. Philadelphia: City of Philadelphia, 1936.

"The Masque of 1916." Program. Philadelphia, 1916.

Philadelphia: "The Workshop of the World." Philadelphia: J. Howard Goodwin, 1919.

"Sesqui to Capital by Air." Philadelphia Rapid Transit Company Service Talks. Vol. 7, No. 15–A. July 14, 1926.

ARTICLES

Amero, Richard. "Colonel D. C. Collier: 'An Inspiration to the Citizens of Today.'" *Journal of San Diego History/San Diego Historical Society Quarterly* 56, no. 4 (2010): 203–216.

———. "The Making of the Panama-California Exposition, 1909–1915." *Journal of San Diego History/San Diego Historical Society Quarterly* 36, no. 1 (1990): 23–39.

Astorino, Samuel J. "The Contested Senate Election of William Scott Vare." *Pennsylvania History* 28, no. 2 (April 1961): 187–201.

Cheney, Lynne Vincent. "1876: The Eagle Screams." *American Heritage* 25, no. 3 (April 1974): 15–35, 98–99.

Ferris, John. "Freel Kendrick of Philadelphia." *Plain Talk* (November 1927): 87–93.

Fox, Bonnie R. "Unemployment Relief in Philadelphia, 1930–1932: A Study of the Depression's Impact on Volunteerism." *PMHB* 93 (January 1969): 86–108.

Hammer, Joshua. "Sifting Sacred Ground." *Smithsonian Magazine* 42, no. 1 (April 2011): 34–44.

Henderson, Alexa Benson. "Richard R. Wright and the National Negro Bankers Association: Early Organizing Efforts among Black Bankers 1924–1942." *PMHB* 117, nos. 1–2 (January–April 1993): 51–81.

Joyce, John St. George. *The Story of Philadelphia*, Philadelphia, PA: Rex Printing House, 1919.

Lippincott, Horace Mather. "Edward T. Stotesbury." *Old York Road Historical Society Bulletin* 6 (October 1942): 3–23.

Miller, Frederic. "The Black Migration to Philadelphia: A 1924 Profile." *PMHB* 108 (July 1984): 315–350.

Petroski, Henry. "The Benjamin Franklin Bridge," *American Scientist* 90, no. 5 (September–October 2002): 406–410.

Pizor, Faith K. "Preparations for the Centennial Exhibition of 1876." *PMHB* 94, no. 2 (1970): 213–232.

Report of the Sesqui-Centennial Committee of the Engineers' Club of Philadelphia on Sites, Philadelphia, PA: Engineer's Club, 1927.

Richardson, Edgar P. "Centennial City." *American Heritage* 23, no. 1 (December 1971): 17–32.

Ryan, Francis. "The Quest for Local Power: John C. Asbury and Black Republican Strategies in Philadelphia in the Early Twentieth Century." Paper presented at the Pennsylvania Historical Association Annual Meeting, Pittsburgh, PA, October 22, 2005.

Selden, Steven. "Transforming Better Babies into Fitter Families: Archival Resources and the History of the American Eugenics Movement, 1908–1930." *Proceedings of the American Philosophical Society* 149, no. 2 (June 2005): 199–225.

Thomas, George E. "From 'Frontier' to Center City: The Evolution of the Neighborhood of the Historical Society of Pennsylvania." *PMHB* 124, nos. 1–2 (January–April 2000): 7–42.

Underkofler, Allen P. "The Philadelphia Improvements. Part I: The Ideas & Projects East of the Schuylkill River." *Magazine of the Philadelphia Chapter of the Pennsylvania Railroad Technical & Historical Society* 2, nos. 2–3 (May 1979): n.p.

Wagner, Albert C., "Crime and Economic Change in Philadelphia, 1923–1934." *Journal of Criminal Law and Criminology* 27, no. 4 (November–December 1936): 483–490.

"Will Urge Hog Island as Site for Exposition," *PI*, February 5, 1922, p. 18.

Wolf, Edwin. "The Origins of Philadelphia's Self-Deprecation, 1820–1920." *PMHB* 104, no. 1 (1980): 58–73.

Yount, Sylvia. "The Jefferson or Declaration House at the Sesqui-Centennial." *Strawbridge and Clothier Store Chat* 19, no. 9 (September 1926): 3–5.

Index

★ ★ ★

Note: Page numbers in *italics* refer to illustrations.

Thomas H. Keels is a historian and lecturer who has authored or co-authored seven books and numerous articles on Philadelphia history, including *Forgotten Philadelphia: Lost Architecture of the Quaker City* (Temple), *Philadelphia Graveyards and Cemeteries, and Wicked Philadelphia: Sin in the City of Brotherly Love.* A confirmed taphophile, Keels has been a tour guide at Laurel Hill Cemetery, Philadelphia's premier Victorian necropolis, for two decades. Visit him online at http://www.thomaskeels.com/.